# SPACE TOURISM

Space tourism has become extremely significant in recent times, especially in pursuance of the new space race among corporate giants such as Virgin Galactic, Blue Origin and SpaceX. Each of these corporate giants has already booked thousands of space enthusiasts for a journey to outer space. Given this wide interest of private space players, space tourists as well as countries in space tourism, it is imperative to understand the legal issues involved in space tourism. This book presents important discussions in the domain of space tourism and its legal implications across the globe. It attempts to find solutions to various challenges like safety and security in space, status of space tourists during emergencies, liability aspects, environmental protection, etc., faced during the recent spurt of space tourism. It also discusses the role of insurance in space tourism, various crimes possible in outer space with the rise of space tourism, the mechanisms for adjudication of such crimes, the aspect of quarantining space tourists, the need to preserve the natural and cultural heritage of space and other topics, besides examining the contemporary legal and policy-oriented issues of privatisation of space.

A must read for scholars and researchers of law, space science, history and other fields who are interested in the space race and outer space law, this book will also be of interest to those exploring space studies, political studies, environmental studies and political economy. It will be useful for policymakers, bureaucrats, think tanks as well as interested general readers looking for fresh perspectives on the future of space.

**Sandeepa Bhat B.** is working as a Professor of Law and Director of the Centre for Aviation and Space Laws at National University of Juridical Sciences, Kolkata. Apart from teaching space law during the last two decades, he has published four books (out of nine) on space law and also published more than 55 articles in journals of international and national repute. He has the distinction of being a member of the Indian Space Research Organisation's Expert Group for drafting the National Space Act for India.

# SPACE TOURISM

## Legal and Policy Aspects

*Edited by*
*Sandeepa Bhat B.*

LONDON AND NEW YORK

Designed Cover Image: Getty Image

First published 2024
by Routledge
4 Park Square, Milton Park, Abingdon, Oxon OX14 4RN

and by Routledge
605 Third Avenue, New York, NY 10158

*Routledge is an imprint of the Taylor & Francis Group, an informa business*

© 2024 selection and editorial matter, Sandeepa Bhat B.; individual chapters, the contributors

The right of Sandeepa Bhat B. to be identified as the author of the editorial material, and of the authors for their individual chapters, has been asserted in accordance with sections 77 and 78 of the Copyright, Designs and Patents Act 1988.

All rights reserved. No part of this book may be reprinted or reproduced or utilised in any form or by any electronic, mechanical, or other means, now known or hereafter invented, including photocopying and recording, or in any information storage or retrieval system, without permission in writing from the publishers.

*Trademark notice*: Product or corporate names may be trademarks or registered trademarks, and are used only for identification and explanation without intent to infringe.

*British Library Cataloguing-in-Publication Data*
A catalogue record for this book is available from the British Library

ISBN: 978-1-032-48862-2 (hbk)
ISBN: 978-1-032-61795-4 (pbk)
ISBN: 978-1-032-61796-1 (ebk)

DOI: 10.4324/9781032617961

Typeset in Times New Roman
by codeMantra

# CONTENTS

| | |
|---|---|
| *List of tables* | *vii* |
| *List of contributors* | *ix* |
| *Preface* | *xiii* |

1 Space Tourism: Outlining the Legal Issues        1
  *Sandeepa Bhat B.*

2 The Kármán Line Controversy and Boundaries of Outer
  Space: Implications for Space Tourism       16
  *Tushar Krishna and Shouvik Kumar Guha*

3 The Effect of Space Tourism on the Concept of
  "Astronaut" Under International Law       28
  *Prof. Melissa de Zwart and Joel Lisk*

4 Need to Clarify the Rescue Norms for Private Space Tourists       42
  *Ankit Kumar Padhy and Divya Tyagi*

5 Keeping Outer Space Safe for Human Presence       55
  *Martha Mejía-Kaiser*

6 State Responsibility and Space Tourism: Customary
  Principles as Modified by Article VI of the Outer Space Treaty       69
  *Ricky J. Lee*

**vi** Contents

7  Legal Framework of Liability in Space Tourism      99
   *Asha P. Soman*

8  The Environmental Effects of Space Tourism      114
   *David Webb*

9  Legal Strategies to Preserve the Natural and Cultural
   Heritage of Space      133
   *Jennifer A. Brobst*

10  Contractual Obligations in the Context of Space Tourism      153
   *Rohan R. Pillai and Arshi Alam*

11  Space Tourism: Possible Crimes and Their Adjudication      167
   *G.S. Sachdeva*

12  Issues of Ownership and Tourism in Outer Space      187
   *Attila Sipos and Simran Upadhyaya*

13  Space Tourism: Learning from the Antarctic Experience      203
   *Aaditya Vikram Sharma*

*Index*      *223*

# TABLES

| | | |
|---|---|---|
| 8.1 | Propellants for current crewed spacecraft | 120 |
| 8.2 | Carbon emissions of crewed spacecraft | 122 |

# CONTRIBUTORS

**Ms. Arshi Alam** is working as a Business Process Associate-Legal at Capgemini India Limited. She did her law graduation from Amity Law School Kolkata, after completing her B.A. Honours in History from Jadavpur University. She is a 2022 LL.M. alumni of the West Bengal National University of Juridical Sciences. She is keenly interested in AI and technology laws.

**Prof. (Dr.) Sandeepa Bhat** is working as a Professor of Law and Director of Centre for Aviation and Space Laws at National University of Juridical Sciences, Kolkata. Apart from teaching space law during the last two decades, he has published four books (out of nine) on space law and also published more than 55 articles in the journals of international and national repute. He has the distinction of being a member of Indian Space Research Organisation's Expert Group for drafting the National Space Act for India.

**Prof. Jennifer A. Brobst** is an Assistant Professor at Cecil C. Humphreys School of Law at the University of Memphis in Tennessee, USA. She has degrees from Victoria University of Wellington, New Zealand (LL.M.); University of San Diego School of Law, USA (J.D.); and University of Cape Town, Republic of South Africa (B.A.). She has lectured and written extensively on the impact of law and technology on society, including in the space law context.

**Dr. Shouvik Kumar Guha** is currently serving as an Associate Professor of Law at the West Bengal National University of Juridical Sciences, Kolkata. His areas of interest include aviation and space laws, law and technology, corporate and financial laws, competition law, and law, literature and popular culture.

**x** contributors

**Tushar Krishna** is a final year law student at the West Bengal National University of Juridical Sciences, Kolkata. He is a convenor of the International Law Student Association, NUJS Chapter, and also a former member of the Centre for Aviation and Space Laws. His deep interest lies in international law and affairs.

**Dr. Ricky J. Lee** is Intellectual Forum Senior Research Associate, Jesus College, University of Cambridge; Adjunct Professor of Law, University of Notre Dame (Australia); Adjunct Professor of International Law, Nirma University (India); and Executive Director, International Academy of Space Law & Policy. Since 1999, Dr. Lee has lectured at universities and acted for launch operators, satellite operators and governments worldwide.

**Joel Lisk** is a Research Associate in space and regulation at Flinders University, Australia. Joel principally researches the content, form and trends related to domestic legal frameworks and regulation for the space sector, with a particular focus on commercial efficacy and operation. Joel has presented on these topics at international conferences and regularly guest lectured at universities across Australia.

**Dr. Martha Mejía-Kaiser**, born in Mexico, is a member of the Board of Directors of the International Institute of Space Law, France. She obtained her Ph.D. on political and social sciences from the National Autonomous University of Mexico. Mejía-Kaiser has published on different space law topics. In 2020, she published the book *The Geostationary Ring – Practice and Law* (Brill/Nijhoff).

**Mr. Ankit Kumar Padhy** is working as an Assistant Professor of Law at the Vellore Institute of Technology, Chennai. He has a keen interest in space law and pursuing Ph.D. in this field from the Gujarat National Law University, Ahmadabad. He has also lectured and published on space law.

**Mr. Rohan R. Pillai** is an Advocate at High Court of Judicature at Bombay, Nagpur Bench. He is also associated with the Sports Authority of India (SAI), Bhopal. He did his graduation from Ambedkar Law College, Nagpur University, and LL.M. from the West Bengal National University of Juridical Sciences, Kolkata. He has a keen interest in space law, sports law and international trade law.

**Prof. (Dr.) G.S. Sachdeva** is one of the pioneer scholars on air and space law in India. Currently, he is Professor Emeritus, Chandigarh University, Punjab, and Adjunct Professor, NALSAR University of Law, Hyderabad. He has written eight books and over 60 articles for edited books and law journals primarily focusing on space law. He has a Doctorate in International Law from JNU, New Delhi.

**Mr. Aaditya Vikram Sharma** is serving as an Assistant Professor at the Vivekananda Institute of Professional Studies – Technical Campus, New Delhi.

Aaditya is fascinated by space law and is pursuing his Ph.D. in Space Law at the WB University of Juridical Sciences, Kolkata. Recently, he also participated in the Southern Hemisphere Space Studies Program of the International Space University, France in Adelaide, Australia.

**Dr. Attila Sipos** worked for MALÉV Hungarian Airlines as Flight Operation and Navigation Officer, Chief Adviser to CEO and Legal Director (1989–2004). He was the Permanent Representative of Hungary on the Council of ICAO (2004–2007) and the Vice-President of the Council of ICAO (2006–2007). He was employed by HungaroControl (ANSP) as Legal Director, Alliance Director and Adviser to the CEO (2008–2014). His passion for academics has driven him to take up teaching assignment at air and space law master's programme of the Sharjah University (UoS).

**Dr. Asha P. Soman** is an Associate Professor at IFIM Law School, Bangalore. She is a member of Study Group 5.20 of IAA Commission 5 on Space Policy, Law and Economy, IAA, France. She obtained her Doctoral degree (Space Law) from NLSIU, Bangalore. She has initiated air and space law committees at previous institutions and developed courses on it. Her research interests are air and space law, technology law, jurisprudence, environmental law, and law and society.

**Dr. Divya Tyagi** is an Assistant Professor of Law at Gujarat National Law University. He teaches air and space laws and serves as the Head of V.S. Mani Centre for Air and Space Law at GNLU. He has organised several editions of distinguished GNLU Air and Space Law Academy as well as accompanying conferences.

**Ms. Simran Upadhyaya** is a final year student at the West Bengal National University of Juridical Sciences, Kolkata. She is an avid reader and pursuer of literary arts. She has been a member of the Centre for Aviation and Space Laws, and is eager to continue exploring the intersections of law, science and technology.

**Prof. (Dr.) David Webb** has a Ph.D. in Space Physics and was made Professor of Engineering at Leeds Beckett University in 2003 and Professor of Peace and Conflict Studies in 2010. He was also chair of the Campaign for Nuclear Disarmament from 2010 to 2021 and has been the Convenor of the Global Network Against Weapons and Nuclear Power in Space for over 30 years.

**Prof. (Dr.) Melissa de Zwart** is Professor of Space Law, Governance and Regulation at Andy Thomas Centre for Space Resources, University of Adelaide, Australia. Professor de Zwart is an expert on laws affecting the military and commercial uses of outer space. She is the Deputy Director of the ARC Centre of Excellence in Plants for Space and a member of the International Institute of Space Law.

# PREFACE

The year 2021 marked the beginning of a race between the private sector giants to catch lucrative space tourism market. It unfolded a new arena as the dominance of State in the space sector has witnessed a serious challenge from the private sector. The space treaties and international policy frameworks in the space sector were drafted at a time when States were the dominant players. Hence, they are oriented towards the regulation of State activities in outer space. With the private sector posing challenge to State dominance, a plethora of legal and policy issues have surfaced at the global level. While on the one hand whether space tourism fits within the ambit of sustainable use of outer space is in question, on the other hand, application of twentieth-century international space treaties' principles to the twenty-first-century private space tourism seems inappropriate.

Given a sudden flurry of activities in the sector of space tourism, one must carefully consider various legal implications and resulting concerns. We are in need of having quick legal response to space tourism to prevent it from being detrimental to the interests of mankind. Issues such as authorisation, supervision, registration, certification of space tourism vehicles and crew, emergency assistance, environmental protection, liability for damage and criminal liability for offences require immediate attention. Most of these aspects are covered under the existing international space treaties, however, in the context of State activities in outer space. Applying them directly to space tourism results in tragedy, but this does not mean that we have to discard them in dealing with space tourism. Hence, while respecting the international treaty obligations, a suitable legal regime needs to be evolved in the context of space tourism. In developing a legal regime in this field, criteria such as *rationae loci* and *ratione materiae* deserve special attention when it comes to ascertaining the role of international and domestic laws.

**xiv** Preface

This book is one of the first comprehensive publications to come in the aftermath of the recent private space tourism race. It decodes the various nuances of space tourism in detail from law and policy perspectives. Starting from the revival of debate on space delimitation to the issue of crimes in outer space, the book covers every issue of concern to a space lawyer in the wake of private space tourism. I am fortunate to receive contributions from some of the best space law experts from different corners of the world. Let me thank them profusely for their contribution despite their hectic schedule. Assistance provided by Ms. Soumya Gupta and Mr. Tushar Krishna is also duly acknowledged herewith. We hope that this book will stand as a bridge between the twentieth-century principles of international space law and the twenty-first-century reality of space tourism.

Prof. (Dr.) Sandeepa Bhat B.
1 January 2024

# 1

# SPACE TOURISM

## Outlining the Legal Issues

*Sandeepa Bhat B.*

### Introduction

The year 2001 marked the beginning of a new chapter in the history of space activities with the introduction of commercial space tourism. Dennis Tito became the first commercial space tourist to visit the International Space Station (ISS) on board a Russian Soyuz vehicle.[1] He spent six days at the ISS during April–May 2001 by spending $20 million.[2] In his testimony submitted during a Joint Hearing on "Commercial Human Spaceflight" 2003, Tito expressed grave concerns about the legal and regulatory aspects of space tourism.[3] He also mentioned it as the primary reason for his lack of interest in planning for investments in the space tourism industry. The concerns expressed by Tito on the legal vacuum still continue to exist; however, his enthusiasm to travel space has not dried up. He has recently signed up with SpaceX for a private trip to Moon.[4]

Between 2001 and 2009, six more private space tourists visited the ISS on board the Russian Soyuz vehicles.[5] Space Adventures was the first private company to be involved with space tourism as it arranged each of the trips between 2001 and 2009.[6] In 2009, Russia took a decision to temporarily halt the private tourism to ISS in the wake of increase in the crew members of the ISS from three to six.[7] This decision gave an impetus to the private entrepreneurs to invest in the development of space tourism industry. The private companies like SpaceX, Blue Origin, Virgin Galactic and Space Adventures intensified their efforts to kick-start private space tourism during the decade following 2010.[8]

The efforts of the private companies to enter into the business of commercial space tourism ranged from the plan of long-term stays in the Earth orbit to short-term stay therein or at a sub-orbital level.[9] Apart from sub-orbital and orbital tourism, plans have also been devised for commercial tourism beyond the Earth

DOI: 10.4324/9781032617961-1

**2** Sandeepa Bhat B.

orbit.[10] Each of these companies also developed different designs and technology for implementing their plans. While some of the companies have developed vertical take-off vehicles, others have banked on the horizontal take-off mechanism similar to the one used in aircraft. For example, Blue Origin uses rocket-type vertical launch and Virgin Galactic's WhiteNightTwo takes off horizontally like an aircraft.[11]

Exactly two decades after the beginning of commercial space tourism, the world witnessed a race between Virgin Galactic, Blue Origin and SpaceX to be the first private company to start space tourism. Virgin Galactic edged this race to operationalise the first space tourism flight on 11 July 2021, which was closely followed by Blue Origin on 20 July 2021.[12] In a race to showcase the safety of their space technologies and to catch the space tourism market, both companies' founders, Richard Branson and Jeff Bezos, took part in their respective first shows. SpaceX didn't fall behind in this race and took a different way to showcase its readiness for space tourism. On 15 September 2021, SpaceX launched its flight 'Inspiration4' for a three days' orbital trip. It was a unique feat as it was the first manned orbital mission without a professional astronaut on board the space vehicle.[13]

After the beginning of the era of space tourism by private operators, the number of instances of space tourism has increased by leaps and bounds. The space tourism market is expected to skyrocket by 2030.[14] Unfortunately, the existing realm of space law doesn't adequately address different nuances of space tourism. While the international space law has been oriented towards the regulation of State activities in outer space, the domestic laws are still to develop for regulating the negative effects of space tourism. Hence, this is the right time to debate on different legal aspects of space tourism to find suitable solutions.

### Debate over the Applicable Law

The first and an overarching legal concern in space tourism is the debate over the application of the legal regime. In order to appreciate this debate, one should understand that aviation law and space law are two distinct fields of laws. While aviation law is based on the principle of State sovereignty over the airspace above its territory,[15] space law is based on the principle of freedom for all States.[16] Given this foundational difference, the elements of aviation law and space law are different and diametrically opposite in several aspects. Just to provide an example, space law fixes liability for any damage caused by space activities on the launching State/s; however, aviation law fixes such liability on private individuals.

Space tourism involves travel through both airspace and outer space. Accordingly, the question of applicable law attains tremendous significance as the simultaneous application of aviation law and space law would result in chaos. The historical debate over the theories of delimitation or demarcation of outer space from airspace has revived with greater significance in the era of space tourism. It is interesting to note that Richard Branson reached an altitude of 86 km,

Space Tourism: Outlining the Legal Issues **3**

triggering the debate on whether he has actually reached space.[17] While many argue that 100 km above the mean sea level should be the line of demarcation between the airspace and outer space, the United States' top agencies like Federal Aviation Administration (FAA) and National Aeronautics and Space Administration (NASA) have considered approximately 80 km above the mean sea level as the starting point of outer space.[18]

The debate over the definition and demarcation of the outer space still remains open-ended from the legal sense. Ever since the beginning of space activities in 1957, the search for a line of demarcation between the airspace and outer space started especially to settle the question of applicable law for activities above the Earth's surface.[19] Theories ranging from spatial approach to functional approach were proposed by different scholars for finding an answer to the question of demarcation as well as applicable law. The spatial approach was an attempt to delineate the outer space on the basis of altitude from the surface of the Earth. It included theories like gravitational force theory, atmosphere theory, aerodynamic lift theory, biological theory, theory of satellite orbit, Kármán line theory, theories based on effective control, interest and national security etc.[20] The functional approach, on the contrary, tries to demarcate the outer space, and more particularly decide on the applicable law by focusing on the function of the object used in the activities above the Earth surface. The functionalists argue that the outer space should start from the region wherever the space activities can be said to have begun.[21] Some of the functionalists believed that there is no need for demarcation of outer space, and what is required is solving the puzzle of applicable law by looking into the function/s of the object.[22]

The spatial approach was bound to fail as there is no natural boundary between the airspace and outer space. Unlike the general misconception, outer space is not a void.[23] As we move upwards, only the density of air reduces. Added to this, the technological developments in both aviation and space sectors have made it difficult to reach a point of clear distinction. With the development in technology, aircraft are in a position to fly at higher altitudes and the space objects are capable of orbiting at lower altitudes.[24] Hence, there would be an area of convergence between the aviation activities and space activities. Application of either aviation law or space law in this zone of convergence remains a matter of debate.

The functional approach is also not free from concerns. Just like demarcating outer space from airspace is difficult, drawing distinction between the aviation activities and space activities is also a complex affair. In most of the space tourism activities the vehicles used are the aerospace vehicles, which are capable of flying like an aircraft with the help of aerodynamic alleviation, and orbit around the Earth like a space object.[25] Hence, deciding the application of aviation law or space law to any activity on board an aerospace vehicle on the basis of its functions is an impossible task. Even if an argument is made for the application of aviation law until the time the aerospace vehicle is flying with aerodynamic alleviation and subsequently applying space law, it would end up in the difficult task

**4** Sandeepa Bhat B.

of finding the function of the aerospace vehicle at the time when the concerned activity happened. Moreover, this would bring more subjectivity and confusion in deciding the question of applicable law.

Thus, the absence of a clear line of demarcation between the airspace and the outer space coupled with the divergence in aviation law and space law stand as major obstacles in the determination of applicable law for aerospace activities. Developing a separate law to govern the aerospace activities, though advocated by some scholars,[26] does not seem to be a feasible option as such a micro level approach would result in disharmony and fragmentation of laws. Moreover, developing such a hybrid law would require an international consensus, which is not expected in the current era of space commercialisation. Hence, developing some guidelines with key factors for the determination of relevant applicable law on a case-by-case basis seems to be a better option available at present to deal with space tourism.

## Concerns in Registration

Registration concerns in space tourism activities are incidental problems arising from the confusion regarding the applicable law. The aerospace vehicles involved in space tourism pose difficulty in deciding the manner of their registration. Even though the aerospace vehicles have the attributes of both aircraft and space objects, it is not possible to register them under both aviation law and space law since there would be conflicting consequences of such registrations. Hence, there remains the difficult question of whether to register the space tourism vehicles under aviation law or under space law.

The registration processes under aviation law and space law are entirely different. Under the aviation law, the Chicago Convention keeps the registration of aircraft as a domestic affair with only a requirement of informing International Civil Aviation Organization (ICAO) and other States about the registration.[27] However, the international space law requires the registration of space objects in both national and international registries.[28] While the registration in case of aircraft is the obligation of owners of the aircraft, the space objects' registration is the responsibility of the launching State/s. Moreover, the aircraft registration is a onetime process, unless there is any attempt to change the registration consequent to sale or other reasons. However, the registration of space objects has to be done by the launching State/s every time they are launched into the Earth orbit or beyond.[29]

Application of space law for registration results in complications. Since the Registration Convention requires the registration of space objects after they have been launched into the Earth orbit or beyond, there is no scope for *a priori* registration of space tourism vehicles. As most space tourism ventures involve a short-time trip to outer space,[30] there would not be sufficient time for registration of space tourism vehicles after they have been launched into the Earth orbit. This would result in situations where even before the entry of particulars in the concerned

Space Tourism: Outlining the Legal Issues **5**

registry, the space vehicles return to the Earth. However, an argument for applying the aviation law for registration simply on the basis of complications of registration under the space law does not find any merit. Since space tourism predominantly involves space-related activities, registration under the aviation law would result in untoward consequences.

### Orbit Allocation and Use

The International Telecommunication Union (ITU) is entrusted with the responsibility to allocate orbits and spectrums for space activities.[31] The orbital allocation by an international agency like ITU is key for proper coordination and ensuring efficient space traffic management. In the absence of such an international allocation system, the outer space would become a realm of chaos.[32] The ITU system of orbital allocation and the Registration Convention together bring transparency in space activities and avoid harmful interferences between multiple space activities. While ITU would not permit the use of same orbital space by more than one player, the Registration Convention helps in planning the space activities in advance to avoid collision or any other disaster in outer space. Under the Registration Convention, the double registration requirement is also supplemented by a provision seeking the State of registry to inform the Secretary General of the United Nations about its space objects that are no longer in outer space.[33] This helps in giving a clear picture about what space objects are in outer space, their orbital parameters and also what objects are no longer in outer space. Accordingly, the ITU system of orbital allocation and the Registration Convention are indispensable for sustainable space developments.

It is pertinent to note here that the ITU system of orbital allocation is primarily based on the radiofrequency allocation, and it is not intended to cover the pleasure trips to outer space.[34] In private space tourism, unlike the scientific expeditions or several other commercial space activities,[35] the operators are not using one particular Earth orbit. Their activities may cut through multiple orbits, though for a short period of time, for providing different views and experiences to tourists as provided generally in every tour operation.[36] This brings forward a two-folded question: First, whether the space tourism operator needs to take permission from ITU, via the State concerned,[37] for all orbital slots to be used in the tour operations? Second, how many orbital slots can be allotted by the ITU for each space tourism operator, especially at a future point in time when many space tourism operators are expected to rule the market?

If we go by the need for effective space traffic management and transparency, the space tourism operator must take permission for the use of each orbital slot. However, many tour operators may be interested in common orbital slots as they provide better views or experiences to the space tourists. This would result in conflicts, and litigations might also reach the courts on the ground of trespassing the orbital slots of one by another tour operator. The second part of the above-mentioned

**6** Sandeepa Bhat B.

two-fold question is further difficult to answer. With the increased competition in the lucrative space tourism market, there will be a race between the space tourism operators for grabbing orbital slots. Every allocation of orbital slot to commercial space tourism will result in cutting down the slots available for scientific missions as well as for other commercial uses of outer space for the common benefit. While the allowance of pleasure trips in outer space brings forward the question of its compatibility with the obligation of carrying on the space activities for the "benefit and interest of all countries" as well as in accordance with the principle of the "province of all mankind" envisaged under Article I of the Outer Space Treaty,[38] granting more orbital slots for space tourism would intensify doubt on its compatibility.

In addition to the concerns in the allocation of orbital slots, space tourism also involves problems in terms of use of orbital slots. Since the space tourism involves intermittent use of orbital slots, the question of whether it constitutes an efficient use of limited resources[39] is difficult to answer. Moreover, the intermittent use of the orbital slots creates problem in maintaining transparency. As highlighted above, the whereabouts of a space tourism vehicle at a given point in time is difficult to assess in the absence of a proper system of registration and deregistration. This would be disastrous from the point of view of space traffic management. Since the private space tourism vehicles may randomly move in different orbits, planning the space launch and ensuring the safety would become a herculean task.

## Authorisation and Continued Supervision

Article VI of the Outer Space Treaty obligates the appropriate State party to authorise and continuously supervise the activities of the private players in outer space. This obligation is sacrosanct as the failure of the State to comply with it would result in attracting international responsibility. However, the Outer Space Treaty does not define the phrase "appropriate State party". Though the subsequent treaties define the "launching State"[40] and "State of registry",[41] they fail to define "appropriate State party". The definition of launching State indicates that there can be multiple States which can come within the ambit of it for the same space object. However, the State of registry for any space object can only be one of the launching States.

Space tourism activities involve multiple players like tour operators, space tourists, launch providers etc. Each of these players may belong to a different State. This brings forward the question as to which is the "appropriate State party" to authorise and continuously supervise space tourism when it involves stakeholders from multiple jurisdictions. One cannot oversimplify this issue to state that all States should take measures, since Article VI of the Outer Space Treaty uses singular rather than plural in imposing the obligation of authorisation and continuing supervision on a State. Moreover, the continuous supervision of increased space tourism activities in future would also be a difficult affair for the "appropriate State party".

## Emergency Assistance

Space activities are inherently risky.[42] Article V of the Outer Space Treaty provides astronauts with an elevated status of being envoys of mankind in outer space. This was based on the presumption that astronauts carry on the activities in outer space for the benefit and interest of all.[43] Being the representatives of mankind in outer space, the astronauts also enjoy the privilege of emergency assistance in the event of accident, distress or emergency landing. This privilege of emergency assistance has been extended to personnel of spacecrafts under the Rescue Agreement.[44] The rescued astronauts or personnel should also be returned safely and promptly to the launching authority.[45] Though the Rescue Agreement stipulates the reimbursement of expenses in case of recovery and return of space objects,[46] it does not contain a similar provision for cost reimbursement in connection with the emergency assistance provided to astronauts or personnel.

In the wake of space tourism, one of the major questions is the status of space tourists in case of emergency. Are they entitled to emergency assistance similar to what is available under the space treaties to astronauts or personnel is the major point in question. Though the scholars are in agreement to deny the status of astronauts to tourists, some of them are of the view that the term 'personnel' is broad enough to include space tourists within its ambit.[47] Such scholars make a reference to Article VIII of the Outer Space Treaty, which confers the jurisdiction and control over the space objects as well as over any personnel thereof to the State of registry of the concerned space object. The reference to 'personnel' under Article VIII could not have been intended to leave out the passengers on board the space object, and accordingly, the reference to 'personnel' under the Rescue Agreement should include passengers is one of the arguments in favour of giving a broad meaning to 'personnel'.[48]

The argument to include the space tourists or any person on board the space object within the meaning of 'personnel' is also buttressed by referring to Article 10 of the Moon Agreement.[49] In order to protect the life and health of any person on the Moon and other celestial bodies, Article 10 of the Moon Agreement mandates the State parties to consider such person as an 'astronaut' under the Outer Space Treaty as well as 'personnel' under the Rescue Agreement. Accordingly, the protection under both Outer Space Treaty and the Rescue Agreement is extendable to any person stands as another argument.[50]

Though the above arguments seem to be flawless at the outset, the concerns would be evident once we dig deep into it. The argument that the meaning of the term 'personnel' under Article VIII of the Outer Space Treaty in the context of exercising jurisdiction and control is wide enough to include any person on board the space object is acceptable. However, basing the interpretation of 'personnel' under the Rescue Agreement on the meaning of 'personnel' under Article VIII of the Outer Space Treaty is an incorrect approach. Every word in a treaty has to be interpreted in light of its context, and object and purpose of the treaty.[51] Attributing the meaning given to a word in a treaty to another treaty, though they form the

**8** Sandeepa Bhat B.

part of treaties in the same domain, without an enquiry into the context and object and purpose of the treaty stands as an incorrect approach of treaty interpretation. This is clearly evident in the approach of the World Trade Organization's (WTO) Dispute Settlement Body (DSB). While interpreting 'like products' under the GATT[52] (interestingly under the same agreement), the WTO DSB has compared the likeness to the image of an accordion to make it clear that the expression 'like products' has different meanings under different provisions of the GATT. It went on to state that:

> The accordion of "likeness" stretches and squeezes in different places as different provisions of the WTO Agreement are applied. The width of the accordion in any one of those places must be determined by the particular provision in which the term "like" is encountered as well as by the context and the circumstances that prevail in any given case to which that provision may apply.[53]

If we carefully go through the preamble and provisions of the Rescue Agreement, importing the meaning of the term 'personnel' from Article VIII of the Outer Space Treaty does not make sense. Even though the preamble of the Rescue Agreement mentions the relevance of "sentiments of humanity", the Agreement is strongly based on the principle of astronauts as envoys of mankind. It is undeniable that the Rescue Agreement is for furthering the mandate of Article V of the Outer Space Treaty rather than to cater to the sentiments of humanity in general. This is adequately reflected in the fact that the Rescue Agreement does not contain any provision regarding the reimbursement of expenses incurred with respect to rescue and return of personnel. A mandate to search, rescue and return without the cost reimbursement would be acceptable only when the 'personnel' is involved in some activities that further the common good. It is illogical to extend such a heavy burden on the States in case of pleasure trips of the space tourists. Moreover, imposing such a burden is also against the spirit of the Rescue Agreement as well as the common intention of the drafters especially when they drafted it during the era of State-oriented space activities. Thus, in the absence of a provision to reimburse the cost, mandating any State to search, rescue and return the private space tourists can never be acceptable.

Argument to import the meaning of 'personnel' from Article 10 of the Moon Agreement is also not a correct approach. On the one hand, the practical implication of the Moon Agreement itself is in question with only 18 States ratifying it.[54] The list of the States also indicates that many of the State parties are not even involved in conducting space activities. Basing a concrete obligation of search, rescue and return of space tourists on such a shaky ground does not make sense. On the other hand, the application of the Moon Agreement is confined to Moon and other celestial bodies, and orbits and trajectories around them.[55] Stretching its coverage to the Earth orbit to argue for providing emergency assistance to space tourists also goes beyond the permissible limits of interpretation.[56]

Drawing analogy from aviation law would also indicate that the term 'personnel' is not wide enough to include everyone on board an object. Aviation personnel are clearly distinguished from the passengers under all laws relating to civil aviation. The Chicago Convention, for example, mandates each aviation personnel to obtain the certificate of competency and licence from the State of registration of the aircraft.[57] Such a certificate or licence is not required for any passenger. This provision is also supplemented with a separate annex on personnel licensing, which also stipulates the coverage of only those persons who are connected with aircraft operations.[58] In light of these aspects, the extension of provisions on emergency assistance under the Outer Space Treaty and the Rescue Agreement to the space tourists still remains at limbo.

## Protection of Environment

There is no denial of the fact that tourism causes damage to environment.[59] While the use of different means of transportation results in emission, the activities of tourists also degrade the environment with waste generation and littering of the waste.[60] In space tourism, the environment of both Earth and the outer space is at stake. A recent study on the emission from one of the SpaceX rocket's launch unveils that approximately 116 tonnes of carbon dioxide was emitted in a span of 165 seconds.[61] This makes a serious inroad into the commitments of the States under international norms to reduce the emission of carbon dioxide and to protect the Earth environment.

The problem of emission is of a greater concern in outer space due to the absence of dense atmosphere. The release of chemical effluents during space missions triggers serious changes in the space environment.[62] Such changes would remain for a long period of time due to less reactions of air. In addition, space tourism is going to add on to the grave concern of space debris.[63] Hence, the question of sustainable use of outer space comes to the forefront especially when we use it extensively for pleasure trips as against scientific investigations or other commercial uses for the common benefit.

The contemporary international regime on the protection of outer space environment is also very weak. The only major direct provision on the protection of space environment is Article IX of the Outer Space Treaty, which is riddled with interpretational concerns. While it requires the State parties to avoid harmful contamination of outer space and prevent adverse changes in the Earth's environment, the provision and the Outer Space Treaty fail to define both "harmful contamination" and "adverse changes". This has resulted in an unending debate over the specifics of obligations of the States under Article IX of the Outer Space Treaty. In addition, both the Outer Space Treaty and the Liability Convention fail to fix liability for causing environmental damage. This is clearly evident from the restricted definition of 'damage' provided under the Liability Convention.[64] Thus, space tourism also poses serious threat to the fulfilment of our environmental commitments in the absence of a proper regulatory mechanism.

## Liability Aspects

The last significant issue to be covered here is the aspect of liability in space tourism. Liability in space tourism has multiple dimensions ranging from civil to criminal as well as between tourists *inter se* to tourists and tour operators/States. As already outlined in the previous section, the application of aviation law or space law for the fixation of liability remains an unclear area. It stands as the most significant concern as the liability norms under aviation law and space law are entirely distinct. Moreover, while the aviation law has several international instruments to deal with different aspects of liability ranging from civil to criminal,[65] the international space law deals only with the third-party civil liability in a limited manner.

Despite the limitations of space law, aviation law cannot be extended laterally upwards to cover all aspects of space tourism. Application of space law to fix liability becomes indispensable, which results in several open-ended questions. In case of any crime or tort committed by one space tourist against another, there would be questions on the jurisdiction and applicable law for fixing the liability. Commission of crime in the outer space has entered the realm of reality with astronaut Anne McClain being accused of hacking into the bank account of her former spouse from the ISS.[66] Since the accused and the victim belonged to the same country, and the offence was alleged to be committed from the United States' module of ISS and the effect was felt within US territory, the questions on jurisdiction and applicable law were not much complicated. However, the determination of jurisdiction and applicable law becomes complicated when the perpetrator and the victim belong to two different States. With the tour operator and space tourism vehicle belonging to yet another State, the complications would multiply.

With respect to criminal jurisdiction on ISS, the Inter-Governmental Agreement on ISS[67] goes primarily by the principle of nationality of the offender, or alternatively, by the jurisdiction of State affected by the offence.[68] However, this approach cannot be considered to be of universal application especially due to its contradiction with Article VIII of the Outer Space Treaty. Article VIII of the Outer Space Treaty stipulates that "A State Party to the Treaty on whose registry an object launched into outer space is carried *shall retain jurisdiction*[69] and control over such object, and over any personnel thereof, while in outer space or on a celestial body." Accordingly, the State of registration of the space object has both right and obligation to exercise jurisdiction over the space objects and the personnel. Since there is no indication to limit the jurisdiction under Article VIII to civil matters, deviation from it does not seem to be justified.

Regarding the aspect of civil liability in space tourism, two major scenarios arise. First is the liability for damage caused to space tourists, and the second is the liability for damage caused to third parties. Both Outer Space Treaty and Liability Convention cover only the liability for damage caused by the 'space object'. They are silent on the liability for damage caused due to the acts of space tourists and tour operators. Moreover, the liability for damage caused by the space objects is also imposed on the launching State/s as against the private operators.[70] Hence, the question on justifiability of holding the State liable for the damage caused by private space activities also comes to the forefront.

## Chapter Conclusion

Commercial space activities are increasing day by day. While some commercial space activities like telecommunication, direct television broadcasting, remote sensing, tele-education, tele-medicine etc. are of common interest, the activity like space tourism only furthers private interests. Whatever may be the arguments made towards the contribution of space tourism to State economy, it is the undeniable fact that space tourism is just the pleasure trip of rich people. More significantly, these pleasure trips are interfering with the beneficial use of outer space by consuming the limited space available for space activities. Compromising the common good in the zeal to promote the interests of select few wealthy space tourists and space tourism operators is not acceptable. Hence, a proper regulatory framework to deal with the plethora of legal issues dealt in this chapter is immediately required before we proceed forward with large-scale commercial space tourism.

## Notes

1 Dennis Tito, 'Testimony Submitted to the Senate Committee on Commerce, Science & Transportation Subcommittee on Science, Technology and Space, and the House Committee on Science, Subcommittee on Space & Aeronautics', *Joint Hearing on "Commercial Human Spaceflight"*, 24 July 2003, p. 1.
2 Mike Wall, 'First Space Tourist: How a US Millionaire Bought a Ticket to Orbit', *space.com*, 27 April 2011, available at <https://www.space.com/11492-space-tourism-pioneer-dennis-tito.html> Last visited, 15 December 2022.
3 *Supra* note 1.
4 Michael Sheetz, 'Space Tourism Pioneer Dennis Tito Books Private Moon Trip on SpaceX's Starship', *CNBC*, 12 October 2022, available at <https://www.cnbc.com/2022/10/12/spacex-starship-seats-space-tourism-pioneer-dennis-tito-books-private-moon-trip.html> Last visited, 15 December 2022.
5 Valerie Stimac, 'A Definitive History of Space Tourism & Human Spaceflight', *Space Tourism Guide*, 5 July 2020, available at <https://spacetourismguide.com/history-of-space-tourism/> Last visited, 15 December 2022.
6 Alex Li, 'The First 20 Years of Space Tourism (2001–2021): A Chronology', *The Space Bar*, available at <https://alexsli.com/thespacebar/2022/2/8/the-first-20-years-of-space-tourism-2001-2021-a-brief-chronology> Last visited, 15 December 2022.
7 'Russia: No More Space Tourists After 2009', *NBC News*, 21 January 2009, available at <https://www.nbcnews.com/id/wbna28773091> Last visited, 15 December 2022; Iansria Novosti, 'Russia to Resume Space Tourist Programme in 2–3 Years', *The Hindu*, 22 March 2010, available at <https://www.thehindu.com/sci-tech/Russia-to-resume-space-tourist-programme-in-2-3-years/article16581083.ece> Last visited, 15 December 2022.
8 Valerie Stimac, '12 Space Tourism Companies That Will Send You to Space', *Space Tourism Guide*, 22 July 2019, available at <https://spacetourismguide.com/space-tourism-companies/> Last visited, 15 December 2022.

9 Stephan Hobe and Jurgen Cloppenburg, 'Towards a New Aerospace Convention? Selected Legal Issues of Space Tourism', *Proceedings of the Forty Seventh Colloquium on the Law of Outer Space*, 2004, pp. 377–385 at p. 377.

10 Ayşe Meriç Yazici and Satyam Tiwari, 'Space Tourism: An Initiative Pushing Limits', *Journal of Tourism, Leisure and Hospitality*, Vol. 3, No. 1, 2021, pp. 38–46 at p. 41.

11 'Blue Origin and Virgin Galactic: Their Space Tourism Flights Explained', *The Planetary Society*, 13 July 2021, available at <https://www.planetary.org/articles/blue-origin-virgin-galactic-space-tourism-flights-explained> Last visited, 15 December 2022.

12 Elizabeth Howell, 'Space Tourism Took a Giant Leap in 2021: Here's 10 Milestones from the Year', *space.com*, 27 December 2021, available at <https://www.space.com/space-tourism-giant-leap-2021-milestones> Last visited, 16 December 2022.

13 Vicky Stein and Scott Dutfield, 'Inspiration4: The First All-Civilian Spaceflight on SpaceX Dragon', *space.com*, 5 January 2022, available at <https://www.space.com/inspiration4-spacex.html> Last visited, 16 December 2022.

14 See 'Space Tourism Market Size, Share & Trends Analysis Report by Type (Orbital, Sub-orbital), by End Use (Government, Commercial), by Region, and Segment Forecasts, 2022–2030', available at <https://www.grandviewresearch.com/industry-analysis/space-tourism-market-report#> Last visited, 16 December 2022; 'Global Space Tourism Market to Reach $8.67 Billion by 2030', *PR Newswire*, 31 August 2022, available at <https://www.prnewswire.com/news-releases/global-space-tourism-market-to-reach-8-67-billion-by-2030--301615597.html> Last visited, 16 December 2022; Vantage Market Research, 'Global Space Tourism Market Size to Hit USD 3622.5 Mn, with a CAGR of 36.4% | The Rapid Advancement of Technology to Drive the Market', *GlobeNewswire*, 21 September 2022, available at <https://www.globenewswire.com/en/news-release/2022/09/21/2520048/0/en/Global-Space-Tourism-Market-Size-to-Hit-USD-3622-5-Mn-with-a-CAGR-of-36-4-The-Rapid-Advancement-of-Technology-to-Drive-the-Market-Vantage-Market-Research.html#:~:text=The%20global%20Space%20Tourism%20Market%20was%20valued%20USD%20562.5%20Million,the%20forecast%20period%202022%2D2028.> Last visited, 16 December 2022.

15 Convention on International Civil Aviation (Chicago Convention) 1944, (1994) 15 U.N.T.S. 295, Art. 1.

16 Treaty on Principles Governing the Activities of States in the Exploration and Use of Outer Space, including the Moon and Other Celestial Bodies (Outer Space Treaty) 1967, 610 UNTS 205, Art. 1.

17 Meenakshi Ray, 'Did Richard Branson Really Fly Into Space? Neil deGrasse Tyson Weighs In', *Hindustan Times*, 16 July 2021, available at <https://www.hindustantimes.com/science/did-richard-branson-really-fly-into-space-neil-degrasse-tyson-weighs-in-101626411110372.html> Last visited, 16 December 2022.

18 Sheena Goodyear, 'Did Richard Branson Really Make It to Space? Technically, It Depends Who You Ask', *CBC Radio*, 12 July 2021, available at <https://www.cbc.ca/radio/asithappens/as-it-happens-the-monday-edition-1.6099336/did-richard-branson-really-make-it-to-space-technically-it-depends-who-you-ask-1.6099854#:~:text=Did%20%5BBranson%5D%20actually%20make%20it,reached%20something%20like%202083%20kilometres.> Last visited, 16 December 2022.

19 Marietta Benko and Jurgen Gebhard, 'The Definition/Delimitation of Outer Space and Outer Space Activities Including Problems Relating to Free ("Innocent") Passage of Spacecraft Through Foreign Airspace for the Purpose of Reaching Orbit and Returning to Earth', in Marietta Benko and Kai-Uwe Schrogl (eds.), *International Space Law in the Making - Current Issues in the UN Committee on the Peaceful Uses of Outer Space*, Vol. 1 (Singapore: Forum for Air and Space Law, 1993) pp. 111–144 at p. 111.

20 Harnam Bhayana, *International Law in the Regime of Outer Space* (Calcutta: R. Cambray and Co. Pvt. Ltd., 2001) pp. 129–137.

21 Vladimir Kopal, 'Issues Involved in Defining Outer Space, Space Object and Space Debris', *Proceedings of the Thirty-Fourth Colloquium on Law of the Outer Space*, 1992, pp. 38–43 at p. 40.

22 Nicolas Matessco Matte, *Aerospace Law* (London: Sweet & Maxwell, 1969) p. 62.

23 'Outer Space Is Not Just an Empty Void', *Financial Review*, 23 November 2016, available at <https://www.afr.com/technology/outer-space-is-not-just-an-empty-void-20161121-gsu385> Last visited, 16 December 2022.

24 Gbenga Oduntan, 'The Never Ending Dispute: Legal Theories on the Spatial Demarcation Boundary Plane between Airspace and Outer Space', *Hertfordshire Law Journal*, Vol. 1, No. 2, pp. 64–83 at p. 74.

25 Rene Joseph Rey, 'Regulatory Challenges, Antitrust Hurdles, Intellectual Property Incentives, and the Collective Development of Aerospace Vehicle-Enabling Technologies and Standards: Creating an Industry Foundation', *Journal of Space Law*, Vol. 35, No. 1, 2009, pp. 75–162 at p. 77, footnote 4.

26 See T.L. Masson-Zwaan, 'The Aerospace Plane: An Object at the Cross-Roads between Air and Space Law', in Henri Abraham Wassenbergh, et al. (eds.) *Air and Space Law: De Lege Ferenda* (Dordrecht: Martinus Nijhoff Publishers, 1992) p. 257.

27 See Chicago Convention, Arts. 17–21.

28 See Convention on Registration of Objects Launched into Outer Space (Registration Convention) 1975, 1023 UNTS 15, Arts. II–IV.

29 *Id.*, Art. II.

30 Molly M. McCue, 'A Regulatory Scheme for the Dawn of Space Tourism', *Vanderbilt Journal of Transnational Law*, Vol. 55, No. 4, 2022, pp. 1087–1116 at p. 1089.

31 'ITU Radio Regulatory Framework for Space Services', available at <https://www.itu.int/en/ITU-R/space/snl/Documents/ITU-Space_reg.pdf> Last visited, 18 December 2022.

32 Martin A. Rothblatt, 'ITU Regulation of Satellite Communication', *Stanford Journal of International Law*, Vol. 18, No. 1, 1982, pp. 1–26 at p. 6.

33 Registration Convention, Art. IV(3).

34 Ryszard Struzak, 'Introduction to International Radio Regulations', pp. 42 & 55, available at <https://www.osti.gov/etdeweb/servlets/purl/20945052> Last visited, 18 December 2022.

35 Satellites involved in commercial space activities like direct television broadcasting, remote sensing of earth, telecommunication etc., would use the same orbit for a long period of time unless the operator decides to manoeuvre them for some operational reasons.

36 See generally Peter Mason, *Tourism Impacts, Planning and Management* (Burlington: Butterworth-Heinemann, 2003).

37 Individuals need to route through the concerned State for obtaining a permit from the ITU to use any orbital slot. See 'Guidelines on the Submission of Application for the Grant of Licence for the Use of Satellite Orbital Slot', available at <https://www.imda.gov.sg/-/media/Imda/Files/Regulation-Licensing-and-Consultations/Licensing/licenses/GuideSatelliteOrbitalSlotLic.pdf> Last visited, 22 December 2022.

38 Outer Space Treaty, Art. I states that "The exploration and use of outer space, including the moon and other celestial bodies, shall be carried out for the benefit and in the interests of all countries, irrespective of their degree of economic or scientific development, and shall be the province of all mankind."

39 Martin L. Stern, 'Communication Satellites and the Geostationary Orbit: Reconciling Equitable Access with Efficient Use', *Law and Policy in International Business*, Vol. 14, No. 3, 1982, pp. 859–884 at p. 861.

40 See Convention on International Liability for Damage Caused by Space Objects (Liability Convention) 1972, 961 UNTS 187, Art. I(c) and Registration Convention, Art. I(a).

**14** Sandeepa Bhat B.

41 See Registration Convention, Art. I(c).
42 Andrea J. Harrington, *Space Insurance and the Law* (Cheltenham: Edward Elgar Publishing Ltd., 2021) p. 2.
43 Aldo Armando Cocca, 'Legal Aspects of Mental and Physical Workload of Astronauts', *Proceedings of the Thirty Seventh Colloquium on the Law of Outer Space*, 1994, pp. 213–221 at p. 216.
44 Agreement on the Rescue of Astronauts, the Return of Astronauts and the Return of Objects Launched into Outer Space (Rescue Agreement) 1968, 672 UNTS 119, Arts. 2 & 3.
45 *Id.*, Art. 4.
46 *Id.*, Art. 5(5).
47 Stephen Gorove, 'Legal and Policy Issues of the Aerospace Plane', *Journal of Space Law*, Vol. 16, No. 2, 1988, pp. 147–156 at p. 151.
48 *Id.*
49 Agreement governing the Activities of States on the Moon and Other Celestial Bodies (Moon Agreement) 1979, 1363 UNTS 3; See James R. Wilson, 'Regulation of the Outer Space Environment through International Accord: The 1979 Moon Treaty', *Fordham Environmental Law Report*, Vol. 2, No. 2, 1991, pp. 173–194 at p. 180; See also Stephen E. Doyle, 'Using Extraterrestrial Resources under the Moon Agreement of 1979', *Journal of Space Law*, Vol. 26, No. 2, 1998, pp. 111–128 at p. 120.
50 Heidi Keefe, 'Making the Final Frontier Feasible: A Critical Look at the Current Body of Outer Space Law', *Santa Clara Computer and High-Technology Law Journal*, Vol. 11, No. 2, 1995, pp. 345–372 at p. 355.
51 Vienna Convention on Law of Treaties 1969, 1155 UNTS 331, Art. 31(1): "A treaty shall be interpreted in good faith in accordance with the ordinary meaning to be given to the terms of the treaty in their context and in the light of its object and purpose."
52 General Agreement on Tariffs and Trade 1994, 1867 UNTS 190.
53 *Japan – Taxes on Alcoholic Beverages* WT/DS8/AB/R, WT/DS10/AB/R, WT/DS11/AB/R, 4 October 1996, p. 21.
54 See 'Status of International Agreements Relating to Activities in Outer Space as at 1 January 2022', *Committee on the Peaceful Uses of Outer Space*, Legal Subcommittee, Sixty-first session, Vienna, 28 March–8 April 2022, UN Doc. A/AC.105/C.2/2022/CRP.10.
55 Moon Agreement, Art. 1.
56 Mark J. Sundahl, 'The Duty to Rescue Space Tourists and Return Private Spacecraft', *Journal of Space Law*, Vol. 35, No. 1, 2009, pp. 163–200 at p. 170.
57 Chicago Convention, Art. 32.
58 Annex 1 to Chicago Convention.
59 Florentina Burlacu, 'Developing Rural Areas in Romania with the Help of Cultural Tourism', *Cogito: Multidisciplinary Research Journal*, Vol. 11, No. 2, 2019, pp. 186–197 at p. 192; Liani Sari, et al., 'The Nature of Management Tourism Area to Embody Welfare Society (Tourism Law Perspective)', *Journal of Law, Policy and Globalization*, Vol. 46, 2016, pp. 74–79 at p. 75.
60 Luz-Aida Martinez Melendez, 'NAFTA, Tourism, and Environment in Mexico', *International Environmental Agreements: Politics, Law and Economics*, Vol. 10, No. 2, 2010, pp. 107–132 at p. 122.
61 Mark Piesing, 'The Pollution Caused by Rocket Launches', *BBC*, 15 July 2022, available at <https://www.bbc.com/future/article/20220713-how-to-make-rocket-launches-less-polluting#:~:text=One%20of%20the%20%22biggest%20surprises,quite%20significant%2C%22%20says%20Drikakis.> Last visited, 23 December 2022.
62 Nicolas M. Matte, 'Environmental Implications and Responsibilities in the Use of Outer Space', *Annals of Air and Space Law*, Vol. 14, 1989, pp. 419–448 at p. 424.

Space Tourism: Outlining the Legal Issues **15**

63 Adrian Taghdiri, 'Flags of Convenience and the Commercial Space Flight Industry: The Inadequacy of Current International Law to Address the Opportune Registration of Space Vehicles in Flag States', *Boston University Journal of Science & Technology Law*, Vol. 19, No. 2, 2013, pp. 405–431 at p. 405.

64 Liability Convention, Art. I(a) states that "The term 'damage' means loss of life, personal injury or other impairment of health; or loss of or damage to property of States or of persons, natural or juridical, or property of international intergovernmental organizations."

65 See Stephan Hobe, 'Legal Aspects of Space Tourism', *Nebraska Law Review*, Vol. 86, 2007, pp. 439–458 at pp. 448–452.

66 Mike Baker, 'NASA Astronaut Anne McClain Accused by Spouse of Crime in Space', *New York Times*, 27 August 2020, available at <https://www.nytimes.com/2019/08/23/us/astronaut-space-investigation.html> Last visited, 23 December 2022.

67 Agreement Among the Government of Canada, Governments of Member States of the European Space Agency, the Government of Japan, the Government of the Russian Federation and the Government of United States of America Concerning Cooperation on the Civil International Space Station, 29 January 1998, TIAS 12927.

68 Inter-Governmental Agreement on ISS, Art. 22.

69 Emphasis added.

70 Yanal Abul Failat, 'Space Tourism: A Synopsis on Its Legal Challenges', *Irish Law Journal*, Vol. 1, 2012, pp. 120–151 at p. 130.

# 2

# THE KÁRMÁN LINE CONTROVERSY AND BOUNDARIES OF OUTER SPACE

## Implications for Space Tourism

*Tushar Krishna and Shouvik Kumar Guha*

### Introduction

Where does outer space begin? This concern first arose in 1972, when Manfred Lachs J. posed two questions: "What are the outer space borders?" and "What are the practical repercussions of such omissions?"[1] He recognised that in the years ahead, technological improvement and increased space operations would lead to volatility and ambiguities, which would slow the rise of commercialised space exploration, including space tourism.[2] This assessment by Lachs appears to be turning into a modern reality, almost half a century later, since no global instrument of space law, including the Outer Space Treaty (OST), has responded to his questions.[3] Such a void poses a significant challenge for the space tourism industry, which is no longer confined to the realm of science fiction.

On 11 July 2021, Richard Branson, founder of Virgin Galactic, claimed to have beaten Jeff Bezos, founder of Blue Origin, one of his main competitors, by reaching 86 km above the Earth and consequently claiming to have pioneered space tourism.[4] This declaration sparked a heated controversy among space experts on whether the height attained by Mr. Branson can even be considered "outer space" and the seemingly trivial question of whether future Virgin Galactic passengers may be recognised as astronauts on reaching such an altitude.[5] Blue Origin, seizing its chance to showcase its dominance over space supremacy, tweeted that

> Virgin Galatic did not overstep the Karman line. New Shepard, on the other hand, was developed to fly over the Karman line, so none of our astronauts' names has an asterisk next to them. Space begins 100 kilometres up at the globally recognised Karman line for 96 per cent of the world's population.[6]

DOI: 10.4324/9781032617961-2

It went on to say that the 80-km limit is defined by only4% of the world as a space border. Therefore, New Shepard would go over 100 km; they would cross both of these limitations, making them preferable to Virgin Galactic flights.[7] However, this clash between two industrial players only demonstrates a very limited facet of the problem, which is multifarious and arose in the absence of any strictly delineated or universal spatial border.

As a result, the authors will examine not only the challenges associated with the lack of such limits but also other aspects of the problem from a broad perspective. Keeping that in mind, the chapter has been divided into the following parts: In Part II, it will look into the overview of the emergence of the question on the space boundary, including the analysis of different outer space origination points, including Kármán Line, Astronaut Badge Line, Mission Intent Line, and Transitionary Outer Space Zone. Subsequently, in Part III, it will delve into the question of why nations abstain from adopting a uniform space boundary. In Part IV, it will consider the reason for having such a delimitation line for outer space. Here, the main focus is on three major factors, i.e. registration and liability, mutual cooperation, non-discrimination, equal usage and exploration of outer space. Finally, the concluding remark is provided in Part V.

## Overview of the Emergence of the Question on Space Boundary

The question of where space originates is one of the earliest in the subject of space law; thus, it is not unusual that various possible explanations have emerged over time. Indeed, proposals ranging from 20 to 15 lakh km were made between 1957 and 1960.[8] The United Nations Committee on the Peaceful Uses of Outer Space has classified these proposals into two separate approaches to determining the boundary of space:[9] The first is the functionalist school, which considers the nature of the action in issue when evaluating whether an entity or individual has reached outer space, rather than taking any determined measurements. The second approach is the spatialist approach, which advocates for a quantifiable or specified boundary regardless of the type or objective of the object conveyed.[10] Both viewpoints, nonetheless, have sparked a lot of discussion and criticism.

Talking about the functionalist approach, it is founded on the contentious premise that "objective evaluation of operations as air or space activities" may be done in the nearspace,[11] which is defined as 20–100 km.[12] This specific assumption magnifies the existing problem, which is exacerbated by technological advancements. Furthermore, the concept of "space objects" cannot be applied to the functionalist method since there appears to be considerable uncertainty surrounding the definition of "space object" other than that it encompasses the components of such objectives.[13] As a result, it is unclear if "space objects" and "things propelled into outer space" are the same things.[14]**One of the most common concepts in the spatialist approach is that nations exert sovereignty in their airspace up to the region

**18** Tushar Krishna and Shouvik Kumar Guha

where "effective control" can be maintained by them.[15] Such a notion clearly invites risks for many countries due to a lack of technology or resources for the expansion of their control over the air space, which they aspire to have in order to secure any prospective encroachment into their sovereignty.[16] Additionally, the Aerodynamic lift theory, which is part of the spatialist approach, states that outer space begins when the aeroplane loses its aerodynamic lift under the atmosphere, which varies between 100 and 130 km, according to different studies.[17] In this context, it appears significant that the two major space boundaries, i.e. Kármán Line and the Astronaut Badge Line, are based on this particular theory itself. Nonetheless, in the following discussion, four major outer space boundaries based on both the approaches – functionalist and spatialist – and a hybrid approach have been analysed.

### Kármán Line

The Kármán Line is one of the most widely acknowledged space lines, also with Fédération Aéronautique Internationale, which is an international record-keeping authority, recognising it.[18] It establishes a spatial line that begins at 100 km (62 miles) above sea level.[19] As previously stated, there is a lack of scholarly or international consensus on the matter of space boundary lines; however, in this scenario, the Kármán Line emerged as the most widely recognised boundary among scholars and State agencies; even the United Nations recognised that space boundary lies something close to the Kármán Line.[20] The Kármán Line is named after its originator, Theodore von Kármán, a scientist from Hungary who worked in both aeronautics and astronautics and was one of the first to attempt to define a space border in the 1960s, eventually establishing the KármánLine.[21] To grasp the origins, it is essential to note that during his 1956 paper presentation, Kármán depicted an aircraft's aerothermal constraints. In other words, as an aircraft attempts to take off, it increases its speed, which creates more heat caused by friction with the atmosphere; using this principle, Kármán estimated the maximum distance an aircraft could fly without becoming overheated, which is 83.82 km (which is different from the current measurement of Kármán Line, i.e. 100 km).[22] It is also pertinent to note that, according to the Kármán chart, the velocity necessary to reach the altitude above such a point is identical to that required to reach orbit.[23] In his book "Space Law and Government",[24] Andrew G. Haley recognised the KármánLine as just an average assessment of the limitations stated by other significant scientists in 1963.[25] Moreover, Haley recognised that the KármánLine I is founded on the aircraft's velocity:weight ratio (Bell X-2), which is extremely flexible depending on technological advancements. Changes in more heat-resistant materials, improvements in jet engines, and so on, for example, can result in considerable changes in predicted distances.[26] The variability of the KármánLine is further demonstrated by the fact that even when using the same aircraft, tracing the outer space boundary on other planets, such as Venus, results in a 250 kmKármánLine.[27] Furthermore, Haely believed the KármánLine to be at 90 km at the conclusion of his work, claiming that this was the lowest height at which the "free radical atomic oxygen occurred".[28]

### Astronaut Badge Line (ABL) –80 km

Institutions in the United States, such as the US Armed Forces, the National Aeronautics and Space Administration (NASA), the National Oceanic and Atmospheric Administration (NOAA) and even the Federal Aviation Administration, have accepted this 80 km ABL between the mesosphere and thermosphere.[29] It's important to note that NASA officially altered their stance about the KármánLine only in 2005 to comply with military and aviation standards.[30] Indeed, three military pilots, William H. Dana, J.A. Walker, and J.B. McKay, were not given astronaut credentials for flying between 90 and 108 km in the 1960s, but were belatedly awarded the same in 2005.[31] Even some well-known scholars, such as Thomas Gangale[32] and Jonathan McDowell,[33] have advocated for an 80-km space frontier based on Kármán's initial study, which implies an 83-km space border.[34] Additionally, the fact that most meteors lose the majority of their mass between the ranges of 70 and 100 km, indicating the growing significance of the atmosphere between these ranges, was used to justify this boundary.[35] Furthermore, artificial satellites with perigees less than 80 km are unlikely to finish their next orbit.[36] At an altitude of 80 km, the free molecular movement, which can only occur in a vacuum (either created artificially or naturally in outer space), begins.[37]

As a result, in comparison to the KármánLine, which has more recognition but not enough empirical backing, there has been strong support for ABL. The ABL does not receive the same level of recognition from other countries. The lack of acknowledgement might be due to the fact that this line is considerably lower than the KármánLine, providing easier accessibility, which ultimately becomes an issue for nations with air dominance. Due to the possibility of other nations' spaceflights, which may be carried out at a lower altitude, the unique sovereignty possessed by these nationals with advancing technology may be jeopardised. On similar grounds, States without air supremacy may have been worried that lowering the border-line would allow technologically sophisticated nations to increase their overhead monitoring. Therefore, it is improbable that the ABL will be universally accepted as the space boundary without such backing.

### Mission Intent Line (MIL)

The MIL is based on a functionalist approach, unlike the Kármán Line and ABL, which are based on a spatialist approach. Thomas Gangale introduced MIL, which determined the space border based on the object's intent rather than any quanti-fiable height. "The anticipated destination of the flying object should determine whether it is classified as a spacecraft or an aircraft", he stated.[38] The most intrigu-ing aspect of his concept is that even if an object does not travel to space (for example, if it fails to travel beyond 20 km) or is unable to be launched, the laws and rules that apply to it are solely those of outer space. Thus, from a commercial standpoint, MIL appears to be aiding in the regulation of space tourism. For example, even if the spacecraft fails to reach outer space due to technical failures or has accidents before reaching the edge of space, the application of MIL offers a way out by allowing the implementation of travel insurance, which would otherwise be unavailable in the current situation.

However, as compared to a physical boundary like Kármán Line or ABL, the fundamental disadvantage of this line is the subjectivity it entails and the added ambiguity it invites. One might misuse the process by explicitly announcing its purpose to reach outer space, which was not the genuine goal in the first place. Similarly, MIL will allow organisations to choose the most advantageous regime from outer space regulation or aviation regulation by just stating their intent. Furthermore, as compared to the spatialist method, the fundamental defect introduced by this mechanism is the satisfactory determination of the goal, which appears to be an additional burden. As a result, in its current state, MIL as a universal concept does not appear to be practical due to its proclivity towards complications rather than solutions.

### Transitionary Outer Space Zone (TOSZ)

Unlike the previously stated boundary lines, which are based on either the spatial or functionalist approaches, this theory focuses on a fusion of both. To put it another way, this technique recommends using both the physical altitude above sea level and the awareness of the object's aim. It considers the zone between 80 km (ABL) and 100 km (Kármán Line) above sea level in order to appreciate the scientific evidence in favour of the 80 km boundary (e.g. Kármán's original calculation, free flow of molecules, etc.) as well as to take into account the 100 kmKármánLine, which is widely accepted worldwide.[39] However, in order to harmonise the two, it proposes utilising a 20-km zone, where only permissible passage may be carried out if the purpose of the object does not come under the scope of unlawful behaviour. By doing so, the fundamental shortcoming of ABL (as stated under the ABL heading) may be addressed while the objective approach is incorporated.

TOSZ is based on the concept of the Exclusive Economic Zone in the United Nations Convention on the Law of the Sea, in which the adjacent nation has exclusive sovereign control over the resources in that zone, while other nations can "enjoy the freedom of navigation, overflights, and other internationally lawful uses of the sea related to these freedoms, such as those associated with the operation of ships, aircraft and submarine cables and pipelines."[40] Similarly, spaceships with a legitimate purpose are free to fly over the TOSZ, whereas restrictions based on purposes do not apply to nations that have a specified section of the TOSZ above them in order to uphold their sovereignty. Under this method, the following purposes can be investigated to ensure legality: eavesdropping on other countries, gaining control of a portion of another country's TOSZ (by creating a space base) and posing a threat to other national security, among others. The technologically advanced as well as the technologically backward countries may rest certain that the distance of up to 80 km will be free of interference, and the remaining 20 km will be under their exclusive control. Although establishing the aims to ensure legitimacy in the TOSZ may be difficult, there is no question that the TOSZ has offered a path forward for countries to consider.

## Why Do Countries Abstain from Choosing a Universal Space Boundary?

The UN Scientific and Technical Subcommittee submitted to the Legal Subcommittee of the UN Committee on the Peaceful Uses of Outer Space in 1968 that "it is difficult to determine any specific concept for the outer space boundary".[41] The subcommittee made this remark because available technology at the time was not evolved enough to demarcate a permanent space boundary, but they also accepted that such a boundary might be defined and approved in the future. Again, in 2004, Hans Haubold, a senior official for Outer Space Affairs, claimed that owing to the imprecise structure of the atmosphere, it is difficult to identify any uniform space border.[42] Indeed, the Earth's atmosphere is "dynamic" and "fluctuates in density", making the establishment of precise borders nearly impossible. However, as described in the prior section, there are options to use TOSZ borders, which contemplate a 20-km range. Although experts may claim that the difficulty is due to the complicated nature of the atmosphere, which prevents the adoption of any universal border, the problem is really due to a "lack of political will to negotiate and agree on a boundary at the international level".[43] The US stance at the UN Committee on the Peaceful Uses of Outer Space's Legal Subcommittee clarifies the above remark:

> With respect to the question of the definition and delimitation of outer space […], our position continues to be that defining or delimiting outer space is not necessary. No legal or practical problems have arisen in the absence of such a definition. On the contrary, the differing legal regimes applicable in respect of airspace and outer space have operated well in their respective spheres. The lack of a definition or delimitation of outer space has not impeded the development of activities in either sphere. We have not been persuaded by the reasons put forth for undertaking such a definition or delimitation. For example, some delegations support the notion of such a definition for its own sake. But without a practical problem to address, undertaking such a definition would be a risky exercise, as explained more fully below. Other delegations suggest that a definition or delimitation is somehow necessary to safeguard the sovereignty of states. However, we are aware of no issue of state sovereignty that would be solved by defining outer space.[44]

The United States will reinstate a similar posture in the years ahead.[45] However, with the advent of space tourism, such a position appears to be absurd, as we can see an expanding number of existing activities of space tourism have been taking place, boosting sub-orbital traffic and thus posing a whole new set of challenges for the legal fraternity, which will be discussed in the next segment.

## Why Do We Need a Universal Outer Space Boundary?

Looking at the UN Scientific and Technical Subcommittee's prognostication that the space boundary will be defined in the future with sufficient technological advancement, in the wake of the emergence of aerospace technologies and the heavy use of near space, there is a pressing need to define the space boundary because of the ambiguities of the rules that apply to these commercial space activities, which go beyond the simple problem of State conflict on the ground of exercising their State sovereignty over the airspace it holds; there could be larger economic ramifications to the ambiguity in the wake of the space race which we saw between the private players (unlike the States during the Cold War).

### Registration and Liability Concerns

The registration and liability mechanism in the OST and other agreements is one of the key regulatory mechanisms that may be attached after settling on a space border.[46] According to current legal standing, registration is only required if the spacecraft is "launched into earth orbit or beyond".[47] Since sub-orbital flights used for space tourism are not meant to enter Earth's orbit, they are exempt from the registration requirement. However, because activities like sub-orbital flights in the form of space tourism "classify themselves as a space activity" and are still excluded from the existing legal process, such a gap is generating a large vacuum in the existing legal mechanism.[48] The fact that the jurisdiction and control aspects of any space object are controlled by the national legislation of the State in which the object has been registered demonstrates the relevance of this registration requirement. Because there is no necessity for sub-orbital flights to be registered, the immediate ramification is the question of which State "exercises jurisdiction and control over such objects".[49]

Furthermore, as the Committee on the Peaceful Uses of Outer Space has recognised, determining the space border is critical in determining the liability of any space action.[50] It is important to note that any space object that damages the Earth's surface or an aircraft in flight is subject to absolute liability.[51] The contrast in "the responsibility convention between absolute culpability for damage to the Earth's surface and to planes in flight[52] and fault-based liability for harm elsewhere[53] implies a physical space boundary", according to a community of scholars.[54] It may even be claimed that the expressions "injury to an aircraft in the flight" and "damage inflicted other than on the Earth's surface" demonstrate the liability convention's leaning towards a spatialist approach.[55] As previously stated, the majority of space flights for the purpose of space tourism will take place in airspace; the chance of harm that such a space flight might inflict is on the surface of an aircraft in flight as compared to other space objects. In the absence of a space boundary, there would be ambiguity as to whether the damage would be classified as "damage to aircraft in flight" or "damage to other space objects", potentially affecting the space tourism sector.

## Maintaining Mutual Cooperation

One of the OST's fundamental ideals is mutual cooperation.[56] According to the concept of mutual cooperation, each State must take into account the space operations of other countries when conducting its own space activities. Furthermore, it necessitates international consultations in circumstances when a State believes that its space operations may jeopardise the space activities of another nation. Since these principles apply in outer space and have "an influence on the rights and obligations of nations carrying out space operations", due to the standing ambiguity regarding the space boundary, the applicability of this concept appears problematic, especially for activities taking place in nearspace, such as space tourism. The current expansion in space tourist operations in this region has most certainly increased "conflict with the traditional aircraft, either during the launch or return process, or owing to failure that may occur during their operation". The growing likelihood of conflict and interference has increased the need for mutual cooperation "to securely sustain space operations while taking into account the interests of other states".

## Freedom to Access and Non-discrimination

According to the OST, all States have the same right to use and explore space.[57] To put it in another way, the State's sovereignty ends in outer space, but it can continue to retain it in the airspace. It can also be interpreted as the proposition of a region of outer space.[58] Similarly, Article I of the OST established the concept of non-discrimination: "space operations should be carried out for the benefit and in the interests of all countries, irrespective of their economic or scientific progress".[59] Many countries (particularly developing countries) have exaggerated the necessity to demarcate the space border in order to ensure that these principles are not being violated.[60] The existing legal structure for the "effective control test" is acting against less technologically proficient countries exercising their rights to explore space,[61] which is in violation of the OST principles.[62]In the wake of the space tourism activities in the near space, there have been increasing chances to have threat towards the national security of the less technologically advanced nations due to the high possibility of the technologically advanced nations using the airspace of these nations by merely saying that this is outer space as per the standard they follow, and thereby they can have right to explore theirs as per the OST freely. Another issue might be that when space tourism becomes more affordable in the future, it will become more accessible to underdeveloped countries, who would wish to exercise their freedom to explore space without prejudice in contrast to technologically advanced nations. The need to establish a well-defined space boundary is critical in such cases.

## Conclusion

Due to the potential for increased space traffic and conflicts in the coming years, the question of having well-defined regulations for outer space has arisen in the contemporary world, when outer space is no longer restrained by governmental entities with the advent of commercial players with technological advancement. One of their concerns was the origin point of space,on which the international nations do not appear to have reached a consensus due totheir political reasons for failing to acknowledge the financial potential of private space enterprises, which raises other questions, such as who is responsible for any action taken in space and under what law? How do you figure out what jurisdiction any space object is in? All of these questions are related, seeing as to how the workaround to all of them is to establish a universal space boundary in order to provide more legal feasibility to the private space industries rather than to maintain the current ambiguities, which will exacerbate the situation in the future as new challenges of space tourism combine with the existing basic problems of no space boundary. In this context, it may be useful to consider whether any cogent customary law can be gleaned from the various State practices in this regard. Domestic legislation such as the Australian Space Activities Act, 1998 (specifically Section 8 thereof) and the South African Republic Space Affairs Act, 1993 (specifically Section 1 thereof) supports the demarcation to remain at 100 km above the mean sea level. In addition, surveys carried out by the UNCOPUOS also revealed nations like Russia and Germany acknowledging this 100 km line as the beginning of outer space and the end of domestic sovereign aerospace jurisdiction; further, organisational practices on both domestic (such as the US Federal Aviation Administration's norms for conferment of astronaut wings) and international studies (conducted by the International Academy of Astronautics and criteria for space flight as determined by the Fédération Aéronautique Internationale) also support such delimitation. Yet, such consonance of practice has till date not been deemed sufficient to declare a clear customary law norm settling the demarcation debate once and for all. Attempts made in the past towards a temporary solution by applying international aviation conventions like the Warsaw Convention or the Montreal Conventionto the so-called sub-orbital flights and bodies like the International Civil Aviation Organization seeking to assume regulatory responsibility for such flights have not been proven to be sustainable in the long run for multiple reasons. When one considers the models provided by the various intercarrier agreements introduced in the equation by the International Air Transport Association, this alternative may assume even further attractiveness. Yet the proponents of such a solution have always acknowledged it to be a short-term one pending international consensus about the spatial boundary. Therefore, the long-term viability of the solution to acknowledge the present and future issues of complexity involving space travel and orbital and sub-orbital flights and to embrace a clear demarcation once and for all appears to be indisputable. Among its alternatives, the TOSZ appears to have the most effectiveness and practicality. By strengthening the legal framework, the operation's hazards, which are now present, might be reduced, making space tourism a more efficient and lucrative enterprise.In light of certain recent developments, such efforts have assumed even more urgency. With the proliferation of space tourism and the need to accord a certain minimum level of protection to such tourists, at least on the same level as astronauts and spacecraft personnel, there is an increasing demand for specific and dedicated laws governing space tourism. Soft law options such as a UN General Assembly Resolution, using international instruments like the International Space Station Inter-Governmental Agreement and the associated Multilateral Crew Operations Panel Agreement as models, as well as hard law options in the form of domestic legislation are all being considered at present. The significance of a properly demarcated boundary of airspace and outer space in the context of the identification of a space tourist is rather obvious. Therefore, for any such legal development and its impact on commercial space tourism, the ascertainment of the aforementioned boundary, be it Kármán Line or any of the other possibilities discussed in this chapter, remains of the utmost importance.

## Notes

1 Manfred Lachs, *The Law of Outer Space: An Experience in Contemporary Lawmaking* (Leiden: Martinus Nijhoff, 2010) pp. 53 &54.
2 Joseph N. Pelton, 'Beyond the Protozone: A New Global Regulatory Regime for Air and Space', presented at *The Manfred Lachs Conference*, McGill University, Air and Space Law Institute, May 2015, p. 6.
3 Treaty on Principles Governing the Activities of States in the Exploration and Use of Outer Space, Including the Moon and Other Celestial Bodies, 27 January 1967, 610 UNTS 205, 18 UST 2410, TIAS No 6347, 6 ILM 386 (entered into force on 10 October 1967) [Outer Space Treaty]; Stephen Gorove, 'Interpreting Article II of the Outer Space Treaty', *Fordham Law Review*, Vol. 37, No. 3, 1969, pp. 349–354.
4 Tom Huddleston Jr., 'Richard Branson vs. Jeff Bezos: How the Two Space-Bound Billionaires Stack Up', *CNBC Make It*, 2 July 2021.
5 *Id.*
6 Blue Origin', 9 July 2021, available at <https://twitter.com/blueorigin/status/1413521 627116032001?ref_src=twsrc%5Etfw%7Ctwcamp%5Etweetembed%7Ctwterm% 5E1413521627116032001%7Ctwgr%5E%7Ctwcon%5Es1_&ref_url=https% 3A%2F%2Fwww.republicworld.com%2Ftechnology-news%2Fscience%2Fjeff-bezos-blue-origin-takes-dig-at-richard-bransons-virgin-galactic-spaceflight.html> Last visited, 5 March 2022.
7 *Id.*

8 Gbenga Oduntan, *Sovereignty and Jurisdiction in the Airspace and Outer Space* (New York: Routledge, 2012) p. 309.

9 UNCOPUOS, The Question of the Definition and/or Delimitation of Outer Space, UN Doc. A/AC.105/C.2/7 (1970), Addendum UN Doc. A/AC.005/C.2/7 Add. 1.

10 Paul Stephen Dempsey, *Public International Air Law* (Montreal: McGill University, 2008) pp. 741–764.

11 S. Neil Hosenball and Jefferson S. Hofgard, 'Delimitation of Air Space and Outer Space: Is a Boundary Needed Now?', *University of Colorado Law Review*, Vol. 57, 1986, pp. 885–893 at p. 888.

12 Michael J. Strauss, 'Boundaries in the Sky and a Theory of Three-Dimensional States', *Journal of Borderlands Studies*, Vol. 28, No. 3, 2013, pp. 369–382 at p. 371.

13 Bin Cheng, *Studies in International Space Law* (Oxford: Clarendon Press, 1997) p. 464.

14 *Id.*, at 493.

15 *Military and Paramilitary Activities in and against Nicaragua* (Nicaragua v. United States of America), [1986] ICJ Rep 14, at para 115.

16 *Supra* note 8, at 310.

17 UNCOPUOS, Report of the Legal Subcommittee on its forty-ninth session, UN Doc. A/AC.105/942, (22 March to 1 April 2010) at 29 [Report of the Legal Subcommittee].

18 S. Sanz Fernández de Córdoba, 'The 100 km Boundary for Astronautics', *Federation Aeronautique International*, June 2004, available at <https://www.fai.org/page/icare-boundary> Last visited, 5 April 2022.

19 Jonathan C. McDowell, 'The Edge of Space: Revisiting the Karman Line', *Acta Astronautica*, Vol. 151, 2018, pp. 668–677 at p. 668.

20 Eric Betzz, 'The Kármán Line: Where Does Space Begin?', *Astronomy*, 5 March 2021, available at <https://astronomy.com/news/2021/03/the-krmn-line-where-does-space-begin> Last visited, 5 April 2022.

21 *Supra* note 18.

22 Theodore von Kármán, *Aerodynamic Heating– The Temperature Barrier in Aeronautics* (Proc. High-Temperature Symposium, Berkeley, California, 1956) pp. 140–142.

23 Thomas Gangale, 'The Non Kármán Line: An Urban Legend of the Space Age', *Journal of Space Law*, Vol. 41, No. 2, 2017, pp. 151–178 at p. 155; Loren Grush, 'Why defining the boundary of space may be crucial for the future of spaceflight', *The Verge*, 13 December 2018, available at <https://www.theverge.com/2018/12/13/18130973/space-karman-line-definition-boundary-atmosphere-astronauts> Last visited, 5 April 2022.

24 Andrew G. Haley, *Space Law and Government* (New York: Appleton-Century-Crofts, 1963) p. 584.

25 *Id.*

26 *Supra* note 23, at 155.

27 Isidoro Martínez, 'Space Environment', 2021, available at <http://imartinez.etsiae.upm.es/~isidoro/tc3/Space%20environment.pdf >Last visited, 16 May 2023.

28 *Supra* note 23, at 155.

29 Raymond Aguilar, 'The Karman line: Separating Space from Sky', *Interesting Engineering*, 23 December 2022, available at <https://interestingengineering.com/science/the-karman-line> Last visited, 16 May 2023.

30 Dennis R. Jenkins, 'NASA – Schneider Walks the Walk', *NASA*, 21 October 2005, available at <https://www.nasa.gov/centers/dryden/news/X-Press/stories/2005/102105_Schneider.html> Last visited, 5 April 2022.

31 Jay Levine, 'A Long-Overdue Tribute', *NASA*, 21 October 2005, available at <https://www.nasa.gov/centers/dryden/news/X-Press/stories/2005/102105_Wings.html>Last visited, 5 April 2022.

32 *Supra* note 23, at 155; Thomas Gangale, 'How High the Sky? The Definition and Delimitation of Outer Space and Territorial Airspace in International Law', *Studies in Space Law*, Vol. 13, 2018, pp. 472–489.

33 Jonathan C.McDowell, 'The Edge of Space: Revisiting the Karman Line', *Acta Astronautica*, Vol. 151, 2018, pp. 668–677.

34 Paul Voosen, 'Outer Space May Have Just Gotten a Bit Closer', *Science*, July 2018, available at <https://www.science.org/content/article/outer-space-may-have-just-gotten-bit-closer>Last visited, 5 April 2022; Brandon Specktor, 'The Edge of Space Just Crept 12 Miles Closer to Earth', *Live Science*, available at <https://www.livescience.com/63166-outer-space-border-karman-line.html>Last visited, 5 April 2022.

35 *Id.*

36 *Id.*

37 T.W.G. Dawson, 'Terminal Velocities of Window Dipoles Used in High Altitude Wind Measurements', *Ministry of Aviation Farnborough Hants*, Royal Aircraft Establishment Technical Report No. 64049, November 1964.

38 *Supra* note 23.

39 Alex S. Li, 'Ruling Outer Space: Defining the Boundary and Determining Jurisdictional Authority', *Oklahoma Law Review*, Vol. 73, 2021, pp. 711–737 at pp. 728–730.

40 The United Nations Convention on the Law of the Sea, 1833 UNTC 3 (entered into force on 10 December 1982) [Law of the Sea], Art. 58, ¶ 1.

41 Treaty on Principles Governing the Activities of States in the Exploration and Use of Outer Space, including the Moon and Other Celestial Bodies, UNGA Res. 2222 (XXI) (19 December 1966).

42 Dan Kois, 'Where Does Space Begin?', *Slate*, 30 September 2004, available at <https://slate.com/news-and-politics/2004/09/where-does-space-begin.html> Last visited, 5 April 2022.

43 Committee on the Peaceful Uses of Outer Space, Legal Subcommittee, 56th Session, Matters Relating to the Definition and Delimitation of Outer Space: Replies of the International Institute of Space Law (IISL), 4 April 2017, U.N. Doc. A/AC.105/C.2/2017/CRP.29, at 1.

44 U.S. Department of State, 'U.S. Statement, Definition and Delimitation of Outer Space and The Character and Utilization of the Geostationary Orbit, Legal Subcommittee of the United Geostationary Orbit, Legal Subcommittee of the United Nations Committee on the Peaceful Uses of Outer Space at its 40th Session in Vienna from April', available at <https://2009-2017.state.gov/s/l/22718.htm> Last visited, 5 March 2022.

45 Richard H. Buenneke, *Personal Communication* (11 September 2014).

46 Outer Space Treaty, Art. VII & VIII; Liability Convention, Art. I(d); Registration Convention, Art. I(b).

47 Registration Convention, Art. I(b) & II.

48 M. Gerhard, 'Space Tourism – The Authorization of Suborbital Space Transportation', in Frans G von der Dunk (ed.), *National Space Legislation in Europe* (Leiden: Martinus Nijhoff Publishers, 2011) pp. 263–290.

49 Outer Space Treaty, Art. 8.

50 Report of the Legal Subcommittee, *supra* note 17, at 12 & 29.

51 Liability Convention, Art. 2.

52 *Id.*, Art. 2.

53 *Id.*, Art. 3.

54 Francis Lyall and Paul B. Larsen, *Space Law: A Treatise* (Burlington, VT: Ashgate Publishing, 2009) p. 171; Paul Stephen Dempsey, 'Liability Caused by Space Objects in International and National Law', *Annals of Air & Space Law*, Vol. 37, 2011, pp. 333–369.

55 Liability Convention, Art. 2 &3.

56 Outer Space Treaty, Art. 9.

57 *Id.*, Art. I.

58 *Id.*, Art II.

59 *Id.*, Art. I.

60 *Supra* note 8, at 290 &291.

61 *Supra* note 1, at 54.

62 Outer Space Treaty, Art I.

# 3

# THE EFFECT OF SPACE TOURISM ON THE CONCEPT OF "ASTRONAUT" UNDER INTERNATIONAL LAW

*Prof. Melissa de Zwart and Joel Lisk*

## Introduction

The year 2021 saw more tourists travel to "space" than ever before from an increasing number of companies, and the number of space tourism missions is expected to continuously rise into the future.[1] The year 2021 also witnessed significant controversy regarding the value, expense and symbolism of these private launches. The "space billionaires" engaged in these activities include Jeff Bezos, Richard Branson and Elon Musk. Bezos and Branson each participated in trips to (the edge of) space via their own companies, Bezos' Blue Origin and Branson's Virgin Galactic.[2] Musk's SpaceX provided the Inspiration4 mission hosting four crew members – Jared Isaacman, billionaire CEO of Shift4 payments, who purchased the mission; artist and scientist Dr Sian Proctor, who had previously applied for the NASA astronaut programme, and data engineer Chris Sembroski, who won their tickets via a contest and lottery respectively; and childhood cancer survivor and physician's assistant, Hayley Arceneaux, who raised $200 million for the St Jude Children's Research Hospital – at an estimated cost of $50 million per passenger.[3] Of course, these billionaires and their paying and non-paying customers are not the only private individuals to participate in space tourism. Dennis Tito purchased a stay on the International Space Station in 2001, as did Greg Olsen in 2005, Anousheh Ansari in 2006, and Charles Simonyi in 2007 and 2009, to name a few.[4]

The year 2022 also witnessed a greater diversity of nations and providers being involved in those launches. However, it saw an escalation in concerns regarding the perception of space tourism as a waste of money in a time of global pandemic and extreme climate change, creating the potential for further environmental harm,

DOI: 10.4324/9781032617961-3

as well as emphasising the disparity between those who can afford even a brief sojourn in space and those who cannot.[5]

This chapter will outline the origins of the concept of astronaut, through a consideration of the identification and training of the first United States astronauts, the original Mercury 7, who conjured up the popular conception of "astronauts". It will then consider the legal treatment of astronauts under international law and the domestic law of the United States, as the State from which the current space billionaire activity is occurring. It will further consider how these concepts are challenged by the activities of the space tourists and conclude by addressing the continuing value of the concept of astronaut in the context of increased commercial use of outer space, including the reliance of civil space agencies upon commercial partners.

## The Concept of Astronaut

As is well known, in the early days of space flight, this exceptionally dangerous activity was regarded as suitable only for those experienced with extreme test conditions. Therefore, the space programmes of both the United States and the (then) Union of Soviet Socialist Republics used Air Force and military test pilots. Notoriously, the original seven pilots of the Mercury 7, the first to be christened with the name "astronauts",[6] were perplexed in having virtually no control over the operation of the spacecraft, as used as they were to actually "flying" the experimental aircraft, which demanded extensive training and skill as well as bravery.[7] The original design for the capsule to be launched into space on top of the Saturn V rocket had very limited manual controls and no windows. Indeed, some design discussions "advocated that man should be anesthetized or tranquilized or rendered passive in some other manner in order that he would not interfere with the operation of the vehicle".[8] These original astronauts, therefore, questioned whether their level of skill was really needed for such a task.[9] They asked for larger windows for improved visibility and increased control over operation of the space object.[10] However, it should be noted that despite these early concerns and the emphasis on the automated systems of the Mercury vehicle, engineers confirmed that "the job demands levels of skill similar to those required in flying high-performance aircraft".[11]

To add insult to injury, these test pilots were preceded by animals as the original astronauts: the first animal to orbit the Earth was the Russian street-dog Laika,[12] although several other animals had been deployed in sub-orbital flights before this including fruit flies, mice, monkeys and dogs.[13] Ham, a 44-month-old chimpanzee, was chosen to be the initial test pilot of the Mercury capsule on 31 January 1961, a few months ahead of Alan Shepherd's flight on 5 May 1961.[14] During this time, Ham was required to operate levers in response to reward and punishment stimuli and could be said to be operating the capsule and its re-entry.

This contentious issue of the extent and complexity of qualities and skills required of an astronaut continued with the development of the NASA Space Shuttle programme, with a recognition that the space for an expanded crew would provide the opportunity for expanded skill sets, including commander, pilot, payload specialists and mission specialists. In 1985 Christa McAuliffe was selected from over 10,000 applicants to be the first teacher and civilian in space as part of the NASA Teacher in Space project. She was put through a NASA training programme and tasked to conduct classes and experiments whilst in space, designated by NASA as a payload specialist. McAuliffe died, along with the rest of the crew, when the Challenger exploded after launch on 28 January 1986.[15] Had the Challenger mission not ended in disaster, there were plans for many more civilians to represent their profession in space. The next programme was to be a journalist in space. It is possible that had the Challenger disaster not occurred, the Space Shuttle age may have resulted in greater access to space for a range of talents and skills, and thus opened up the debate over the meaning of "astronaut" at that time.

Current space tourism providers offer a largely autonomous operation of the space vehicle, leaving the participants to enjoy the view or engage in various experiments and activities. Again, questions may be raised if these ancillary activities affect their recognition as astronauts. Anousheh Ansari spent her nine self-funded days on the International Space Station conducting science experiments.[16] Should this be regarded as a distinct activity from private space adventurer who spends their time gazing back on Earth?

What does it mean to be an astronaut in the time of the successful test flights by the space billionaires in 2020/2021? Tronchetti notes that space tourism has always been more about the flight than the destination.[17] The experience of being in space, being weightless, has, until now, been the major focus of the tourist. However, now there are plans to journey to the Moon and beyond, and possibly later to Mars. Do these extended journeys raise new issues for the characterisation of the space tourist and the consequent benefit of space tourism? Certainly, as will be discussed further below, some of the attractions of participating in space tourism are fundamentally to be recognised as an astronaut. Thus, it is worth considering the effect of what it means to be an astronaut in the context of space tourism.

## The Legal Treatment of Astronauts

Article V of the Outer Space Treaty 1967 (OST) provides the primary legal obligations with respect to astronauts. At its simplest, Article V contains four key concepts, the provision:

- deems astronauts to be "envoys of mankind in outer space";
- requires that States Parties to the OST "render to [astronauts] all possible assistance in the event of [an] accident, distress or emergency landing";

- requires that where astronauts make a landing in the circumstances of an accident, distress or emergency landing, they are returned to jurisdiction in which their space object is registered; and
- requires States Parties to notify other States of any phenomena that may constitute a danger to the life or health of astronauts.[18]

This article is an expansion of paragraph 9 of the UNGA Resolution 1962 (XVIII); Declaration of Legal Principles Governing the Activities of States in the Exploration and Use of Outer Space, which provided

> States shall regard astronauts as envoys of mankind in Outer Space and shall render to them all possible assistance in the event of accident, distress, or emergency landing on the territory of a foreign State or on the high seas. Astronauts who make such a landing shall be safely and promptly returned to the State of registry of their space vehicle.[19]

Hence the concept of astronaut as an envoy of mankind and as a human who should be subject to special obligations was a foundational principle of international space law. But how can such principles be given legal content and shape?

Despite the content of Article V, Article VIII of the OST refers to "personnel" of a space object with respect to jurisdiction and control: does this suggest there is a qualitative difference between astronauts and personnel? Are astronauts a sub-set of personnel? Where the specific word "astronaut" is used, does this suggest an enhanced status of astronauts and a distinction from other personnel who may be carried on a space object?

The Rescue and Return Agreement 1968 uses the word "astronaut" in the name of the treaty and in the preamble.[20] However, the remainder of the Rescue and Return Agreement uses the term "personnel of a spacecraft", imposing broad obligations to notify of risks to personnel and to render assistance in the event of accident or emergency. Specifically, the Rescue and Return Agreement imposes the following obligations on Contracting Parties:

- Notification with respect to accidents, conditions of distress or emergency or unintended landing of personnel of a spacecraft in territory under that jurisdiction of that State or on the high seas or any place not under the jurisdiction of any State to the launching authority and the United Nations[21];
- Provision of rescue and all necessary assistance to personnel of a spacecraft in territory under the jurisdiction of a State Party due to accident, distress, emergency or unintended landing[22];
- Provision of search, rescue and assistance where possible when personnel of a spacecraft have alighted on the high seas or any place not under jurisdiction of any State[23]; and
- Safe and prompt return of such personnel to the launching authority.[24]

## 32   Prof. Melissa de Zwart and Joel Lisk

The Moon Agreement 1984 goes well beyond the scope of both the OST and the Rescue and Return Agreement with respect to application of the obligations of both protection and rescue of people in space.[25] It deems all persons on the Moon or another Celestial Body, in orbit around the Moon or other Celestial Body to be both an "astronaut" and "personnel of a spacecraft", thus incorporating the language and obligations of both the Outer Space Treaty and the Rescue and Return Agreement.

Article 10 imposes two primary obligations on States Party to the Moon Agreement: they must safeguard the life and health of people in space and offer shelter to persons in distress. Article 1 of the Moon Agreement extends these principles to other celestial bodies and orbits and trajectories around the Moon. Whilst these obligations are extensive, the low acceptance rate of the Moon Agreement indicates that this attempted extension is unlikely to reflect international law.

There has been extensive academic analysis of the interpretation of these terms. The general consensus of academic opinion is that the term "astronaut" applies to professionals conducting work in outer space, whereas the term "personnel of spacecraft" applies to a crew or those with a professional function on a spacecraft.[26] Those people with no such roles would not fall into either category. As already noted, whilst the Moon Agreement seeks to extend this definition to all people in space, it is unlikely that this would be accepted. Academic discourse has certainly also addressed the complexity of adopting a narrow definition of such terms in the context of the expansion of space tourism.[27]

### Domestic Space Regulation and Other State Practice

The application of the concept of "astronaut" or "personnel of a spacecraft" to space tourists has also been influenced by the introduction of domestic practice and conventions with respect to categorising participants in spaceflight or missions. For example, as discussed above, the size of the Space Shuttle created room and roles for multiple crew, including those not involved in the operation of the Shuttle. The NASA Space Transportation System User Handbook (June 1977) sets out guidance on a wide range of matters relevant to the operation of the United States' Space Shuttle, including the roles of personnel. The Handbook states that the "[o]rbiter crew consists of the commander and pilot. Additional crew members who may be required to conduct Orbiter and payload operations are a mission specialist and one or more payload specialists".[28] The Handbook expanded on the idea of "payload specialists" by stating that

> the concept of noncareer crew members permits vis[i]ting payload operators to fly as payload specialists … These payload specialists, if they are provided by the user, are required to undergo the minimum STS training considered necessary for them to function efficiently as members of a flight crew.[29]

The International Space Station similarly has adopted its own classifications. The Principles Regarding Processes and Criteria for Selection, Assignment, Training and Certification of ISS (Expedition and Visiting) Crew members create two classes of ISS crew member: "Professional Astronaut/Cosmonaut" and "Spaceflight Participant". Professional Astronaut/Cosmonauts are individuals who have been selected and trained by an ISS partner agency and who are employed by that agency as an astronaut or cosmonaut. Comparatively, "Spaceflight Participants" are those individuals on the ISS that have been sponsored by an ISS partner agency, but are not necessarily permanent astronauts or cosmonauts. The crew member selection principles specifically mention crew members of non-partner space agencies, engineers, scientists, teachers, journalists, filmmakers or tourists as types of "Spaceflight Participants".[30]

The Principles Regarding Processes and Criteria for Selection, Assignment, Training and Certification of ISS (Expedition and Visiting) Crewmembers go further to also identify Expedition (Increment) and Visiting Crewmembers. These classifications apply to the main crew of the ISS that are responsible for the activities that take place on the ISS, and the crew that travel to and from the ISS but do not form part of the core crew of the ISS, respectively. Professional astronauts/cosmonauts and spaceflight participants may fall into either category depending on their role.

Looking to domestic law, the United States' Commercial Space Launch Act (as amended) adopts another set of definitions and concepts related to human participation in spaceflight. By necessity, the Commercial Space Launch Act has needed to reflect the ambitions of the commercial launch sector and include references to both "traditional" and non-traditional involvement in space activities. The Commercial Space Launch Act contemplates three classes of human involvement in spaceflight activities:

- "Crew" is defined expansively to include employees of an entity licensed to launch space objects and that entity's contractors involved in activities directly relating to the launch, re-entry or operation of a launch or re-entry vehicle. Unlike other definitions and conceptualisations discussed above, "crew" in this context includes more than just those going into outer space (i.e. individuals involved in a launch as ground crew).
- Government astronaut" takes on a more traditional character, being an individual who is designated by the United States' National Aeronautics and Space Administration, is carried into or from space in the course of their employment, and is either an employee of the US Government or an "international astronaut partner". This last phrase: "international astronaut partner" is a reference to individuals designated as ISS crew members under the International Space Station Intergovernmental Agreement.
- Space flight participants" are those individuals who do not fit within the above categories, but are carried into or from outer space on a launch or re-entry vehicle.[31]

The United Kingdom passed its revised regulatory framework for space activities, the Space Industry Act, in 2018 and supported that legislation with additional regulations in 2021.[32] The Space Industry Regulations 2001 introduces a range of terms relevant to human spaceflight including "crew", "cabin crew", "flight crew", "human occupant" and "spaceflight participant".[33] Crew is used as a collective term to cover both "cabin crew" and "flight crew". "Flight crew" are pilots or flight engineers who take part in spaceflight activities. "Cabin crew" are those individuals performing duties assigned to them by the pilot, but are not pilots or flight engineers. Finally, "spaceflight participants" are "individual[s], other than [...] member[s] of the crew, who [are] to be carried on board a launch vehicle".[34] The definitions of "flight crew" and "cabin crew" are unique to the United Kingdom, but the definition of "spaceflight participant" takes on a recognisable character when considering the content of the United States' Commercial Space Launch Act.

Looking at further recent State practice with respect to the characterisation of the concept of astronaut or personnel of a spacecraft, the Artemis Accords impose an obligation with respect to "personnel in outer space". Section 6 (Emergency Assistance) provides[35]:

> The Signatories commit to taking all reasonable efforts to render necessary assistance to personnel in outer space who are in distress and acknowledge their obligations under the Rescue and Return Agreement.

Clearly, this would encompass civilian and commercial operations. However, this does not specifically address space tourists. It does reflect the reality that space is incredibly hostile to human life, and the survival of any individual is entirely dependent upon the facilities and services brought with them from Earth. The restatement of the obligations under the Rescue and Return Agreement may be said to be one of basic humanity.[36]

However, with respect to paying customers, one must pause and consider if the arrangements are the same for a tourist and a professional astronaut. Should they expect a higher level of safety, or are they forfeiting their usual consumer rights by undertaking such a risky activity? One of the major impediments in developing a large space tourism industry is the spectre of liability. In order to provide a period of time in which the space tourism industry can develop with limited liability and consequent minimal regulation, the United States Federal Aviation Administration (FAA) has imposed a moratorium which prohibits issuing regulations to protect the health and safety of crew and spaceflight participants until 1 January 2024, regarded as an industry in the nascent growth phase. This is an important marker of the maturity and nature of space tourism.

Another traditional indicium of being an astronaut is the award of "wings", which has been done, for example, in the United States for civilian, government and military astronauts. The various branches of the United States Military apply differing requirements according to service branch with respect to qualification for the award of wings. For the Air Force, Navy and Marines, the requirement is the completion of training and having travelled beyond 50 miles (approximately 80 km) above sea level; for the Army, the qualification is the completion of training and undertaking orbit of the Earth.[37] For NASA astronauts, silver pins are awarded to those who have completed astronaut training and gold pins for those who have flown in space.[38]

Since 2004 the FAA has awarded Commercial Space Astronaut Wings to individuals who reach 50 miles above the surface of the Earth. The purpose of the programme was to bring attention to space activities and celebrate the achievements of those brave enough to venture into space and "promote the development of vehicles designed to carry humans into space". However, in December 2021, the FAA announced that with the significant expansion of space tourism, it would no longer be awarding wings but would rather recognise those who launch on an FAA-licensed or permitted launch and reach 50 statute miles above the surface of the Earth by listing those individuals on a website.[39] The FAA announced that:

> Before the Wings program ends, the FAA will award Commercial Space Astronaut Wings to those who had qualifying space travel in 2021, including 15 individuals who have already travelled beyond 50 statute miles above the surface of the Earth on a FAA-licensed launch. Individuals on qualifying flights occurring prior to the end of the year are also eligible to receive Wings.
> In addition, the FAA is making an honorary award of Commercial Space Astronaut Wings to two individuals who flew on a FAA-permitted experimental test flight in a space launch vehicle that broke up during flight in 2014.[40]

It is noted that all of the space tourists who launched with Bezos and Branson in 2021 (including William Shatner) are listed on the FAA site and made wings before the December cut-off.[41] Interestingly, and possibly an indicium of the regard with which wings are held, both Bezos and Branson commissioned and had made their wings before their respective flights.[42]

## Envoys of Mankind

Article V of the OST uses the phrase "envoys of mankind in outer space". It has been suggested that this designation is intended to impact the treatment of astronauts, potentially giving them some status such as that conferred on diplomats. A consideration of primary sources, such as the *travaux preparatoires*, and the discussions before UNCOPUOS reveals no clear understanding of this concept. For example, the Statement by the Representative of the Austrian delegation, Mr. Zemanek, observes that it would be doubtful that the reference to astronauts as envoys in mankind in outer space "could give rise to a legal obligation". Zemanek continues that "it would be first necessary to determine whether the word 'envoys' was to bear its normal meaning under international law, and to consider whether

States which are not space Powers should not have a hand in the way astronauts were launched into space".[43] Other discussions highlighted the need to protect and assist astronauts in distress[44] and to acknowledge the "heroic role they were playing as pioneers in the exploration and peaceful uses of space".[45]

The academic analysis largely concurs that the phrase was "inserted as political rhetoric" and had "already served its purpose and outlived its utility".[46] As observed by the authors of "Article V" of the Cologne Commentary, it is regarded by the international community as a "figure of speech" and further:

> Given the evolution of commercial spaceflight, with a view to the completely different motivations of the individuals concerned to travel to and in outer space, the assumptions of the drafters that humans in space would, by definition, be working there fundamentally for a greater public common good (even if often limited to one or more nations) are no longer valid today. It is unlikely that the rather lofty status of "envoy of mankind" in this context refers to commercial spaceflight participants who travel to outer space primarily for private leisure purposes ("space tourists").[47]

It may be argued that this special status is indeed one of the measures sought by space tourists, but as Sreejith suggests, this may be a sentiment of romance rather than international law.[48]

## Future Developments

In June 2019, NASA issued an Interim Directive (NID) to allow private astronauts to make short duration visits to the ISS to undertake commercial or marketing activities.[49] Noting that "NASA Strategic Objective 2.1 directs the Agency to lay the foundation for America to maintain a constant human presence in low-Earth orbit (LEO) to be enabled by a commercial market." As part of this developing economy, NASA is using the ISS to stimulate both the supply and demand of a robust commercial marketplace, with the vision of a sustained LEO human spaceflight presence where NASA could be one of many customers.[50] Permitted activities are currently limited to projects which:

1 Require access to the unique microgravity environment for manufacture, production or development of a commercial application;
2 Have a nexus to the NASA mission; or
3 Support the development of a sustainable LEO economy.

ISS resources are made available by NASA in return for payment and/or reimbursement dependent upon the activities undertaken, according to a predetermined pricing schedule and execution of a standard form agreement. The NID further

Effect of Space Tourism on the Concept of "Astronaut"  **37**

outlines the obligations imposed on private astronauts approved for a mission on the ISS, and the US Government astronauts supporting such activities.

Certainly, commercial activities are rapidly increasing. In April 2022, SpaceX carried four private astronauts to the ISS under a contract with AXIOM.[51] Initially intended to be aboard the ISS for eight days, due to unfavourable weather for their return, they spent 15 days on the ISS. Each passenger undertook various activities and experiments for their sponsoring organisation whilst onboard the ISS. Axiom has announced that they will continue to bring more private astronauts to the ISS and have a contract with SpaceX for three more missions. These activities are a precursor to Axiom's intended construction of a private LEO space station to replace the ISS when it is decommissioned at the end of this decade.[52]

NASA has a contract with Axiom to build a module to attach to the ISS, which may be deployed as early as 2024.[53] UK-based Space Entertainment Enterprise has contracted Axiom to build an inflatable "content and environment module" for the ISS called SEE-1, scheduled for launch in 2024.[54] This module is intended to be used for filming and other content creation.[55] Tom Cruise was scheduled to travel to the ISS in 2021 to film his foreshadowed space movie. However, his trip was delayed allowing a Russian film crew, including actress Yulia Peresild and producer Klim Shipenko, to be the first movie makers on the ISS in 2021, landing with cosmonaut Oleg Novitskiy on 17 October 2021.[56]

In addition to activities in LEO, NASA also has plans for crewed missions to the Moon, including, ultimately, commercial missions. SpaceX had announced a plan to fly a space tourist around the Moon as early as 2023.[57] Other plans relate to sub-orbital travel. SpaceX flagged the use of its rockets for point-to-point travel anywhere on Earth in less than 30 minutes.[58] A Chinese space plane company has announced that it will be providing sub-orbital tourism and point-to-point travel via a reusable rocket by 2025.[59]

All of these ventures will raise new issues. Still, it seems evident that as space tourism becomes more popular, attracting greater numbers and wider consumer options, the application of the term "astronaut" to such people becomes more remote.

## Chapter Conclusion

What can we learn from the concept of astronauts and the experiences of space tourism? It appears inevitable that we will have to change the concept of who we consider being an "astronaut", but it remains worth considering attributes and factors that we have traditionally considered that would make someone an astronaut and addressing what we can learn from that.

Sreejith has observed that the heroic characterisation of astronauts in international space law as reflecting the very best in terms of bravery and skills – the "envoys of all of humanity in outer space" – evolved over time into the more pragmatic "personnel of a spacecraft". Despite this, much of the motivation to go into space is to re-enact or experience what it means to be an "astronaut". This reflects the disconnect between "astronaut" in international space law and "astronaut" in popular culture.[60]

Much has been said regarding the transformative value of the "overview effect": the unique experience of seeing the whole Earth against the background of space is said to create a significant change in all who witness the vulnerability and beauty of our blue planet. Beth Moses, the chief astronaut instructor at Virgin Galactic, has identified it as an "indescribable and magical experience". William Shatner, reflecting on his flight on Blue Origin, described it as "profound".[61]

It is certainly to be hoped that as more people venture into space, they can bring back any new insight that they gain from their journey to space in a time of increasing space debris and catastrophic climate change. Whilst the current voyagers are people of exceptional wealth and their beneficiaries, like all new opportunities, over time, this will likely bring technological advancements which will open up the possibility of access for others. This is a period of adventure and learning and the spirit of the astronauts who have led the way off the Earth now inspire us to venture forward.

## Notes

1 Elizabeth Howell, 'Space Tourism Took a Giant Leap in 2021: Here's 10 Milestones from the Year', *Space.com*, 27 December 2021, available at <https://www.space.com/space-tourism-giant-leap-2021-milestones> Last visited, 10 August 2022.
2 Ramin Skibba, '2021 Was the Year Space Tourism Opened Up. But for Whom?', *Wired*, 29 December 2021, available at <https://www.wired.com/story/2021-was-the-year-space-tourism-opened-up-but-for-whom> Last visited, 10 August 2022.
3 Adam Mann, 'Space Is All Yours -For a Hefty Price', *MIT Technology Review*, 21 February 2022, available at <https://www.technologyreview.com/2022/02/21/1044909/commerical-space-tourism-cost/> Last visited, 10 August 2022; Jeffry Kluger, 'Meet the All-Civilian Crew of Inspiration4, From a St. Jude's Physician Assistant to a Lockheed Martin Engineer', *Time,* 10 August 2021, available at <https://time.com/6083979/meet-inspiration4-crew-members/> Last visited, 10 August 2022.
4 Mike Wall, 'Q & A: World's First Space Tourists Reflect on Dawn of Private Spaceflight', *Space.com*, 26 April 2011, available at <https://www.space.com/11481-space-tourist-reflections-private-spaceflight.html> Last visited, 10 August 2022.
5 Dharna Noor, 'Space Tourism Is a Waste', *Gizmodo*, 19 July 2021, available at <https://www.gizmodo.com.au/2021/07/space-tourism-is-a-waste/> Last visited, 10 August 2022.
6 Loyd S. Swenson, Jr, James M. Grimwood and Charles C. Alexander, *This New Ocean: A History of Project Mercury* (Washington D.C.: National Astronautical and Space Administration, 1966), p. 160: "They were to be called 'astronauts' as the pioneers of ballooning had been called 'aeronauts', and the legendary Greeks in search of the Golden Fleece were called 'Argonauts', for they were to sail into a new uncharted ocean."
7 *Id.*, at 160: "The astronauts were first and foremost test pilots, men accustomed to flying alone in the newest, most advanced, and most powerful vehicle this civilization had produced."
8 *Id.*, at 195, quoting Jones, 'Man's Integration into the Mercury Capsule', Paper presented at the 14th Annual Meeting of the American Rocket Society, 1959.

9 *Id.*, at pp. 190–199.

10 Robert B. Voas, 'Manual Control of the Mercury Spacecraft', *Astronautics*, March 1962, pp. 18–38 at p. 18.

11 Robert B. Voas, 'A Description of the Astronaut's Task in Project Mercury', *Human Factors*, Vol. 3, No. 3, 1961, pp. 149–165 at p. 149.

12 Alice George, 'The Sad, Sad Story of Laika, the Space Dog, and Her One-Way Trip into Orbit', *The Smithsonian Magazine*, 11 April 2018, available at <https://www.smithsonianmag.com/smithsonian-institution/sad-story-laika-space-dog-and-her-one-way-trip-orbit-1-180968728/> Last visited 10 August 2022.

13 'What Was the First Animal Sent into Space?' *Royal Museums Greenwich*, available at <https://www.rmg.co.uk/stories/topics/what-was-first-animal-space#:~:text=orbit%20the%20Earth.-,What%20was%20the%20first%20animal%20in%20space%3F, rocket%20on%2020%20February%201947> Last visited, 10 August 2022.

14 *Supra* note 6, at 310–318.

15 National Aeronautics and Space Administration, 'S. Christa Corrigan McAuliffe, Teacher in Space Participant (Deceased): Biographical Data', April 2007, available at <https://www.nasa.gov/sites/default/files/atoms/files/mcauliffe.pdf> Last visited, 10 August 2022.

16 Chelsea Whyte, 'Anousheh Ansari Interview: Why Everyone Should See Earth from Space', *New Scientist,* 9 September 2020, available at <https://www.newscientist.com/article/mg24732990-800-anousheh-ansari-interview-why-everyone-should-see-earth-from-space/#ixzz7VaFhFHUh> Last visited, 10 August 2022.

17 See Fabio Tronchetti, 'Legal Aspects of the Military Uses of Outer Space', in Frans von der Dunk and Fabio Tronchetti (eds.) *Handbook of Space Law* (Cheltenham: Edward Elgar Publishing, 2015) pp. 331–382.

18 Treaty on Principles Governing the Activities of the States in the Exploration and Use of Outer Space, including the Moon and Other Celestial Bodies, 27 January 1967, 610 UNTS 205 (entered into force 10 October 1967) ('Outer Space Treaty') Art V.

19 UNGA Res. 18/1682, (13 December 1963) para. 9.

20 Agreement on the Rescue of Astronauts, the Return of Astronauts and Return of Objects Launched into Outer Space, 22 April 1968, 672UNTS 331 (entered into force 3 December 1968) ('Rescue and Return Agreement').

21 *Id.*, Art. 1.

22 *Id.*, Art. 2.

23 *Id.*, Art. 3.

24 *Id.*, Art. 4.

25 Agreement Governing the Activities of States in the Moon and Other Celestial Bodies, 18 December 1979, 1363 UNTS 3 (entered into force 11 July 1984) ('Moon Agreement').

26 See, for example, Frans von der Dunk and Gerardine Goh, 'Article V' in Stephan Hobe, Bernhard Schmidt-Tedd and Kai-Uwe Schrogl (eds.) *Cologne Commentary on Space Law*, Vol. 1 (Köln: Carl Heymanns Verlag, 2009) pp. 94–102 at p. 94; Irmgard Marboe, Julia Neumann and Kai-Uwe Schrogl, 'Article 1 (Notification of Accidents/ Distress/Emergency or Unintended Landing', in Stephan Hobe, Bernhard Schmidt-Tedd and Kai-Uwe Schrogl (eds.) *Cologne Commentary on Space Law*, Vol. 2 (Köln: Carl Heymanns Verlag, 2013) pp. 38–48 at p. 42; Frans von der Dunk 'International Space Law', in Frans von der Dunk and Fabio Tronchetti (eds.) *Handbook of Space Law* (Cheltenham: Edward Elgar Publishing, 2015) pp. 29–126 at p. 80; Carla Sharpe and Fabio Tronchetti, 'Legal Aspects of Public Manned Spaceflight and Space Station Operations', in Frans von der Dunk and Fabio Tronchetti (eds.) *Handbook of Space Law* (Cheltenham: Edward Elgar Publishing, 2015) pp. 618—661 at pp. 647–650; E Kamenetskaya '"Cosmonaut" ("Astronaut"): An Attempt of International Legal Definition', *Proceedings of the 31st Colloquium on the Law of Outer Space*, 1988, pp. 177–178 at p. 178; Yuri Baturin, 'The Astronaut's Legal Status', *Advanced Space Law*, Vol. 5, 2020, pp. 4–13.

27 See, for example, Ram Jakhu and Raja Bhattacharya, 'Legal Aspects of Space Tourism', *Proceedings of the 45th Colloquium on the Law of Outer Space*, 2002, pp. 112–133 at pp. 118 & 119; Ling Yan, 'Does the Rescue Agreement Apply to Space Tourists', *Proceedings of the International Institute of Space Law*, Vol. 54, 2011, pp. 192–201 at p. 195; Stephen Hobe, 'Legal Aspects of Space Tourism', *Nebraska Law Review*, Vol. 86, 2007, pp. 439–458 at p. 454; Yanal Abul Failat, 'Space Tourism: A Synopsis on Its Legal Challenges', *Irish Law Journal*, Vol. 1, 2012, pp. 120–151 at pp. 123 & 124.

28 National Aeronautics and Space Administration, *Space Transportation System User Handbook* (Washington: NASA, 1977) pp. 4–22.

29 *Id.*

30 Multilateral Crew Operations Panel, *Principles Regarding Processes and Criteria for Selection, Assignment, Training and Certification of ISS (Expedition and Visiting) Crewmembers*, November 2001, Revision A.

31 Title 51, United States Code §50902 (2022); Definitions were added to the Commercial Space Launch Act by the Commercial Space Launch Amendments Act of 2004, Pub. L. No. 108-492, 118 Stat. 3974, §2(b).

32 See, Space Industry Act 2018 (UK).

33 Space Industry Regulations 2021 (UK) Reg. 2(1).

34 *Id.* Reg. 2(1)

35 National Aeronautics and Space Administration, *The Artemis Accords: Principles for Cooperation in the Civil Exploration and Use of the Moon, Mars, Comets and Asteroids for Peaceful Purposes*, 13 October 2020.

36 Irmgard Marboe, Julia Neumann and Kai-Uwe Schrogl, 'Preamble', in Stephan Hobe, Bernhard Schmidt-Tedd and Kai-Uwe Schrogl (eds.) *Cologne Commentary on Space Law*, Vol. 2 (Köln: Carl Heymanns Verlag, 2013) pp. 31–37 at pp. 36 & 37.

37 'Jeff Bezos and Sir Richard Branson May Not Be Astronauts, US Says', *BBC News*, 23 July 2021, available at <https://www.bbc.com/news/world-us-canada-57950149> Last visited, 10 August 2022.

38 Federal Aviation Administration, 'Commercial Human Spaceflight Recognition', 9 June 2022, available at <https://www.faa.gov/space/human_spaceflight/recognition/> Last visited, 10 August 2022.

39 Federal Aviation Administration, 'FAA Ends Commercial Space Astronaut Wings Program, Will Recognise Individuals Reaching Space on Website', 10 December 2021, available at <https://www.faa.gov/newsroom/faa-ends-commercial-space-astronaut-wings-program-will-recognize-individuals-reaching> Last visited, 10 August 2022.

40 *Id.*

41 *Id.*

42 *Supra* note 38.

43 UN Doc A/AC.105/C.2/SR.58 (20 October 1966) pp. 2 & 3.

44 UN Doc A/AC.105/PV.26 (7 December 1964) 16; UN Doc A/C.1/PV.1500 (19 October 1967) p. 11, para 109.

45 UN Doc A/C.1/SR.1343 (3 December 1963) p. 171, para. 36.

46 G.S. Sachdeva, 'Outer Space Treaty: An Appraisal', in AjeyLele (ed.) *50 Years of the Outer Space Treaty* (New Delhi: Pentagon Press, 2017) pp. 24–47 at p. 24.

47 Frans von der Dunk and Gerardine Goh, 'Article V', in Stephan Hobe, Bernhard Schmidt-Tedd and Kai-Uwe Schrogl (eds.) *Cologne Commentary on Space Law*, Vol. 1 (Köln: Carl Heymanns Verlag, 2009) pp. 94–102 at p. 94.

48 S.G. Sreejith, 'The Fallen Envoy: The Rise and Fall of Astronaut in International Space Law', *Space Policy*, Vol. 47, 2019, pp. 130–139 at p. 133.

49 National Aeronautical and Space Administration: Human Exploration and Operations Mission Directorate, *NASA Interim Directive (NID): Use of International Space Station (ISS) for Commercial and Marketing Activities*, 6 June 2019.

50 *Id.*

51 Michael Sheetz, 'SpaceX Returns Private Ax-1 Astronaut Crew to Earth after Extended Space Station Stay', *CNBC,* 25 April 2022, available at <https://www.cnbc.com/2022/04/25/spacex-ax-1-splashdown-private-axiom-astronaut-crew-returns-from-iss.html> Last visited, 10 August 2022.

52 Michael Sheetz, 'Private Spaceflight Specialist Axiom Space Raises $130 Million to Become the Latest Space Unicorn', *CNBC*, 16 February 2021, available at <https://www.cnbc.com/2021/02/16/axiom-space-raises-130-million-and-becomes-the-latest-space-unicorn.html> Last visited, 10 August 2022.

53 *Id.*

54 Scott Snowden, 'Axiom Space Plans to Build a Movie Studio Module for the International Space Station by 2024', *Space.com*, 26 January 2022, available at <https://www.space.com/axiom-space-station-movie-studio-module> Last visited, 10 August 2022.

55 Michael Sheetz, 'Tom Cruise Space Movie Producers Sign Deal with Axiom to Build Studio in Orbit', *CNBC*, 20 January 2022, available at <https://www.cnbc.com/2022/01/20/tom-cruise-movie-producers-sign-axiom-deal-for-space-production-studio.html> Last visited, 10 August 2022.

56 Agence France-Presse, 'Russian Film Crew Return to Earth after Shooting the First Movie in Space', *The Guardian,* 17 October 2021, available at <https://www.theguardian.com/science/2021/oct/17/russian-film-crew-return-to-earth-after-shooting-the-first-movie-in-space> Last visited, 10 August 2022.

57 Mike Wall, 'SpaceX Plans to Fly Humans Around the Moon in 2023', *Scientific American*, 18 September 2018, available at <https://www.scientificamerican.com/article/spacex-plans-to-fly-humans-around-the-moon-in-2023/> Last visited, 10 August 2022.

58 SpaceX, 'Earth to Earth Transportation' 2022, available at <https://www.spacex.com/human-spaceflight/earth/index.html> Last visited, 10 August 2022.

59 Andrew Jones, 'Chinese Space Plane Company Targets Suborbital Tourism, Point-to-Point Travel by 2025', *Space.com*, 27 January 2022, available at <https://www.space.com/private-chinese-space-plane-tourism-travel?utm_source=SmartBrief&utm_medium=email&utm_campaign=58E4DE65-C57F-4CD3-9A5A-609994E2C5A9&utm_content=6DEE0CB3-9956-4057-9558-88F42BD2A28A&utm_term=faa8398e-4676-4916-b8ee-b8258d7b8b17> Last visited, 10 August 2022.

60 *Supra* note 52, at 137.

61 *Supra* note 2.

# 4

# NEED TO CLARIFY THE RESCUE NORMS FOR PRIVATE SPACE TOURISTS

*Ankit Kumar Padhy and Divya Tyagi*

### Introduction

Since the first space object was launched into space in 1957, mankind has made constant efforts to realise its ultimate aim of human space flight. One of the most important milestones in this direction has been the development and innovation of space technology that enables space travel by humans on a commercial basis.[1]

The Ansari X-prize and Virgin Galactic's SpaceShipOne drew the global community's attention to commercial space tourism.[2] Dennis Tito was the first private citizen to fly to space in 2001. He travelled to International Space Station on a Soyuz spacecraft from Russia. He paid approximately $20 million for his eight-day trip.[3] Until now, more than ten civilians have travelled to space. Recently, SpaceX successfully completed the first all-civilian spaceflight to outer space and back, known as the Inspiration4 mission, whereby four private passengers were launched to Earth's orbit (at the height of approximately 575 km) and stayed there for three days before returning back safely to Earth. Boeing, Virgin Galactic and Blue Origin are a few other dominant players in the space tourism industry. Currently, more than a dozen companies have the technological know-how and capability to operate space tourism flights. Recently, Blue Origin CEO Jeff Bezos and Virgin Galactic CEO Richard Branson travelled to sub-orbital space, symbolically marking the beginning of the commercial space tourism era.

Space tourism can be described as any commercial activity that provides passengers with the opportunity to go to outer space. It may alternatively be defined as "the actions of individuals travelling to and staying in locations beyond their typical environment for no more than one year in a row for recreational purposes". In simple terms, it is the act of travelling to space for recreational, commercial or pleasure objectives.

DOI: 10.4324/9781032617961-4

There are numerous types of space tourism, including sub-orbital, orbital, lunar and orbital space tourism that includes a stay at the International Space Station or a space hotel.[4] While companies such as Blue Origin and Virgin Galactic concentrate on sub-orbital travel, SpaceX intends to build orbital and inter-planetary tourism. SpaceX has tentative plans to fly humans and spacecraft to Mars by 2050.

Space tourism is emerging as a new commercial business arena for the aerospace industry. Commercial space tourism allows people to closely associate with outer space at a personal level, providing them with the first-hand experience of space travel. Further, the elite class of people, the millionaires and billionaires, usually find it comparatively easier to earn a few million than to become a government astronaut. However, in the coming decades, with the further evolution of space technology and an increase in the number of space flights, human space travel would no longer be restricted to government-trained astronauts and rich billionaires.

The space tourism market in 2019 was estimated at around $550 million.[5] In the coming five years, the global market for commercial space tourism is projected to reach between $1,130 million and $1,180 million, with a compound annual growth rate of between 12% and 15%.[6] Commercial space tourism flights would account for a substantial portion of the overall revenue share of the space companies during the period 2020–2025.[7] In the next five years, the costs of space tourism flights have been forecasted to witness a significant decline with the advancement of technology.[8] Further, the trends project the growth of the tourism market in the space sector to $1,700 million by 2027. United States, Europe and China would be home to the leading space tourism service providers, with the USA having the largest share.[9]

The technology pertaining to space travel has advanced dramatically over the past few decades, making regular and cost-effective space flights possible and enabling space companies to accommodate a continual stream of passengers. Reusable Launch Vehicle technology can substantially reduce the cost of each space trip. Currently, companies like SpaceX and Blue Origin have made good progress towards improving the technology in order to make RLVs fully reusable. Also, an increasing number of spaceports worldwide is adding to the infrastructural capabilities for operating regular space flights. Development of advanced aerospace planes, especially for sub-orbital tourism, like that of Blue Origin and Virgin Galactic, can further make travelling to the edge of space affordable and accessible for Earthlings.[10]

The future possibilities and potential of this new adventure arena create difficult and intriguing legal issues. On the technological, financial and market demand fronts, the private space tourism industry continues to grow at an exponential rate. However, the legislative framework governing the commercial space tourism industry appears to have fallen behind. The five space treaties that govern contemporary space tourism are the Outer Space Treaty, the Rescue Agreement, the Liability Convention, the Registration Convention and the Moon Agreement.[11] The last space treaty, that is, Moon Agreement, came back in 1979, around four decades ago. The space treaties were drafted during the Cold War, when governments had

**44** Ankit Kumar Padhy and Divya Tyagi

sole authority over space flight and the use of outer space for commercial tourism was merely science fiction or a distant, unattainable goal.

Given that this industry has the potential to become a billion-dollar industry in the near future, it is crucial to have a comprehensive legal framework in place, which will help in bolstering the confidence of the involved stakeholders (including customers, insurers, States and private companies) in commercial space tourism by clearly defining their legal status and rights. One of the most fundamental legal concerns confronting space tourism is the legal situation of space travellers under the current international legal system. Another question linked to the earlier one is whether the duty to rescue of astronauts and personnel under space treaties is relevant to the space tourists as well. Consequently, it is essential to analyse the major legal challenges that have evolved in this emerging field of adventure.

## Legal Norms Regulating Rescuing Space Tourists under Current International Space Law

### Historical Evolution of Rescue Obligation under International Space Law

The 1959 UNCOPOUS Report underlined the major challenges that may arise during the emergency or distress landing of a spacecraft. It drew the attention of the nations to the necessity for a comprehensive legal framework for the speedy rescue and return of the spacecraft and its crew to the launching nation in the case of a distress landing. The report acted as a catalyst and provided the necessary incentive for the formulation of the Rescue Agreement.[12]

In 1962, the United States and USSR agreed, through the means of exchanged letters, on the imminent need to codify rescue and return standards for astronauts and the prompt return of space vehicles in emergency scenarios. In furtherance of the consensus achieved among space powers to draft rescue norms, the United States and the Soviet Union engaged in extensive debates that ended in the insertion of Principle 9 into the 1963 Declaration of Principles. It stipulated that States shall recognise astronauts as representatives of humanity and provide them with all possible support in the event of an emergency landing on the territory of a foreign State or in international waters. It also provides for the safe and expeditious return of astronauts to the State where the spacecraft is registered. The rescue and return requirements outlined in Principle 9 of the 1963 Declaration of Principles became part of hard law and customary international law when Article V of the Outer Space Treaty was ratified in 1967. The adoption of the Rescue Agreement further refined and crystallised the Outer Space Treaty's (OST) rescue and return criteria.

### Existing Norms of Rescue under Space Treaties

OST provides an elementary framework to regulate exploratory endeavours in outer space, the Moon and other celestial bodies. Article V of OST refers to astronauts as "envoys of mankind" and imposes a binding duty on State parties to provide all practicable aid to astronauts in case of any accident, crisis or emergency landing on another State party's territory or on high seas. Article VIII of the OST stipulates that the State of registry shall retain control and jurisdiction over space objects launched into outer space and provides for the return of such space objects or their component parts when discovered beyond the territorial limits of the State of registry upon the provision of identifying data. Article VI of the OST stipulates international accountability for national space operations conducted by government or non-government organisations.

The Rescue Agreement was adopted in an effort to clarify any ambiguities left by the OST regarding astronauts.[13] Articles 2 to 4 of the Rescue Agreement describe the rescue standards for spacecraft personnel. According to the Rescue Agreement, in case of any emergency landing in a foreign State's territory, that State must take all practicable means to rescue the spacecraft's crew.[14] In addition, if a State discovers information regarding personnel of a spacecraft in distress that has landed on the high seas or beyond the territorial limits of such foreign State and is in a position to assist the personnel, that State shall provide all possible assistance in search and rescue operations. The Agreement also mandates the prompt and safe return of the rescued crew of a malfunctioning spacecraft to the launching authority. In addition, Article 5 of the Rescue Agreement requires the State parties to notify the launching State and the United Nations Secretary-General if they receive information about a space object in distress landing on their territory, on the high seas, or in any other location not under the jurisdiction of another nation.

The commitment to rescue has been fully considered in Moon Agreement. Article 10 of the Moon Agreement stipulates that every practicable measure be taken to safeguard the life and health of people on the Moon. It also requires the parties to give space travellers in distress with shelter in their lunar infrastructure. In addition, Article 13.2 of the Moon Agreement specifies that the obligation to rescue under the OST and Rescue Agreement applies to everyone on board the Moon. While the Moon Agreement provisions regarding rescue norms are more comprehensive as compared to other space treaties, it also has certain limitations. The application of the agreement is limited to the Moon only; thus, it would not cover the initial phases of the space tourism flight. Also, the low number of ratifications of the Moon Agreement reduces its significance as a hard law.

### Legal Conundrums Relating to Rescue Norms of Astronauts under OST and Rescue Agreement

In this part, we will try to scrutinise the legal issues spurred by the OST and Rescue Agreement and analyse the extent to which Rescue Agreement has been successful in rectifying the legal gaps left by the OST.

Article V of OST requires parties to provide all possible assistance to astronauts in accident, distress and emergency scenario. However, OST does not provide much clarity on the term "all possible assistance".[15] The Rescue Agreement not only fails to define the term but also fails to use this term. Rather, it uses terms like all necessary assistance, all possible steps and assistance if necessary. It seems that frequent use of the term 'necessary' has slightly diluted the high burden imposed by the OST.

An interesting issue the rescue norms present is whether the launching State can enter into the territory of any Contracting party to look for any astronauts who might have faced emergency landing. Article 2 of the Rescue Agreement states that the search and rescue endeavours shall take place under the direction and control of the Contracting party. Such party can consult and seek assistance from the launching State. Thus, literal interpretation of Article 2 of the Rescue Agreement reflects that the launching State has not been given unfettered right to enter any other State's territory where the space object with astronauts in distress might have landed, if such Contracting party objects to the same. Ultimately, the final discretion to take a call on the assistance from the launching State has been left with the territorial Contracting party in whose territory the distressed space object with astronauts might have landed.[16]

Another critical issue the rescue norms under the two conventions present is the definition of the terms accident, distress and emergency landing. OST and Rescue Agreement do not provide any definition or clarity on the precise meaning of these terms. However, as per Doolittle, the terms may be given ordinary general meaning. He tries to clarify the meaning of the terms. An accident may be defined as "an unintended random event without deliberate design". A distress scenario may be defined as "a state of danger or dire necessity" and an emergency landing may be comprehended as "an unexpected landing caused by unforeseeable conditions". Unintended landing would surely include any landing caused by astronaut's own fault or negligence, and also any landing caused by navigational error.[17]

Another debatable issue relevant to rescue of astronauts presented by the space treaties is the ascertainment of liability to pay the search and return cost of astronauts in distress. As per the Rescue Agreement, launching State needs to pay the search and return cost of the space object.[18] However, nothing has been mentioned with regard to the search, rescue and return cost incurred by the Contracting State party. The Contracting State parties would have expressly manifested any requirement to compensate the search, rescue and return of the astronauts if they intended to. It is pertinent to note that the rescue operations are generally very costly and take a lot of time. Also, there are no established norms and procedure regarding calculation of the costs involved in such rescue operations. The lack of any express incentive for the Contracting State parties to save the astronauts in distress can prove to be a hurdle faced by commercial space tourism industry in the long run.

A crucial issue with regard to rescue of the astronauts is whether astronauts have been conferred some diplomatic immunity considering the fact that they have been given 'envoys of mankind' status by Article V of OST. Whether the astronauts would be immune from any prosecution of illegal trespass which the Contracting State party where they have landed in distress may bring against them. Article V of the OST read with the Rescue Agreement obligates the State parties to return the astronauts to the launching State. This obligation is absolute in nature and reflects that the astronauts cannot be arrested and prosecuted on the charges of trespassing.[19]

Another question related to the previous issue is whether the astronauts would have to be repatriated even if they commits an offence after landing in the territory of another Contracting party and whether the general immunity to the astronauts applies in such a scenario as well. Space law jurists have argued that the astronauts would have to be repatriated even if they commit some criminal offence after landing and it is the launching State which is the appropriate authority to prosecute and punish the astronauts for such criminal charges.[20]

One of the pertinent questions regarding the return of astronauts is whether astronauts need to be returned by the territorial Contracting State party where the distress landing has taken place if the space object was involved in surveillance mission of the Contracting State party. Under international law and space treaties, surveillance operations through space objects are considered legal. Thus, astronauts would have to be returned to the launching State even if the space object was being used for spying purpose. However, as per Article 4 of the Rescue Agreement, even if the astronauts are involved in aggressive military activities, they would still have to be returned to the launching State in spite of the fact that such aggressive military activities are contrary to the norms of international law and space treaties. Article 4 of the Rescue Agreement has removed any subjective considerations or discretion from the obligation to promptly and safely return the astronauts in case of accident, distress scenario or emergency landing.[21] Under Article 3 of the Rescue Agreement, it is an obligation of the Contracting State party which comes to know of any astronauts in distress outside its territory to communicate the same to the launching State and Secretary-General of the United Nations. However, the time frame within which they should make this communication to the launching State is not as stringent as Article 1 of the Rescue Agreement. As per Article 1, the Contracting State party needs to immediately communicate any information it received regarding astronauts in distress to the said authorities. The alertness expected from the Contracting State party is higher when the distress landing takes place within its territorial boundaries.

Also, in times of commercial space tourism, where the private space companies would have every minute details about the space tourism flight to the extent of the pulse rate of the astronauts, whether casting the obligation of notification for commercial space objects and passengers in distress would be an obsolete and unnecessarily over-burdening requirement for the Contracting State parties should be pondered upon.

### Limitations of the Duty to Rescue under the Contemporary Body of Space Law

OST and Rescue Agreement fail to provide an exact definition of the term 'astronaut' and 'personnel', leaving uncertainty as to space travellers. It is uncertain from the provisions of the OST and Rescue Agreement whether space passenger falls

## 48 Ankit Kumar Padhy and Divya Tyagi

under the ambit of astronaut or personnel of spacecraft.[22] OST also fails to provide any precise norms for regulating private commercial space tourism activities in outer space.

## Analysis of Rescue Obligations towards Space Tourists in Accordance with the Vienna Convention on the Law of Treaties' Interpretational Rules (VCLT)

According to the VCLT,[23] the terms of a treaty should be given their ordinary meaning in the light of their 'context' and 'object and purpose' of the treaty.[24] Additional tools of interpretation, such as treaty's *travaux preparatoires*, historical circumstances surrounding the signing of the treaty and internationally recognised maxims of treaty interpretation, may be used if the ordinary meaning of a term in the treaty is unclear. When the conventional meaning of a term in a treaty results in a plainly ridiculous or unreasonable interpretation, supplementary means may also be invoked.[25] When treaties are verified in more than two languages, each is equally authoritative.[26]

### *Arguments for Classifying Space Tourists as 'Astronauts' under the Outer Space Treaty and 'Personnel' under the Rescue Agreement*

Article V of the OST describes astronauts as envoys of humanity. However, no clear definition of the term 'astronaut' is provided by OST. The preamble of the OST recognises the shared interest of all humanity in the peaceful utilisation of outer space. This language of Article V, when read in conjunction with the OST's preamble, recognises the far-reaching impact of space exploration efforts on mankind as a whole and seems to suggest a broad reading of the terms 'astronaut' and 'personnel' to cover all civilian spacefarers. This interpretation is consistent with the overarching goal of the OST, which is to promote the welfare of humanity.

The Rescue Agreement's elementary objective is to establish standards for the rescue of persons in emergency or crisis circumstances, highlighting the fact that it is inspired by similar humanitarian principles as OST. Thus, it would be irrational and would lead to absurdity to distinguish space tourists from personnel for the rescue purpose. It cannot be the intention of the drafters that only crew members should be rescued, and civilian space tourists should be left unaided during an emergency rescue operation. This viewpoint is further corroborated by the Italian delegation's statement on the proposed wording of the Rescue Agreement, which states that the phrase 'personnel' applies to everyone on board, not just astronauts, and that 'everyone on board' has the right to aid for humanitarian reasons. In addition, the absence of any legal compensation obligation by the launching authority to the State rescuing the stranded spacecraft demonstrates the humanitarian nature of the Rescue Agreement and supports this approach.

### Arguments Against Classifying Space Tourists as 'Astronauts' under the Outer Space Treaty and 'Personnel' under the Rescue Agreement

Astronauts have been regarded as 'envoys of mankind' because they work for the greater common good of the public.[27] The benefits of the new knowledge emerging from the research and scientific studies conducted by the astronauts are available to all the States, irrespective of their contribution to such research studies. Such ancillary benefits from the new scientific research and developments in outer space by the exploration activities of astronauts constitute a balancing consideration for the obligations to rescue and return imposed by the OST on all nations. However, no such scientific benefits are accrued by all nations by private space tourism undertaken by space passengers for their own leisure, and therefore, space tourists do not fit under the 'envoys of mankind' as no greater public good is served by their space travel for their own enjoyment. Thus, the responsibility to rescue and return space tourists cannot be disproportionately imposed on all States without a balancing consideration.[28]

Personnel refers to employees of any work, enterprise or service. The literal and plain interpretation of the word "personnel" restricts its meaning to employed crew members supporting space vehicles and astronauts, providing some kind of service for the functioning and support of the space vehicle, and would not include space passengers within the ordinary meaning of the term. The translations of the term "personnel" in authenticated Chinese, French and Spanish versions of the Rescue Agreement also restrict the scope of the term to crew members and service providers on board and thus exclude space tourists from its ambit.[29]

When the OST and Rescue Agreement were drafted, space travel was the exclusive domain of the government, and private commercial space tourism was regarded as almost impossible. Thus, considering the historical context, it becomes apparent that the framers only intended to apply the rescue norms to astronauts and personnel of spacecraft (i.e. crew members) and did not envisage their applicability to space tourists. This standpoint further gets strengthened by the comment of the French delegate during the presentation of the Rescue Agreement to the United Nations General Assembly. In the said comment, the French delegate clearly stated that the rescue obligations of the Rescue Agreement are only applicable to flights experimental and scientific in nature and not to those of commercial nature.

Also, the argument that the rescue and return rules of the OST and Rescue Agreement are based on humanistic values is fundamentally wrong. Idealistic sentiments and moral values to save human lives in case of an emergency during a space operation are not enough to make the States legally obligated to do something, because they are not part of customary international law or the rules of the existing space treaties.

## Suggestions and Way forward

The legal status of space tourists, especially the applicability of the obligation to rescue and return, evidently remains contested under the contemporary space treaties. These unsolved legal uncertainties have the potential to severely impede the development of the nascent commercial space travel industry. Therefore, it is imperative to urgently resolve these legal issues.

While there are multiple approaches under international law through which the relevant issues may be resolved, new treaty, resolution or subsequent agreement, the feasibility of these approaches varies. However, there are a few common points that must be adequately addressed in any such reformatory measure. The terms 'astronaut', 'personnel' and 'space tourists' should be clearly defined, and clear differentiation should be done between the aforesaid terms. Also, it should be made clear that space tourists are 'astronauts' according to the OST and 'personnel of spacecraft' according to the Rescue Agreement. Further, reference to ISS Intergovernmental Agreement and MCOP Agreement may provide the guiding light for defining these terms.[30]

In the future, the rescue operations with regard to space passengers might involve crew members and tourists of multiple nationalities, and the operation might be conducted in the territory of a third State, raising several legal questions, including the definitional issues, the applicability of duty to rescue and return, and applicable law. Thus, a new comprehensive treaty regulating commercial space tourism devised under the umbrella of the United Nations would be an ideal and durable solution to the legal conundrums surrounding space tourism.[31] However, considering the low ratification of the Moon Agreement and the hesitant approach of major space-faring nations like the United States and Russia towards hard law adoption in the outer space sector in the last few decades, it seems a highly improbable task to achieve in the current scenario.

An international fund to compensate the State undertaking the rescue operations of the space passengers in case of emergency or distress landing situations in the territory of such rescuing State or on high seas needs to be created. The fund may have a sponsoring system similar to the IMF, wherein space-faring nations party to the treaty may contribute sums proportionate to their respective GDPs. The space-faring nations may also charge space passengers a certain sum for the fund. This fund would ensure sufficient compensation for the rescuing State.[32]

Since the negotiation and adoption of a multilateral international treaty is a slow-paced mechanism under international law, considering the stalemate with respect to the development of hard law under space law and the imminent need for clarity on rescue norms, the adoption of the UNGA resolution clarifying the existing ambiguities can be a useful initial step to improve legal certainty and sustainable development of the space tourism industry. Additionally, it can also expressly provide that the rescuing State would be compensated for the expenses incurred by it during the rescuing and return operations. Although such resolution would be non-binding in nature, it can act as an ice breaker, serve as a model framework, and may become part of customary international law on widespread inclusion in domestic laws regulating space tourism.

Alternatively, the States Parties to the OST and Rescue Agreement could also come to an international agreement that clarifies what 'astronaut' and 'personnel of spacecraft' mean and makes it clear that space tourists are included in the definitions of these terms for the purpose of the duty to rescue and return. Such a subsequent agreement interpreting the provisions of an existing treaty has been mandated by the VCLT.[33]

### Space Rescues by Private Space Companies: Need to Extend the Law of Salvage to Outer Space

The current space treaties require the Contracting State parties to take all feasible measures to assist astronauts and personnel of spacecraft in distress. However, with the increasing participation of private space companies in the space tourism sector, the said companies would also have the means and know-how to conduct rescue operations in space. It remains unsettled under the space treaties whether any private space company having requisite technical capability and undertaking rescue operation to assist astronauts in distress may receive any compensation.

The maritime laws of salvage may provide a good reference point for incentivising rescue operations by private space companies. Salvage is made up of three main parts. First, the property that is the subject of a salvage claim must have been in danger. Second, the people who saved the property must have done so on their own free will. Third, the rescue must have worked out at least partially. If a rescuer can show that it did all three things, it is entitled to be paid for its rescue work. However, space law in the current form instead of rewarding the salvage operations by private space companies might actually punish them for any failure to carry out a successful rescue operation.

An international instrument like UNGA resolution extending the refined version of maritime salvage laws to outer space can be an ad hoc solution till an exhaustive permanent settlement is reached regarding the said issue. However, the admiralty law of salvage would need minor modifications to better suit the outer space environment.

Normally, in admiralty law, salvage cannot be awarded if only persons have been rescued. When both persons and property are successfully rescued, then salvage award may be made (if required, out of the proceeds from the sale of the rescued property). However, to incentivise rescue of stranded astronauts, personnel in spacecraft and space tourists by private space ventures, a slight exception needs to be made for 'pure life salvage'.

'No cure no pay' is one of the crucial principles of maritime salvage law. According to the said rule, no award or recovery of expenses may be granted in case of unsuccessful salvage mission. A minor exception may also be made to the salvage concept of 'no cure no pay' rule under the admiralty law while extending it to outer space by allowing reasonable expenses plus a stipulated percentage of expenses (as incentive) for private space companies demonstrating technical capability to carry out space rescue operations and diligently undertaking the said rescue mission even if the rescue attempt does not succeed. Also, space rescue in the form of bringing medicines or other vital items necessary for the survival of stranded space tourists may be brought under the concept of salvage law for outer space. Additionally, a private space rescue operation which may be unable to save the spacecraft but succeed in neutralising a substantial potential health hazard should be allowed compensation for benefitting the launching State from avoiding huge liability under the Liability Convention if the risk would not have been averted.

In the long run, the best way to incorporate the law of salvage to space rescue operations is through an Outer Space Salvage Convention. Such a convention may take inspiration from the Brussels Convention on Salvage at Sea. As an international treaty on space salvage may take a long time to be negotiated, and ratified by the States, meanwhile space salvage law may also be developed by having reference to relevant national laws and practice and incorporating the same in international soft law instruments.

## Chapter Conclusion

Gone are the days when space travel would be undertaken by the national governments to reflect their space power. Since the early twenty-first century, participation of private companies in the space sector has considerably increased. Space is becoming the next billion-dollar market platform for the companies to make big profits on their investments. Space tourism will be a common phenomenon in inter-continental air travel in the near future. Private space companies will be torchbearers of human space travel in the coming decades. With increasing number of spacecrafts carrying tourists to outer space and back would increase, it will increase the potential for accidents, distress situations or mishaps. Few of the said emergency situations may need rescue operations to protect the space tourists and the spacecraft. However, people must perceive space tourism as safe for sustainable growth in the number of passengers willing to undertake this adventurous journey. Having clear rules for rescue and return in case of an emergency during space travel can be an essential step in this direction. Detailed legal norms need to be also formulated to incentivise and support rescue operations by private space ventures possessing the required technical capability and willing to carry out diligent salvage mission. Under the current space treaties, it is still unclear what the legal status of space tourists is and whether or not there is a duty to rescue and return space tourists. Clarity about who is responsible for space tourists' rescue and return is important not only for the customers but also for private space companies and governments.

There is an imminent need to remove the superficial distinctions made between astronauts, crew members and space tourists with regard to their rescue and return in distress and extend their applicability to everyone on board. Proactive steps at the international level are required to harmonise the archaic space treaties to the modern-day legal challenges posed by new space activities like commercial space tourism and create a well-defined predictable legal regime.

In the long term, a new comprehensive treaty regulating commercial space tourism would be the best way to deal with legal issues related to space tourism. However, a United Nations General Assembly resolution clearing up existing ambiguities and being well adopted by domestic laws, or a multilateral agreement explicitly stating that space tourists would fall under the definition of astronauts under OST and personnel under Rescue Agreement can be a workable icebreaker.

## Notes

1 Steven Freeland, 'Space Tourism and the International Law of Outer Space', in Sandeepa Bhat B. (ed.) *Space Law in the Era of Commercialisation* (Lucknow: Eastern Book Company, 2010) pp. 15–38 at p. 15.
2 Tanja Masson Zwaan and Steven Freeland, 'Between Heaven and Earth: The Legal Challenges of Human Space Travel', *ActaAstronautica*, Vol. 66, 2010, pp. 1597–1607 at p. 1597.
3 Steven Freeland, 'Fly Me to the Moon: How Will International Law Cope with Commercial Space Tourism?', *Melbourne Journal of International Law*, Vol. 11, 2010, pp. 1–29 at p. 7.
4 Frans G. Von Der Dunk, 'Space Tourism. Private Spaceflight and the Law: Key Aspects', *Space Policy*, Vol. 27, No. 3, 2011, pp. 146–152 at p. 147.
5 'Global Space Tourism Market Growth (Status and Outlook) 2019–2024', available at <https://www.fiormarkets.com/report/global-space-tourism-market-growth-status-and-outlook-372490.html> Last visited, 20 March 2022.
6 *Id*; 'Space Tourism Market Forecast 2022–2027', available at <https://www.industryarc.com/Report/19394/space-tourism-market.html> Last visited, 20 March 2022.
7 'Space Tourism Market Forecast 2022–2027', available at <https://www.industryarc.com/Report/19394/space-tourism-market.html> Last visited 20 March 2022.
8 *Id.*
9 'Global Space Tourism Industry', available at <https://www.reportlinker.com/p05960156/Global-Space-Tourism-Industry.html?utm_source=GNW> Last visited, 20 March 2022.
10 Dylan Taylor, 'The Future of Space Tourism: op-ed', available at <https://www.space.com/future-of-space-tourism-op-ed> Last visited, 20 March 2022.
11 Treaty on Principles Governing the Activities of States in the Exploration and Use of Outer Space, Including The Moon and Other Celestial Bodies 18 UST 2410 (1967) (Outer Space Treaty); Agreement on the Rescue of Astronauts, the Return of Astronauts and the Return of Objects Launched into Outer Space (Rescue Agreement); Convention on International Liability for Damage Caused by Space Objects 672 UNTS 119 (1968) 24 UST 2389 (1972) (Liability Convention); Convention on Registration of Objects Launched into Outer Space 28 UST 695 (1975) (Registration Agreement); and Agreement Governing the Activities of States on the Moon and Other Celestial Bodies 1363 UNTS 3 (1979) (Moon Agreement).
12 Manfred Lachs, Tanja L. Masson-Zwaan and Stephan Hobe, *The Law Of Outer Space* (Netherlands: Martinus Nijhoff Publishers, 2010) pp. 87 & 88.

13 Robert M. Jarvis, 'The Space Shuttle Challenger and the Future Law of Outer Space Rescues', *International Lawyer (ABA)*, Vol. 20, No. 2, 1986, pp. 591–622 at p. 600.

14 Zeldine Niamh O' Brien, 'The Rescue Agreement and Private Space Carriers', *Proceedings of the Fifty-First Colloquium on the Law of Outer Space*, 2008, pp. 126–136 at pp. 127 & 128.

15 R. Cargill Hall, 'Rescue and Return of Astronauts on Earth and in Outer Space', *American Journal of International Law*, Vol. 63, No. 2, 1969, pp. 197–210 at p. 205.

16 Stephen Gorove, 'International Protection of Astronauts and Space Objects', *DePaul Law Review*, Vol. 20, No. 3, 1971, pp. 597–617 at p. 601.

17 J. William Doolittle, 'Man in Space: The Rescue and Return of Downed Astronauts', *United States Air Force JAG Law Review*, Vol. 9, No. 5, 1967, pp. 4–7 at p. 7.

18 Rescue Agreement. Art. 5(5).

19 Charles A Riccio Jr., 'Another Step for Mankind-The Agreement of the Rescue of the Astronauts and the Return of Objects Launched into Outer Space', *United States Air Force JAG Law Review*, Vol. 12, No. 2, 1970, pp. 142–153 at p. 147.

20 Paul G. Demling and Daniel M. Arons, 'The Treaty on Rescue and Return of Astronauts and Space Objects', *William and Mary Law* Review, Vol. 9. No. 3, 1968, pp. 630–663 at p. 653.

21 Rescue Agreement, Art. 4.

22 Steven A. Mirmina, 'Astronauts Redefined: The Commercial Carriage of Humans to Space and the Changing Concepts of Astronauts under International and U.S. Law', *FIU Law Review*, Vol. 10, No. 2, 2015, pp. 669–678 at p. 671.

23 Vienna Convention on the Law of Treaties, Art. 31, May 23, 1969, 1155 U.N.T.S. 331.

24 *Id.*

25 *Id.*

26 VCLT, Art. 33(4).

27 Carl Quimby Christol, *The Modern International Law of Outer Space* (New York: Pergamon Press, 1982) pp. 178–180.

28 Tanvi Mani, 'The Applicability of the Norms of Emergency Rescue of Astronauts to Space Tourists', *King's Student Law Review*, Vol. 7, No. 1, 2016, pp. 28–39 at p. 30.

29 Mark Sundahl, 'The Duty to Rescue Space Tourists and Return Private Spacecraft', *Journal of Space Law*, Vol. 35, 2009, pp. 163–200 at pp. 185–189.

30 Megan McCauley, 'Astro-Not?-How Current Space Treaties Could Fall Short of Protecting Future Space Tourists', *The University of the Public Law Review*, Vol. 50, 2019, pp. 453–488 at pp. 479 & 480.

31 George Robinson, 'Astronauts and a Unique Jurisprudence: A Treaty for Spacekind', *Hastings International & Comparative Law Review*, Vol. 7, No. 3, 1984, pp. 483–499 at p. 494.

32 *Supra* note 28, at 37.

33 VCLT, Art. 31(3)(a).

# 5

# KEEPING OUTER SPACE SAFE FOR HUMAN PRESENCE

*Martha Mejía-Kaiser*

## Introduction

Before the first humans were sent to outer space, there were many concerns if they could survive. Once astronauts successfully reach space, they are exposed to natural conditions that can damage their health and even cost their lives. Concepts and technologies were developed to protect astronauts from the hostile space environment, such as spaceships and spacesuits that offer some level of protection against micrometeoroids, the extreme temperatures in space, as well as the lack of oxygen and atmospheric pressure. However, the increase of space activities in the last years has created new threats not only to traditional human spaceflight, but also to the emerging space tourism industry. This writing addresses these man-made threats and focuses on the 'Low Earth Orbits' (LEO) as the orbital area that so far has been visited by a few tourists.

## Small Satellites

To enable the development of space tourism, it is necessary to understand the threat of an increasing number of satellites orbiting the Earth. A 'satellite' is "[a] body which revolves around another body of preponderant mass and which has a motion primarily and permanently determined by the force of attraction of that other body".[1] In the year 2022, almost 2,400 space objects were launched,[2] which is a record number since the beginning of the space era. Of all launched space objects in 2022, about 2,350 were sent to Low Earth Orbits, and about 95% of these space objects are small satellites.[3]

With the development of new technologies, such as miniaturisation and light materials, the size, weight and cost of the integration of spacecraft can be strongly

DOI: 10.4324/9781032617961-5

**56** Martha Mejía-Kaiser

reduced. The International Standardization Organization, a non-governmental organisation of national standards bodies, classifies 'very small spacecraft' and gives recommendations for their design and operation.[4] The mass of this category of space object ranges between 0.01 and 600 kg.[5] Very small space objects usually do not have manoeuvrable capabilities.

### Satellites without Propulsion and Guidance Systems

To save weight, very small satellites do not have propulsion and guidance systems. Objects orbiting at very Low Earth Orbits do not represent a big problem at the moment. With short-duration missions, they have a short orbital life of only some weeks. However, the higher the satellites without propulsion systems are orbited, the longer they will take to naturally descend and re-enter the atmosphere. The US Government considered limiting the orbital altitude to 400 km for satellites that have no propulsion systems, with the aim to protect the International Space Station and other crewed spacecraft.[6] This proposal faced resistance from satellite manufacturers and operators who already had planned years ahead for the production and launch of their satellites and feared a drop in their business performance.

This US Government's proposal is under scrutiny.[7] It is highly probable that this proposal will be adopted as a requirement for the licensing conditions of US and foreign satellite operators. This rule would benefit the safety of manned spaceflight and space stations of other countries at and above 400 km altitude.[8]

### Satellites with Propulsion and Guidance Systems

Small satellites with propulsion and guidance systems can correct their orbits and also perform evasive manoeuvres. This group includes satellites that form part of large constellations, like the US SpaceX Starlink[9] and the British OneWeb[10] constellations. Some close encounters of Starlink satellites with other space objects have already taken place. In 2020, a Starlink satellite had a close encounter with a satellite of the European Space Agency.[11] One year later, Starlink satellites had two close encounters with the manned Chinese Space Station.[12]

Usually, institutions that provide data on 'conjunctions'[13] inform satellite operators about collision risks. However, operators have a limited time for coordinating evasive manoeuvres, which are largely undertaken manually, after email communication among the involved operators.[14] As a complicating factor, satellite ground stations are not suitable as surveillance infrastructure to find and track the increasing number of space objects.

Four space treaties enjoy vast recognition of States performing space activities. For the protection of the health and life of astronauts, Article V of the Outer Space Treaty stipulates, "States Parties to the Treaty shall regard astronauts as envoys of mankind in outer space and shall render to them all possible assistance in the event of accident, distress, or emergency landing [...]".[15] The Rescue Agreement, which contains more specific norms to protect astronauts, stipulates in its Article 2 that

> [i]f, owing to accident, distress, emergency or unintended landing, the personnel of a spacecraft land in territory under the jurisdiction of a Contracting Party, it shall immediately take all possible steps to rescue them and render them all necessary assistance.[16]

However, these treaties do not contain specific obligations to protect humans in space at all times. Lacking international space traffic rules that give priority to the safety of astronauts and their spacecraft, and lacking prompt surveillance and alert infrastructure, outer space has become an increasingly dangerous place for human presence.

In some fora the topic of space traffic coordination is discussed. Since 2006, the European Commission has undertaken studies on space situational awareness.[17] In 2014, the 'European Union Space Surveillance and Tracking Consortium' was established to "[...] provide data, information and services related to the surveillance and tracking of space objects orbiting the Earth".[18] In 2022, this consortium was providing collision avoidance services to operators of 260 satellites. In 2021, the European Commission established a 'Union Space Programme' and the 'European Union Agency for the Space Programme'. Both are relevant for a European Space Traffic Management.[19] At the beginning of 2022, the European Union released a joint communication on space traffic management.[20] This joint communication highlights the need for a coordinated approach to space traffic management. For this purpose, the European Commission has started a process of consultations with all stakeholders to protect the space objects of the European Union Space Program and those of the EU Member States. One part of the strategy for space traffic management aims to improve the infrastructure on the surface of the Earth and to develop space-based monitoring for better tracking of space objects. It is also planned to develop a toolbox with standards for space traffic management to support national authorities when licensing satellite operators who wish to provide services to EU Member States. The joint communications acknowledge that some EU Member States have already implemented in their national legislation some norms that contribute to the coordination of space traffic. For the medium term, it is foreseen that the standards proposed by the European Commission will become obligatory in the European Union.

In the Committee on the Peaceful Uses of Outer Space (COPUOS) of the United Nations, States' delegates discuss the development and implementation of "[...] technical and regulatory provisions to promote safe access to outer space, the safety of operations in outer space, and the safe return from outer space [...]".[21]

At the national level, some rules are under development. For example, a new rule of the US licensing requirements will require operators to "[...] mitigate the collision risk [...]" in general.[22] Based on the strong commercial relationship between

NASA and SpaceX, in 2021, they concluded a bilateral agreement to give a priority right-of-way to all NASA space assets, such as the International Space Station.[23]

This agreement could become a model to protect human spaceflight, also of other countries. However, the dominance of a few private firms with an increasing number of space objects in Low Earth Orbits may render it difficult to protect manned spaceflight of countries which do not license these dominating private ventures. There is a chance for concluding such agreements if there is a strong commercial relationship between a foreign private company and a State, like a relationship between the US private company Tesla and China.[24] Without strong commercial ties, the private companies have stronger bargaining power.

Humans in outer space are facing the growing collision risk with operational spacecraft. Another threat is the collision with space debris.

## Space Debris

The launch activity of satellites to Low Earth Orbits also generates space debris. Space debris results from items that detach during normal launch operations, rocket stages that separate after they propelled a space object into space, satellites whose fuel is used up and cannot any longer be manoeuvred, those that suffer system ruptures[25] and release fragments,[26] those that suffer catastrophic explosions and those that are intentionally destroyed.[27] Over time, several thousands of tonnes of space debris have accumulated in outer space.[28]

Before large constellations were deployed, researchers considered that 5%–10% of satellites would suffer malfunction right after their deployment in outer space. This was later confirmed by the first batch of Starlink satellites.[29] The deployment of large constellations of small satellites thus creates large amounts of space debris that endangers manned space objects.[30]

### *Mitigation of Space Debris*

Being concerned about a growing space debris population, researchers of space agencies engaged with collision warnings to protect their assets decided to establish a common forum, the Inter-Agency Space Debris Coordination Committee (IADC). This group of experts first identified two critical regions where most of the satellites are orbited: the Low Earth Orbit Region (from the surface of the Earth until 2,000 km altitude) and the Geosynchronous Orbit Region (at about 36,000 km altitude). In 2002, the IADC published a set of recommendations to mitigate the creation of space debris in these regions.[31] These recommendations served later as a basis for a set of guidelines at COPUOS which were endorsed by a UN General Assembly Resolution in 2007.[32] The COPUOS Guidelines applicable to the Low Earth Orbit Region include actions to:

- Limit debris released during normal operations
- Minimise the potential for break-ups during operational phases

Keeping Outer Space Safe for Human Presence **59**

- Limit the probability of accidental collision in orbit
- Limit the long-term presence of spacecraft and launch vehicle orbital stages in the Low Earth Orbit (LEO) region after the end of their mission
- Minimise the potential for post-mission break-ups resulting from stored energy
- Avoid intentional destruction

The limitation of debris released during normal operations refers to all items that are released during the deployment of space objects in orbit, such as thermal blankets, protection covers of sensors, restraint cables of solar panels, etc. Conformity with this recommendation can be verified through surveillance systems from Earth. This is of relevance for owners of satellites who have contracted the services of satellite integrators to follow this recommendation.

The guideline to minimise the potential for break-ups during operational phases advises operators to plan and execute measures if their space system is malfunctioning and there is a probability that a break-up will take place. In this case it is recommended to immediately take action, such as initiating disposal measures and passivating energies that may cause a catastrophic fragmentation. Although it is not possible to verify with independent external systems if space actors are following this recommendation, this guideline is further developed to give technical guidance on how to reduce potential break-ups.[33]

The guideline to limit the probability of accidental collision in orbit is related to space traffic coordination. Space object operators are encouraged to watch the orbital data of other space objects and to apply collision avoidance manoeuvres. Although this measure is directed to space object operators, collision avoidance measures are a collective effort. It can only be accomplished if there is a reliable world-wide infrastructure to constantly track all space objects (functional and space debris), to adequately manage the data gathered, to timely provide/acquire conjunction warnings and to apply collision avoidance manoeuvres with high probability of success.

Another guideline recommends to lower the orbit of launch vehicle orbital stages and satellites in LEO when they have fulfilled their mission. This manoeuvre of lowering the orbit to reduce the time span space objects take to enter into the Earth atmosphere is known as 'de-orbiting'. Although the COPUOS Guidelines are not specific as to where to de-orbit, the IADC Guidelines recommend to lower the orbit of space objects so they take 25 years or less to naturally decay and to re-enter the Earth atmosphere.[34] This corresponds to about 600 km. The lower they are, the faster they will re-enter the atmosphere. However, this IADC Guideline of 2002 is no longer adequate to meet the requirements of present LEO activities. The International Space Station, the Chinese Space Station and all manned space objects transit at about 400 km altitude. All these space objects are in the middle of a 'slosh area', exposed to space objects that have ended their operational life and are no longer manoeuvrable. A revision of the altitude to lower the limit below the 400 km altitude becomes urgent to protect manned space objects from an increasing collision risk.

**60** Martha Mejía-Kaiser

The guideline that recommends minimising the potential of post-mission break-ups resulting from stored energy calls upon operators of space objects to passivate after de-orbiting. Before turning off communication links with the space object for decommissioning, it is recommended to apply passivation measures, such as disconnecting the batteries from solar panels, to discharge the rest of energy in batteries, to release fuel remnants, to vent gases under pressure and to neutralise power in the momentum wheels.

The last recommendation, to avoid intentional destruction, has been ignored by some space-faring countries,[35] as demonstrated by the recent anti-satellite test (ASAT) of the Russian Federation.[36] Fragments of this destroyed satellite posed a threat to the International Space Station (ISS). Astronauts and cosmonauts onboard the ISS were directed to take preventive safety measures, like closing hatches and taking shelter, while the debris cloud was approaching.[37] The Chinese Space Station also had a close encounter with a fragment resulting from this Russian ASAT.[38]

For the mitigation of other kinds of debris, a growing number of States are adopting national legislation that obligates the application of the IADC Mitigation Guidelines for private companies that obtain a licence.[39]

### Applicability of Space Law

The start of space tourism in Low Earth Orbits coincides with the deployment of large constellations and at a time when States keep performing anti-satellite tests. Since neither the Outer Space Treaty nor other treaties impose an express obligation to protect humans in outer space, and given that States have been reluctant to enter into new treaty obligations, it is necessary to look which provisions in the space treaties can be used to counteract the growing congestion. The Outer Space Treaty offers several provisions that could apply.

### *Can States Place an Unlimited Number of Space Objects in Earth Orbit?*

Article I of the Outer Space Treaty guarantees that "Outer space [...] shall be free for [...] use by all States [...]".[40] By placing large constellations of small satellites in Low Earth Orbits, States make use of this right. However, Article IX of the same treaty sets limits to this freedom. This Article stipulates that "[i]n the [...] use of outer space, [...] States Parties to the Treaty [...] shall conduct all their activities in outer space, [...] with due regard to the corresponding interests of all other States Parties to the Treaty". States have thus the freedom to place a large number of space objects as long as they do not hinder the activities of other space actors.[41]

So far, within the large dimensions of outer space few collision incidents have occurred. In addition to that, no State has raised protests based on the 'due regard' principle of Article IX of the Outer Space Treaty by claiming that its interests have been ignored by other States when carrying out their space activities.

Keeping Outer Space Safe for Human Presence **61**

Should the trend of deploying large constellations of satellites continue without any international coordination and/or restriction, at a certain point the line will be reached when a safe place becomes dangerous for space navigation. When evasive manoeuvres and collisions become frequent, all States will be hindered from performing safe space activities. Crewed space missions will no longer be possible. Space stations would need to be permanently evacuated. We may even reach the tipping point, from where it will be impossible to return to the prior situation.

Article VI of the Outer Space Treaty stipulates that "States Parties [...] shall bear international responsibility for national activities in outer space, [...] [and that the] activities of non-governmental entities in outer space, [...] shall require authorization and continuing supervision".[42] In order to fulfil this primary responsibility, a growing number of States are authorising the launching and private operation of satellites through licensing systems. The States then 'supervise' the compliance of the licence requirements. However, the 'continuous supervision' obligation also entails the primary responsibility of States to provide adequate infrastructure to satellite operators to enable them to comply with their duties.

States are rising the collision risk when they grant an unlimited number of authorisations without an efficient information system to assist satellite operators in undertaking evasive manoeuvres. Collisions could possibly be attributed to the failure of States in fulfilling their supervision obligations. They are not only putting their own national space assets at risk, but as well the space assets of other satellite operators. This lack of supervision will raise a secondary responsibility of the State.

### Have States a Right to Perform Anti-satellite Tests in Outer Space?

Article I of the Outer Space Treaty specifies that "Outer space [...] shall be free for exploration [...] by all States [...] in accordance with international law".[43] However, the term 'exploration' can be understood in a wide manner, including the anti-satellite tests that serve to observe the robustness of materials, devices and procedures. Researcher Hobe comments that "[the] broad range of activities shows how difficult it is to come up with a precise understanding of the area of freedoms granted by Article I".[44] On the other hand, Article IX of the Outer Space Treaty stipulates that "States Parties to the Treaty shall [...] conduct exploration [...] so as to avoid [its] harmful contamination [...]." Despite the limitation to avoid the harmful contamination of outer space with the resulting fragments of anti-satellite tests, and the principle of Article I that "[t]he exploration and use of outer space, [...] shall be carried out for the benefit and in the interests of all countries [...]", no State has raised protests, based on the Outer Space Treaty, against the anti-satellite tests of the United States,[45] the Russian Federation (and the former USSR), China[46] and India.[47] It can be assumed that States currently interpret anti-satellite tests not to be forbidden under space law, and under international law in general. However, it is obvious that anti-satellite tests, so far only performed in Low Earth Orbit, will contribute to the collapse of a valuable region of outer space, which is an area of collective interest.

There are growing calls for the adoption of a legally binding instrument that forbids such tests.[48] The latest Russian anti-satellite test motivated the UN General Assembly to adopt a resolution to this effect at the end of 2021.[49] In 2022, the US Vice-President announced the United States was self-imposing a ban to "[…] conduct destructive, direct-ascent anti-satellite (ASAT) missile testing […]". The Vice-President mentioned that "the United States seeks to establish this [ban] as a new international norm for responsible behaviour in space".[50] Canada,[51] New Zealand[52] and Japan[53] followed the United States with declarations announcing to observe this ban. If this initiative continues to be supported by more States, and all of them abide to this commitment, the ban to conduct direct-ascent anti-satellites tests may become a minimum standard of care, or as Vice-President Harris mentioned, 'a new international norm for responsible behaviour in space'.

The proposed ban is limited to direct-ascent missiles. So far, anti-satellite tests were undertaken only by launching missiles from Earth. However, one should not discard the possibility that new ways of anti-satellite test can be performed, like directing a space object in orbit intentionally against another. Such type of anti-satellite tests could continue creating space debris. For this reason, it is important to ban all types of intentional destruction of space objects in Earth orbits.

## Consultation Rights

Taking into consideration a growing number of space objects launched into outer space, two provisions of Article IX of the Outer Space Treaty need a closer look.

### Consultation Rights Regarding Large Constellations

One provision of Article IX of the Outer Space Treaty concerns to States that perform space activities that may hinder other space actors:

> If a State Party to the Treaty has reason to believe that an activity or experiment planned by it or its nationals in outer space, […] would cause potentially harmful interference with activities of other States Parties in the peaceful exploration and use of outer space, […] it shall undertake appropriate international consultations before proceeding with any such activity or experiment.[54]

The large number of satellites launched in the past two years has been unprecedented.[55] Researchers are warning that the Low Earth Orbital region is endangered. At the same time, States deploying satellite constellations do not consult the States Parties to the Outer Space Treaty about this activity 'before' the placement of large numbers of satellites, as provided in Article IX. These States perceive their activities as 'business as usual'. They give priority to their commercial goals and disregard a global vision of the consequences of their behaviour with the potential to cause harmful interference to the space activities of other States.

The last sentence of the same Article IX provides that:

> A State Party [...] which has reason to believe that an activity or experiment planned by another State Party in outer space, [...] would cause potentially harmful interference with activities in the peaceful exploration and use of outer space, [...] may request consultation concerning the activity or experiment.

So far, no State has made this request under Article IX, although the plans and details of satellite constellations are publicly known.[56] If States that deploy large constellations of satellites do not voluntarily offer consultations, they should be requested to legitimise their activities by submitting how they will control the space traffic of their operational space objects, and what are their concrete plans and actions to remove the resulting space debris. States that request consultation need to be supported by hard data, to support the 'reason to believe' criterion with evidence. Surveillance information and the assessment of the international scientific community can contribute to this objective element for the consultation request.

### Consultation Rights Regarding Anti-satellite Tests

As military activities, States planning to undertake anti-satellite tests usually do not release their plans beforehand to the international community. On grounds of military secrecy, States do not offer consultations following Article IX of the Outer Space Treaty.

Although Article IX of the Outer Space Treaty stipulates that consultation can only be requested for 'planned' activities, members of the international community should nevertheless demand the few States that have performed anti-satellite tests, and are likely to repeat such activities, to explain their past behaviour and inform about the impact of such tests on the space environment in the short and long term. States that play down the threats resulting from anti-satellite tests[57] should be publicly challenged in international fora with solid evidence and statements of experts and of States that submit the request.

The importance of exercising the consultation procedure comes at a time when there is a disconnection between the political, military and commercial decisions on one side, and the scientific and technical consensus about the consequences of the increase of space objects in outer space on the other.

### Concluding Remarks

It becomes obvious that manned space objects should enjoy priority and that operators of non-manned space objects should take all measures to avoid their orbital paths. States need to agree, ideally by treaty, that all manned spacecraft should have the right-of-way and that the safety of persons in outer space is paramount.

Several States are authorising the launch of large numbers of satellites without any limit. Large numbers of satellites are licensed in Low Earth Orbit, but the licensing States do not hold appropriate surveillance infrastructure and conjunction assessment capabilities in proportion to the number of satellites. States need to limit the number of space objects to the level of capabilities of ground and spatial surveillance infrastructure that enable satellite operators to timely receive information on conjunction alerts and to reduce collision risks.[58] This can only be accomplished with international cooperation with a larger number of tracking ground stations positioned all around the Earth.

Another urgent measure that needs to be adopted is a ban on anti-satellite tests. If States continue testing destructive capabilities, we will lose navigable Low Earth Orbits, and the door to other orbital altitudes may be closed for many decades.

States that operate space objects in outer space have the primary responsibility to act with due regard towards other States and to keep the orbital environment of the Earth operational. Just like we have only one Earth, we have only one Low Earth Orbital region that needs to be protected for human presence. Not only for tourists that temporally visit outer space, but for those who permanently live and work there…and for those who will venture to the Moon and beyond.

## Notes

1 International Telecommunication Union (ITU), *Radio Regulations*, Vol. 1, edition of 2020, p. 24, Art. 1.179, available at <https://www.itu.int/pub/R-REG-RR-2020> Last visited, 9 May 2023.
2 See ESA, *Space Environment Statistics*, updated 27 March 2023, available at <https://sdup.esoc.esa.int/discosweb/statistics/> Last visited, 9 May 2023. See in particular the last two graphs about payload launches in LEO and GEO.
3 See "Smallsats by the Numbers 2023", *Bryce Tech Reports*, available at <https://brycetech.com/reports> Last visited, 9 May 2023.
4 ISO standard 'Space Systems – Requirements for Small Spacecraft', ISO/TS 20991:2018, available at <https://www.iso.org/standard/74109.html?browse=tc> Last visited, 9 May 2023.
5 See the classification of satellites according to their mass by the United States, Federal Aviation Administration (FAA), *The Annual Compendium of Space Transportation: 2018*, Table 11, p. 94, available at <https://www.faa.gov/about/office_org/headquarters_offices/ast/media/2018_ast_compendium.pdf> Last visited, 9 May 2023.
6 See United States, Federal Register, *Rule by* the *Federal Communications Commission*, 20 July 2020, available at <https://www.federalregister.gov/documents/2020/07/20/2020-12013/streamlining-licensing-procedures-for-small-satellites> Last visited, 9 May 2023.
7 See Jon Brodkin, 'FCC Moves Cautiously in Plan to Prevent Space Debris and Satellite Collisions', *Ars Technica*, 23 April 2020, available at <https://arstechnica.com/tech-policy/2020/04/fcc-plan-to-regulate-space-debris-scaled-back-to-avoid-conflicts-with-nasa/> Last visited, 9 May 2023.

Keeping Outer Space Safe for Human Presence **65**

8  The Chinese Space Station is at an altitude of 390 km. See the orbital path of the China Space Station at *n2yo.com* (Live Real Time Satellite Tracking and Predictions), core module Tianhe-1 (search: 2021-035A), or available at <https://www.n2yo.com/satellite/?s=48274#results> Last visited, 9 May 2023.

9  Space Exploration Technologies Corp (SpaceX) is deploying the Starlink satellite constellation at about 560 km altitude, with expectation to offer commercial broadband internet service that will include rural and remote locations all around the world. Each Starlink satellite weights about 260 kg. See 'Starlink – Dynamic 3D Orbit Display' (real time updated), *Heavens Above*, available at <https://heavens-above.com/Starlink.aspx> Last visited, 9 May 2023.

10  OneWeb satellites weigh about 150 kg each. The first batch with six OneWeb satellites was launched on 27 February 2019. See Gunter D. Krebs, 'Orbital Launches of 2019', *Gunter's Space Page*, available at <https://space.skyrocket.de/doc_chr/lau2019.htm> Last visited, 9 May 2023. The OneWeb satellites orbit is at about 1,200 km altitude. See the orbital path of a OneWeb satellite (search: 2021-025A) at *n2yo.com*, or available at <https://www.n2yo.com/satellite/?s=48042#results> Last visited, 9 May 2023.

11  Predicted Near Miss between Aeolus and Starlink 44', *ESA*, 3 September 2019, available at <https://www.esa.int/ESA_Multimedia/Images/2019/09/Predicted_near_miss_between_Aeolus_and_Starlink_44> Last visited, 9 May 2023. In 2020, OneWeb operators claimed that a Starlink satellite had a close encounter with a OneWeb satellite, but SpaceX disputed this. See SpaceX filing to the US Federal Communications Commission on the event, *Space Exploration Holdings, LLC, IBFS File No. SAT-MOD-20200417-00037*, 9 September 2020, available at <https://fcc.report/IBFS/SAT-MOD-20200417-00037/2729898.pdf> Last visited, 9 May 2023.

12  See UN Doc. A/AC.105/1262(6 December 2021), available at <https://www.unoosa.org/res/oosadoc/data/documents/2021/aac_105/aac_1051262_0_html/AAC105_1262E.pdf> Last visited, 9 May 2023.

13  See Quentin Verspieren, 'Military Influence on International Regime-Making for Space Traffic Management: Explaining the Evolution of SSA Data Transparency at the US Department of Defense', *Proceedings of the IISL Colloquium on the Law of Outer Space*, IAC-19.E7.4.1, 2019. ESA's definition of conjunction is: "[…] a conjunction is understood as a geometric close approach between two objects, irrespective of their activity status, triggering an operator analysis but not necessarily an avoidance manoeuvre nor implying a collision." ESA, Environment Report, 2022, p. 68, available at <https://www.sdo.esoc.esa.int/environment_report/Space_Environment_Report_latest.pdf> Last visited, 9 May 2023.

14  See ESA, Predicted near miss between Aeolus and Starlink 44, *supra* note 11.

15  *Treaty on Principles Governing the Activities of States in the Exploration and Use of Outer Space, Including the Moon and Other Celestial Bodies*, 27 January 1967, 610 UNTS 205, 18 UST 2410, TIAS 6347, 6 ILM 386 (entered into force on 10 October 1967) [Outer Space Treaty], Art. V.

16  *Agreement on the Rescue of Astronauts, the Return of Astronauts, and the Return of Objects Launched Into Outer Space*, 22 April 1968, 672 UNTS 119, 19UST 7570, TIAS 6559,7 ILM151 (entered into force on 3 December 1968) [Rescue Agreement], Art. 2.

17  See Ludovica Ciarravano, "The European Space Situational Awareness Legal Framework as an Example of Top-Down Approach Applicable to Future European Space Traffic Management-Related Initiatives", *Proceedings of the IISL Colloquium on the Law of Outer Space*, IAC-21.E7.1.11, 2021.

18  European Union, *Joint Communication: An EU Approach for Space Traffic Management - An EU Contribution Addressing a Global Challenge*, 15 February 2022, available at <https://ec.europa.eu/info/files/joint-communication-eu-approach-space-traffic-management-eu-contribution-addressing-global-challenge_en> Last visited, 9 May 2023, p. 6.

66 Martha Mejía-Kaiser

19 See *Regulation (EU)2021/696 of the European Parliament and of the Council of 28 April 2021 Establishing the Union Space Programme and the European Union Agency for the Space Programme*, available at <https://eur-lex.europa.eu/eli/reg/2021/696/oj> Last visited, 9 May 2023.
20 See EU, *Joint Communication, supra* note 18.
21 See UN Doc. A/76/20 (25 August–3 September 2021), at 23–24, available at <https://www.unoosa.org/res/oosadoc/data/documents/2021/a/a7620_0_html/A_76_20E.pdf> Last visited, 9 May 2023.
22 The License Applicant "[…] will mitigate the collision risk […]. [S]teps to assess and mitigate the collision risk should include, but are not limited to: Contacting the operator of any active spacecraft involved in such a warning; sharing ephemeris data and other appropriate operational information with any such operator; and modifying space station attitude and/or operations." US, *Code of Federal Regulations*, US Government Printing Office, Title 47 - Telecommunication, US 47CFR25, awaiting approval by the Office of Management and Budget., § 25.114 (d)*** (14)(iv)(A)(5), e-CFR, available at <https://www.ecfr.gov/current/title-47/chapter-I/subchapter-B/part-25> Last visited, 9 May 2023.
23 "Partner will use reasonable efforts to: 1) Perform evasive action by on-orbit Starlink satellites to mitigate close approaches and avoid collisions with all NASA assets". *Nonreimbursable Space Act Agreement Between The National Aeronautics and Space Administration and Space Exploration Technologies Corp for Flight Safety Coordination with NASA Assets*, NASA, 2021, available at <https://www.nasa.gov/sites/default/files/atoms/files/nasa-spacex_starlink_agreement_final.pdf> Last visited, 9 May 2023. See the orbital path of the International Space Station at *n2yo.com* (search: 1998-067A), or at <https://www.n2yo.com/satellite/?s=25544> Last visited, 9 May 2023.
24 Elon Musk is founder and CEO of SpaceX, and is co-founder and CEO of Tesla Inc., an electrical car manufacturer. See *Tesla – Elon Musk*, 2023, available at <https://www.tesla.com/elon-musk> Last visited, 9 May 2023. A Tesla factory was established in the city of Shanghai, China. It is claimed that Tesla received political concessions and extensive government support to build the factory. See Eva Dou, 'Tesla, Elon Musk face backlash in China after Beijing's complaint against SpaceX', *The Washington Post*, 28 December 2021, available at <https://www.washingtonpost.com/world/2021/12/28/elon-musk-tesla-china-spacex/> Last visited, 9 May 2023.
25 See one-minute video of the rupture of the Indonesian satellite Telkom-1 in 2017: 'Telkom-1 Satellite Debris Incident', Exo Analytic Space Operations Center, 30 August 2017, available at <https://www.youtube.com/watch?v=4FXX1kSNljU> Last visited, 9 May 2023.
26 See the 12 worst explosions of space objects in outer space, from 1965 (US transtage OV-2-I) to 2019 (Indian Microsat-R), in Chris Daehnick and Jess Harrington, 'Look Out Below: What Will Happen to Space Debris in Orbit?', *McKinsey & Company*, 1 October 2021, exhibit 4, available at <https://www.mckinsey.com/industries/aerospace-and-defense/our-insights/look-out-below-what-will-happen-to-the-space-debris-in-orbit> Last visited, 9 May 2023.
27 "Satellites were deliberately destroyed in space. There were several reasons for doing this, e.g., to avoid disclosing the design, or the testing of anti-satellite weaponry." ESA, Space Environment Statistics, *supra* note 2. See also Francesca Letitzia, 'ESA Environmental Report on Space Debris', 19 September 2019, slide 4, available at <https://www.sdo.esoc.esa.int/publications/ESA%20Environmental%20Report%20on%20Space%20Debris%20Mitigation_slides.pdf> Last visited, 9 May 2023.
28 See ESA, *Space Debris by the Numbers*, 2023, available at <https://www.esa.int/Safety_Security/Space_Debris/Space_debris_by_the_numbers> Last visited, 9 May 2023.
29 See Jonathan O'Callaghan, "'Not Good Enough' - SpaceX Reveals That 5% of Its Starlink Satellites Have Failed in Orbit so Far', *Forbes*, 30 June 2019, available at <https://www.

forbes.com/sites/jonathanocallaghan/2019/06/30/not-good-enough-spacex-reveals-that-5-of-its-starlink-satellites-have-failed-in-orbit/> Last visited, 9 May 2023.

30 In 2017, the Inter-Agency Space Debris Coordination Committee (IADC), published a statement with recommendations for the design and operation of large satellite constellation in Low Earth Orbits, with the aim to mitigate the generation of space debris. See IADC, *Statement on Large Constellations of Satellites in Low Earth Orbits*, IADC-15-03 (last revision July 2021), available at <https://www.iadc-home.org/documents_public> Last visited, 9 May 2023.

31 See Inter-Agency Space Debris Coordination Committee (IADC), *Space Debris Mitigation Guidelines*, 15 October 2002 (last revised in 2021), IADC-02-01, available at <https://www.iadc-home.org/documents_public/view/id/82#u> Last visited, 9 May 2023.

32 See UNGA Res. A/RES/62/217(22 December 2007), paragraphs 26 to 28, available at <https://undocs.org/A/RES/62/217> Last visited, 9 May 2023.

33 See ISO Standard 'Space Debris Mitigation Requirement', ISO 24113:2019 (published in 2011, last revision in 2023), abstract available at <https://www.iso.org/standard/83494.html> Last visited, 9 May 2023.

34 See Guideline 5.3.2, IADC, Space Debris Mitigation Guidelines, *supra* note 31.

35 A publication of the Secure World Foundation lists anti-satellite tests of several countries. See *Global Counterspace Capabilities: An Open-Source Assessment*, Secure World Foundation, 2021, section 10 (online page: 182), available at <https://swfound.org/media/207162/swf_global_counterspace_capabilities_2021.pdf> Last visited, 9 May 2023.

36 An ascending missile destroyed the satellite Cosmos-1408 at 480 km altitude. See Nivedita Raju, 'Russia's Anti-Satellite Test Should Lead to a Multilateral Ban', *Stockholm International Peace Research Institute* (SIPRI), 7 December 2021, available at <https://www.sipri.org/commentary/essay/2021/russias-anti-satellite-test-should-lead-multilateral-ban> Last visited, 9 May 2023.

37 *Id. Cf.* 'NASA Administrator Statement on Russian ASAT Test', *NASA*, 15 November 2021, available at <https://www.nasa.gov/press-release/nasa-administrator-statement-on-russian-asat-test> Last visited, 9 May 2023.

38 The fragment approached the Chinese Space Station within 14.5 m. See 'Chinese Satellite Narrowly Misses Debris from Russian Explosion', *Aviation Week & Space Technology*, 24 January-6 February 2022, p. 8.

39 See UN *Compendium on Space Debris Mitigation Standards Adopted by States and International Organizations*, UN Office of Outer Space Affairs, 1 March 2023, available at <https://www.unoosa.org/documents/pdf/spacelaw/sd/Space_Debris_Compendium_COPUOS_20_March_2023.pdf> Last visited, 9 May 2023.

40 Outer Space Treaty, Art. I, *supra* note 15.

41 Researcher Sergio Marchisio considers that 'due regard' connotes not to compromise the safety of the space operations of other countries, which means in principle to follow a minimum standard of care. See Sergio Marchisio, 'Article IX, Outer Space Treaty', in Stephan Hobe, Bernhard Schmidt-Tedd and Kai-Uwe Schrogl (eds.) *Cologne Commentary on Space Law*, Vol. 1 (Cologne: Heymanns, 2009), pp. 169–182 at p. 175.

42 Outer Space Treaty, Art. VI, *supra* note 15.

43 Outer Space Treaty, Art. I, *supra* note 15.

44 Stephan Hobe, 'Article I, Outer Space Treaty', in Stephan Hobe, Bernhard Schmidt-Tedd and Kai-Uwe Schrogl (eds.) *Cologne Commentary on Space Law*, Vol. 1 (Cologne: Heymanns, 2009), pp. 25–43 at p. 34.

45 One of the latest deliberate destructions in orbit of the United States took place on February 2008. Despite the claims of the United States that this event did not produce long-lasting orbital debris, the European Space Agency assessed that some debris were catapulted into higher orbits and endangered the International Space Station. "In the

short-term, however, the risk of penetration of the shields of the ISS manned modules by USA-193 fragments larger than 1 cm increased by about 30%." ESA, 'Space Debris, Frequently Asked Questions', 20 April 2013, available at <http://www.esa.int/Our_Activities/Operations/Space_Debris/FAQ_Frequently_asked_questions> Last visited, 9 May 2023. *Cf. Global Counterspace Capabilities: An Open-Source Assessment*, Secure World Foundation, Brian Weeden and Victoria Samson (eds.), April 2019, pp. 6-3, available at <https://swfound.org/counterspace/> Last visited, 9 May 2023.

46 As a reaction to the anti-satellite test of China in 2007, proposals were submitted at different fora for the creation of codes of conduct calling "[…] States to refrain from intentional action which will or might bring about, directly or indirectly, the damage or destruction of objects in outer space". Marchisio, *supra* note 41, at 181.

47 The Russian Space Agency Roscosmos informed that the collision risk of the ISS rose by 5% after the deliberate destruction of the satellite Microsat-R of India. See 'ISS Faces Mounting Threat of Being Struck by Indian Satellite Junk', *TASS*, 29 May 2019, available at <https://tass.com/science/1060628> Last visited, 9 May 2023.

48 The Stockholm International Peace Research Institute expressed its hopes that the anti-satellite test of the Russian Federation in 2021 will motivate States to agree on a multilateral ban of this sort of tests. SIPRI, *supra* note 36.

49 See UNGA Res. 76/231, *Reducing Space Threats Through Norms, Rules and Principles of Responsible Behaviours* (30 December 2021), available at <https://documents-dds-ny.un.org/doc/UNDOC/GEN/N21/417/21/PDF/N2141721.pdf?OpenElement> Last visited, 9 May 2023.

50 The US White House. *Fact Sheet: Vice President Harris Advances National Security Norms in Space*, 18 April 2022, available at <https://www.whitehouse.gov/briefing-room/statements-releases/2022/04/18/fact-sheet-vice-president-harris-advances-national-security-norms-in-space/> Last visited, 9 May 2023.

51 See Permanent Mission of Canada to the United Nations in Geneva, *Canadian Statement*, 9–13 May 2022, available at <https://documents.unoda.org/wp-content/uploads/2022/05/Canada-General-Statement-for-Translators-OEWG-Space-Threats-Session-bilingual.pdf> Last visited, 9 May 2023.

52 See Nanaia Mahuta (New Zealand, Foreign Affairs Minister), 'Otago Foreign Policy School, Opening Address', *Beehive.govt.nz*, 1 July 2022, available at <https://www.beehive.govt.nz/speech/otago-foreign-policy-school-opening-address> Last visited, 9 May 2023.

53 See Ministry of Foreign Affairs of Japan, Decision Not to Conduct Destructive Direct-Ascent Anti-satellite Missile Testing, 13 September 2022, available at <https://www.mofa.go.jp/press/release/press3e_000451.html> Last visited, 9 May 2023.

54 Outer Space Treaty, Art. IX, *supra* note 15.

55 See the penultimate graph about launches in LEO, *supra* note 2.

56 Miraslava Kazlouskaya, 'Large Satellite Constellations', *German Journal of Air and Space Law*, No. 4, 2021, pp. 571–585 at pp. 574–575.

57 Sergei Lavrov, Russian Foreign Affairs Minister, admitted the deliberated destruction of a satellite at 480 km altitude, but denied that it endangered the ISS or represented any other danger. It is claimed that the destruction produced 1,500 fragments. See Maya Yang, 'Russia Admits to Anti-satellite Missile Test But Denies "Dangerous Behavior"', *The Guardian*, available at <https://www.theguardian.com/science/2021/nov/16/russia-defends-anti-satellite-missile-test> Last visited, 9 May 2023.

58 See section 'NASA Lacks Direct Measurement Data on Debris near the International Space Station', in NASA Office of Inspector General, *NASA'S Efforts to Mitigate the Risks Posed by Orbital Debris*, 27 January 2021, p. 25, available at <https://oig.nasa.gov/docs/IG-21-011.pdf> Last visited, 9 May 2023.

# 6

# STATE RESPONSIBILITY AND SPACE TOURISM

## Customary Principles as Modified by Article VI of the Outer Space Treaty

*Ricky J. Lee*

## Introduction

The spectacular developments in human spaceflight in the first two decades of the present century have transformed both the prospects and the realities of space tourism. In this short span of time, human spaceflight has evolved from having been the exclusive province of a handful of States to a world of competing private businesses all rushing to send "commercial astronauts" into space. Meanwhile, the space tourism sector has transformed itself from a government-controlled revenue-generating Russian enterprise for a few multimillionaires,[1] as it was in the 1990s, into an industry in which competing private and commercial ventures have been offering trips into low Earth orbit for potentially less than one million US dollars.[2] In 2021, in particular, multiple launches by private ventures in the so-called "billionaires' space race" have sent both men and women, young and old, into the small but rapidly growing company of space tourists or commercial astronauts.[3]

Indeed, the diversity in gender, age, sexual orientation and ethnicity of the modern corps of commercial astronauts is such that their only common characteristic is their wealth.

For better or worse, one other constant is the relevant principles of space law and public international law, particularly those dealing with state responsibility for space activities. Remarkably in a sector of such a rapid pace of technological development, the existing legal principles concerning state responsibility for space activities have remained unchanged since 13 December 1963,[4] the almost forgotten time in the history of human spaceflight when no more than 11 men and one woman crossed the final frontier,[5] and well before 12 men (and no woman) walked on the Moon.[6] In discussing the principles of state responsibility that apply to private human spaceflight, one must first consider the content and effect of the relevant customary principles of international law, a task greatly assisted by their codification

DOI: 10.4324/9781032617961-6

**70** Ricky J. Lee

by the International Law Commission in the Articles on Responsibility of States for Internationally Wrongful Acts (the "State Responsibility Articles").[7] This must then be followed by an analysis of how the substantive effect of such principles are affected or modified by Article VI of the Treaty on Principles Governing the Activities of States in the Exploration and Use of Outer Space, including the Moon and Other Celestial Bodies (the "Outer Space Treaty").[8] Finally, any such discussion would be incomplete without consideration of the adequacy of this framework of state responsibility on the practical realities of private and commercial human spaceflight.

## State Responsibility under Customary International Law

### Responsibility for Internationally Wrongful Acts

#### Overview

The customary principles of state responsibility are some of the most frequently invoked and applied legal principles of public international law.[9] Throughout the history of international jurisprudence of the Permanent Court of International Justice and the International Court of Justice, the legal and financial responsibility of a State for an internationally wrongful act committed against another State has been one of the most highly litigated issues.[10] Consideration, albeit a brief one, of the relevant customary principles of state responsibility, perhaps, is best achieved by analysis of the judgments in the following three cases:

1 the decision of the Permanent Court of International Justice in the *Case concerning the Factory at Chorzów (Germany* v. *Poland) (Merits)*, relating to the responsibility of a State for an internationally wrongful act by the State itself[11];
2 the decision of the International Court of Justice in *Military and Paramilitary Activities in and against Nicaragua (Nicaragua* v. *United States of America)*, relating to the responsibility for acts on the territory of one State that is attributable in fact to another State[12]; and
3 the often-cited decision of the International Court of Justice in the *Corfu Channel Case (Merits) (United Kingdom* v. *Albania)*, relating to the responsibility for acts within the territory of one State that is not attributable to another State but could not have been carried out without the knowledge of the territorial State.[13]

Each of these cases is now discussed in turn.

### The Chorzów Factory Case

In 1915, the German Empire entered into an agreement with Bayerische Stickstoffwerke A.G., under which a nitrate factory was to be built at Chorzów, in Upper Silesia, by the German Reich, to be operated by the company, in effect, under licence.[14] After the end of the First World War, a continuing dispute arose between Germany and the newly created States of Czechoslovakia and Poland as to the territory of Upper Silesia and its eventual division. Meanwhile, in 1919, a new company, Oberschlesische Stickstoffwerke A.G., was established, and the new Weimar Republic of Germany transferred the land, factory, buildings, installations, raw materials, reserves, equipment and stock at Chorzów to this new company.[15]

On 15 May 1922, after a war between Czechoslovakia and Poland, a series of plebiscites and multiple uprisings, the Geneva Convention of 15 May 1922 concerning Upper Silesia was concluded between Germany and Poland, pursuant to which the area around Chorzów was ceded to Poland, Article 6 of which stated[16]:

> Poland may expropriate in Polish Upper Silesia, in conformity with the provisions of Articles 7 to 23, undertakings belonging to the category of major industries, including mineral deposits and real estates. Except as provided in these clauses, the property, rights, and interests of German nationals or of companies controlled by German nationals may not be liquidated in Polish Upper Silesia.

On 1 July 1922, the Polish Court at Huta Krolewska cancelled Oberschlesische Stickstoffwerke's ownership and Bayerische Stickstoffwerke's operation and control of the factory at Chorzów and ruled that its ownership was to be registered in the name of the Polish Government; officials from the Polish Treasury took control and possession of the factory two days later.[17] In an earlier judgment of the Permanent Court of International Justice, Poland was held to have contravened Article 6 of the Geneva Convention of 15 May 1922 by its unlawful seizure of the factory and its economic benefits from both Bayerische Stickstoffwerke and Oberschlesische Stickstoffwerke.[18] The straightforward consequence of this internationally wrongful act by the Polish Government was that Poland was liable to Germany for the damage caused resulting from that wrongful act[19]:

> [It] is a principle of international law, and even a general conception of law, that any breach of an engagement involves an obligation to make reparation. … the Court has already said that reparation is the indispensable complement of a failure to apply a convention, and there is no necessity for this to be stated in the convention itself.

What is interesting (and complex) for the purposes of the present discussion is the pains to which the Court took to identify the actual wrongful act in question. In one view, Poland had expropriated the factory and associated economic rights and has failed to pay reparation for them; as such, the wrongful act in this view would be the failure to pay reparation for the expropriation. On the other view, Poland cannot lawfully expropriate the factory without contravening Article 6 of the Geneva Convention, and so the internationally wrongful act is the seizure itself. This is not a distinction without a difference: if the expropriation itself is lawful,

Poland would only be liable to compensate for the value of the property taken; however, if the seizure itself is unlawful, Poland must pay reparations not only for the value of the property taken but also to consider the full economic effects of Bayerische Stickstoffwerke and Oberschlesische Stickstoffwerke having been deprived not only of the factory but its continuing operation over the life of the factory.[20] Accordingly, in place of a simple valuation of the value of the factory and other physical property on-site as on 3 July 1922, the Court posed three questions[21]:

I. -
    A. What was the value, on 3 July 1922, ... of the undertaking for the manufacture of nitrate products of which the factory was situated at Chorzów in Polish Upper Silesia, in the state in which that undertaking (including the lands, buildings, equipment, stocks and processes at its disposal, supply and delivery contracts, goodwill and future prospects) was, on the date indicated, in the hands of the Bayerische and Oberschlesische Stickstoffwerke?
    B. What would have been the financial results ... (profits or losses), which would probably have been given by the undertaking thus constituted from 3 July 1922, to the date of the present judgment, if it had been in the hands of the said Companies?
II. What would be the value at the date of the present judgment ... of the same undertaking (Chorzów) if that undertaking ... had remained in the hands of the Bayerische and Oberschlesische Stickstoffwerke, and had either remained substantially as it was in 1922 or had been developed proportionately on lines similar to those applied in the case of other undertakings of the same kind ...?

The legal basis of these questions is the need for the reparations payable by Poland to compensate Germany, to the extent possible, to restore it to the position it would have been in if the Polish wrongful act had not occurred (*restitutio in integrum*).[22] The amount ultimately paid by the Polish Government to Bayerische Stickstoffwerke and Oberschlesische Stickstoffwerke was negotiated and settled between them.[23]

### The Nicaragua Case, the Iran-US Claims Tribunal and Tadić

By 1979, President Anastasio Somoza Debayle, together with his father and brother, had ruled Nicaragua continuously since 1936.[24] In that year, his administration was overthrown by and replaced with the "Junta of National Reconstruction" dominated by the Frente Sandinista de Liberación Nacional, also known as the "Sandinistas".[25] Armed opposition to the new regime was concentrated in two main groups, the Fuerza Democrática Nicaragüense that operated in the area bordering Honduras, and the Alianza Revolucionaria Democrática that operated in the region bordering Costa Rica; they became known together as the "Contras" (being a shortened form of *Contrarevolucionarios*). The United States, under President Ronald

Reagan, sought to isolate the Sandinista regime by supporting the Contras through financial, logistical, matériel and planning support, eventually escalating to covert tactical support and military operations.[26]

In *Nicaragua*, the International Court of Justice distinguished between acts carried out by individuals not being *de jure* organs of the United States but were acting on behalf of the United States in that they were totally dependent on the United States by being paid, equipped, supported and directed by organs of the United States (referred to as "Unilaterally Controlled Latino Assets", or "UCLAs"). Those individuals were also paid, financed, equipped and supported by the United States but retained a degree of autonomy or independence from the United States and its state organs (the Contras falling within this category). The Court held that acts of the UCLAs were clearly and directly attributed to the United States, including:

- laying mines in Nicaraguan ports, in particular El Bluff, Corinto and Puerto Sandino, the process involving clashes between speedboats and helicopters of the UCLAs with Nicaraguan patrol boats;
- blowing up an underwater oil pipeline and part of the oil terminal at Puerto Sandino;
- an air and sea attack on the port of Corinto that destroyed five oil storage tanks, which led to substantial loss of fuel and the evacuation of civilian population;
- rocket attacks by speedboats and helicopters on the Nicaraguan naval base at Potosí;
- attacks by speedboats and helicopters on the oil storage facility at San Juan del Sur;
- conducting high-altitude reconnaissance overflights;
- conducting low-altitude overflights that caused sonic booms in their wake; and
- conduct of military manoeuvres jointly with Honduras near the Nicaraguan border.[27]

As for the Contras, the Court held that the acts of the United States in paying, financing, arming, equipping, training, supplying, supporting and aiding them are attributed to the United States, and they were internationally wrongful acts as they involved and/or led to the use of military force in Nicaragua against the territorial sovereignty and political integrity of that State.[28] However, the specific acts of the Contras themselves, particularly those that allegedly contravened international humanitarian law, could not be attributed to the United States in the absence of direct knowledge, control or direction by the United States over the Contras.[29] As the Court stated[30]:

> The Court has taken the view ... that United States participation, even if preponderant or decisive, in the financing, organising, training, supplying and equipping of the Contras, the selection of its military or paramilitary targets, and the

74   Ricky J. Lee

planning of the whole of its operation, is still insufficient in itself, on the basis of the evidence in the possession of the Court, for the purpose of attributing to the United States the acts committed by the Contras in the course of their military or paramilitary operations in Nicaragua. All the forms of United States participation mentioned above, and even the general control ... over a force with a high degree of dependency on it, would not in themselves mean, without further evidence, that the United States directed or enforced the perpetration of the acts contrary to human rights and humanitarian law alleged by [Nicaragua]. Such acts could well be committed by members of the Contras without the control of the United States. For this conduct to give rise to legal responsibility of the United States, it would in principle have to be proved that that State had effective control of the military or paramilitary operations in the course of which the alleged violations were committed.

Antonio Cassese commented that the above extracted paragraph suggests that the Court required the acts of the Contras themselves to have been ordered or compelled by the United States for such acts to be attributed to the United States as being subject to its "effective control".[31] This view is supported by the decisions of the Iran-US Claims Tribunal, which held on repeated occasions the imputability of a private act to the State would depend on an objective determination of any influence over, or benefit derived from, the activity that may be attributed to the State, such that if the acts are conducted by private persons or entities without the direction or influence of the State, such acts are generally not imputable to the State.[32] In *Foremost Tehran Inc.* v. *Iran*, an Iranian company decided not to pay dividends to its shareholders, one of which was the claimant company registered in the United States. The Tribunal imputed that decision to the State because the company acted under the influence of some of its directors appointed by the Iranian Government and the company was implementing government policy concerning the financial interests of foreigners.[33] Further, it was held in *Flexi-Van Leasing Inc.* v. *Iran* that, even if the relevant entity was under the control of the State, it must be demonstrated that the specific conduct itself was directed or influenced by the State for it to be imputable to the State.[34]

This need for specificity in the direction given by the State to amount to "effective control" is contrasted with the decision of the Appeals Chamber of the International Criminal Tribunal for the Former Yugoslavia in *Prosecutor* v. *Tadić*,[35] in which it is suggested that attribution for the purposes of state responsibility may also be made by the application of an "overall control" test[36]:

... another degree of control over actions by organised and hierarchically structured groups, such as military or paramilitary units; in this case overall control by the state over the group was sufficient, hence specific instructions were not required for each individual operation.

State Responsibility and Space Tourism  **75**

As seen in the discussion below, the International Law Commission and the International Court of Justice will both embrace the "effective control" test from *Nicaragua* and reject the "overall control" test in *Tadić*.[37]

## The Corfu Channel Case

Between 1943 and 1949, the Greek Civil War was fought between the Kingdom of Greece, supported by the United Kingdom and the United States, and the Communist Party of Greece (Κομμουνιστικό Κόμμα Ελλάδας) with its Democratic Army of Greece (Δημοκρατικός Στρατός Ελλάδας), supported by the Soviet Union and Yugoslavia.[38] On 16 May 1946, during the Greek Civil War in Greece, British cruisers *H.M.S. Orion* and *H.M.S. Superb* sailed into the Corfu Channel, a narrow body of water separating the Greek island of Corfu from the Albanian and Greek mainland coast, and the Albanian shore batteries opened fire but missed both vessels.[39] On 22 October 1946, British cruisers *H.M.S. Leander* and *H.M.S. Mauritius* and destroyers *H.M.S. Saumarez* and *H.M.S. Volage* sailed into the Corfu Channel.[40] The *Saumarez* struck a mine in the bay near Saranda, being in Albanian waters, and serious damage resulted with the loss of 36 lives.[41] When the *Volage* had the *Saumarez* in tow, it also struck a mine, and another eight people were killed. The *Saumarez* was damaged beyond repair.[42]

The International Court of Justice determined that the mine laying could not have been done without being visible from the Albanian coast, particularly given the vigilance shown by Albania towards British warships entering the Corfu Channel (as demonstrated by Albania firing on the *Orion* and the *Superb* earlier), and concluded that the laying of the minefield in the channel could not have been accomplished without the knowledge of Albania[43]:

> In the present case, two series of facts, which corroborate one another, have to be considered: the first relates to Albania's attitude before and after the disaster of October 22nd, 1946; the other concerns the feasibility of observing minelaying from the Albanian coast. … From all the facts and observations mentioned above, the Court draws the conclusion that the laying of the minefield which caused the explosions on 22 October 1946, could not have been accomplished without the knowledge of the Albanian Government.
>
> …
>
> The obligations incumbent upon the Albanian authorities consisted in notifying, for the benefit of shipping in general, the existence of a minefield in Albanian territorial waters and in warning the approaching British warships of the imminent danger to which the minefield exposed them. Such obligations are based … on certain general and well-recognised principles, namely: elementary considerations of humanity, even more exacting in peace than in war; the principle of the freedom of maritime communication; and every State's obligation

**76** Ricky J. Lee

not to allow knowingly its territory to be used for acts contrary to the rights of other States.

...

The Court therefore reaches the conclusion that Albania is responsible under international law for the explosions which occurred on 22 October 1946, in Albanian waters, and for the damage and loss of human life which resulted from them, and that there is a duty upon Albania to pay compensation to the United Kingdom.

In a later judgment, the Court assessed the amount of compensation payable by Albania to the United Kingdom and arrived at £843,947 as the fixed quantum.[44]

### The State Responsibility Articles

The adoption of the State Responsibility Articles in 2001 brought to a conclusion over 40 years of work by the International Law Commission (the ILC) to codify the customary principles concerning state responsibility.[45] As Robert Rosenstock, then president of the Commission, stated[46]:

The State Responsibility Articles are bound to clarify and organize legal thinking, planning, and States' conduct for the foreseeable future. It may be possible to criticize the articles for not being more detailed. However, it will not be possible to deny that here, as in the case of the ILC's work on privileges and immunities, the law of the sea, and the law of treaties, the Commission has constructed a solid foundation for future development of the law in the light of changing circumstances.

Reflecting the legal principles laid down in *Chorzów Factory* and the authorities preceding and following it, Articles 2 and 4 of the State Responsibility Articles state:

Article 2

There is an internationally wrongful act of a State when conduct consisting of an action or omission:

(a) is attributable to the State under international law; and
(b) constitutes a breach of an international obligation of the State.

Article 4

1 The conduct of any State organ shall be considered an act of that State under international law, whether the organ exercises legislative, executive, judicial or any other functions, whatever position it holds in the organization of the State, and whatever its character as an organ of the central Government or of a territorial unit of that State.

2 An organ includes any person or entity which has that status in accordance with the internal law of the State.

More relevant for the purposes of the present study in the context of private and commercial human spaceflight and reflecting in part the principles contained in *Nicaragua* and *Tadić* is Article 8 of the State Responsibility Articles:

The conduct of a person or group of persons shall be considered an act of a State under international law if the person or group of persons is in fact, acting on the instructions of, or under the direction or control of, that State in carrying out the conduct.

James Crawford suggested that the most clear-cut situation in which state responsibility arises under Article 8 is where a State instructs a private person or entity to commit an act on its behalf.[47] This is further supported by the Commentary to the State Responsibility Articles, which clarified the ambit of Article 8 as follows[48]:

Where a State has authorized an act ... questions can arise as to the State's responsibility for actions going beyond the scope of the authorization ... Such cases can be resolved by asking whether the unlawful or unauthorized conduct was really incidental to the mission or clearly went beyond it. In general, a State, in giving lawful instructions to persons who are not its organs, does not assume the risk that the instructions will be carried out in an unlawful way. On the other hand, where persons or groups have committed acts under the effective control of a State, the condition for attribution will be met even if particular instructions may have been ignored.

However, the International Court of Justice, in the *Case concerning Application of the Convention on the Prevention and Punishment of the Crime of Genocide (Bosnia and Herzegovina* v. *Serbia and Montenegro)* held that state responsibility is invoked only if the instructions are given for each operation that constitutes the internationally wrongful acts, and not generally as regards the overall actions taken by the person(s) or group(s) that committed the acts.[49] The Court went on to repudiate explicitly the "overall control" test suggested in *Tadić*:

The "overall control" test has the major drawback of broadening the scope of State responsibility well beyond the fundamental principle governing the law of international responsibility: a State is responsible only for its own conduct, that is to say the conduct of persons acting, on whatever basis, on its behalf. That is true of acts carried out by its official organs, and also by persons or entities which are not formally recognized as official organs under internal law but which must nevertheless be equated with State organs because they are in a relationship of complete dependence on the State. Apart from these cases, a

**78** Ricky J. Lee

State's responsibility can be incurred for acts committed by persons or groups of persons – neither State organs nor to be equated with such organs – only if, assuming those acts to be internationally wrongful, they are attributable to it under the rule of customary international law reflected in [Article 8]. This is so where an organ of the State gave the instructions or provided the direction pursuant to which the perpetrators of the wrongful act acted or where it exercised effective control over the action during which the wrong was committed. In this regard the "overall control" test is unsuitable, for it stretches too far, almost to breaking point, the connection which must exist between the conduct of a State's organs and its international responsibility.

Crawford stated that, "this determination effectively ends the debate as to the correct standard of control to be applied" under Article 8 of the State Responsibility Articles.[50]

## Article VI of the Outer Space Treaty

### *Elements of Article VI*

*Overview*

Surprisingly, Article VI of the Outer Space Treaty, which deals with state responsibility for space activities, would not be in the top ten list of subject matters of inter-governmental and academic discussions on space law. Specifically, Article VI states that:

State Parties to the Treaty shall bear international responsibility for national activities in outer space, including the Moon and other celestial bodies, whether such activities are carried on by governmental agencies or by non-governmental entities, and for assuring that national activities are carried out in conformity with the provisions set forth in the present Treaty. The activities of non-governmental entities in outer space, including the Moon and other celestial bodies, shall require authorisation and continuing supervision by the appropriate State Party to the Treaty. When activities are carried on in outer space, including the Moon and other celestial bodies, by an international organisation, responsibility for compliance with this Treaty shall be borne by the international organisation and by the State Parties to the Treaty participating in such organisation.

It is clear from this that Article VI of the Outer Space Treaty imposes the following obligations on States as regards space activities:

to incur state responsibility for "national" activities in outer space regardless of whether such activities are carried out by public or private entities and to assure that "national" activities are conducted in conformity with the Outer Space Treaty and, through Article III, with international law;

to authorise and continually supervise, where appropriate, the activities of non-governmental entities in outer space; and

to share international responsibility for the activities of international organisations of which the State is a participant.

It is prudent to consider each of these provisions of Article VI in turn and in the context of the existing body of international law on state responsibility.

### Responsibility for "National" Space Activities

Given that States incur responsibility under Article VI of the Outer Space Treaty for national space activities regardless of whether such activities are carried out by public or private persons or entities, taking the first sentence of Article VI of the Outer Space Treaty at its highest, then state responsibility is engaged for private space activities regardless of whether such activities are attributable to the State by operation of the customary principles set out in *Nicaragua* and/or under Article 8 of the State Responsibility Articles. In other words, state responsibility adheres to all non-governmental space activities of a State without any need or regard for such activities to be attributable to the State.

However, to take such a lofty interpretation of this provision in Article VI would ignore the qualified nature of the provision, in that States are to incur responsibility for "national" space activities. In effect, the provision appears to be substituting the distinction between governmental and private space activities with the requirement that the activities, regardless of the nature of the actor, be "national" in nature. It is respectfully contended that this is a distinction without a difference. In the context of state responsibility, the concept of attribution is to deem a private act to be a state act. In essence, attribution makes a private act "national" in nature. As such, it is appropriate to regard the provision as being no more than a pre-*Nicaragua* restatement of the customary principle of attribution.[51] This is supported by the effect of the prevailing application of international law to space activities under Article III of the Outer Space Treaty and the obligation of States in this sentence of Article VI to ensure that "national" space activities of non-state actors conform with the Outer Space Treaty and international law.

### Duty to Authorise and Continually Supervise Space Activities

If the first sentence of Article VI of the Outer Space Treaty does no more than introduce and apply the existing customary principles of attribution for state responsibility to space activities carried out by non-State actors, the second sentence presents an effective shortcut in establishing the requisite "effective control" over such private space activities. The second sentence, in requiring that

**80** Ricky J. Lee

private space activities be authorised and continually supervised by the "appropriate State", applies regardless of whether the space activities are "national" in character – the qualification found in the first sentence is not found in the rest of Article VI. In a practical sense, this means that for every private or otherwise non-governmental space activity, including those not "national" in character, one or more States would have:

1  authorised it;
2  continually supervised it; and
3  been aware of it.

Where a private activity is authorised and continually supervised by a State agency, particularly if a licensing and/or regulatory framework is involved, the activity must necessarily come within the effective control of that State. The activity cannot be carried on lawfully without the authorisation by the State, and the continual supervision must result in the State being able to give directions, impose conditions and otherwise subject the activity to its administrative and regulatory control. The licensing of private space activities is no exception. For example, under the space licensing frameworks enacted under the Outer Space Act 1986 of the United Kingdom or Space (Launches and Returns) Act 2018 (Cth.) of Australia:

- launching a space object from their territory cannot be done without a licence[52];
- launching a space object by their nationals outside their territory cannot be done without a licence[53];
- a licence may subject the activity to conditions to which the licensee must comply[54]; and
- a licensee must assure the State of compliance with all international obligations of the State in relation to the activity.[55]

Similar provisions may be found in the equivalent legislation in many States.[56] Any such licensing, authorisation, supervision, compliance and enforcement by States of private space activities pursuant to Article VI of the Outer Space Treaty, regardless of the weight of the regulatory burden imposed, would amount to "effective control" for the purposes of the attribution tests under *Nicaragua* and Article 8 of the State Responsibility Articles. If a State fails or omits to authorise or continually supervise a private space activity for which it is the "appropriate State", this failure or omission would constitute an international wrongful act for which state responsibility would be engaged.[57] In this context, the fact that the obligations to authorise and continually supervise private space activities are found in the same Article VI dealing with state responsibility cannot be an accident or coincidence.

Even if, *arguendo*, the actions of a State in supervising and continually supervising a private space activity are insufficient to amount to "effective control", or the relevant State is not the "appropriate State" for the purposes of Article VI, the fact remains that, in the interconnected modern world, the State must be aware of the activity, especially if it is being carried out from its territory and transits through its airspace over which a State has exclusive and sovereign control.[58] Just as the International Court of Justice held that Albania was responsible for the third-party mining of its territorial waters in the Corfu Channel, as it must have been aware of it at the time,[59] a State would be responsible for any private space activity of its nationals or from its territory that it must have been aware of at the time it takes place.[60]

In practice, the net effect of the operation of Article VI of the Outer Space Treaty against the background of the customary principles of state responsibility is that a State would have international responsibility for its governmental space activities as well as all non-governmental space activities (regardless of whether they have a national character or otherwise), carried out from its territory or by its nationals, because:

- as the "appropriate State", it would have exercised effective control over the non-governmental activity by the acts of authorisation and continuing supervision as required under Article VI;
- as the "appropriate State", it failed to authorise and/or continually supervise the non-governmental activity as required under Article VI; or
- not being the "appropriate State", the non-governmental activity cannot have been carried out in its territory and/or by its nationals without its knowledge.

This conclusion has two ancillary effects. The first is that this international responsibility would apply to the State even if the relevant private space activity was conducted outside the territory of the State because the State is either the "appropriate State" and/or it must have had knowledge of it. Not only is this consistent with the position following *Nicaragua* and Article 8 of the State Responsibility Articles, this also accords with the approach in the Convention on International Liability for Damage Caused by Space Objects (the "Liability Convention"),[61] which imposes liability on a State for the launch activities of its nationals, even if these activities take place outside the sovereign territory of that State.[62] The second, being the effect on the concept of the "appropriate State", is discussed in greater detail below.

### Dealing with Minor Controversies

#### Responsibility versus Liability

Some commentators had sought to distinguish the "responsibility" prescribed under Article VI of the Outer Space Treaty with "liability" as imposed under Article VII and the provisions of the Liability Convention.[63] From this perspective, Article VI would do no more than to prescribe a regulatory obligation and moral responsibility on States without the imposition of any liability. It is respectfully submitted that this interpretation must be incorrect; to begin with, this would represent a significant mischaracterisation of the content of state responsibility under public international law, which has been connected with liability for damages since time immemorial.[64]

Even if, *arguendo*, the use of the term "responsibility" in Article VI of the Outer Space Treaty is not meant to have any correlation with the concept and principles of state responsibility, recent commentators have placed much emphasis on the use of terms in other languages that are equally authentic to interpret the Outer Space Treaty.[65] This in particular, considering Article 33(3) of the Vienna Convention on the Law of Treaties, provides that the terms used in a treaty are presumed to have the same meaning in each authentic text.[66] In the French text, the term «*responsabilité internationale*» is used in both Articles VI and VII of the Outer Space Treaty in place of both "international responsibility" and "international liability" in the English text. Similarly, the Chinese term 「国际责任」, the Russian term «международнуюответственность» and the Spanish term «*responsables internacionalmente*» are used as the equivalent terms for both "international responsibility" and "international liability" in Articles VI and VII.

Accordingly, if "responsibility" under Article VI and "liability" under Article VII have the same meaning, Article VI must be interpreted to mean that States are to be internationally liable for space activities for which those State(s) have state responsibility for the purposes of international law.[67] For the above reasons, the proposition that Article VI of the Outer Space Treaty has no liability effects on States cannot be supported.

## Meaning of "Appropriate State"

The second ancillary controversy relating to Article VI of the Outer Space Treaty is that the State of nationality may find itself in a situation where it is unable to supervise the space activities of its private nationals because they are being conducted outside its territory. For example, if a Belgian national is domiciled in Brazil and conducts their space activities in Brazilian territory, it would be difficult, if not impossible, for Belgium as the State of nationality to authorise and continually supervise those space activities or to impose civil penalties or criminal sanctions for non-compliance. However, there are several reasons why the State of nationality would not be excluded from being the "appropriate State" simply because its nationals or the relevant space activity are outside its territorial control.

First, taking the regulatory obligations of Article VI of the Outer Space Treaty at its highest, Armel Kerrest suggested that asserting this difficulty is in itself a breach of international law[68]:

This is of course in total breach of international law. States have personal jurisdiction over their nationals. They must keep the capacity to implement international law in general and space law in particular and to make it applicable to their citizens whether they are natural or legal persons.

When considered in the context of the duties imposed under Article VI of the Outer Space Treaty being implemented through domestic legislation that carries criminal sanctions, Kerrest's view is supported by elements of general international law. Most notably, such support can be found in the *S.S. Lotus* case, which related to the collision between the French steamer *S.S. Lotus* and the Turkish vessel *S.S. Bozkourt* that resulted in the death of eight Turkish crew.[69] The Permanent Court of International Justice held that Turkey was capable of extending its criminal jurisdiction over French nationals arrested in Turkey for committing a crime under Turkish law, even though the alleged crime took place on the high seas and, as such, France asserted exclusive jurisdiction over the incident onboard as the law of the flag.[70] As the Court stated[71]:

> Though it is true that in all systems of law, the principle of the territorial character of criminal law is fundamental, it is equally true that all or nearly all of these systems of law extend their action to offences committed outside the territory of the State which adopts them. ... The territoriality of criminal law, therefore, is not an absolute principle of international law and by no means coincide with territorial sovereignty.

Further, Edwin Dickinson stated in his introductory comment on the Harvard Research Draft Convention on Jurisdiction with Respect to Crime that[72]:

> The competence of the State to prosecute and punish its nationals on the sole basis of their nationality is based upon the allegiance which the person charged with crime owes to the State of which he is a national. ... If international law permits a State to regard the accused as its national, its competence is not impaired or limited by the fact that he is also a national of another State.

Second, the States Parties to the Outer Space Treaty have accepted their exposure to international liability if the damage is caused to a third State due to the conduct of space activities by its nationals, both under Article VII of the Outer Space Treaty and the provisions of the Liability Convention, without territorial delimitation. In the case of damage caused to the surface of the Earth or to aircraft in flight, the Liability Convention imposes absolute liability on the launching States, including the territorial State and the State of nationality, for which no assertion of ignorance, powerlessness or *non est factum* would excuse a State from liability.[73] It would be surprising that the States intended to subject themselves to specific treaty provisions concerning liability for damage caused by space objects in such circumstances, even absolute liability, but would exclude themselves from state responsibility in the same situation.

**84** Ricky J. Lee

Third, many States have not shied away from enacting domestic legislation that apply to their nationals extraterritorially, even some that contain criminal sanctions. For example, legislation relating to sexual exploitation of children,[74] bribery,[75] modern slavery[76] and even those relating to space activities[77] are often stated to apply to nationals both within and outside their territorial jurisdictions.[78] However, it must be noted that it is not the legal or jurisdictional competence of the State of nationality but rather its physical inability to enforce its laws over nationals domiciled outside its territory that causes difficulties for the State of nationality to act as the "appropriate State". Even in *Lotus*, which James Brierly suggested to be "based on the highly contentious metaphysical proposition of the extreme positivist school",[79] the Court stated that the "exclusively territorial character of law relating to this domain constitutes a principle which, except as otherwise expressly provided, would *ipso facto*, prevent States from extending the criminal jurisdiction of their courts beyond their frontiers".[80] In other words, the personal jurisdiction that the State of nationality has over its nationals would allow for the later prosecution of any crimes committed by that national when they return to its territory but would not allow that State from fulfilling its duty to authorise and continually supervise the space activities of that national carried on outside its territory.

That is not to suggest that the State of nationality must always be the "appropriate State" for the purposes of Article VI of the Outer Space Treaty. If the "appropriate State" is intended always to be the State of nationality, it is doubtful that the drafters of the Outer Space Treaty would have found it necessary to invent a new term to describe it but then omitted to define it. Indeed, the term "appropriate" is best read with reference to the context in which it is placed, namely the act of authorising and continually supervising the space activities of non-governmental entities. For instance, in the *travaux préparatoires* of the Principles Declaration, there was a proposal tabled by the United States that contained the following provision[81]:

> A state or international organisation from whose territory or with whose assistance or permission a space vehicle is launched bears international responsibility for the launching, and is internationally liable for personal injury, loss of life or property damage caused by such vehicle on the Earth or in air space.

It may be concluded from the above discussion that the "appropriate State" is the State in the best position to assert direct and immediate control over the non-governmental space activities to authorise and continually supervise them. Accordingly:

- in the case of a space activity conducted by a private entity within the territory of its State of nationality, the "appropriate State" is clearly that State;
- in the case of a private entity conducting a space activity outside its State of nationality but within the territory of another State, the State in the best position

to authorise and continually supervise is the State with territorial jurisdiction over the activities of that private entity; and

- for a space activity conducted by a private entity outside the territorial jurisdiction of any State, the State of nationality would likely remain the most "appropriate State".[82]

In practice, however, the existing body of domestic laws relating to licensing of non-governmental space activities suggest that States would rather err on the side of caution and require all non-governmental activities conducted in their territory by anyone and conducted by their nationals anywhere to be authorised and continually supervised by the State.[83] The history of operations of Sea Launch L.L.C. illustrates this point perfectly. Sea Launch was a consortium of four companies, one each of Norway (20%), Russia (25%), Ukraine (15%) and the United States (40%).[84] Sea Launch operated a launch facility comprising a converted ocean drilling platform (*Ocean Odyssey*), and its operational centre (*Sea Launch Commander*) was located on another vessel. Both vessels were located on the high seas during launches (albeit often close to the territorial waters of Kiribati). The vessels were registered in Liberia, and the primary launch vehicle used was the Ukrainian *Zenit-3SL*. Originally incorporated in the Cayman Islands, Sea Launch was subject only to licensing and regulation under British law[85] until the United States amended its law so that it would apply to any foreign company with no less than 40% shareholding held by US nationals, after which Sea Launch transferred its corporate registration to the United States to avoid double regulation.[86] In 2017, the assets of Sea Launch were purchased by the parent company of Siberia Airlines, also known as S7 Airlines. However, the prospect of Sea Launch returning to commercial operations is much diminished, if not extinguished, following the 2022 Russian invasion of Ukraine.[87]

In defining the term "appropriate State" as the State best placed to assert legal and regulatory control as per the formulation above, there are three implications that should be noted:

1 this is a fairer outcome as the State of nationality should not be placed in a position where it must fulfil an impossible legal obligation due to the need to act extraterritorially;
2 the problem of "double jeopardy" is avoided as the "appropriate State," and only that State is responsible under the Outer Space Treaty for authorising and continually supervising the space activities conducted by private entities within its territorial jurisdiction, even though the prevailing state practice is to embrace that double jeopardy[88]; and
3 although such a definition would have an effect on the imposition of state responsibility under Article VI of the Outer Space Treaty, this definition does not affect or prejudice the effect of Article VII or the provisions of the Liability Convention in imposing liability on the launching States, regardless of whether it had authorised and continually supervised the activity or otherwise.

## International Transfer of Satellite Registration and Implications on State Responsibility

### Article VIII of the Outer Space Treaty

The launching of space objects remains an important aspect of space activities and its corresponding state responsibility and liability, with the application of the Liability Convention as well as Article VII of the Outer Space Treaty. However, liability for the operation of space objects is such that if a satellite operator manoeuvred a satellite into a collision with another satellite or its re-entry and led to damage on the surface of the Earth, liability under those treaty provisions would rest with the "launching States".[89] While the satellite operator would be regarded as having procured the launch of a satellite, the situation becomes a little more complex if the satellite operator was not one of the original launching States.

Article VIII of the Outer Space Treaty provides that:

> A State Party to the Treaty on whose registry an object launched into outer space is carried shall retain jurisdiction and control over such object, and over any personnel thereof, while in outer space or on a celestial body. ...

While Article VI of the Outer Space Treaty would apply to impose state responsibility on the State operating a satellite for any internationally wrongful acts or omissions in the course of doing so, the vesting of jurisdiction and control over a satellite on the State of registry under Article VIII means that state responsibility and the corresponding international liability may also vest in the State of registry.

### The Registration Convention

In the case where only one State is involved in the launch of a particular space object, this does not pose any difficulties. On the United Nations Register of Space Objects, almost all States have registered nearly all their space objects, either pursuant to the Convention on Registration of Objects Launched into Outer Space (the "*Registration Convention*"),[90] or on a voluntary basis under General Assembly Resolution 1721B (XVI).[91] However, where there is more than one launching State, Article II(2) of the Registration Convention provides that:

> Where there are two or more launching States in respect of any such space object, they shall jointly determine which one of them shall register the object ..., bearing in mind the provisions of Article VIII of the [Outer Space Treaty] and without prejudice to appropriate agreements concluded or to be concluded among the launching States on jurisdiction and control over the space object and over any personnel thereof.

For example, the United States adopted the position that it will only register all space objects that are owned by US governmental or private entities, regardless of where they were launched, and that non-US payloads launched from the United States should be registered by the State whose nationals own the payload.[92] This is consistent with what is expected under Article VIII of the Outer Space Treaty and is a positive development in terms of clarifying the practice of States in deciding on the appropriate State of registry between multiple launching States, as it reflects the commercial reality that it is the owner of the payload, rather than the other launching States, that would most desire the retention of jurisdiction and control.

## Transfer of Registration

What remains a subject of substantial debate is the problem of the transfer of registrations of space objects and, along with that transfer, the jurisdiction and control over the space object under Article VIII of the Outer Space Treaty. Neither the Outer Space Treaty nor the Registration Convention contains any provision for the transfer of the registration of a space object. This was an issue during the 1997 handover of sovereignty over Hong Kong to the People's Republic of China[93] and the 1999 privatisation of Inmarsat.[94] In the former case, China was not a launching State for any of the space objects registered by the United Kingdom on behalf of Hong Kong, it is then the Crown Colony; and in the latter case, the United Kingdom was not a launching State of the Inmarsat satellites. In both cases, the United Nations Register for Space Objects proceeded pragmatically to give effect to the transfers of registration.

Several commentators have suggested an amendment to the Registration Convention, pursuant to Article IX, to address the issue of transferring the registration of space objects to a State that was not a launching State.[95] This position may be unnecessary when due consideration is given to existing State practice, for recently, in addition to the examples given above, the Netherlands has sought to register space objects with the U.N. Register for which it was not a launching State.[96] In that case, the Netherlands asserted the view that it was not obliged to furnish any of the orbital parameters required under the Registration Convention as it was not a launching State but, having placed the satellites on its national register, it was entitled to assert jurisdiction and control over the space object pursuant to Article VIII of the Outer Space Treaty.[97]

It is obvious that a *duty* to register the space object is imposed under the Registration Convention, and such a duty is imposed only on the launching States. Accordingly, in order to register a space object as a non-launching State, one must find a legal *right* to register it. As the Registration Convention does not provide this right, the other logical candidate is General Assembly Resolution 1721B.[98] As such, it is not necessary to amend the Registration Convention; any new State of registry that was not a launching State can seek to register the transferred space object pursuant to General Assembly Resolution 1721B to assert jurisdiction and control over the space object under Article VIII of the Outer Space Treaty.[99]

### Implications of Jurisdiction and Control on State Responsibility

Given that the State of registry retains jurisdiction and control over a satellite under Article VIII of the Outer Space Treaty, any international wrongful act or omission arising out of the operation of that satellite would engage the state responsibility of the State of registry, even if the relevant satellite operator is a non-governmental entity of the State of registry, a non-governmental entity elsewhere or even a foreign State. This is because:

- following *Nicaragua*, the State of registry has formal and effective control over the satellite and, by necessity, includes all acts or omissions in its control and operation;
- following *Corfu Channel*, no act or omission in operation and control of the satellite can occur without the knowledge of the State of registry;
- applying Article 8 of the State Responsibility Articles, the State of registry has and retains control over the satellite, including all acts or omissions in its control and operation; and
- most relevantly in the context of space law, the State of registry, by necessity the "appropriate State" for the purposes of Article VI of the Outer Space Treaty, must authorise and continually supervise the activities of governmental and non-governmental entities in the operation of a satellite on its registry.

Accordingly, this presents a second shortcut to the attribution of non-State acts and omissions to non-governmental actors or even foreign actors. By operation of both Articles VI and VIII of the Outer Space Treaty, the registration of a space object by the State of registry would result in that State assuming responsibility for the international wrongful acts and omissions in the course of the operation and control of that space object, regardless of the nationality or character of the person or entity involved. The US policy in relation to the registration of satellites with multiple launching States discussed above suggests that States are well aware of this necessary consequence under the Outer Space Treaty following their registration of space objects.[100]

## State Responsibility for Commercial Space Tourism

### The Appropriate State in Practice

As with the example of Sea Launch discussed above, commercial space tourism operators would want to avoid licensing requirements from multiple States by ensuring that they are subject to regulation by only one State – as such, the

State of nationality, State of registry, the territorial State and thus the "appropriate State" under Article VI would be the same. The content of the authorisation and continual supervision exercised by the State is particular to commercial space tourism. Although a significant number of States have enacted domestic laws and regulations for the licensing of space activities,[101] some are too specific to apply to either human spaceflight or a reusable launch vehicle that returns to Earth after the flight. For example, the licences, permits and offences for non-compliance under the Outer Space and High-Altitude Activities Act 2017 of New Zealand do not apply to the return to Earth of a reusable launch vehicle; and almost none of the existing domestic space laws deal specifically with private human spaceflight. If a commercial space tourism operator is to operate from any State without specific laws or regulations concerning human spaceflight, the relevant State would be responsible for its acts and omissions regardless of the adequacy of its laws and regulations.

### Contents of Specific Regulations

In the United States, as an example of the form of authorisation and continuing supervision of space tourism ventures, domestic legislation has been enacted concerning human spaceflight,[102] and the Federal Aviation Administration (the FAA) has adopted regulations on human spaceflight.[103] Although there are suggestions that tighter regulation by the FAA is required,[104] the current Commercial Spaceflight Regulations address the following requirements:

- training and qualifications of the flight crew[105];
- life support and safety systems[106];
- contents of the information to be given to commercial astronauts and space tourists to inform them of the relevant risks[107]; and
- execution of cross-waivers of claims between the FAA and the commercial astronauts and space tourists.[108]

Similarly, the Law on the Regulation of the Space Sector 2019 of the United Arab Emirates provides for licensing of "manned spaceflight, or long-term human residence in space", with some brief operational requirements and the expectation that they will be supplemented in greater detail by the Emirates Space Agency later.[109]

### Absence of Specific Regulations

Even if a State lacks specific laws and regulations concerning commercial or private human spaceflight or space tourism, such as those in the United States, it does not follow that authorisation and continuing supervision under Article VI of the Outer Space Treaty cannot occur. Most domestic space laws are wide enough in scope to apply to any space activity, such as the Outer Space Act 1986 of the

United Kingdom,[110] or the Space Affairs Act 1993 of South Africa,[111] and there are no content or qualitative requirements under Article VI as to the authorisation or continuing supervision. Further, as Article VI requires not licensing and regulation but rather authorisation and continuing supervision, nothing in Article VI would prevent such authorisation or continuing supervision from being carried out by executive action where permissible as a matter of domestic law.

Most importantly, the absence of domestic laws and regulations does not affect the attribution of commercial and private space tourism activities to the "appropriate State" and, as discussed above, the failure or omission by the appropriate State to authorise and continually supervise private space activities would be in and of itself an international wrongful act for which the appropriate State would be responsible internationally.

## The Last Word on State Responsibility for Commercial and Private Space Tourism

It follows from the above discussion that, by operation of Article VI of the Outer Space Treaty, States bear international responsibility for the space activities of their non-governmental entities, including commercial space tourism operators. In this context, a commercial and private space tourism operator is no different to any other non-State actor engaged in space activities; its acts and omissions are attributable to the State under Article VI, whether by:

- the space activities of the operator being "national" in character;
- the State instructing, directing or controlling the operator and its activities;
- the State exercising "effective control" generally over the operator and its activities;
- the State exercising "effective control" through authorisation and continual supervision of the operator's activities;
- the State failing or omitting to authorise and continually supervise the operator and its space activities;
- the State having knowledge of the operator's activities, acts and omissions; and
- the State being the State of registry for the operator's launch vehicles and space objects.

Far from wishing to avoid responsibility, the prevailing State practice is that States prefer to license and regulate private space activities in all circumstances that they may find themselves liable for them – whether by operation of the Liability Convention or under Article VI of the Outer Space Treaty. The dawn and growth of the commercial space tourism sector are unlikely to affect this trend, such that more States will join the United Arab Emirates and the United States in ensuring that their existing or new domestic space laws and regulations cover the licensing and regulation of commercial space tourism, accepting the state responsibility they bear internationally.

## Notes

1 Chris Dubbs and Emeline Paat-Dahlstrom, *Realizing Tomorrow: The Path to Private Spaceflight* (Lincoln: University of Nebraska Press, 2011); Albert A. Harrison, *Spacefaring: The Human Dimension* (Berkeley: University of California Press, 2001); Alexis Bautzmann and Thomas Delage, 'En route vers le cosmos?', *Diplomatie*, Vol. 16, 2005, at p. 50; and Craig Mellow, 'Space Trippers', *Air & Space Magazine*, November 2006, available at <https://www.smithsonianmag.com/air-space-magazine/space-trippers-12987104/> Last visited, 18 March 2022.

2 Dave Lee, 'Ten-Minute Space Trip with Bezos Sells for $28m', *Financial Times*, 14 June 2021, p. 6; and Neil Vigdor and Kenneth Chang, 'What Will It Cost to Fly Virgin Galactic to Space?', *The New York Times*, 15 September 2021, available at <https://www.nytimes.com/2021/07/11/science/cost-to-fly-virgin-galactic-space.html> Last visited, 18 March 2022.

3 John Herrman, 'Billionaires Reach for the Stars', *The New York Times*, 10 October 2021, p. ST2; Marcia Dunn, 'Star Trek's Shatner to Get Real-Life Taste of Space Abroad Blue Origin Capsule', *The Globe and Mail*, 5 October 2021, p. A2; Denis Lafay, 'Branson, Bezos, et Musk, les fossoyeurs de l'espace', *La Tribune*, 1 October 2021, p. 1; Joey Roulette, 'Short Flight Makes Star of 'Star Trek' the Oldest Space Tourist', *The New York Times*, 14 October 2021, p. A19; Sinéad O'Sullivan, 'Privatising Space Means More Astronauts Will Boldly Go', *Financial Times*, 2 November 2021, p. 17; and Dieter Sürig, Auf und davon; Amazon-Gründer Jeff Bezos erlebteinpaarMinutenSchwerelosigkeit an Bord seines eigenenRaumschiffs. Die Rekordeaberbricht seine Crew, *Süddeutsche Zeitung*, 21 July 2021, p. 17. See also Henry Wismayer, 'Space Tourists Won't Find the Awe They Seek', *The New York Times*, 29 November 2021, p. A23; and Ollie A. Williams, 'Billionaire Space Race Turns into a Publicity Disaster', *Forbes*, 21 December 2021, available at <https://www.forbes.com/sites/oliverwilliams1/2021/12/21/billionaire-space-race-turns-into-a-publicity-disaster/?sh=4121af0b5e4d> Last visited, 18 March 2022.

4 Declaration of Legal Principles Governing the Activities of States in the Exploration and Use of Outer Space, UNGA Resolution 1962 (XVIII), (13 December 1963) at paragraph 5.

5 The human space flight programme of the Soviet Union began on 12 April 1961 with the launch of Yuri Gagarin in Vostok 1, paused with the launch of Valentina Tereshkova in Vostok 6 on 16 June 1963, and did not resume until the Voskhod programme began crewed launches on 12 October 1964: see Rex Hall and David Shayler, *The Rocket Men: Vostok & Voskhod, the First Soviet Manned Spaceflights* (Dordrecht: Springer, 2001); and Colin Burgess and Rex Hall, *The First Soviet Cosmonaut Team: Their Lives, Legacy, and Historical Impact* (Berlin, Germany: Springer, 2009). The Mercury programme of the United States began with the launch of Alan B. Shepard, Jr. in Freedom 7 on 5 May 1961 and ended with L. Gordon Cooper, Jr. in Faith 7 on 15 May 1963; the first crewed launch of the Gemini programme did not take place until 23 March 1965: see Donald K. Slayton and Michael Cassault, *Deke! U.S. Manned Space: From Mercury to the Shuttle* (New York: St. Martin's Press, 1994); and Gene Kranz, *Failure Is Not an Option: Mission Control from Mercury to Apollo 13 and Beyond* (New York: Berkeley Books, 2000).

6 The Apollo 11 landing on the Moon took place on 20 July 1969: see Andrew Chaikin, *A Man on the Moon: The Triumphant Story of the Apollo Space Program* (New York: Penguin, 1994); Slayton and Cassault, *supra* note 5; and James Schefter, *The Race: The Uncensored Story of How America Beat Russia to the Moon* (New York: Doubleday, 1999).

7 Articles on Responsibility of States for Internationally Wrongful Acts, UNGA Resolution 56/83, UN Doc. A/56/10, (12 December 2001) [the "State Responsibility Articles"]. See James Crawford, *The International Law Commission's Articles on State Responsibility: Introduction, Text, and Commentaries* (Cambridge: Cambridge

University Press, 2002). See also David D. Caron, 'The I.L.C. Articles on State Responsibility: The Paradoxical Relationship between Form and Authority', *American Journal of International Law*, Vol. 96, 2002, pp. 857–873.

8 Treaty on Principles Governing the Activities of States in the Exploration and Use of Outer Space, Including the Moon and Other Celestial Bodies, 27 January 1967, 610 UNTS 205, 18 UST 2410, TIAS. No. 6347, 6 ILM 386 (entered into force on 10 October 1967) [the "Outer Space Treaty"]. See Paul G. Dembling and Daniel M. Arons, 'The Evolution of the Outer Space Treaty', *Journal of Air Law and Commerce*, Vol. 33, 1967, pp. 419–456; and Ivan A. Vlasic, 'The Space Treaty: A Preliminary Evaluation', *California Law Review*, Vol. 55, 1967, pp. 507–519.

9 See Pierre-Marie Dupuy, 'The International Law of State Responsibility: Revolution or Evolution?', *Michigan Journal of International Law*, Vol. 11, 1989, pp. 105–126; Yoshiro Matsui, 'The Transformation of the Law of State Responsibility', in René Provost (ed.) *State Responsibility in International Law* (London: Routledge, 2002) pp. 3–65; Katja Creutz, *State Responsibility in the International Legal Order: A Critical Appraisal* (Cambridge: Cambridge University Press, 2020), pp. 53–107; G. Sidney Buchanan, 'A Conceptual History of the State Action Doctrine: The Search for Governmental Responsibility', *Houston Law Review*, Vol. 34, 1997, pp. 333–424; Martins Paparinskis, 'The Once and Future Law of State Responsibility', *American Journal of International Law*, Vol. 114, 2020, pp. 618–626; Robert Latham, 'The Politics and History of Responsibility Across Boundaries', *Brown Journal of World Affairs*, Vol. 7, 2000, pp. 173–184; and Mahnoush H. Arsanjani, 'The Codification of the Law of State Responsibility', *American Society of International Law Proceedings*, Vol. 83, 1989, pp. 225–229.

10 See Rosalyn Higgins, 'The International Court of Justice: Selected Issues of State Responsibility', in Maurizio Ragazzi (ed.) *International Responsibility Today: Essays in Memory of Oscar Schacter* (The Hague: Martinus Nijhoff, 2005) pp. 271–286; James Crawford S.C., 'The International Court of Justice and the Law of State Responsibility', in Christian J. Tams and James Sloan (eds.) *The Development of International Law by the International Court of Justice* (Oxford: Oxford University Press, 2013) pp. 70–86 at p. 81; Enrico Milano, 'Territorial Disputes, Wrongful Occupations, and State Responsibility: Should the International Court of Justice Go the Extra Mile', *The Law and Practice of International Courts and Tribunals*, Vol. 3, 2004, pp. 509–541; and KajHober, 'State Responsibility and Investment Arbitration', *Journal of International Arbitration*, Vol. 25, 2008, pp. 545–568.

11 *Case concerning the Factory at Chorzów (Germany v. Poland) (Claim for Indemnity) (Merits)* [1927] P.C.I.J. Rep. (Ser. A) No. 9.

12 *Military and Paramilitary Activities in and against Nicaragua (Nicaragua v. United States of America.)* [1986] I.C.J. Rep. 14.

13 *Corfu Channel Case (United Kingdom v. Albania) (Merits)* [1949] I.C.J. Rep. 4.

14 *Supra* note 11, at 18 & 19.

15 *Id.*, at 19 & 20.

16 Geneva Convention concerning Upper Silesia, 5 May 1922, 9 L.N.T.S. 46 (entered into force on 15 May 1922). See *Rights of Minorities in Upper Silesia (Minority Schools) (Germany v. Poland)* [1928] P.C.I.J. (Ser. A) No. 15, Annex 1. See also Joseph F. Harrington, Jr., 'The League of Nations and the Upper Silesian Boundary Dispute, 1921–1922', *Polish Review*, Vol. 23, 1978, pp. 86–101; Bernhard Gröschel, *Themen und Tendenzen in Schlagzeilen der Kattowitzer Zeitung und des OberschlesischenKuriers 1925–1939: Analyse der Berichterstattungzur Lage der deutschenMinderheit in Ostoberschlesien* (Berlin: Gebr. Mann, 1993); and F. Gregory Campbell, 'The Struggle for Upper Silesia, 1919–1922', *Journal of Modern History*, Vol. 42, 1970, pp. 361–385.

17 *Supra* note 11, at 21 & 22.

State Responsibility and Space Tourism **93**

18 *Case concerning Certain German Interests in Polish Upper Silesia (Merits) (Germany v. Poland)* [1926] P.C.I.J. Rep. (Ser. A) No. 7.
19 *Supra* note 11, at 29.
20 *Id.*, at 49–54.
21 *Id.*, at 50 & 51.
22 *Id.*, at 47. See Felix E. Torres, 'Revisiting the Chorzów Factory Standard of Reparation – Its Relevance in Contemporary International Law and Practice', *Nordic Journal of International Law*, Vol. 90, 2021, pp. 190–227; Muthucumaraswamy Sornarajah, *The Pursuit of Nationalized Property* (The Hague: Martinus Nijhoff, 1986) pp. 140–147; and Patrick J. Smith, 'Determining the Standard Compensation for the Expropriation of Naturalised Assets: Themes for the Future', *Monash University Law Review*, Vol. 23, 1997, pp. 159–170.
23 *Case concerning the Factory at Chorzów (Germany v. Poland) (Order of 25 May 1929)* [1929] P.C.I.J. Rep. (Ser. A) No. 19.
24 See Dan La Botz, *What Went Wrong? The Nicaragua Revolution – A Marxist Analysis* (The Hague: Brill, 2016) pp. 74–108; Bernard Diedreich, *Somoza and the Legacy of U.S. Involvement in Central America* (New York: Dutton, 1981); Andrew Crawley, *Somoza and Roosevelt: Good Neighbour Diplomacy in Nicaragua, 1933–1945* (Oxford: Oxford University Press, 2007); and David Schmitz, *Thank God They're on Our Side: The United States and Right-Wing Dictatorships* (Chapel Hill: University of North Carolina Press, 1999).
25 Matilde Zimmerman, *Sandinista: Carlos Fonseca and the Nicaraguan Revolution* (Durham: Duke University Press, 2000); Lynn Horton, *Peasants in Arms: War and Peace in the Mountains of Nicaragua, 1979–1994* (Athens: Ohio University Center for International Studies, 1991) pp. 95–117; and Susan Meiselas, *Nicaragua: June 1978 – July 1979* (New York: Pantheon Books, 1981).
26 Sam Dillon, *Commandos: The C.I.A. and Nicaragua's Contra Rebels* (New York: Henry Holt, 1991) pp. 49–56; and James P. Rowles, 'U.S. Covert Operations Against Nicaragua and their Legality under Conventional and Customary International Law', *The University of Miami Inter-American Law Review*, Vol. 17, 1986, pp. 407–508.
27 *Supra* note 12, at 48–53.
28 *Id.*, at 63–65.
29 *Id.*
30 *Id.*
31 Antonio Cassese, 'The Nicaragua and Tadić Tests Revisited in Light of the I.C.J. Judgment on Genocide in Bosnia', *European Journal of International Law*, Vol. 18, 2007, pp. 649–668 at 653. See also Remy Jorritsma, 'Where General International Law Meets International Humanitarian Law: Attribution of Conduct and the Classification of Armed Conflicts', *Journal of Conflict and Security Law*, Vol. 23, 2018, pp. 405–431.
32 The Iran-U.S. Claims Tribunal was established under the Algiers Declaration of 19 January 1981 to resolve claims between governments and nationals of the two countries following the Iranian Revolution. See David D. Caron, 'The Nature of the Iran-United States Claims Tribunal and the Evolving Structure of International Dispute Resolution', *American Journal of International Law*, Vol. 84, 1990, pp. 104–156; and Allahyar Mouri, 'Aspects of the Iran-United States Claims Tribunal', *Asian Yearbook of International Law*, Vol. 2, 1992, pp. 61–85 at 73.
33 *Foremost Tehran Inc.* v. *Iran* (1986) 10 Iran-U.S.C.T.R. 228.
34 *Flexi-Van Leasing Inc.* v. *Iran* (1986) 12 Iran-U.S.C.T.R. 335. In that case, a private Iranian company under the control of the Iranian Government committed acts of expropriation, but the Iran-US Claims Tribunal held that they were not imputable to the State as it could not be demonstrated that the acts themselves were under the direction or influence of the State.

94 Ricky J. Lee

35 *Prosecutor* v. *Tadić* (1999) 124 I.L.R. 61.
36 Cassese, *supra* note 31, at 657.
37 *Id.*; Kitty Felde, Gabrielle Kirk McDonald, Alan Tieger, and Michail Wladimiroff, 'The Prosecutor v. DuskoTadić', *American University International Law Review*, Vol. 13, 1998, pp. 1441–1468; Louis G. Maresca, 'Case Analysis: The Prosecutor v. Tadić: The Appellate Decision of the I.C.T.Y. and Internal Violations of Humanitarian Law as International Crimes', *Leiden Journal of International Law*, Vol. 9, 1996, pp. 219–231; Dino Kritsiotis, 'The Tremors of Tadić', *Israel Law Review*, Vol. 43, 2010, pp. 262–300; and Phenyo Keiseng Rakate, 'The Characterisation of Conflicts in International Law: Applying *Tadić* to the Kosovo Crisis', *Stellenbosch Law Review*, Vol. 11, 2000, pp. 276–283.
38 See John O. Iatrides and Nicholas X. Rizopoulos, 'The International Dimension of the Greek Civil War', *World Politics Journal*, Vol. 17, 2000, pp. 87–103; Amikam Nachmani, 'Civil War and Foreign Intervention in Greece: 1946–49', *Journal of Contemporary History*, Vol. 25, 1990, pp. 489–522; T. L. Chrysanthopoulos, 'British and Greek Military Occupations of the Dodecanese – 1945–1948', *Revue Hellenique de Droit International*, Vol. 2, 1949, pp. 227–236; and Athanasios D. Sfikas, *British Labour Government and the Greek Civil War: 1945–1959* (Edinburgh: Edinburgh University Press, 2019).
39 James P. Delgado, 'Cold War in the Corfu', *Military History*, Vol. 31, 2014, pp. 36–39. See also Aristotles Constantinides, 'The Corfu Channel Case in Perspective: The Factual and Political Background', in Karine Bannelier, Theodore Christakis, and Sarah Heathcote (eds.) *The I.C.J. and the Evolution of International Law: The Enduring Impact of the Corfu Channel Case* (London: Routledge, 2012) pp. 41–59; Harding F. Bancroft and Eric Stein, 'The Corfu Channel Case', *Stanford Law Review*, Vol. 1, 1949, pp. 646–657; and Hector A. Munro, 'The Case of the Corfu Minefield', *Modern Law Review*, Vol. 10, 1947, pp. 363–376.
40 *Supra* note 13.
41 *Id.*
42 *Id.*
43 *Id.*, at 18–20 & 23. There was some evidence to suggest that the mines in the Corfu Channel were laid by Yugoslav vessels on Albanian request, but the Court did not accept this as proven: Owen Pearson, *Albania as Dictatorship and Democracy: From Isolation to the Kosovo War* (London: Bloomsbury Academic, 2006) p. 154.
44 *The Corfu Channel Case (Albania v. United Kingdom) (Assessment of Compensation)* [1949] I.C.J. Rep. 244.
45 See Robert Rosenstock, 'The I.L.C. and State Responsibility', *American Journal of International Law*, Vol. 96, 2002, pp. 792–797.
46 *Id.*, at 797.
47 James Crawford, *State Responsibility: The General Part* (Cambridge: Cambridge University Press, 2013) p. 144. See discussion above on *Nicaragua*; and *United States Diplomatic and Consular Staff in Tehran (United States v. Iran)* [1980] I.C.J. Rep. 3 at 29 & 30.
48 Crawford, *supra* note 7, Article 8, § 8. See also Charlotte Beaucillon, Julian Fernandez, and Hélène Raspail, 'State Responsibility for Conduct of Private Military Companies Violating jus ad bellum', in Francesco Francioni and Natalino Ronzitti (eds.) *War by Contract: Human Rights, Humanitarian Law, and Private Contractors* (Oxford: Oxford University Press, 2011), pp. 396–420 at p. 406; and Hannah Tonkin, *State Control over Private Military and Security Companies in Armed Conflict* (Cambridge: Cambridge University Press, 2011) p. 115.
49 *Case concerning Application of the Convention on the Prevention and Punishment of the Crime of Genocide (Bosnia and Herzegovina* v. *Serbia and Montenegro)* [2007] I.C.J. Rep. 43 at 208.

50 Crawford, *supra* note 47.
51 See for example, Elisabeth Back-Impallomeni, 'Article VI of the Outer Space Treaty', in United Nations (ed.) *Proceedings of the United Nations/Republic of Korea Workshop on Space Law* (Vienna: United Nations, 2003), at pp. 348–351; and Ricky J. Lee, 'Liability Arising from Article VI of the Outer Space Treaty: States, Domestic Law, and Private Operators', *Proceedings of the Colloquium on the Law of Outer Space*, Vol. 48, 2005, pp. 216–228.
52 Outer Space Act 1986 (U.K.), Sec. 3; and Space (Launches and Returns) Act 2018 (Australia), Sec. 12.
53 *Id.*; and *id.*, Sec. 14.
54 *Id.*, Sec. 4; and *id.*, Sec.s 29–31 and 46C & 46D.
55 *Id.*, Sec. 4(2)(da); and *id.*, Sec.s 28 and 46B.
56 See for example, Law on Space-Related Activities 2020 of Armenia; Law on the Activities of Launching, Flight Operation or Guidance of Space Objects 2005 of Belgium; Outer Space Act 409/2016 of Denmark; Act on Space Activities 63/2018 of Finland; Loi relative aux opérations spatiales 518/2008 of France; Law on Space Activities 21/2013 of Indonesia; Law on Space Activities 2012 of Kazakhstan; Space Liability Act 2007 of the Republic of Korea; Loiportant sur les activités spatiales 2020 of Luxembourg; Rules Concerning Space Activities and the Establishment of a Registry of Space Objects 2006 of The Netherlands; Outer Space and High-Altitude Activities 2017 of New Zealand; Decree-Law no. 16/2019 on Legal Regime of Access to and Exercise of Space Activities of Portugal; Law about Space Activity 1993 of the Russian Federation; Space Activities Act 2022 of Slovenia; Space Affairs Act 1993 of South Africa; Act on Space Activities 1982: 963 of Sweden; Ordinance on Space Activity 1996 of Ukraine; Law on the Regulation of the Space Sector 12/2019 of the United Arab Emirates; Title 51, United States Code; and Outer Space Ordinance 1997 of Hong Kong. See also Ricky J. Lee, 'The Liability Convention and Private Space Launch Services – Domestic Regulatory Responses', *Annals of Air & Space Law*, Vol. 31, 2006, pp. 351–380.
57 *Supra* note 13, at 18–20 & 23; and State Responsibility Articles, Art. 2.
58 See Małgorzata Polkowska, 'Limitations in the Airspace Sovereignty of States in Connection with Space Activity', *Security and Defence Quarterly*, Vol. 20, 2018, pp. 42–56; and Amad Sudiro and Jeannette Natawidjaja, 'State Sovereignty over the Airspace on the Perspective of International Air Law: A Study of the Delegation of Airspace Management of Batam and Natuna Island to Singapore', *Advances in Social Science, Education and Humanities Research*, Vol. 478, 2020, pp. 726–729.
59 *Supra* note 13, at 18–20.
60 Harding F. Bancroft and Eric Stein, 'The Corfu Channel Case', *Stanford Law Review*, Vol. 1, No. 4, 1949, pp. 646–657; Hector A. Munro, 'The Case of the Corfu Minefield', *Modern Law Review*, Vol. 10, No. 4, 1947, pp. 363–376; Jan Arno Hessbrügge, 'The Historical Development of the Doctrines of Attribution and Due Diligence in International Law', *New York University Journal of International Law and Politics*, Vol. 36, 2004, pp. 265–306; and Bojan Milisavljević, 'Odgovornost Države Za Međunarodne Protivpravne Akte – Opšti Osvrt' ('Responsibility of States for Internationally Wrongful Acts – A General Overview'), *Harmonius: Journal for Legal and Social Studies in South East Europe*, 2013, pp. 204–217.
61 Convention on International Liability for Damage Caused by Space Objects, 29 March 1972, 961 U.N.T.S 187; 24 U.S.T. 2389; T.I.A.S. 7762 (entered into force on 1 September 1972) [the "Liability Convention"].
62 Liability Convention, Art. I.
63 See for example, Ian Awford, 'Commercial Space Activities: Legal Liability Issues', in V. S. Mani, S. Bhatt, and V. Balakista Reddy (eds.) *Recent Trends in International Space Law and Policy* (New Delhi: Lancers Books, 1997) pp. 383–424 at 388.

64 Richard M. Buxbaum, 'A Legal History of International Reparations', *Berkeley Journal of International Law*, Vol. 23, 2005, pp. 314–346; Wladyslaw Czaplinski, 'The Concept of War Reparations in International Law and Reparations after World War II', *Polish Quarterly of International Affairs*, Vol. 14, 2005, pp. 69–80; Marco Sassòli, 'State Responsibility for Violations of International Humanitarian Law', *International Review of the Red Cross*, Vol. 84, 2002, pp. 401–434; Eric A. Posner and Alan O. Sykes, 'An Economic Analysis of State and Individual Responsibility under International Law', *American Law and Economics Review*, Vol. 9, 2007, pp. 72–134; Dinah Shelton, 'Righting Wrongs: Reparations in the Articles on State Responsibility', *American Journal of International Law*, Vol. 96, 2002, pp. 833–856; and Patrycja Sobolewska, 'The Question of War Reparations in Polish-German Relations After World War II', *Review of International, European, and Comparative Law*, Vol. 17, 2019, pp. 139–159.

65 Article XVII of the Outer Space Treaty provides that the Chinese, English, French, Russian, and Spanish texts are equally authentic. For an example of commentaries that have made this observation, see Armel Kerrest, 'Remarks on the Responsibility and Liability for Damage Other Than Those Caused by the Fall of a Space Object', *Proceedings of the Colloquium on the Law of Outer Space*, Vol. 40, 1997, pp. 134–140; and Ricky J. Lee, 'Liability Arising from Article VI of the Outer Space Treaty: States, Domestic Law, and Private Operators', *Proceedings of the Colloquium on the Law of Outer Space*, Vol. 48, 2005, pp. 216–228.

66 Article 33(4) of the Vienna Convention on the Law of Treaties further provides that, where there is a difference in meaning across different texts, the meaning that best reconciles the texts is to be adopted.

67 Some commentators have also noted that the *travaux préparatoires* and many domestic laws in civil law jurisdictions do not draw a distinction between "responsibility" and "liability". See for example, Bin Cheng, 'Article VI of the Outer Space Treaty Revisited: "International Responsibility", "National Activities" and "The Appropriate State"', *Journal of Space Law*, Vol. 26, 1998, pp. 7–32 at 10; and Motoko Uchitomi, 'State Responsibility/Liability for "National" Space Activities: Towards Safe and Fair Competition in Private Space Activities', *Proceedings of the Colloquium on the Law of Outer Space*, Vol. 44, 2001, pp. 51–60.

68 Armel Kerrest, 'Commercial Use of Space, including Launching', *I.I.S.L. Space Law Conference: Paper Assemble* (Beijing: China Institute of Space Law, 2004) p. 199.

69 *S.S .Lotus (France* v. *Turkey)* (1927) P.C.I.J. Rep. (Ser. A), No. 10.

70 *Id.*

71 *Id.*, at 20.

72 Edwin D. Dickinson, 'Introductory Comment to the Harvard Research Draft Convention on Jurisdiction with Respect to Crime', *American Journal of International Law*, Vol. 29, 1935, pp. 443–447.

73 Liability Convention, Art. II.

74 18 U.S.C. § 2423; Melissa Curley and Elizabeth Stanley, 'Extraterritorial Jurisdiction, Criminal Law, and Transnational Crime: Insights from the Application of Australia's Child Sex Tourism Offences', *Bond Law Review*, Vol. 28, 2016, pp. 169–197; Sara Sun Beale, 'Prosecuting Sexual Exploitation and Trafficking Abroad: Congress, the Courts, and the Constitution', *Duke Journal of Gender Law and Policy*, Vol. 27, 2020, pp. 25–43; Patrick Vrancken and Kasturi Chetty, 'International Child Sex Tourism: A South African Perspective', *Journal of African Law*, Vol. 53, 2009, pp. 111–141; Martin Ratcovich, 'Extraterritorial Criminalisation and Non-Intervention: Sweden's Criminal Measures against the Purchase of Sex Abroad', *Nordic Journal of International Law*, Vol. 88, 2019, pp. 398–428; and Kathy J. Steinman, 'Sex Tourism and the Child: Latin America's and the United States' Failure to Prosecute Sex Tourists', *Hastings Women's Law Journal*, Vol. 13, 2002, pp. 53–76.

75 See Bribery Act 2010 (U.K.); Foreign Corrupt Practices Act (U.S.); Criminal Code (France), Art. 113; and Sarah C. Kaczmarek and Abraham L. Newman, 'The Long Arm of the Law: Extraterritoriality and the National Implementation of Foreign Bribery Legislation', *International Organization*, Vol. 65, 2011, pp. 745–770.

State Responsibility and Space Tourism **97**

76 See Modern Slavery Act 2018 (Cth.) of Australia; Loi sur le devoir de vigilance of February 2017 of France; Modern Slavery Act 2015 of the U.K.; Trafficking Victims Protection Act 2000 of the U.S.A.; etc.
77 See Space (Launches and Returns) Act; Outer Space Act; and the domestic laws listed at note 55.
78 See Edward M. Morgan, 'Criminal Process, International Law, and Extraterritorial Crime', *University of Toronto Law Journal*, Vol. 38, 1988, pp. 245–277; Michael Farbiarz, 'Extraterritorial Criminal Jurisdiction', *Michigan Law Review*, Vol. 114, 2016, pp. 507–558; Julian D. M. Lew, 'The Extraterritorial Criminal Jurisdiction of English Courts', *International and Comparative Law Quarterly*, Vol. 27, 1978, pp. 168–214; and Janice Brabyn, 'The Extraterritorial Reach of Hong Kong Criminal Law and the Hong Kong Court of Appeal', *Hong Kong Law Journal*, Vol. 23, 1993, pp. 178–206, and Danielle Ireland-Piper, 'Extraterritorial Criminal Jurisdiction: Does the Long Arm of the Law Undermine the Rule of Law?', *Melbourne Journal of International Law*, Vol. 13, 2012, pp. 1–36.
79 James L. Brierly, 'The Lotus Case', *Law Review Quarterly*, Vol. 44, 1928, pp. 154–163 at p. 155.
80 *Supra* note 69, at 20.
81 U.N. Doc. A/C1/881, (14 October 1962).
82 See for example, Istvan Herczeg, 'Interpretation of the Space Treaty of 1967 (Introductory Report)', *Proceedings of the Colloquium on the Law of Outer Space*, Vol. 10, 1967, pp. 105–112 at 107; Stephen Gorove, 'Liability in Space Law: An Overview', *Annals of Air & Space Law*, Vol. 8, 1983, pp. 373–380 at 377; and Michel Bourély, 'La commercialisation des activitésspatiales: aspects juridiques', *Annales de l'Université des sciences sociales de Toulouse*, Vol. 37, 1989, pp. 43–56.
83 See Space (Launches and Returns) Act; and Outer Space Act.
84 Specifically, the original shareholders of Sea Launch L.L.C. were Aker Kværner A.S.A. (Norway, 20%), Boeing Launch Services Inc. (U.S., 40%), S. P. Korelev Rocket and Space Corporation Energia (Russia, 25%), and Yozhnoye Design Office and P.A. Yuzhmash (Ukraine, 15%).
85 The Cayman Islands is a self-governing British Overseas Territory and Outer Space Act 1986 (Imp.) applied as extended to the Cayman Islands under the Outer Space Act 1986 (Cayman Islands) Order 1998.
86 51 U.S.C. § 50902(1)(C).
87 Yuliya Federinova and Andrey Lemeshko, 'Russian Airline Owner to Challenge Musk, Bezos in Space', *Bloomberg News*, 27 September 2016, available at <https://www.bloomberg.com/news/articles/2016-09-27/russian-airline-owner-moves-to-challenge-musk-bezos-in-space> last visited, 25 January 2022; and Jeff Foust, 'Sea Launch 'frozen' after ships moved to Russia', *Space News*, 24 April 2020, available at <https://spacenews.com/sea-launch-frozen-after-ships-moved-to-russia/> last visited, 12 April 2022.
88 As the Sea Launch example discussed above demonstrates, domestic space legislation and regulations are not uniform in scope and applicability, so it is possible for the same space activity to be subject to licensing and regulation by more than one State, without resolving the question of which is the "appropriate State" for the purposes of Article VI of the Outer Space Treaty.
89 Liability Convention, Art. I.
90 Convention on the Registration of Objects Launched into Outer Space, 1023 U.N.T.S. 15; 28 U.S.T. 695; T.I.A.S. 8480 (entered into force on 1 September 1972).
91 U.N.G.A. Resolution 1721B (XVI), (20 December 1961).
92 See Kenneth Hodgkins, 'International Cooperation in the Peaceful Uses of Outer Space', *Remarks on Agenda Item 75 in the Fourth Committee of the United Nations General Assembly*, 9 October 2002, available at <http://www.state.gov/g/oes/rls/rm/2002/14362.htm> last visited, 9 April 2004.
93 See Julian Hermida, 'Transfer of Satellites in Orbit – An International Law Approach', *Proceedings of the Colloquium on the Law of Outer Space*, Vol. 46, 2003, pp. 189–192;

and Yun Zhao, 'Current Legal Status and Recent Developments in Hong Kong Law and Its Relevance to Pacific Rim Space Law and Activities', *Journal of Space Law*, Vol. 35, 2009, pp. 599–614.

94  See David Sagar, 'The Privatisation of Inmarsat: Special Problems', in Ray A. Harris (ed.) *International Organisations and Space Law: Proceedings of the Third E.C.S.L. Colloquium* (Noordwijk: European Space Agency, 1999) pp. 127–142; Maury J. Mechanick, 'The Role and Function of Residual International Intergovernmental Satellite Organisations Following Privatisation', in Patricia McCormick and Maury J. Mechanick (eds.) *The Transformation of Intergovernmental Satellite Organisations: Policy and Legal Perspectives* (Leiden: Brill, 2013) pp. 175–222; George Huang, 'International Satellite Organisations Facing the Challenge: INTELSAT and INMARSAT', *Singapore Journal of International & Comparative Law*, Vol. 3, 1999, pp. 186–236; and Bernhard Schmidt-Tedd and Michael Gerhard, 'How to Adapt the Present Regime for Registration of Space Objects to New Developments in Space Applications', *Proceedings of the Colloquium on the Law of Outer Space*, Vol. 48, 2005, pp. 353–359.

95  See Kai-Uwe Hörl and Julian Hermida, 'Change of Ownership, Change of Registry? Which Objects to Register, What Data to Be Furnished, When, and Until When?', in United Nations, *Proceedings of the I.I.S.L./E.C.S.L. Symposium: Reinforcing the Registration Convention* (Vienna: United Nations, 2003) p. 18.

96  U.N.Doc. A/AC.105/806, (22 August 2003) for the purchase of satellites by New Skies Satellites, a Dutch company; and U.N. Doc. ST/SG/Ser.E/417, (25 September 2002) for the registration of satellites of the privatised Inmarsat Limited, which became a British company.

97  U.N.Doc. A/AC.105/806, (22 August 2003).

98  U.N.G.A. Resolution 1721 (XVI), (20 December 1961).

99  Article VIII of the Outer Space Treaty does not impose any requirement on any State of registry to be a launching State to carry a space object on its domestic register; General Assembly Resolution 1721B calls upon "States launching objects into orbit" to furnish information to the U.N. "for the registration for launchings". While the language of Resolution 1721B would suggest that only a launching State may register a space object with the U.N., there is no specific obstacle to a launching State providing information to the U.N. that specified another State as the State of registry, thus completing the circle of legal technicalities in enabling a non-launching State to be the State of registry and assert jurisdiction and control over a space object.

100  *Supra* note 92.

101  See Space (Launches and Returns) Act and Outer Space Act.

102  U.S. Code, Title 51.

103  Code of Federal Regulations, Title 14, Part 460.

104  See Christian Davenport, 'Richard Branson and Jeff Bezos Will Fly to Space at Their Own Risk. Does That Make It Right for Everyone?', *The Washington Post*, 23 June 2021, available at <https://www.washingtonpost.com/technology/2021/06/23/space-tourism-faa-regulation/> last visited, 14 April 2022.

105  14 C.F.R. § 460.5 and § 460.7 (U.S.A.).

106  *Id.*, § 460.11 and § 460.13.

107  *Id.*, § 460.45.

108  *Id.*, § 460.49.

109  Law on the Regulation of the Space Sector, Federal Law No. 12 of 2019, Article 16.

110  Outer Space Act 1986, Sec. 1.

111  Space Affairs Act 1993, Sec. 11.

# 7

# LEGAL FRAMEWORK OF LIABILITY IN SPACE TOURISM

*Asha P. Soman*

## Introduction

The journey of space tourism was not a smooth road. It has travelled a long road since 2001. There have been many objections and confusion to taking tourists to outer space, but it has become a reality, and it is gaining momentum too. Space tourism has more impact than normal space activities. It has a significant impact on the economic, social, health, entertainment and investment industry. So far, one of the major criticisms against the huge investments in space missions was that the investment could be done in the other basic necessity areas for nation-building, especially in developing and underdeveloped countries. The benefits of space technologies are so significant now that it has become a necessity to invest in this sector. Space tourism is attracting many to explore the frontiers of space and be space travellers, and at the same time, filmmakers started their journey even to the International Space Station (ISS) to shoot their movies.[1] Hence, with the space tourism sector, the entertainment industry also becomes a part of future space missions.

Age-old criticism of investing enormous amounts in space activities is diluted by the emergence of space tourists. The richest people in the world are now in a race to mark their name as space travellers and for this, they are ready to pay the national space agencies and private space entities many dollars.[2] This will result in increased investment in the space sector, in multiple dimensions. If the number of space tourists is increasing, it will also attract the insurance sector to such missions, as it is always to take insurance while going to such risky tourist destinations.

Though space tourism can change the dimensions of the age-old space activities done only for sovereign purposes, it takes in its wings many legal complexities, which need a proper legal framework. One such complicated area of space tourism

DOI: 10.4324/9781032617961-7

is the liability regime. The definition of space tourists, the difference between astronauts and space tourists, laws applicable to space tourists, liability and compensation are a few issues relating to space missions with space tourists. The main issue analysed in this chapter is the need for a liability framework for space tourism at the international and national levels.

## Definition of Space Tourism

Earlier space activities were aimed at understanding the cosmos in a better way, but space tourism is also gaining momentum along with other space activities. Space tourism can be defined as an individual except an astronaut[3] going to outer space for non-sovereign purposes and to enjoy their holidays. I want to give this definition to space tourism, and this has been framed keeping in mind the basic ideology of "tourism" and the sovereign duties performed by the astronauts in each space mission. Spending holidays as a tourist and performing employment responsibilities cannot be clubbed together and compared. Space tourism[4] is recreational space travel, either on established government-owned vehicles such as the Russian Soyuz and the International Space Station (ISS) or on vehicles fielded by private companies.[5]

## Space Tourists

Dennis Tito, an American businessman, is the world's first orbital space tourist. He was launched by a Russian Soyuz spacecraft in April 2001. He travelled to the International Space Station, and the mission was a $20 million deal brokered by the Virginia-based firm Space Adventures.[6] Space tourism has been popular for a very long time and can be divided into orbital, sub-orbital, and lunar space tourism. During the period from 2001 to 2009, seven space tourists made eight space flights aboard a Russian Soyuz spacecraft to the International Space Station. The publicised price was in the range of $20–25 million per trip.[7] The commercialisation of the space sector got another face through the expanding wings of space tourism, and the number of space tourists is also increasing.[8] This marked a new era in the history of space activities and the "tourism". This travel took with it the legal complexities related to space tourism, and the need for international and national space legislation to have a relook at the existing framework.

Though Russia supported Tito, there was strong opposition from the National Aeronautics and Space Administration (NASA) and space agencies from Canada, Europe and Japan. They were against the idea to take a private person to the ISS. NASA officials were not satisfied that Tito's training would be sufficient, as his arrival was scheduled at the time of complex and crucial station operations. Tito was a nonprofessional crew member and was not trained to act on all critical systems that may arise in space; hence, there was the need for constant supervision from the astronauts. This would create a significant burden on the expedition, and affect the overall safety of the International Space Station.[9]

Even though Dennis Tito takes the credit, he may not have been the first space tourist. Before Tito went to space, Toyohiro Akiyama[10] and Helen Sharman,[11] two private citizens, were selected to travel to the Russian Space Station in the early 1990s. But they are often not considered space tourists because they did not pay for their rides themselves, these intrepid space flyers helped pave the way for the space tourism industry that is taking shape today.[12]

During the 1990s, a deal between MirCorp and Space Adventures Ltd. started the advent of space tourism. To generate income for the maintenance of the Space Station, MirCorp decided to sell a trip to Mir, and Tito became its first paying passenger. Tito paid $20 million for his flight on the Russian spacecraft Soyuz TM-32, and spent seven days onboard the ISS. Thus, Tito became the world's first space tourist. However, given the arduous training required for his mission, Tito objected to the use of the word tourist, and since his flight, the term spaceflight participant has been more often used to distinguish commercial space travellers from career astronauts.[13]

The year 2021 marked a turning point in the saga of space tourism – Virgin Galactic launched Richard Branson, Blue Origin launched Jeff Bezos, William Shatner and Good Morning America's host, Inspiration4 launched four civilians, a Russian film crew shoots drama on ISS, Japanese billionaire Yusaku Maezawa flew to ISS.[14] SpaceX has created history through its Inspiration4 – all-civilian spaceflight.[15] Billionaire Jared Isaacman privately chartered the spaceflight and it became the first crewed orbital mission with no professional astronauts on board. Four civilian-occupied spaceflights circled the Earth for three days and the main purpose of this mission was to raise awareness and funds for a paediatric cancer research hospital[16] and to begin a new era for human spaceflight and exploration.[17]

Russia is taking the lead in the space tourism sector, pointing towards another form of the space race with the backup of commercialisation of space missions. Russia proposed a "Luxury Hotel" for the International Space Station. The NEM-2 module would have four cabins, two bathrooms, exercise equipment, Wi-Fi and a lounge with a 16-inch window.[18]

## Space Tourism: Issues and Perspectives

When the complexities in any area expand, there needs to be a change in the law also; and the space sector is not an exemption from this fact. Starting from the first space mission to all the missions so far, the existing legal framework at the international and national levels is inadequate to meet the challenges, adding to the complexities of space tourism, which calls for an urgent need for reconsideration of the space legal framework. As far as the existing international space law is considered, although there are five basic treaties and agreements, most nations have not become a part of these agreements. Analysis of different national space legislations will also make it a point that laws differ from a wider perspective. Intellectual property rights and space insurance are two areas which have not been properly dealt with by most of the national space laws and policies. The year 2021 witnessed several missions where space tourists were taken on space missions, and this included missions with a private person from the entertainment industry. Considering the future scope of space tourism, it is necessary to have laws at the international and national levels to deal with the diverse issues relating to safe tourism.

The dynamic emergence of the private sector in outer space activities was an undeniable fact that created new challenges to be addressed at the multilateral level.[19] Legal issues relating to space tourism include:

a  laws need to regulate private entities involved in space tourism,
b  insurance for space tourists,
c  crimes by space tourists during the mission, and the liability regime and claims or jurisdiction by different nations,
d  medical emergency or death of a space tourist,
e  increasing environmental damages due to normal space missions and missions solely for space tourists,
f  increasing missions affecting ozone layer depletion and climate change,
g  liability of nations in case of accidents during space tourist missions and deciding the matters relating to compensation,
h  extra-terrestrial application of national laws for space tourists,
i  the clash between aviation law and space law, and
j  dispute settlement and space tourism.

One of the pertinent questions which need to be addressed while considering several legal issues relating to space tourism is the need for the extension of protection provided to the astronauts also to space tourists. Both astronauts and space tourists are on the space mission to travel to space, but with different objectives. Astronaut is under the 'pressure of employment', whereas space tourists are under the 'pleasure of enjoying an adventurous tourist destination'. This primary differentiation itself points to the argument that space tourists cannot be treated with the same legal protections provided to astronauts.

Not only the difference in the functioning but also the selection process and training of astronauts are different and tough compared to tourists to space. The Principles Regarding Processes and Criteria for Selection, Assignment, Training and Certification of ISS (Expedition and Visiting) Crewmembers, 2001[20] (ISS Crew Criteria Document) defines the processes, standards and criteria for selection, assignment, training and certification of Space Station crew for flight. All the partners of the International Space Station (ISS) shall be using these principles for the professional astronauts/cosmonauts or spaceflight participants as ISS (Expedition

Legal Framework of Liability in Space Tourism **103**

and Visiting) crew members. It defines two types of crew members – (a) professional astronauts/cosmonauts and (b) spaceflight participants. Former is an individual who has completed the official selection and has been qualified as such at the space agency of one of the ISS partners and is employed on the staff of the crew office of that agency. Latter are individuals[21] sponsored by one or more partner(s), mostly for a temporary assignment that is covered under a short-term contract.

As per the above categorisation, space tourist comes under the definition of "spaceflight participants" and not astronauts. Under the principles, astronauts are expedition crew members – who are the main crew of the ISS and perform planned activities for an increment.[22] Space tourists are not expedition members.

ISS Crew Criteria Document also mentions the factors for disqualification as a crew member, which include the following:

a  delinquency or misconduct in prior employment/military service;
b  criminal, dishonest, infamous or notoriously disgraceful conduct;
c  intentional false statement or fraud in examination or appointment;
d  habitual use of intoxicating beverages to excess;
e  abuse of narcotics, drugs or other controlled substances;
f  membership or sponsorship in organisations that adversely affect the confidence of the public in the integrity of, or reflecting unfavourably in a public forum on, any ISS partner, partner State or cooperating agency.

Behavioural requirement mentioned in the ISS Crew Criteria Document is also not something that can be related to the space tourist, these include relevant operational experience, demonstrated performance under stress, ability to function as a team member, high moral integrity, adaptability/flexibility and motivation consistent with the programme mission. The above-mentioned matters are not required for the tourists, as their main aim is not any operational mission. Also, the tourists do not need to understand and comply with the provisions of the ISS Crew Code of Conduct (CCOC).

Training aspects for the professional expedition of the crew members are mentioned in Volume 7 of the Station Program Implementation Plan (SPIP). Before the start of increment-specific training, recommended members of the crew undergo advanced training for nearly 12 months. The International Training Control Board (ITCB) designs a minimum ISS training programme for the visiting crew and spaceflight participants. As a rule, the visiting crew should train with the increment crew that will be in orbit during their visit.[23] Even though space tourists can be included under the category of spaceflight participants, still the professional training of astronauts and the training provided to a space tourist are different; hence the training needs to be regulated separately by well-written rules and guidelines. The compulsory training required to be a space tourist also differentiates space tourism from other forms of tourism, which do not demand any form of training or formal acceptance.

**104** Asha P. Soman

For astronaut training, the main objective of the Chinese Astronaut System is to ensure the health and performance of astronauts during long-term space flights. The primary task of this system includes training and support to the astronauts[24] and human space life science research. The purpose of astronaut training is to establish a competent Astronaut Corps with excellent conduct, rational structure and appropriate scale, to select and train qualified crew for human spaceflight missions.[25] It is very well reflected under the system that astronauts are related to professionally trained individuals, but space tourists are going through these kinds of rigorous training and selection processes to board a spacecraft. The argument that astronauts and space tourists need to be treated separately hence gets a strong moot point.

Another reason for arguing space tourists cannot be treated as astronauts is that the training given for the astronauts is very complex, and they are trained to survive all the unforeseen events which will happen during the mission and for many months. But while considering the training provided to an individual for a space tourist mission, it does not include all those pieces of training to make them equipped to meet and survive all the calamities and casualties they need to face as part of the mission.

Another issue related to space tourism is space insurance. The insurance sector is one area that will be benefited from the increasing number of space tourist missions. But, the lack of clarity on the insurance coverage provided to the astronauts does have an impact on the implications on space tourism and the tourists. Most of the risks like fire, accident and theft are covered by insurance, and the premium depends upon various factors – the more the risk, the more premium needs to be paid.

Space missions are very risky. Considering the general principles of insurance, even if an individual wants to get this protection, the premium will be very high, and may also warrant good health conditions. An increase in space tourism[26] will most probably showcase a boom in the insurance sector also, and one of the reasons for this will be because most such missions will be undertaken by private players, and also by the entertainment industry. But if the space tourists are going only within the limit of air space, then there needs to be clarity as to whether the insurance type is aviation insurance or space insurance. This dilemma also needs to be settled by the international and national air and space law community.

Huge investment is needed for every space mission, and taking tourists to space is also expensive, as they need to undergo training to survive the mission, and to face unforeseen situations, which is not a prerequisite for other types of tourism. Economic investment is a constraint to taking forward the idea of space tourism.

### Liability in Space Tourism

Liability for space activities is one of the major concerns for each of the space missions, and it is a complex area for all the nations involved in the space race too. The Convention on International Liability for Damage Caused by Space Objects, 1972

(Liability Convention) mainly deals with the liability for space activities, and the inclusion of space tourism under the ambit of this convention itself is a debatable matter.

While considering the legality, space tourism itself has been taken as a serious concern. The main lacunae in this area is that almost all laws relating to outer space at the international level are silent about the different legal issues relating to space tourism. As many of the national space legislations are also framed based on international documents, the complexities of space tourism are not incorporated in the national laws too.

Astronauts are considered the "envoys of mankind in outer space" by the Outer Space Treaty of 1967, but the same status cannot be designated to space tourists, and, hence, similar legal protection also cannot be given to tourists to outer space. Space tourists are not on a national mission to explore the cosmic world for the betterment of mankind; on the other hand, astronauts are specially trained government employees who are on a national mission. One of the cardinal principles of international space law is cooperation between nations, and the same has been mentioned in various treaties and agreements for space missions. Space tourists are not on a national mission, and they are not bound by the principle of cooperation with others, as far as sharing information about their private missions are considered. Hence, space tourists cannot be given the status of "envoys of mankind in outer space".

The Agreement on the Rescue of Astronauts, the Return of Astronauts and the Return of Objects Launched into Outer Space, 1968 (the Rescue Agreement) under Article 1[27] makes the member nations duty to assist the astronauts during an emergency and on landing on their territory. If this obligation of member nations is extended to space tourism also, in the future, with the increase of space tourism missions by public and private enterprises, it will be troublesome for the nations to take up the responsibilities under the Registration Convention and give the same assistance that is required for the astronauts.

Based on the above arguments, this chapter tries to bring up the argument that the legal position enjoyed by astronauts cannot be extended to space tourists. Astronauts are professionally competent persons on national missions to do scientific experiments and other space activities in outer space. Space tourists are not professionally proficient persons. Because of this prima facie difference, the same legal protections provided to the astronauts cannot be extended to space tourists. Hence, the existing international space laws as such cannot be related to space tourism. So there is a need for the international and national space community to develop a proper legal framework for space tourism.

Countries like India, which has its national space legislation (Draft Space Activities Bill, 2017)[28] still not passed by the Parliament, do not include provisions for space tourism and liabilities relating to space tourism. In the Bill of 2017, the Department of Space does not mention space tourism as one of the major concern areas for space activities in India, and the Draft does not have any provision relating to space tourism. In the Explanatory Note[29] to the Draft Bill, the Government of India does accept its obligation under the international legal documents for outer space activities, basically under international responsibility and regarding the liability for damages caused by space activities and space objects. Under the present regime, nations are responsible for the space activities done by the non-governmental or private sector enterprises in those nations; hence, this Bill has incorporated provisions for licence[30] or authorisation and continuous supervision by the State over non-sovereign entities. So far, there is no proper international legal commitment towards space tourism, and so these are not being incorporated into the space law statutes. Currently, India does not have the international responsibility of incorporating provisions relating to space tourism and the liability of India on space tourism.[31] Regarding liability for commercial space activities, under the Bill, the licensee needs to indemnify the Central Government of the claims brought against the government for the damage or loss arising out of commercial space.

Another issue relating to the liability aspect of space tourism is the clash that can arise between Air or Aviation Law and Space Law. Sovereignty rights are the main point of conflict. Article 1 of the Convention on International Civil Aviation, 1944 (the Chicago Convention) recognises the 'complete and exclusive sovereignty of member nations over the airspace above its territory'.[32] Under international law and international aviation law, air space is under the jurisdiction of each nation's sovereign right. If a nation allows space tourism in its national space legislation or policy, maintaining the balance between its aviation law and space law will become difficult. For instance, under the Indian aviation law, there are several statutes passed by the Parliament to protect the sovereignty of the country by regulating the air space above the country: the Airport Authority of India Act of 1994. The Airports Authority of India maintains the airspace and altitude restrictions in India.[33] Further, there are several statutory bodies[34] like the Directorate General of Civil Aviation (DGCA), the Bureau of Civil Aviation Security (BCAS), the Airports Economic Regulatory Authority of India (AERA), Aircraft Accident Investigation Bureau (AAIB) established by the Ministry of Civil Aviation to investigate aircraft accidents and crimes against aircraft, and these are also backed by statutory protection. Indian aviation laws agree with the Convention on International Civil Aviation of 1944 (the Chicago Convention)[35] which recognises the right of nations over their air space.

Complete and exclusive sovereignty of the nations over the air space is mentioned in the Chicago Convention solely related to international civil aviation. Hence, providing a legal framework, particularly for the liability of space tourism under international and national aviation law is also not an easy task. This aspect also demands a separate set of laws framed for space tourism, maintaining the balance between air and space law.

Further, the competitions which offer the winner to get a ticket as space tourists also mention the trip will be within the air space and not to outer space – calling for

Legal Framework of Liability in Space Tourism **107**

the application of aviation or air law. For instance, one such competition mentions taking

> 14 people from all over the world for a space training competition and the winner can fly a MIG 29/31 for a free trip to the stratosphere. The competition will take place in Russia in June 2018 during celebrations of both UNISPACE+50 and FIFA 2018 world cup.[36]

The stratosphere is the second layer of the atmosphere.[37] Hence, the organisers are not taking the winners to outer space but the air space. While considering such competitions and taking the space tourist within the air space limits, the conflict between air and space law arises; and this also creates difficulty in determining a legal framework for liability under neither aviation law nor space law.

Organisers of the competitions are offering the chance of being a space tourist and are not providing proper training to individuals.[38] One week or a few months of training provided to the individuals selected for space tourism cannot be compared at par with the professional training astronauts are getting.[39] This also calls for the non-application or non-extension of the existing international and national space laws applicable to the astronauts, to the space tourists, particularly the Liability Convention, 1972 and the Convention on Registration of Objects Launched into Outer Space, 1976 (the Registration Convention).

Even if the United Nations Office for Outer Space Affairs (UNOOSA) and other outer space communities/organisations can come up with laws or guidelines for space tourism, it cannot be taken affirmatively that the member nations of the UNOOSA and other communities/organisations will adopt those laws. For instance, the binding effect of the European Code of Conduct for Space Debris Mitigation, 2004[40] is that the application of the Code is voluntary.[41] Profit is the main motive for scheduling space missions for taking tourists. Hence, all the countries and private entities will be looking forward to flexible laws supporting their needs and demands.

### Need for Legal Framework at International and National Level for Space Tourism

From 1969[42] onwards humans have lived and worked continuously aboard the International Space Station, advancing scientific knowledge and demonstrating new technologies, making research breakthroughs not possible on Earth. As a global endeavour, 244 people from 19 countries have visited the unique microgravity laboratory that has hosted more than 3,000 research and educational investigations from researchers in 108 countries and areas.[43]

Though space explorations and human beings staying on the International Space Station are from decades back, space tourism is in its infancy and needs to go a long road. Space tourism is not a new concept, but the contradiction between space activities and space tourism is that technological advancements and all the intrusions into the cosmos aim at knowing more about the hidden outer space for the betterment of human life on Earth; whereas space tourism is not on the exploration side but on the luxury of the luxurious people to make their name manifest on the history as space travellers. Space activities need huge investments, and space tourism sets aback on the money that can be used for space activities for space explorations.

International and national laws relating to space insurance (insurance for life, life insurance for astronauts, life insurance for space tourists), extra-terrestrial application of space laws, intellectual property rights and training for astronauts, visiting crew and space tourists need to be laid down with clarity. As far as space missions by nations are considered, there are international and national legal frameworks, but the same is lacking in the case of space tourists. Hence, there is a need for the international space law community to place properly a legal framework for the same.

Further, the "Space2030" Agenda and implementation plan[44] submitted by the Committee on the Peaceful Uses of Outer Space to the General Assembly is a forward-looking strategy for reaffirming and strengthening the contribution of space activities and space tools to the achievement of global agendas, addressing long-term sustainable development concerns of humankind. This Agenda also aimed at promoting equal opportunities in the space sector by encouraging, in particular, young people and women to consider careers in science, technology, engineering and mathematics.[45]

Objectives of this Agenda include facilitating and promoting the integration of the space sector with other sectors like energy, public health, the environment, climate change, the management of resources and information and communication technology, as well as the development of multi-stakeholder partnerships leading to innovative space-based solutions for social and economic development that can be integrated into mechanisms for implementing the Sustainable Development Goals. The objective also includes the long-term sustainability of outer space, promoting the development of the space industry, with a particular focus on small and medium-sized enterprises, increasing investment in the space sector and creating high-quality jobs, and promoting the spin-off benefits of space technologies to the non-space sector.[46] Agenda 2030 does not cover anything on space tourism, rather one of the objectives is going against space tourism as such; "enable space activities for all, based on international law, by promoting an international framework that facilitates equal access to space for all, including non-spacefaring nations, and encourages safety and innovation". Space tourism is not something that can be related to the benefit of mankind, which is the basic principle behind space exploration, which now has also become the luxury enjoyed by the richest people of the world, whereas the Agenda is focused on space activities except tourism.

One objective of the Agenda which can be narrowly related to space tourism is: Promote and facilitate collaboration and partnership between the private and public sectors, academic institutions and research and development centres in the field of the utilisation of space for achieving Sustainable Development Goals, as well as in the area of the long-term sustainability of outer space activities.[47] Here also, there is no implication of the international space law community reflecting its view on space tourism.

Though 2021 has been marked by the name of several space tourists,[48] it has not been reflected in the several committees and drafts[49] under the UNOOSA in 2021. Similarly to Agenda 2030, the Report of the Sixty-Fourth Sessions of the Committee on the Peaceful Uses of Outer Space held from 25 August to 3 September 2021 does not mention space tourism and its legal implications. The report also emphasised the need for the inclusion of private and public stakeholders in the development of strategies and regulatory frameworks,[50] but nothing directly on space tourism.

One of the main reasons for the increasing number of space tourists is the privatisation of the space sector. Privatisation has become something that cannot be avoided in current and future space missions. NASA, the Indian Space Research Organisation (ISRO) and many space agencies have tied up several private entities for their missions. NASA has a Commercial Crew Program (CCP), which has been formed to facilitate the development of a US commercial crew space transportation capability to achieve safe, reliable and cost-effective access to and from the International Space Station and low Earth orbit. Multiple American companies that are designing and developing transportation capabilities to and from low Earth orbit and the International Space Station are part of the CCP. By supporting the development of human spaceflight capabilities, NASA is laying the foundation for future commercial transportation capabilities.[51] NASA and SpaceX also have several joint missions together.[52]

The European Space Agency (ESA) has also taken initiatives in favour of space tourism. According to the ESA, the interest of the general public in sub-orbital flying has become substantial, and it could offer a realistic opportunity to 'touch' space by experiencing weightlessness and seeing the curvature of the Earth's limb. "Being so closely related to ESA's core business, the agency is observing these developments with interest, and is now presenting its position on privately-funded suborbital spaceflight". The private partnership is encouraged by the ESA and provides the necessary environment for private entities to flourish in this field.[53]

Space activities are based on the international legal regime and generally accepted principles, and the national space legislation and policies catered for the need of each nation, and without compromising the security and sovereignty aspects, most nations have come up with their laws in this regard.

## Chapter Conclusion

Presently, space tourism has become an emblem of millionaires, but it is not too late when this will be accessible to the common people also, like what happened with the aviation sector – earlier travelling in flight was a luxury, but now it has become accessible for the common people also. After the boon of the private sector in the space industry, most nations including India have introduced in their policies and legislations rules and regulations for the private players in the space sector. With the cumulative number of space tourists, now, there is a need to relook at the international and national space laws and policies to include the legal framework for space tourists too.

Space tourism is an activity with economic implications and a revenue-generating mission for national space agencies. Affluent people to get a view of the Earth from space are ready to give money to the space agencies, and if there is the proper legal framework by the national and the international community, nations could look forward to framing laws affirmatively for the space tourism sector. But, profit comes secondary when the safety of humanity itself is considered, so there needs to be a balance that should be achieved conceiving the principle of sustainable development and protection of the Earth's atmosphere. Few people's luxurious curiosity must not be a reason for the future generation to have a struggling life on Earth.

Space tourism is separate from the normal tourism industry or business, the issues relating to this type of tourism are also specific, and hence, need specific laws. Rather than extending or amending the existing international space law principles for space activities, it is suggested that a new law for space tourism is the need of the hour. National space legislation also needs reconsideration in this respect. As the Draft Space Activities Bill, 2017 is still pending, the Government of India can incorporate the provisions relating to space tourism into its space legislation.

## Notes

1 'In Historic First, Russian Film Crew Lands after Shoot Aboard ISS', available at <https://www.nbcnews.com/news/world/historic-first-russian-film-crew-lands-shoot-iss-rcna3148> Last visited, 10 October 2022.

2 See, Jackie Wattles, '2021: The Year of Space Tourism', available at <https://edition.cnn.com/2022/01/01/tech/space-business-year-in-review-scn/index.html> Last visited, 10 October 2022.

3 The term "Astronaut" has been originated from Greek (*naut* from *nautes*), which means "space sailor", and *astro* from the Greek word *Astron*, which means "star". Together these Greek words make an astronaut a "star sailor". Russian space explorers are known as *cosmonauts*, *cosmo* in Greek for "universe", so both *cosmo* and *kosmos* have the same meaning. *See* 'Astronaut Biographies', available at <https://www.nasa.gov/astronauts> Last visited, 19 December 2021. *See* Root *naut*, from *nautes*, Greek words for "sailor". This suffix can be used to create many travel-specific words. For example, Argonauts were mythical Greek sailors on the ship named the Argo, available at <https://www.vocabulary.com/dictionary/astronaut> Last visited, 19 December 2021.

4 One of the definitions or explanation for the word "tourist" is one who makes a journey for pleasure, stopping here and there; "tour" means "a turn, a shift on duty", available at <https://www.etymonline.com/word/tourist> Last visited, 18 January 2022. Tourism is the act and process of spending time away from home in pursuit of recreation, relaxation and pleasure, while making use of the commercial provision of services. As such,

tourism is a product of modern social arrangements, beginning in Western Europe in the seventeenth century, although it has antecedents in Classical antiquity, available at <https://www.britannica.com/topic/tourism> Last visited, 8 January 2022.

5 'Britannica', available at <https://www.britannica.com/topic/space-tourism> Last visited, 18 January 2022.

6 Tito made it to orbit, spent about six days aboard the International Space Station, and then landed in Kazakhstan on 6 May 2001. See, Mike Wall, 'First Space Tourist: How a U.S. Millionaire Bought a Ticket to Orbit', available at <https://www.space.com/11492-space-tourism-pioneer-dennis-tito.html> Last visited, 19 January 2022.

7 'Space Tourism', available at <https://dbpedia.org/page/Space_tourism> Last visited, 3 January 2022.

8 'Space Tourism Market Size, Share & Trends Analysis Report by Type (Orbital, Sub-orbital), By End Use (Government, Commercial), By Region, and Segment Forecasts, 2022–2030', available at <https://www.grandviewresearch.com/industry-analysis/space-tourism-market-report> Last visited, 13 October 2022.

9 See, Mike Wall, 'First Space Tourist: How a U.S. Millionaire Bought a Ticket to Orbit', available at <https://www.space.com/11492-space-tourism-pioneer-dennis-tito.html> Last visited, 19 January 2022.

10 Toyohiro Akiyama was a Japanese journalist.

11 Helen Sharman was a British chemist.

12 Denise Chow, 'Before Tito, Russia Flew 2 Paying Passengers to Space', available at <https://spacenews.com/tito-russia-flew-2-paying-passengers-space/> Last visited, 19 January 2022.

13 'Space Tourism', see available at <https://www.britannica.com/topic/space-tourism> Last visited, 18 January 2022. MirCorp was a private venture in charge of the space station Mir. Before Tito could make his trip, the decision was made to deorbit Mir, and— after the intervention of Space Adventures Ltd.—the mission was diverted to the ISS.

14 See Elizabeth Howell, 'Space Tourism Took a Giant Leap in 2021: Here's 10 Milestones from the Year', available at <https://www.space.com/space-tourism-giant-leap-2021-milestones> Last visited, 19 January 2022.

15 Launched on 15 September 2021.

16 St. Jude Children's Research Hospital.

17 See Vicky Stein, 'Inspiration4: The First All-Civilian Spaceflight on SpaceX Dragon', available at <https://www.space.com/inspiration4-spacex.html> Last visited, 19 January 2022.

18 Jason Daley, 'Russia Proposes "Luxury Hotel" for the International Space Station', available at https://www.smithsonianmag.com/smart-news/russia-proposes-luxury-hotel-international-space-station-180967674/> Last visited, 19 January 2022.

19 Report of the Committee on the Peaceful Uses of Outer Space, General Assembly Official Records Seventy-sixth Session Supplement No. 20, available at <https://www.unoosa.org/res/oosadoc/data/documents/2021/a/a7620_0_html/A_76_20E.pdf> Last visited, 24 December 2021.

20 Multilateral Crew Operations Panel, November 2001, available at <https://esamultimedia.esa.int/docs/isscrewcriteria.pdf> Last visited, 3 January 2022.

21 Individuals include, e.g. commercial, scientific and other programmes; crew members of non-partner space agencies, engineers, scientists, teachers, journalists, filmmakers or tourists. A sponsoring agency is one of the five ISS partners (CSA, ESA, NASA, GOJ and Rosaviakosmos) that provide crew flight opportunities.

22 *Supra* note 20.

23 *Id.*

24 Astronaut support refers to the construction of the health support system, the living support system and the work support system, setting the medical/ergonomic require-ments for human-rated spacecraft and implementing the evaluation, thus providing support for astronauts during orbital flight. Human space life science research refers to the

exploration and solution of space life science issues related to human being, developing advanced health support and human factors engineering technologies, so as to provide sustained theoretical and technological support for innovative development of manned spaceflight and future human deep space exploration.

25 'Astronauts', available at <http://en.cmse.gov.cn/constitutes/astronautsystem/> Last visited, 12 January 2022.

26 Andrew Ross Sorkin, Jason Karaian, Sarah Kessler, Stephen Gandel, Michael J. de la Merced, Lauren Hirsch and Ephrat Livni, 'The Space Race for Insurers', available at <https://www.nytimes.com/2021/07/09/business/dealbook/branson-bezos-space-race-insurance.html> Last visited, 16 October 2022.

27 'Ares', available at <https://www.unoosa.org/pdf/gares/ARES_22_2345E.pdf> Last visited, 16 October 2022.

28 'Draft Space Activities Bill, 2017', Available at <https://prsindia.org/billtrack/draft-space-activities-bill-2017> Last visited, 2 January 2022.

29 Explanatory Note on Draft Space Activities Bill, 2017, II. International Treaty Obligations on Outer Space Activities, p. 2, available at <https://prsindia.org/files/bills_acts/bills_parliament/1970/Draft%20Space%20Activities%20Bill%202017.pdf> Last visited, 16 October 2022.

30 Draft Space Activities Bill, 2017. Section 2 (b) defines licence. Chapter II deals with Space Activity Regulatory Mechanism - Sections 3(d), (k). Chapter III deals with Authorisation and Licence for Commercial Space Activity – Sections 5 to 10.

31 No.E.11020/2/2015-Sec-VI Government of India Department of Space, available at <https://prsindia.org/files/bills_acts/bills_parliament/1970/Draft%20Space%20Activities%20Bill%202017.pdf> Last visited, 2 January 2022.

32 'Convention on International Civil Aviation Done at Chicago on the 7th Day of December 1944', Available at <https://www.icao.int/publications/documents/7300_orig.pdf> Last visited, 16 October 2022.

33 Establishment of Minimum Flight Altitudes, F. No. 9/38/2009-IR, Civil Aviation Requirements. Section 9 – Air Space and Air Traffic Management Series 'R', Part I Issue II, 8th January 2010, Office of Director General of Civil Aviation, Government of India, available at <http://164.100.60.133/cars/D9R-R1.pdf> Last visited, 16 October 2022.

34 'Organization Setup', available at <https://www.civilaviation.gov.in/en/aboutus/orgsetup> Last visited, 16 October 2022.

35 Available at <https://www.icao.int/publications/Documents/7300_orig.pdf> Last visited, 2 January 2022.

36 Details of the Competition Is', available at <https://www.unoosa.org/documents/pdf/psa/activities/2017/SamaraWorkshop/presentations/2-3-6.<Aurthur_Tomas_Sustainable_Space_Exploration_through_Space_tourism.pdf> Last visited, 5 January 2022.

37 'The Stratosphere', available at <https://scied.ucar.edu/learning-zone/atmosphere/stratosphere#:~:text=The%20stratosphere%20is%20a%20layer,the%20stratosphere%20is%20the%20mesosphere> Last visited, 5 January 2022.

38 '14 People Will Be Selected on the Basis of Mobile Gaming App. These 14 People Will Be Given Extensive Training for One Week as an Astronaut @GCTC', available at <https://www.unoosa.org/documents/pdf/psa/activities/2017/SamaraWorkshop/presentations/2-3-6._Aurthur_Tomas_Sustainable_Space_Exploration_through_Space_tourism.pdf> Last visited, 5 January 2022.

39 For example, Virgin Galactic, on its website, mentions the training for space tourists, but it does not mention how many and the process. "Our pre-flight Space Readiness Program consists of specific events, activities, and training designed to leave you physically, mentally and spiritually ready for space", available at <https://brochure.virgingalactic.com/preflight> Last visited, 16 October 2022.

40 'ESA-27560, European Code of Conduct for Space Debris Mitigation', available at <https://archives.eui.eu/en/fonds/475516?item=ESA-27560> Last visited, 16 October 2022.

41 Article 2.2 of the Code, available at <https://www.unoosa.org/documents/pdf/spacelaw/sd/European_code_of_conduct_for_space_debris_mitigation.pdf> Last visited, 16 October 2022.

42 First rudimentary station was created in 1969 by the linking of two Russian Soyuz vehicles in space, followed by other stations and developments in space technology until construction began on the ISS in 1998. 'History and Timeline of the ISS', available at <https://www.issnationallab.org/about/iss-timeline/#:~:text=The%20first%20rudimentary%20station%20was,ever%20developed%3A%20the%20American%20shuttles.> Last visited, 17 October 2022.

43 'Two Astronauts Receive Assignments for NASA's SpaceX Crew-6 Mission', available at <https://www.nasa.gov/press-release/two-astronauts-receive-assignments-for-nasa-s-spacex-crew-6-mission> Last visited, 18 January 2022.

44 Fifty-seventh session, Vienna, 3–14 February 2020.

45 The "Space2030" Agenda: Space as a Driver of Sustainable Development, Seventy-Sixth Session of the UN General Assembly, Recalling Its Resolution 73/6 of 26 October 2018, available at <https://www.unoosa.org/documents/pdf/copuos/2021/A_73_L3.pdf> Last visited, 24 December 2021.

46 *Id.*

47 *Id.*

48 Virgin Galactic's First Flight (11 July 2021), Blue Origin's First Flight (20 July 2021), Inspiration4 Mission (15 September 2021), Beam Me Up, Scotty (13 October 2021), Japanese billionaire Yusaku Maezawa (8 December 2021), Good Morning Earth (11 December 2021). Valerie Stimac, 'Space Tourism Took Off In 2021, Here's How It Happened', available at <https://www.forbes.com/sites/valeriestimac/2021/12/31/space-tourism-took-of-in-2021-heres-how-it-happened/?sh=175c9b4e4011> Last visited, 17 October 2022.

49 For example, the "Space2030" Agenda, Report on the United Nations/Mongolia workshop on the applications of global navigation satellite systems (Ulaanbaatar, 25–29 October 2021), available at <https://documents-dds-ny.un.org/doc/UNDOC/GEN/V21/083/02/PDF/V2108302.pdf?OpenElement> Last visited, 17 October 2022.

50 Report of the Committee on the Peaceful Uses of Outer Space, General Assembly Official Records Seventy-Sixth Session Supplement No. 20, available at <https://www.unoosa.org/res/oosadoc/data/documents/2021/a/a7620_0_html/A_76_20E.pdf> Last visited, 24 December 2021.

51 'Commercial Crew Program Essentials', available at <https://www.nasa.gov/content/commercial-crew-program-the-essentials> Last visited, 18 January 2022.

52 *Supra* note 43.

53 'ESA and Space Tourism', available at <https://www.esa.int/Enabling_Support/Preparing_for_the_Future/Discovery_and_Preparation/ESA_and_space_tourism> Last visited, 4 April 2022.

# 8

# THE ENVIRONMENTAL EFFECTS OF SPACE TOURISM

*David Webb*

### In the Beginning

As long ago as the 1960s, Pan American World Airways had been pushing the idea of private spaceflight – and a model of an Orion III Space clipper with a Pan Am logo was used in the 1968 film "2001: A Space Odyssey".[1] At that time the idea was more fantasy than fiction, but Austrian journalist Gerhard Pistor asked to book a flight to the Moon, and Pan Am announced that they were going to offer commercially operated passenger lunar flights – five years before Apollo 11 landed on the lunar surface. During the Apollo missions, interest grew, and eventually, Pan Am had a waiting list for tickets of about 100,000 people.[2] However, the company went bust in 1991.

Space tourism started at the end of the 1990s when Mir Corp, a private Russian company in charge of the Mir Space Station, needed to raise funds to help maintain it. They joined with Space Adventures Ltd and sold a trip to Mir Space Station to an American businessman, Dennis Tito.[3] However, before Tito's planned launch date, it was decided to scrap Mir and deorbit it. So, the trip was reorganised with the International Space Station (ISS) as the destination, and Tito left Earth on a Russian Soyuz spacecraft on 28 April 2001 to spend seven days on the ISS,[4] becoming the first space tourist to fund his own trip.

Space Adventures Ltd went on to organise a few more flights from 2002 to 2009, arranging for a further six tourists to ride on Russian Soyuz rockets for a fee reported to be up to $50 million per person.[5] Each of these trips involved spending a few days onboard the ISS. So, South African computer millionaire Mark Shuttleworth flew to the ISS in 2002[6] and American businessman Gregory Olsen in 2005,[7] followed by Iranian-born American entrepreneur Anousheh Ansari in September 2006.[8] American billionaire Charles Simonyi followed in 2007 with a

DOI: 10.4324/9781032617961-8

ride on a Soyuz TMA-10 spacecraft to spend ten days on the ISS.[9] He also made a second trip in 2009. Then, in October 2008, Richard Garriott, an American video game developer and former astronaut's son, paid $30 million to become the sixth space traveller.[10] Before the Russians suspended the use of its spacecraft for tourists, the last tourist to travel to the ISS was Canadian entrepreneur Guy Laliberté, who visited in 2009.[11]

There was then a ten-year gap between trips to the ISS, but in 2019 NASA announced that tourists could visit the space station for $35,000 per night (not including transport).[12] This was, therefore, the first space hotel opportunity, and in December 2021, Japanese billionaire Maezawa Yusaku and his production assistant Hirano Yozo became paying passengers on a Soyuz spacecraft and spent 12 days on the space station.[13] It is reported that the tickets cost $88 million and Maezawa has a further ambition to fly around the Moon and hopes to do this with six to eight guests in the next few years, flying with Elon Musk's SpaceX corporation for around $100 million.[14] Earlier in 2021, there were the well-publicised sub-orbital passenger flights of Virgin Galactic and Blue Origin who took passengers into space and back in a few short trips.

Virgin Galactic made the first of these flights on 11 July 2022 with Richard Branson and three employees on board.[15] The spacecraft was air-launched from a carrier airplane called White Knight Two and reached an altitude of 86 km – just above the 80 km height which NASA designates for travellers to be classed as astronauts.[16] Virgin expected commercial flights to begin in 2023, and from 2005 to 2014, the company sold around 600 tickets for $200,000–$250,000 each.[17] Sales resumed after Branson's flight at a higher price of $450,000, and another 100 were quickly sold.[18] The company's aim is to eventually launch as many as 400 flights per year with two pilots and six passengers.[19]

On 20 July 2021, Blue Origin's New Shepard rocket took off with Jeff Bezos, his brother Mark, 18-year-old student Oliver Daemen, the son of a Dutch financier, and 82-year-old Wally Funk for a sub-orbital space ride.[20] Daemen had previously held a seat on the second flight but was able to get on the first one after the anonymous bidder, who paid $28 million at a public auction for a ticket, had to pull out.[21] A second Blue Origin flight took actor William Shatner (Star Trek's Captain Kirk), aged 90, into space on 13 October.[22] These two trips reached an altitude of 107 km, just above the 100 km Kármán Line, where aeronautics gives way to astronautics, and which is deemed by many to be the edge of space.[23] Indeed, 'where space actually starts' has led to some disagreement between Bezos (who declares the Kármán Line as the start of space) and Branson (who uses the NASA definition for astronauts).[24]

Blue Origin is looking to launch paying travellers into space, using the reusable New Shepard rocket and a passenger capsule on top, for a reported $200,000 and $300,000 ticket price.[25] Blue Origin has already stated its intention of more than doubling the number of tourists it flies by adding another vehicle to its fleet.[26] It is also planning to have a lunar lander, Blue Moon, ready for 2024.[27]

Because sub-orbital space tourism does not go through the US Government (as a journey to the ISS would) different US States are now competing to attract companies who offer them. Virginia was the first to support commercial space activities but others, such as Florida and New Mexico, Texas and California, are also adopting comparable legislation.[28]

Elon Musk's SpaceX company appears to be focussing on the longer trips and is offering up its Crew Dragon spacecraft for chartered orbital flights.[29] On 16 September 2021, it carried four American citizens (Jared Isaacman, Sian Proctor, Hayley Arceneaux and Chris Sembroski) into Earth's orbit for three days. The flight was called Inspiration4 and was privately chartered by billionaire Jared Isaacman to raise awareness and funds for a children's research hospital – it became the first private citizen crewed orbital mission.[30]

SpaceX has also been delivering cargo to and from the ISS since 2012, and in 2020 it began transporting astronauts there.[31] It is estimated that NASA will be paying SpaceX an average of $58 million per astronaut, compared with the $81 million it cost for flights on Soyuz rockets.[32]

SpaceX is also offering commercial trips to orbit the Earth and the Moon, and Elon Musk's ambitions are far-reaching. He plans to use SpaceX's huge Starship rocket to fly as many as 100 people around the world in minutes.[33] Claims are that a flight from New York to Shanghai would take 39 minutes, rather than the 15 hours it takes by airplane.[34] Musk also has plans for colonies on the Moon and Mars which would likely also eventually include hotels for tourist trips.[35]

So, there does not seem to be a shortage of people willing to pay a lot of money to go into space, and a number of other companies are joining in to help them. For example, Axiom Space Inc is looking to construct its own space station in the near future and provide spaceflight services to individuals, corporations and space agencies.[36] As things develop and launch systems become cheaper, one may not even need to be a billionaire to afford a ticket – just very wealthy.

A recent report by the Swiss multinational investment bank UBS sees the space tourism industry growing rapidly, with high-speed travel via outer space competing with long-distance airline flights. They anticipate an annual market of at least $20 billion, with space tourism having a $3 billion share by 2030.[37]

However, as the number of launches increases, effects on the environment also increase, and there are some important environmental issues now being raised.

## Environmental Concerns

During the launch process, rockets use a huge amount of fuel, and there is a range of different propellants used.[38] Orbital rockets employ multiple stages to achieve enough thrust to travel through the Earth's atmosphere. As each stage ends, it separates from the launch vehicle and is burnt up by atmospheric friction as it falls back to Earth.[39] Propulsion is achieved through the burning of a propellant, which consists of a fuel and an oxidiser. The four most common fuels are kerosene, hypergolic fuels, liquid hydrogen and solid fuels.[40]

## Overcrowding

A growing number of mega-constellations of satellites in Low Earth Orbit (LEO) are being planned and developed by broadband providers such as SpaceX's Starlink system and Amazon's Project Kuiper. They aim to provide global high-speed broadband services for commercial and military use *via* a huge number of satellites orbiting close to the Earth to enhance the speed of communications.[41]

Starlink already has licences to operate over 11,000 satellites (another 30,000 may follow[42] and with others could lead to a total of over 60,000 satellites in orbit) from three different altitudes around 1,200 km (above the ISS), 550 km and very low at 340 km.[43] At these low altitudes, satellites do not last forever (maybe five to ten years)[44] because they are subject to atmospheric drag. LEO is also a graveyard orbital area, and satellites are often moved there so that their orbits decay and they then burn up in the upper atmosphere, damaging it and creating pollution.[45] All this activity results in satellite collisions, and satellite operators often must move their satellites to avoid possible collisions from occurring.[46]

The European Space Agency (ESA) estimates that as of 5 January 2022, about 6,170 space launches have taken place (excluding failures) since 1957, with 12,470 satellites being placed into Earth orbit. Of those, some 7,840 are still in space and 5,100 are still functioning.[47] In addition, they estimate that there are over 1,036,500 pieces of space debris greater than 1 cm in size. Space debris consists of discarded objects in orbit around Earth, such as abandoned satellite fragments, solidified liquids, products of erosion etc. As launch numbers rise and as tens of thousands of satellites with a limited lifetime are placed in LEO, the problem will increase significantly. According to the ESA, even a tiny 1-cm sized object travelling at orbital velocities of 36,000 km an hour would have the kinetic energy of an exploding grenade.[48]

This was a problem noted some time ago, in 1978, by NASA scientist Donald J. Kessler. Kessler proposed a situation where two colliding objects in space could generate debris that then collides with other objects, creating a growing number of pieces of debris. This has become known as the Kessler Syndrome,[49] and such a self-sustaining cascade of collisions could eventually result in a cloud of debris that rockets may not be able to penetrate.

Another problem presented by placing so many satellites in orbit is the threat to the night sky, which is being scarred by the trails of satellites as they pass overhead. Astronomers investigating very distant, and therefore very faint, objects need long exposures of the sky, and these are already being photo-bombed by satellites in LEO. They are calling for operators and observatories to collaborate to manage and monitor constellations and look for ways to make LEO satellites less reflective.[50]

**118** David Webb

The overpopulation of Low Earth Orbit by mainly commercial satellites is therefore generating a number of problems for the near-space environment. Overcrowding is increasing the likelihood of collisions and debris creation or adding to atmospheric pollution through satellite de-orbiting. Disturbing effects are also being created for observers on the Earth.

### Launch Accidents

Accidents at launch can cause a considerable amount of environmental destruction and contamination. For example, an accident during a flight test of the US military Advanced Hypersonic Weapon at the launch site on Kodiak Island in Alaska in 2014 resulted in such heavy damage that the site was not reopened for two years.[51]

The rush for space and the increase in satellite launches is also accompanied by an increase in places to launch from, and an increasing number of new spaceports are being established around the world.[52] The construction of these spaceports is often opposed by local residents who are concerned about the effects on their environment and the destruction of local ecologies, but their arguments are usually drowned out by promises of jobs and prosperity for their communities. For example, things seemed to be going well for the establishment of a spaceport proposal submitted in July 2018 by Maritime Launch Services (MLS) at Canso in Nova Scotia. However, the Nova Scotia environment minister did not give approval and asked for a detailed Focus Report. MLS submitted a 475-page report in March 2019 which seemed to satisfy the Nova Scotia environment minister who approved the undertaking.[53] However, the report included a description of how the hydrazine fuel to be used to propel their cheap Ukrainian rockets was "a strong irritant" that could cause eye damage and it also stated that repeated exposures could even result in liver and kidney damage.[54] As plans were for eight of these rockets to be launched per year from the site which is just a few kilometres from local residences and the town's hospital, residents became concerned and formed an opposition group calling itself "Action Against Canso Spaceport". They were also concerned about the potential damage to the environment and traditional way of life of the community.

The Municipal and Provincial governments repeatedly claimed that there was local support for the spaceport and when a pro-spaceport petition was tabled by local politician Lloyd Hines in April 2019, "Action Against Canso Spaceport" declared that 60% of the names on the petition were not even from the Canso community. They therefore started their own petition to the Canadian government to stop supporting the project.[55]

However, after MLS declared that it would fly 'green' rockets and use 'green' technology to construct the spaceport,[56] construction was eventually approved in August 2022.[57]

Many spaceports are situated in remote areas, away from large population centres and these are usually places where local wildlife has been left to flourish. However,

Environmental Effects of Space Tourism **119**

they also tend to lack employment opportunities and experience difficulties in retaining a steady population. An example of how various concerns can clash over development can be found in County Sutherland, Scotland.

The UK Space Agency announced its backing for a spaceport on the A'Mhoine peninsula in Sutherland County in July 2018. The Highlands and Islands Enterprise development agency supported the idea and granted £17.3 m to help design and build the spaceport and predicted a reversal in the decline in the local economy and the population.[58]

However, environmental groups raised objections because the site is next to protected peatland, part of the largest blanket bog in Europe and which has an estimated 400 million tonnes of carbon locked within it, playing an important role in combating climate change.[59] The Mhoine is also a Site of Special Scientific Interest (SSSI) and is seeking to become a UNESCO World Heritage Site. A local study expressed concerns that the development of the spaceport would result in destruction of the environment and local traditions, disruption of the peat bog and possible large-scale release of carbon to the atmosphere. Problems could also arise from the use of hazardous substances such as rocket fuel and other substances.[60]

However, although the Highland Council received 457 objections to the plans, with 118 in support, it granted planning permission for the spaceport in August 2020,[61] and this decision was fought at the Scottish Land Court and a Judicial Review was called. The Judicial Review was initiated by Wildland Ltd, a company owned by billionaires Anders and Anne Holch Povlsen who are local landowners. The construction of the spaceport on the Melness Estate was supported by the Melness Crofters' Estate who emphasised the job creation and local investment opportunities. They also suggested that the spaceport would be small and is designed to be carbon-neutral, and the plan is for rockets to use renewable bio-fuel.[62] In addition, the environmental impact would be mitigated by the restoration of areas where peat has been collected in the past using that displaced by the spaceport construction. Eventually, recognising that the Polvsens had a £1.4 m investment in a rival spaceport planned for the Shetland Isles and that the few crofters who had objected to the scheme were being funded by Polvsen, the Scottish Land Court rejected the challenge and approved the plans in September 2021.[63]

## Rocket Propellants

The combustion emissions common to all types of propellants include water vapour ($H_2O$) and nitrogen oxides ($NO_x$, $NO + NO_2$), and other pollutants include black carbon (BC) from carbon-based solid and hypergolic fuels and kerosene, and alumina particles ($Al_2O_3$) and gaseous chlorine (Cl) from solid fuels.[64] Rockets inject these pollutants directly into all atmospheric layers. Space objects re-entering the atmosphere through the mesosphere also emit thermal $NO_x$ from the vaporisation process.[65]

**120** David Webb

**TABLE 8.1** Propellants for current crewed spacecraft

| Organisations | Country | Launch vehicle | Propellants |
|---|---|---|---|
| Roscosmos/RSC Energia | Russia | Soyuz 2 | Refined kerosene/liquid oxygen |
| SpaceX/NASA | USA | Falcon 9 | Refined kerosene/liquid oxygen |
| Blue Origin | USA | New Shepard 4 | Liquid hydrogen/liquid oxygen |
| Virgin Galactic | USA | SpaceShipTwo | HTPB/$N_2O$ |
| CASC | China | Long March 2 | UDMH/NTO |
| NASA | USA | Space Launch System | Liquid hydrogen/liquid oxygen PBAN/APCP |

*Note:* Stuart Parkinson, 'The climatic impacts of spaceflight', *Scientists for Global Responsibility*, 2 October 2021, available at <https://www.sgr.org.uk/sites/default/files/2021-10/SGR_Climatic_impacts_spaceflight_Oct21.pdf> Last visited, 24 February 2022.

Table 8.1 shows the various fuels used by spacecraft that are currently used to transport people. Hypergolic propellants consist of two components, a fuel and an oxidiser that spontaneously ignite when they come into contact. One such combination is UDMH (unsymmetrical dimethylhydrazine) and TCO (nitrogen tetroxide).[66] UDMH was called 'devil's venom' by Soviet scientists. A UN Development Programme report in 2004 reported that it had caused severe environmental damage to a huge area around the Baikonur Cosmodrome launch site in Kazakhstan.[67] A study of accidents at the cosmodrome revealed that the day after a serious accident in 2013, the content of carcinogenic UDH and NDMA (nitro dimethyl amine) exceeded their maximum permissible concentrations by 8,900 and 6,100 times, respectively.[68] An unpublished study led by epidemiologist Sergey Zykov and seen by the scientific journal *Nature* confirms pollution fears raised by environmental groups.[69] Zykov said that Russian space agency officials had a "negative attitude" to studies from outside the agency. The article also claims that another scientist who had campaigned against launches is alleged to have been harassed by security officials.

UDMH is highly carcinogenic and is emitted as the first and second stages of Russia's Proton rockets are released and fall back to the ground.[70] Very little research has been published on this but according to the UN review, UDMH and by-products can stay in the soil for decades.[71] Although Russia no longer uses it, UDMH also powers the first four generations of China's Long March rockets and generations 2–4 are still being used.[72]

NASA used APCP (ammonium perchlorate composite propellant) mixed with polybutadiene acrylonitrile (PBAN) to give the extra thrust required to launch the space shuttles.[73] Following several shuttle launches, large numbers of fish were found dead in nearby waters, and investigations showed that the space shuttle emissions may have temporarily made the water mildly acidic.[74]

Rocket exhaust clouds generated during launch also contain reactive chemicals such as hydrochloric acid and aluminium oxide that become mixed with the water used to cool down the launch pad and rocket. This cloud then spreads out, affecting soil and water quality, and damaging vegetation.[75] In 2005 there were reports that levels of perchlorate in breast milk and vegetables were high in many areas around the United States.[76] Perchlorates occur naturally, but indications were that rockets were contaminating water supplies, and is considered particularly dangerous to children.[77]

## Impacts on the Atmosphere

The Kármán Line is situated at the bottom of the thermosphere, and to get there and beyond, rockets travel through the stratosphere which contains the ozone layer, through the mesosphere and into the thermosphere, where the temperature rises quite rapidly in the extremely sparse atmosphere. Approximately two-thirds of the rocket exhaust from the burning fuel is released into the stratosphere and mesosphere, and the exhaust particles are so small that they stay there and accumulate for 3–4 years.[78]

### Ozone Depletion

Researchers at the University College London (UCL) have measured the mass of pollutants emitted from rocket launches and debris re-entries for each month of 2019. The key pollutants are $NO_x$, $HCl + Cl$, $Al_2O_3$ (aluminium oxide or alumina) and black carbon (BC or soot).[79] These pollutants have a number of harmful effects on the atmosphere. For example, the nitrogen oxides, alumina and chemicals produced from the breakdown of water vapour convert the ozone present into oxygen, which diminishes the ozone layer, and its shielding of dangerous solar UV radiation from the Earth's surface. The water vapour present also produces stratospheric clouds that further speed up the ozone removal process by providing a surface for the reaction to take place. The research at UCL[80] found that rocket pollution had the potential to undermine ~20% of the gains made by the Montreal Protocol to protect the ozone layer by phasing out the many substances that have been causing its depletion. They also found that BC emissions at these very high altitudes produce substantial global warming effects, around 500 times more than surface and aviation sources.[81] It has been calculated that solid-fuelled rockets have emitted over 1,400 tonnes of alumina particles into the stratosphere.[82]

### Climatic Effects

Space travel's contribution to global warming comes from the release of significant amounts of $CO_2$, alumina particles, BC and water vapour into the stratosphere. The amounts of each pollutant are dependent on the type of propulsion used.[83]

Blue Origin's liquid oxygen/hydrogen propellant produces large quantities of water vapour, and the combustion of both the Virgin Galactic and Falcon

**122** David Webb

fuels produce $CO_2$, BC and some water vapour. Rockets that use kerosene, as in SpaceX's Falcon 9 and Russia's Soyuz rockets, emit alumina and BC particles into the stratosphere.[84]

Water vapour is a big contributor to the natural greenhouse effect. Although it has a small effect at ground level, at high altitudes the effects are large as they impact the mesosphere and ionosphere.[85] High-altitude cloud blooms have often been seen that can be attributed to particular launches.[86]

It has been found that BC plays a major role in global warming, and when rockets travel through the stratosphere, a few percent of the emissions they leave behind can be in the form of BC – whereas only about 1% of the emissions of modern jet engines is in the form of BC.[87] However, in 2018 rockets were responsible for depositing about 225 tonnes of BC particles into the stratosphere, which is similar to the amount of BC emitted annually by global air travel. At the same time, the stratosphere received 1,400 tonnes of alumina particles emitted by solid-fuelled rockets.[88]

Virgin Galactic's nitrogen-based oxidant is also responsible for producing nitrogen oxides and compounds that contribute to air pollution. The very high temperatures generated during the launch process and on re-entry of discarded components and/or returning crafts also convert the nitrogen in the atmosphere to nitrogen oxides.[89] Three years of space tourism launches have contributed 6% to global radiative forcing, considerably more than the 0.02% contribution from all other BC sources.[90]

The overall impact of BC and alumina particles is complex as they also slightly reduce the reflective power of the Earth. BC particles absorb and alumina particles reflect solar radiation at the top of the atmosphere and so they both have a cooling effect on the Earth's surface and lower atmosphere. To resolve the complex situation and accurately measure the effects of the sudden rise in rocket emissions will require a sophisticated computer model which has yet to be devised.[91]

**TABLE 8.2** Carbon emissions of crewed spacecraft

| Organisations | Launch vehicle | No. of crew | Carbon emissions per launch ($tCO_2e$) | Carbon emissions per person ($tCO_2e$) |
|---|---|---|---|---|
| Roscosmos/RSC Energia | Soyuz 2 | 3 | 290 | 95 |
| SpaceX/NASA | Falcon 9 | 4 | 510 | 125 |
| NASA | Space Launch System | 4 | 3,660 | 915 |

*Note:* Stuart Parkinson, 'The climatic impacts of spaceflight', presented at 'Linking militarised space and the climate crisis', 2 October 2021 – organised by the *Global Network Against Weapons and Nuclear Power in Space,* available at <https://www.sgr.org.uk/sites/default/files/2021-10/SGR_Climatic_impacts_spaceflight_Oct21.pdf> Last visited, 24 February 2022.

Table 8.2 shows conservative estimates for carbon emissions of space tourism flights by Soyuz and Falcon 9 spacecraft. The Space Launch System example is for the Artemis 1 lunar mission which is due to be launched in 2023.[92] There is no publicly available comparable data for Virgin or Blue Origin vehicles. However, very high carbon emissions are associated with the liquid oxygen and hydrogen fuels used by Blue Origin because the liquification process takes place at temperatures below −253°C at normal atmospheric pressure. This means that very energy-intensive processes are required to create the fuel and then to store it at these temperatures and it has been estimated that, for each tonne of liquid hydrogen used, about 25 tonnes of carbon dioxide equivalent ($tCO_2e$) is emitted.[93] This compares with about 3 $tCO_2e$ for aviation fuel. It has also been estimated that the launch of Blue Origin's New Shepherd spacecraft is responsible for 330 $tCO_2e$ being released.[94]

These are very conservative carbon emission estimates. Other stratospheric heating by the effects of water vapour and other gases could be significant but are not included, and neither are the carbon emissions produced by obtaining the raw materials needed and the manufacture of the rocket and associated infrastructure. The 'carbon emissions per person' category includes essential crew (e.g. the pilot) – so the 'carbon emissions per tourist' is higher.

Space tourism is one of the big drivers behind spacecraft development. However, the burning of the fuels and the journey through the atmosphere are environmentally harmful and are contributing to the global tragedy of climate change. And it is not states that are pushing this industry so much – it is mainly the work of billionaire entrepreneurs who are exploiting the general excitement of exploration and adventure that comes with travelling to the unknown, to grow their space activities, their egos and their income.

Until fairly recently, the space industry has been relatively small and relatively stable and so rocket launches have not been considered to be much of a threat to the global environment. However, the rapid growth of the industry and the lack of research and oversight are now causing some concern.[95]

### Sustainability

Scientists generally agree that more research programmes are needed to investigate the effects of space launches on the Earth's atmosphere and how much they contribute to climate change. One very important question emerges – how sustainable is space tourism in terms of the dangers posed to the planet from climate change? We can measure the contribution to climate change that an activity makes through its carbon footprint. Here, the total greenhouse gas emissions caused by an individual or some activity are expressed in terms of carbon dioxide equivalent ($CO_2e$), as mentioned previously.

The annual carbon footprint of 1 UK citizen is estimated to be 10 $tCO_2e$,[96] and the annual carbon footprint of one person living with a 2030 sustainable lifestyle

**124** David Webb

is estimated as 2.5 $tCO_2e$.[97] Table 8.2 indicates that the carbon footprint of a space tourist flight for one person is at least 100 $tCO_2e$, which means that 1 space tourist flight is equivalent to ten times the annual carbon footprint of a UK citizen and 40 times that required for a sustainable lifestyle in 2030.

Therefore, although it is no surprise perhaps, space tourism can be seen as just another example of global inequality, with the richest 10% of the world population being responsible for almost half of the total emissions and the poorest 50% responsible for 10%.[98]

Space tourism then is set to grow significantly, possibly causing considerable environmental damage. The question of whether there are any laws, treaties, international agreements etc., that might limit the harmful effects of the billionaire space race then arises.

## The Legal Dimension

The 1967 "Outer Space Treaty on Principles Governing the Activities of States in the Exploration and Use of Outer Space, including the Moon and other Celestial Bodies (OST)"[99] is internationally accepted as the multilateral agreement that lays down the foundations of international space law. It came into force in 1967 and states that: "the exploration and use of outer space shall be carried on for the benefit and in the interests of all mankind", stating explicitly that the use of space should be for the benefit of all – not just a few of the super-wealthy.

Article 7 of the OST states that State Parties are "internationally liable for damage [...] on the Earth, in air space or in outer space, including the Moon and other celestial bodies." However, when the treaty was drafted, the environmental effects of space launches themselves were not seen as an issue and so are not explicitly covered.

Article 9 does state that State Parties should "conduct [...] so as to avoid their harmful contamination and also adverse changes in the environment of the Earth resulting from the introduction of extra-terrestrial matter and, where necessary, shall adopt appropriate measures for this purpose" but this refers to the introduction of objects from beyond the Earth into the Earth's environment. So, it does not include space travel originating from the Earth.

The 1972 Convention on International Liability for Damage Caused by Space Objects[100] refers to loss of life, personal injury, or loss of or damage to property – but not to the environmental effects caused by launches or re-entries. In addition, the core objectives of the United Nations Environment Programme (UNEP) are "to serve as an authoritative advocate for the global environment, to support governments in setting the global environmental agenda, and to promote the coherent implementation of the environmental dimension of sustainable development within the UN system".[101] Most of the concern on this subject has however, focussed on space debris, and there is nothing included concerning measuring, monitoring or controlling the effects of spaceflight on the environment.

Therefore, there seem to be no environmental safety standards for space launches and no system to monitor them and ensure that launches and journeys through the atmosphere do not cause environmental damage.

So, until we know a lot more about the environmental effects of space travel, it seems that the best way to proceed is to adopt the precautionary approach:

> In order to protect the environment, the precautionary approach shall be widely applied by States according to their capabilities. Where there are threats of serious or irreversible damage, lack of full scientific certainty shall not be used as a reason for postponing cost-effective measures to prevent environmental degradation.[102]

This approach was adopted by the 1992 Rio Declaration (also the first international instrument to include a definition of the precautionary principle),[103] and should be used as widely as possible; otherwise, the richest few will continue to endanger the survival of the poorest many.

The growing activities of the military in space and concerns of an arms race in space have been of some concern for a long time,[104] and the effects of these activities on space tourism could be very significant.[105] After many years of failure to agree on any treaty to ensure the Prevention of an Arms Race in Outer Space (PAROS),[106] some limited progress was made in November 2021 when the United Nations First Committee approved a new working group to develop rules of the road for military activities in space. Any agreements reached could perhaps even form the basis of a new treaty and, although discussions would be more focussed on activities associated with the military, they are also very likely to include such things as space debris and should also tackle wider environmental concerns and the responsible and sustainable use of space. However, recent history has shown that agreements on these issues are very difficult to achieve, and further talks have already stalled due to the invasion of Ukraine.

## Chapter Conclusion

The recent ventures into space tourism by billionaire entrepreneurs do not bode well for the environment, especially if this activity is extended to become more affordable and more readily available. Indications are that space launches are already causing problems to the Earth's environment – although the extent of these problems may not be totally understood currently. The best way to deal with poorly understood problems is to proceed with caution. The best time to deal with the problem is when it is still small and manageable – and this is especially true when the problem can linger and accumulate over a long period of time.

It is a matter of some urgency therefore that states join together to recognise the environmental problems associated with space launches and space travel. More research needs to be carried out to fully understand the chemistry and the mechanisms of the upper atmosphere and the effects that spacecraft can have on them. More funding and international collaboration is required to enable the complex models to be developed.

It is in everyone's interests to understand the mechanisms involved and take steps to enable the international regulation and monitoring of space launches. All space-faring nations (and would-be spacefarers) should remember the words of the internationally agreed Outer Space Treaty, "the exploration and use of outer space shall be carried on for the benefit and in the interests of all mankind", the excitement and wonder at travelling into space must be considered alongside concerns for environmental sustainability and our responsibility as stewards for life on the planet.

## Notes

1 Karl Tate, 'Fantastic Flight: The Orion III Spaceplane from "2001: A Space Odyssey"', *Space.com*, 15 March 2016, available at <https://www.space.com/32258-orion-space-plane-2001-space-odyssey-photo-essay.html> Last visited, 12 October 2022.

2 Sian Brett, 'How Much Does a Ticket to Space Cost', *Royal Museums Greenwich*, 18 December 2019, available at <https://www.rmg.co.uk/stories/blog/how-much-does-ticket-space-cost-future-space-tourism> Last visited, 24 February 2022.

3 M. Wall, 'First Space Tourist: How a U.S. Millionaire Bought a Ticket to Orbit', *Space.com*, 27 April 2011, available at <https://www.space.com/11492-space-tourism-pioneer-dennis-tito.html> Last visited, 24 February 2022.

4 Harald Sack, 'Dennis Tito, the Very First Space Tourist', *SciHi Blog*, 28 April 2020, available at <http://scihi.org/dennis-tito-space-tourist/> Last visited, 12 October 2022.

5 Emile A. Margolis, 'Space Tourism: Then and Now', Editorial, *Smithsonian National Air and Space Museum*, 25 October 2021, available at <https://airandspace.si.edu/stories/editorial/space-tourism-then-and-now> Last visited, 24 February 2022.

6 'Mark Shuttleworth South African Entrepreneur, Philanthropist, and Space Tourist', *Britannica*, 14 September 2022, available at <https://www.britannica.com/biography/Mark-Shuttleworth> Last visited, 12 October 2022.

7 G.B. Leatherwood, 'Interview with Gregory Olsen', *Space Future,* 8 May 2008, available at <https://www.spacefuture.com/journal/journal.cgi?art=2008.05.08.gregory_olsen_interview> Last visited, 12 October 2022.

8 'Anousheh Ansari American Businesswoman', *Britannica*, 8 September 2022, available at <https://www.britannica.com/biography/Anousheh-Ansari> Last visited, 12 October 2022.

9 'Charles Simonyi American Software Executive and Space Tourist', *Britannica*, 6 September 2022, available at <https://www.britannica.com/biography/Charles-Simonyi> Last visited, 12 October 2022.

10 Catherine Clifford, 'What It's Like to Travel to Space, from a Tourist Who Spent $30 Million to Live There for 12 Days', *CNBC*, 19 October 2018, available at <https://www.cnbc.com/2018/10/19/what-its-like-in-space-from-a-tourist-who-spent-30-million-to-go.html> Last visited, 12 October 2022.

11 Clara Moskowitz, 'Circus Billionaire Says Space Trip Worth Every Penny', *Space.com*, 6 October 2009, available at <https://www.space.com/7375-circus-billionaire-space-trip-worth-penny.html> Last visited, 12 October 2022.

12 'NASA to Open International Space Station to Tourists', *BBC News*, 7 June 2019, available at <https://www.bbc.com/news/world-us-canada-48560874.amp> Last visited, 24 February 2022.

13 Vishwam Sankaran, 'Japanese Billionaire and His Producer Arrive at ISS as First Self-Funded Space Tourists in Over a Decade', *The Independent*, 9 December 2021, available at <https://www.independent.co.uk/space/japanese-billionaire-yusaku-maezawa-iss-b1972647.html> Last visited, 12 October 2022.

14 'Japanese Billionaire Blasts Off to International Space Station', *BBC News*, 8 December 2021, available at <https://www.bbc.co.uk/news/world-asia-59544223> Last visited, 24 February 2022.

15 Steve Gorman, 'Billionaire Branson Soars to Space Aboard Virgin Galactic Flight', *Reuters*, 12 July 2021, available at <https://www.reuters.com/lifestyle/science/virgin-galactics-branson-ready-space-launch-aboard-rocket-plane-2021-07-11> Last visited, 24 February 2022.

16 Leah Crane, 'Who Counts as an Astronaut? Not Jeff Bezos, Say New US Rules', *New Scientist*, 22 July 2021, available at <https://www.newscientist.com/article/2285017-who-counts-as-an-astronaut-not-jeff-bezos-say-new-us-rules/> Last visited, 12 October 2022.

17 Time Levin 'Virgin Galactic Announces Tickets to Space Will Start at $450,000', *yahoo! finance*, 6 August 2021, available at <https://uk.finance.yahoo.com/news/virgin-galactic-sets-ticket-prices-210011652.html> Last visited, 12 October 2022.

18 Richard Speed, 'Another 100 Space Tourists Buy a Ride from Virgin Galactic: $25k of That Ticket Deposit Is "Non-refundable"', *The Register*, 9 November 2021, available at <https://www.theregister.com/2021/11/09/virgin_galactic_q3/> Last visited, 24 February 2022.

19 'Virgin Galactic Sells Tickets to Space', *RT.com*, 16 February 2022, available at <https://www.bignewsnetwork.com/news/272301158/virgin-galactic-sells-tickets-to-space> Last visited, 24 February 2022.

20 Lia De La Cruz, 'Jeff Bezos' Blue Origin Flight Soars to the Edge of Space', *Earth Sky*, 20 July 2021, available at <https://earthsky.org/space/jeff-bezos-blue-origin-flight-on-july-20/> Last visited, 24 February 2022.

21 Chris Ciaccia, 'Luckiest Boy in the World? Private Equity Boss's Son, 18, Replaces Anonymous Bidder Who Paid $28m to Fly on Jeff Bezos's Blue Origin Rocket but Had to Pull Out After "Scheduling Conflict"', *Mail Online*, 15 July 2021, available at <https://www.dailymail.co.uk/sciencetech/article-9792075/18-year-old-physics-student-takes-place-28M-auction-winner-fly-Jeff-Bezos-space.html> Last visited, 12 October 2022.

22 Michael Sheetz, 'Jeff Bezos' Blue Origin Successfully Launches Crew with William Shatner to Space and Back', *CNBC*, 13 October 2021, available at <https://www.cnbc.com/2021/10/13/watch-william-shatner-go-to-space-with-jeff-bezos-blue-origin.html> Last visited, 24 February 2022.

23 Eric Betz, 'The Karman Line: Where Does Space Begin?', *Astronomy*, 5 March 2021, available at <https://astronomy.com/news/2021/03/the-krmn-line-where-does-space-begin> Last visited, 12 October 2022.

24 Lia De La Cruz, 'The Billionaire Space Race and the Karman Line', *Earth Sky*, 14 July 2021, available at <https://earthsky.org/human-world/the-billionaire-space-race-and-the-karman-line> Last visited, 24 February 2022.

25 Eric M. Johnson, 'Jeff Bezos Plans to Charge at least $200,000 for Space Rides', *Reuters*, 13 July 2018, available at <https://www.reuters.com/article/us-space-blueorigin-exclusive-idUSKBN1K301R> Last visited, 24 February 2022.

26 Jeff Foust 'Blue Origin to Increase New Shepard Launches in 2022', *Spacenews*, 18 February 2022, available at <https://spacenews.com/blue-origin-to-increase-new-shepard-launches-in-2022/> Last visited, 12 October 2022.

27 "Blue Moon", *Blue Origin*, available at <https://www.blueorigin.com/blue-moon/> Last visited, 12 October 2022.

28 'State Support for Commercial Space Activities', *Federal Aviation Administration*, available at <https://www.faa.gov/about/office_org/headquarters_offices/ast/media/State

128 David Webb

%20Support%20for%20Commercial%20Space%20Activities.pdf> Last visited, 24 February 2022.

29 Stephen Clark, 'NASA Formally Certifies SpaceX's Crew Dragon for "Operational" Astronaut Flights', *Spaceflight Now*, 7 October 2022, available at <https://spaceflightnow.com/2020/11/10/nasa-formally-certifies-spacexs-crew-dragon-for-operational-astronaut-flights/> Last visited, 12 October 2022.

30 'The First All-Civilian Mission to Orbit', available at <https://inspiration4.com/> Last visited, 12 October 2022.

31 Space Station', *SpaceX website*, available at <https://www.spacex.com/human-spaceflight/iss/index.html> Last visited, 24 February 2022.

32 'Commercial Crew Transportation', *NASA factsheet*, available at <https://www.nasa.gov/sites/default/files/atoms/files/ccp_olia_fact_sheet_final_508-10-27.pdf> Last visited, 24 February 2022.

33 Simon Thomsen, 'Elon Musk Wants to Fly People Around the World in Under an Hour', *Business Insider Australia*, 29 September 2017, available at <https://www.businessinsider.com.au/elon-musk-wants-to-fly-people-around-the-world-in-under-an-hour-2017-9> Last visited, 24 February 2022.

34 Patrick May, 'New York to Shanghai in 39 Minutes? Elon Musk's Latest Revolution', *The Mercury News*, 29 September 2017, available at <https://www.mercurynews.com/2017/09/29/new-york-to-shanghai-in-39-minutes-elon-musks-latest-revolution/> Last visited, 12 October 2022.

35 Leah Crane, 'Elon Musk's New Plans for a Moon Base and a Mars Mission by 2022', *New Scientist*, 29 September 2017, available at <https://www.newscientist.com/article/2149003-elon-musks-new-plans-for-a-moon-base-and-a-mars-mission-by-2022/> Last visited, 12 October 2022.

36 Mike Wall, 'Axiom Space: Building the Off-Earth Economy', *Space.com*, 17 January 2022, available at <https://www.space.com/axiom-space> Last visited, 24 February 2022.

37 Michael Sheetz, 'Super Fast Travel Using Outer Space Could Be $20 Billion Market, Disrupting Airlines, UBS Predicts', *CNBC*, 18 March 2018, available at <https://www.cnbc.com/2019/03/18/ubs-space-travel-and-space-tourism-a-23-billion-business-in-a-decade.html> Last visited, 24 February 2022.

38 Robert A. Braeunig, 'Rocket Propellants', *Rocket & Space Technology*, 2008, available at <http://www.braeunig.us/space/propel.htm> Last visited, 12 October 2022.

39 'Booster Staging', NASA, available at <https://www.grc.nasa.gov/www/k-12/rocket/rktstage.html> Last visited, 12 October 2022.

40 *Id.*

41 Eytan Tepper and Jean-Frédéric Morin, 'The Mega Disruption: Satellite Constellations and Space-based Internet', *Centre for International Governance Innovation*, 31 August 2020, available at <https://www.cigionline.org/articles/mega-disruption-satellite-constellations-and-space-based-internet/> Last visited, 12 October 2022.

42 Jonathan O'Callaghan, 'SpaceX's Application for 30,000 Extra Starlink Satellites Highlights Concerns About Regulation', *Forbes*, 16 October 2019, available at <https://www.forbes.com/sites/jonathanocallaghan/2019/10/16/spacex-accused-of-evading-rules-with-proposal-for-30000-extra-starlink-satellites/> Last visited, 24 February 2022.

43 Jeff Foust, 'Astronomers Warn About Effects of Other Satellite Megaconstellations', *SpaceNews*, 4 June 2020, available at <https://spacenews.com/astronomers-warn-about-effects-of-other-satellite-megaconstellations/> Last visited, 12 October 2022.

44 Desmond King-Hele, *Satellite Orbits in an Atmosphere – Theory and Applications* (Glasgow: Blackie, 1987).

45 Ashish, 'Graveyard Orbit: What Happens When Artificial Satellites Die?', *Science ABC*, available at <https://www.scienceabc.com/nature/universe/graveyard-orbit-what-happens-when-artificial-satellites-die.html> Last visited, 12 October 2022.

46 Aayesdha Arif, 'This Is How Satellites Avoid Colliding into Each Other', *Wonderful Engineering.*, 15 February 2017, available at <https://wonderfulengineering.com/satellite-collision/> Last visited, 12 October 2022.

47 'Space Debris by Numbers', *European Space Agency*, 5 January 2022, available at <https://www.esa.int/Safety_Security/Space_Debris/Space_debris_by_the_numbers> Last visited, 24 February 2022.

48 Nicole Mortillaro, 'Space Junk Threatens to Disrupt Our Daily Lives. Here's What Experts Are Trying to do About It', *CBC News*, 26 February 2018, available at <https://www.cbc.ca/news/science/space-debris-1.4545467> Last visited, 24 February 2022.

49 Donald J. Kessler and Burton G. Cour-Palais, 'Collision Frequency of Artificial Satellites: The Creation of a Debris Belt', *Journal of Geophysical Research*, 1 June 1978, available at <https://doi.org/10.1029/JA083iA06p02637> Last visited, 24 February 2022.

50 Constance Walker, Jeffrey Hall, Lori Allen et al. 'Impact of Satellite Constellations on Optical Astronomy and Recommendations Toward Mitigation', *Bulletin of the AAS*, Vol. 52, No. 2, 25 August 2020, available at <https://baas.aas.org/pub/2020i0206/release/1> Last visited, 24 February 2022.

51 George Chambers, 'Kodiak Island Spaceport Reopens Following 2014 Launch Failure', *NASA Spaceflight*, 25 August 2016, available at <https://www.nasaspaceflight.com/2016/08/kodiak-spaceport-reopens-2014-failure/> Last visited, 24 February 2022.

52 Jeff Foust, 'More Spaceports, More Problems', *Space News*, 25 February 2022, available at <https://spacenews.com/more-spaceports-more-problems/> Last visited, 12 October 2022.

53 'Canso Spaceport Facility Project', *Nova Scotia Canada*, available at <https://www.novascotia.ca/nse/ea/canso-spaceport-facility/> Last visited, 12 October 2022.

54 Joan Baxter, 'Opposition to Canso Spaceport Grows', *Halifax Examiner*, 5 August 2019, available at <https://www.halifaxexaminer.ca/province-house/opposition-to-canso-spaceport-grows/> Last visited, 24 February 2022.

55 'Stop the Canso Spaceport Project', *change.org*, October 2021, available at <https://www.change.org/p/justin-trudeau-stop-the-canso-spaceport-project-60e96b97-f70d-4778-b22f-ce51d127d3f8> Last visited, 12 October 2022.

56 Elizabeth Howell, 'Nova Scotia Spaceport Project Aims to Launch Clean-Tech Rockets', *Space.com*, 2 September 2022, available at <https://www.space.com/spaceport-america-private-space-competition-canada> Last visited, 12 October 2022.

57 Maritime Services, 'Maritime Launch to Begin Construction of Spaceport Nova Scotia', 29 August 2022, available at <https://www.maritimelaunch.com/news/maritime-launch-begin-construction-spaceport-nova-scotia> Last visited, 12 October 2022.

58 Dani Garavelli, 'The Battle to Build UK's First Spaceport in Sutherland', *The Scotsman*, 20 June 2021, available at <https://www.scotsman.com/news/environment/insight-the-battle-to-build-scotlands-spaceport-3279541> Last visited, 12 October 2022.

59 Ellie Howard, 'Scotland's 10,000-Year-Old Wild Heartland', *BBC*, 3 August 2020, available at <https://www.bbc.com/travel/article/20200802-scotlands-10000-year-old-wild-heartland> Last visited, 12 October 2022.

60 M. Danson, G. Whittam, and J. Wyper, "Satellites to Sutherland-Not-Quite Coals to Newcastle!'. *17th Rural Entrepreneurship Conference, Impact Hub Inverness/UHI*, 17–19 June 2019.

61 'Sutherland Space Hub Secures Planning Permission', *BBC*, 19 August 2020, available at <https://www.bbc.co.uk/news/uk-scotland-highlands-islands-53834962> Last visited, 12 October 2022.

62 'Scotland's Sustainable Spaceport', *Melness Crofters' Estate*, 4 October 2021, available at <https://www.melness.scot/news/scotlands-sustainable-spaceport> Last visited 12 October 2022.

63 'Scottish Land Court Rules in Favour of Space Hub Sutherland', *Scottish Legal News*, 14 September 2021, available at <https://www.scottishlegal.com/articles/scottish-land-court-rules-in-favour-of-space-hub-sutherland> Last visited, 12 October 2022.

64 J.A. Dallas, S. Raval, J.P. Alvarez Gaitn, S. Saydam, and A.G. Demspter, 'The Environmental Impact of Emissions from Space Launches: A Comprehensive Review', *Journal of Cleaner Production*, Vol. 255, 28 January 2020, available at <https://www.sciencedirect.com/science/article/pii/S0959652620302560> Last visited, 24 February 2022.

65 See for example, C. Park and J.V. Rakich, 'Equivalent-Cone Calculation of Nitric Oxide Production Rate during Spaceshuttle Re-entry', *Atmospheric Environment*, Vol. 14, No. 8, 1967, pp. 19–72.

66 Beverly Perry, 'We've got (rocket) Chemistry', *NASA*, 21 April, 2016, available at <https://blogs.nasa.gov/Rocketology/tag/rocket-fuel/> Last visited, 12 October 2022.

67 'Environment and Development Nexus in Kazakhstan', *United Nations Development Program*, Technical Report UNDPKAZ 06, 2004.

68 T.V. Koroleva, et al. 'Ecological Consequences of Space Rocket Accidents in Kazakhstan between 1999 and 2018', *Environmental Pollution*, Vol. 268, Part A, January 2021 *Journal of Cleaner Production*, 255, 28 January 2020, available at <https://www.sciencedirect.com/science/article/abs/pii/S0269749120364009> Last visited, 24 February 2022.

69 Jim Giles, 'Study Links Sickness to Russian Launch Site', *Nature*, 12 January 2005, available at <https://rdcu.be/cHAM7> Last visited, 24 February 2022.

70 Tereza Pultarova, 'The Environmental Impact of Rocket Launches: The "dirty" and the "green"', *Space.com*, 28 October 2021, available at <https://www.space.com/rocket-launches-environmental-impact> Last visited, 24 February 2022; more information on the environmental damage around Baikonur at <https://factsanddetails.com/central-asia/Kazakhstan/sub8_4f/entry-4685.html#chapter-0> Last visited, 24 February 2022.

71 *Id.*

72 *Id.*

73 *Id.*

74 *Id.*

75 *Id.*

76 Robert Roy Britt, 'Rocket Fuel Chemical Found in Breast Milk of Women in 18 States', *Live Science*, Vol. 24, February 2005, available at <https://www.livescience.com/177-rocket-fuel-chemical-breast-milk-women-18-states.html> Last visited, 24 February 2022.

77 *Id.*

78 Eloise Marais, 'Space Tourism: Rockets Emit 100 Times More CO2 per Passenger Than Flights – Imagine a Whole Industry', *The Conversation*, 19 July 2021, available at <https://theconversation.com/space-tourism-rockets-emit-100-times-more-co-per-passenger-than-flights-imagine-a-whole-industry-164601> Last visited, 24 February 2022.

79 *Id.*

80 *Id.*

81 R. G. Ryan, et al. 'Impact of Rocket Launch and Space Debris Air Pollutant Emissions on Stratospheric Ozone and Global Climate', *Earth and Space Open Archive*, 12 February 2022, available at <https://doi.org/10.1002/essoar.10510460.1> Last visited, 24 February 2022.

82 M.N. Ross and D.W. Toohey, 'The Coming Surge of Rocket Emissions', *Eos*, 24 September 2019, available at <https://eos.org/features/the-coming-surge-of-rocket-emissions> Last visited, 24 February 2022; E.J. Marc et al. 'Global Civil Aviation Black Carbon Emissions', *Environment, Science & Technology*, Vol. 47, No. 18, 2013,

pp. 10397–10404, available at <https://pubs.acs.org/doi/abs/10.1021/es401356v> Last visited, 24 February 2022.

83 'How Much Air Pollution Do Rocket Launches Cause?' *Breeze Technologies*, 22 October 2021, available at <https://www.breeze-technologies.de/blog/how-much-air-pollution-do-rocket-launches-cause/> Last visited, 12 October 2022.

84 *Id.*

85 Jonathan H. Jiang, et al. 'An Assessment of Upper Troposphere and Lower Stratosphere Water Vapor in MERRA, MERRA2, and ECMWF Reanalyses Using Aura MLS Observations', Journal of Geophysical Research, Vol. 120, No. 22, 27 November 2015, pp 11,468–11,485, available at <https://doi.org/10.1002/2015JD023752> Last visited, 12 October 2022.

86 Michael H. Stevens, et al. 'Bright Polar Mesospheric Clouds Formed by Main Engine Exhaust from the Space Shuttle's Final Launch', Journal of Geophysical Research, Vol. 117, D19, 5 October 2012, available at <https://doi.org/10.1029/2012JD017638> Last visited, 24 February 2022.

87 Frederick Simmons, *Rocket Exhaust Plume Phenomenology* (Reston: The Aerospace Press, 2000).

88 *Supra* note 83.

89 R.G. Ryan, E.A. Marais, C.J. Balhatchet, and S.D. Eastham, 'Impact of Rocket Launch and Space Debris Air Pollutant Emissions on Stratospheric Ozone and Global Climate', *Earth and Space Open Archive*, 12 February 2022, available at <https://doi.org/10.1002/essoar.10510460.1> Last visited, 24 February 2022.

90 'Radiative forcing' is defined by the IPCC as a measure of the influence a given climatic factor has on the amount of downward-directed energy transferred to the Earth's surface by electromagnetic and thermal radiation. See for example, Martin N. Ross and Patti M. Sheaffer, 'Radiative Forcing Caused by Rocket Engine Emissions', *Earth's Future*, Vol. 2, 2014, pp. 177–196, available at <https://doi.org/10.1002/2013EF000160> Last visited, 24 February 2022.

91 *Id.*

92 'Artemis 1', *NASA*, available at <https://www.nasa.gov/artemis-1> Last visited, 24 February 2022.

93 Robert Rapier, 'Estimating the Carbon Footprint of Hydrogen Production', *Forbes*, 6 June 2020, available at <https://www.forbes.com/sites/rrapier/2020/06/06/estimating-the-carbon-footprint-of-hydrogen-production/?sh=6722565424bd> Last visited, 12 October 2022.

94 M. Berners-Lee, *How Bad Are Bananas?* (London: Profile books, 2020) p. 150.

95 Jocelyn Timperley 'Billionaire Space Race: What Does It Mean for Climate Change and the Environment?', *Science Focus*, 12th August 2021, available at <https://www.sciencefocus.com/news/billionaire-space-race-what-does-it-mean-for-climate-change-and-the-environment> Last visited, 24 February 2022.

96 'Carbon Footprint: Exploring the UK's Contribution to Climate Change', *WWF*, 2020, available at <https://www.wwf.org.uk/sites/default/files/2020-04/FINAL-WWF-UK_Carbon_Footprint_Analysis_Report_March_2020%20%28003%29.pdf> Last visited, 24 February 2022.

97 '1.5-Degree Lifestyles', *IGES*, 2019, available at <https://www.iges.or.jp/en/pub/15-degrees-lifestyles-2019/en> Last visited, 24 February 2022.

98 'Extreme Carbon Inequality: Why the Paris Climate Deal Must Put the Poorest, Lowest Emitting and Most Vulnerable People First', *Oxfam*, 2015, available at <https://policy-practice.oxfam.org/resources/extreme-carbon-inequality-why-the-paris-climate-deal-must-put-the-poorest-lowes-582545> Last visited, 24 February 2022.

99 'The Outer Space Treaty on Principles Governing the Activities of States in the Exploration and Use of Outer Space, Including the Moon and other Celestial Bodies',

*United Nations Office for Outer Space Affairs*, available at <https://www.unoosa. org/oosa/en/ourwork/spacelaw/treaties/introouterspacetreaty.html> Last visited, 24 February 2022.

100 'International Liability for Damage Caused by Space Objects', *United Nations Office for Outer Space Affairs*, available at <https://www.unoosa.org/oosa/en/ourwork/ spacelaw/treaties/introliability-convention.html> Last visited, 24 February 2022.

101 'United Nations Environment Programme', *Climate ADAPT*, available at <https:// climate-adapt.eea.europa.eu/metadata/organisations/united-nations-environment-programme> Last visited, 24 February 2022.

102 Science for Environment Policy, 'The Precautionary Principle: Decision-Making Under Uncertainty', *European Commission*, Issue 18, September 2017, available at <https:// ec.europa.eu/environment/integration/research/newsalert/pdf/precautionary_principle_ decision_making_under_uncertainty_FB18_en.pdf> Last visited, 24 February 2022.

103 Jose Felix Pinto-Bazurco, 'The Precautionary Principle', *IISDO Earth Negotiations Bulletin*, October 2020 <https://www.iisd.org/system/files/2020-10/still-one-earth-precautionary-principle.pdf> Last visited, 24 February 2022.

104 See for example: S. Ghoshroy (ed.) 'Missile Defense Systems and Weapons in Space – Serious Consequences for Global Peace and Security', *The International Network of Engineers and Scientists*, October 2021 <http://inesglobal.net/2021/10/06/ international-group-of-scientists-and-academics-issues-urgent-call-to-ban-missile-defense-and-space-weapons/> Last visited, 24 February 2022.

105 K. Grossman, 'Can Space Tourism Co-exist with Space Being Turned into a War Zone?', presented at the *Space Tourism: Legal Dimensions Conference*, January 29, 2022 available at <http://space4peace.org/can-space-tourism-co-exist-with-space-being-turned-into-a-war-zone/>Last visited, 24 February 2022.

106 D. Webb and J. Scheffran, 'Prevention of an Arms Race in Outer Space (PAROS): Obstacles and Options', International Working Group, Moving Beyond Missile Defense, *The International Network of Engineers and Scientists*, October 2021 available at <http:// inesglobal.net/wp-content/uploads/2021/10/section-10-webb-scheffran-space-ban.pdf> Last visited, 24 February 2022.

# 9

# LEGAL STRATEGIES TO PRESERVE THE NATURAL AND CULTURAL HERITAGE OF SPACE

*Jennifer A. Brobst*

## Introduction

Tourism on Earth and beyond is motivated by a number of interests, from a sense of adventure or desire for luxury to more intellectual pursuits. When tourism relates to an interest in natural and cultural heritage, legal intervention is ordinarily required to ensure its continued enjoyment and preservation as a public commons.[1] The Budapest Declaration of 2002, adopted by members of the United Nations Educational, Scientific and Cultural Organization (UNESCO), states that "[t]he properties on the World Heritage List are assets held in trust to pass on to generations of the future as their rightful inheritance".[2] The UNESCO World Heritage Convention recognises "that parts of the cultural or natural heritage are of outstanding interest and therefore need to be preserved as part of the world heritage of mankind as a whole".[3]

In the last 20 years, the first space tourism events focused on adventure and luxury, largely antithetical to the notion of a public commons. Legal concerns for the initial wealthy space tourists focus primarily on personal liability and safety, often resolved through liability waivers acceptable to the affluent clientele.[4] In 2022, Virgin Galactic's marketing as the first commercial space flight enterprise or "spaceline" touts that passengers, who can afford the 90-minute journey, will "[e]xperience weightlessness, breathtaking views of Earth, and a life-changing transformation through our unique and innovative spaceflight system, all in unparalleled comfort".[5] NASA has recently hosted wealthy guests for brief tourist visits to the International Space Station, launched by commercial spaceflights such as SpaceX. In addition, "Russia has been hosting tourists at the space station – and before that the Mir station – for decades".[6]

DOI: 10.4324/9781032617961-9

**134** Jennifer A. Brobst

While ongoing commercial space tourism for the wealthy is now a reality, nascent planning by State actors for the preservation of natural and cultural heritage in space will soon follow, from conservation of the first landing site on the Moon to space parks, on-site memorials and museums in space. In the competition for luxury spaceflight, entrepreneurs will "be happy if the Federal government just leaves space alone".[7] However, as discussed below, the public's common interest in space heritage will demand more governmental intervention and oversight from individual states and the international legal community. The parallel history of the national parks movement, international treaties related to the law of the high seas and Antarctica, and the implementation of the UNESCO World Heritage Convention offer some guidance on a potential legal framework that would help preserve the natural and cultural heritage of orbital and outer space.

## The Parks Movement Extending into Space

Since the late nineteenth century, most countries have engaged in conservation efforts through the formation of public parks, funded and maintained by their governments. Some have critically argued this is an extension of colonialist, imperialist sentiment.[8] The very act of carving boundaries for protection on Earth is a national effort to control both nature and property.[9] For space-faring nations such as the United States, conceptualising a Space Frontier arguably reflects "an ideology of American exceptionalism and reinforced longstanding beliefs in progress, growth, and capitalist democracy" which would involve "the colonization, exploitation, and development of space".[10] In Russia, the Museum of Cosmonautics displays an "outstanding city landmark" of architectural design entitled "The Monument to the Conquerors of Space".[11] Also, if Earth's creation of parks was initially a Western construct imposed on developing nations without recognition of their diversity of viewpoints, as a result, it "denies the value of non-Western sensibilities towards nature and obscures significant differences in the way parks were incorporated into non-Western societies".[12] As of 2010, almost 13% of the land surface of the Earth was governed as a park or other protected space by governmental bodies.[13] However, none of the expanses of orbital and outer space is currently designated for preservation or established as a park.

Despite such criticism, efforts to preserve cultural heritage and the environment's biodiversity and unique beauty also demonstrate humanity's intellectual curiosity and care for the environment and future generations. The expressions of astronauts reflecting on their experience also should not be dismissed as sentimental or superficial merely because they are optimistic. Sally Ride, the first American woman in space, remarked: "Studying whether there's life on Mars or studying how the universe began, there's something magical about pushing back the frontiers of knowledge. That's something that is almost part of being human, and I'm certain that will continue."[14] China's first astronaut in space, Yang Liwei, reportedly said to his wife upon his return, "I saw our planet … It's so beautiful, like you."[15]

Legal Strategies to Preserve the Natural and Cultural Heritage **135**

The parks movement reflects humanity's complex understanding of itself and its environment, in a simultaneously selfish, cooperative and selfless manner. Over time, the World Heritage Convention has also adapted to a better understanding of cultural diversity and the problematic history of human conquest. For example, the Budapest Declaration on World Heritage asserted the need to ensure that the 1972 UNESCO World Heritage Convention "applies to heritage in all its diversity, as an instrument for the sustainable development of all societies through dialogue and mutual understanding".[16]

An interest in space heritage cannot be denied.[17] Quietly, dark sky parks have arisen across the Earth as preserved spaces in more industrialised nations. The International Dark-Sky Association designates public and private regions as "a land possessing an exceptional or distinguished quality of starry nights and a nocturnal environment that is specifically protected for its scientific, natural, educational, cultural heritage, and/or public enjoyment".[18] Of course, many less populated nations continue to enjoy the nightly spectacle of a starry sky without significant light pollution – an experience that human ancestors experienced for millions of years. UNESCO, along with organisations such as the UN World Tourism Organization, has supported similar work based on the 2007 Declaration in Defence of the Night Sky and the Right to Starlight.[19] This Declaration asserts that "an unpolluted night sky that allows the enjoyment and contemplation of the firmament should be considered an inalienable right of humankind equivalent to all other environmental, social, and cultural rights[.]"[20] The United Nations soon after declared 2009 as the International Year of Astronomy in a proclamation defining the night sky as a part of the common and universal heritage of humankind.[21]

In addition to appreciation of the scenic beauty and educational value of personally seeing celestial bodies from Earth, UNESCO has acknowledged the relevance of astronomy on Earth to the world's cultural heritage, such as Mayan and Incan observatories in Central and South America.[22] Heritage preservation on Earth of human space travel appears in museums around the world, allowing members of the public to see the first rockets on display at the Museum of Cosmonautics in Moscow or at the Smithsonian's National Air and Space Museum in Washington, D.C.[23] Finally, the use of space exploration already benefits conservation and park preservation efforts on Earth through the use of satellite imagery of protected areas of land and sea.[24] Extending these efforts into space itself is a natural next step but one which requires careful discussion of the legal implementation and requisite international cooperation.

## The UNESCO Framework for Natural and Cultural Preservation

National parks and world heritage sites on Earth are circumscribed by property rights, but protection of space beyond Earth's atmosphere requires a different analysis. The widely adopted Outer Space Treaty of 1967 provides that outer space and celestial bodies are not subject to national appropriation by claim of sovereignty.[25] Moreover, exploration and use of outer space must be "in accordance with international law, including the Charter of the United Nations, in the interest of maintaining international peace and security and promoting international co-operation and understanding".[26] Thus, existing international frameworks addressing heritage preservation should be examined if natural and cultural heritage in outer space is to be protected. The most relevant instrument is the UNESCO World Heritage Convention.[27] However, this requires recognition that cultural heritage subject to property ownership, such as the International Space Station, will more easily fit within existing frameworks than natural heritage in areas of space that, by definition, legally belong to everyone and no one.

Without legal protection, space heritage potentially is vulnerable to permanent destruction and loss from competing interests, misuse and neglect. In 2023, the UN World Heritage Committee listed 55 world heritage sites in danger, an increase of three new endangered sites since 2022.[28] These are primarily located in Africa and the Middle East, and are subject to destruction due to climate change, mining, lack of resources and human conflict.[29] Fortunately, before humanity engages in more extensive space flight, anticipatory efforts to ensure protection of valuable sites and artefacts can be made, with the understanding that looting and exploitation would likely occur without legal measures.[30] As the American jurist Oliver Wendell Holmes stated, "[a]s long as the 'possessory' instinct remains, it will be more comfortable for the law to satisfy it in an orderly manner, than to leave people to themselves".[31]

The 1972 World Heritage Convention, seeking the preservation of natural and cultural human heritage, has been ratified by nearly 200 nations.[32] Its 50-year history parallels that of humanity's history of space exploration. In 1977, the World Heritage Committee put forth its first Operational Guidelines, which stated: "The cultural and natural heritage are for each nation and the international community amongst their most important and priceless possessions".[33] As of July 2021, there were 1,154 world heritage sites among 167 States Parties, of which 897 are cultural, 218 are natural and 39 are mixed.[34]

Again, some have been critical of the endeavour, asserting that

> [i]nternational conservationists like the founding director of UNESCO, Julian Huxley, used [national parks] as a moral yardstick to remind the colonies recently released into independence that in the modern world, a country without a national park can hardly be recognized as civilized.[35]

In fact, the first inscribed heritage site was L'Anse aux Meadows National Historic Park in 1978, in Newfoundland, Canada[36] – a site of human exploration and conquest as an eleventh-century Viking landing site, and the first known European presence in the New World.[37] Many spectacular natural and cultural heritage sites exist across Earth today, such as Tikal National Park in Guatemala, Sundarbans National Park in West Bengal, India, and Victoria Falls in Zimbabwe.[38]

As a matter of public interest, a UNESCO framework that already recognises human exploration and unique, spectacular natural settings would work well in preserving the history of space exploration and settlement. Although most cultural world heritage sites have been located in well-populated regions, quite unlike the human experience in space to date, first landing sites and settlements frequently have been subjects of preservation, such as the first UNESCO cultural heritage site in Canada. On Earth, designated natural world heritage sites are often in less populated regions where humanity has appreciated the beauty of lush, hospitable landscapes, as well as stark and inhospitable but exquisite landscapes. For example, the Ténéré Desert in Niger, Antarctica, and the world's vast oceans have all been the focus of UNESCO preservation efforts.[39] Unique space objects and other planetary landscapes should attract similar interest in receiving human protection.

### The Promise and Limitations of the UNESCO World Heritage Convention in Space

Under the UNESCO World Heritage Convention, only States Parties to the Convention may nominate a natural or cultural heritage site, and the site must exist under their territorial boundaries.[40] Nominations are reviewed by intergovernmental bodies which inform the UN World Heritage Committee's decision.[41] Under its Operational Guidelines, a designated world heritage site must meet certain criteria for inscription, regardless of whether a site relates to natural or cultural heritage. First, it must demonstrate "Outstanding Universal Value".[42] That is, it must be "so exceptional as to transcend national boundaries and to be of common importance for present and future generations of all humanity".[43] Second, it must meet at least one of ten criteria which support a finding of outstanding universal value, such as the following, which are most applicable in the outer space environment:

i represent a masterpiece of creative genius;
ii exhibit an important interchange of values, over a span of time or within a cultural area of the world, on developments in architecture or technology, monumental arts, town-planning or landscape design;
vii contain superlative natural phenomena or areas of exceptional natural beauty or aesthetic importance;
viii [provide a record of Earth's history, as well as a record of life and geological processes].[44]

The last criterion could easily be amended to include a record of the history of Earth "and other celestial bodies". Similarly, the term "world" in the World Heritage

**138** Jennifer A. Brobst

Convention should be amended to connote the totality of the human experience, which is no longer bound by gravity to the planet's surface.

*Protection of Cultural Space Heritage through UNESCO and National Sovereignty*

As members of the World Heritage Convention, individual States are obligated under Articles 4 and 5 to protect their world heritage sites and under Article 6 to cooperate with and assist other Member States in protecting their sites.[45] Articles 19 through 26 address international assistance through the World Heritage Committee and Fund.[46] However, Article 25 states:

> As a general rule, only part of the cost of work necessary shall be borne by the international community. The contribution of the State benefiting from international assistance shall constitute a substantial share of the resources devoted to each programme or project, unless its resources do not permit this.[47]

While reporting on the progress of State preservation of designated world heritage sites to UNESCO is required,[48] there is no enforcement mechanism other than a mutual interest in cooperation and public attention via the highly publicised List of World Heritage in Danger.[49] For example, one of the listed World Heritage in Danger sites is the Tropical Rainforest of Sumatra (Indonesia), and UNESCO's analysis is public but not prescriptive:

> The State Party's commitment not to grant permits for geothermal energy exploration within the property is *welcomed*, and the State Party should be *encouraged* to reflect this commitment through legislation to rule out the possibility of future geothermal development proposals within World Heritage properties.[50]

Article VI of the Outer Space Treaty also requires, but cannot enforce, that "States Parties to the Treaty shall bear international responsibility for national activities in outer space, including the Moon and other celestial bodies, whether such activities are carried on by governmental agencies or by non-governmental entities[.]"[51]

The protection and preservation of cultural heritage in space, such as landing equipment left on the Moon, may fit this framework, but conservation of scenic beauty of outstanding universal value in space, in the interests of preventing human activity, would require a new international agreement if no State appropriation of territory is permitted. That is, no State sovereign could designate a world heritage site in space if it held no authority to assert sovereignty. Here, international agreements for the use and protection of public commons, such as those related to the high seas, are instructive.

## A Need for a New International Agreement to Preserve the Natural Heritage of Space

A new international agreement is necessary to preserve the natural heritage of space, such as a future tourist destination to the Olympus Mons on Mars, the solar system's largest volcano.[52] Under the UN Convention on the Law of the Sea, "innocent passage" is permitted to all States in territorial waters if made without threat to the territorial sovereign State or pollution or exploitation of its territory.[53] However, like space travel, "[t]he high seas are open to all States, whether coastal or land-locked. Freedom of the high seas is exercised under the conditions laid down by this Convention [on the Law of the Sea] and by other rules of international law".[54] Importantly, Article 89 asserts that "[n]o State may validly purport to subject any part of the high seas to its sovereignty".[55] Yet cooperative preservation of resources is required. "All States have the duty to take, or to cooperate with other States in taking, such measures for their respective nationals as may be necessary for the conservation of the living resources of the high seas".[56] Even if UNESCO's World Heritage Convention, with its emphasis on national nomination and responsibility, would not easily apply to natural heritage sites in space, the type of international cooperative purpose that would be required to protect such sites could still rely on determinations of outstanding universal value.[57]

The Convention on the Law of the Sea promises territorial freedom and lays out specific duties of preservation and conservation. However, it does not provide an easy solution to ensuring adequate enforcement. Although the high seas comprise two-thirds of the world's oceans, only around 1% of the high seas is reportedly protected.[58] According to one researcher, the "patchwork approach to high seas governance" raises significant concerns, including the absence of an available international legal mechanism to create comprehensive marine protection or even environmental impact assessment.[59] States are, instead, expected to regulate themselves when they cause harm to the environment on the high seas,[60] subject to international law.[61] In the early days of space exploration, there has been little need for policing or protection from theft and vandalism. However, as discussed below, heritage sites may offer both a target of international conflict as well as a promising opportunity for finding common ground.

## Promoting International Peace and Cooperation through Respect for Common Heritage

The UNESCO World Heritage Convention seeks to preserve a legacy of cultural and natural heritage, but it also offers an indirect benefit as a reminder of a shared, common humanity, an understanding critical to peacekeeping. This mutual understanding of common identity between nations through heritage preservation and tourism could serve a similar purpose in space travel.

**140** Jennifer A. Brobst

One important example is offered through the International Polar Heritage Committee of the International Council on Monuments and Sites (ICOMOS), led by Secretary-General Dr. Bryan Lintott, which has designated numerous historic sites and monuments in Antarctica.[62] These include, for example, Captains Scott's and Shackleton's huts, and memorials to scientists from India.[63] Before the 1959 Antarctic Treaty, competing nations had defaced each other's historic sites on the continent, which led to cultural and natural heritage preservation as a topic at the first Antarctic Treaty System discussion.[64] At the first discussion, it was agreed that there was a universal interest in the preservation of heritage in Antarctica, which has promoted both peace and preservation in the region.[65]

A guiding precautionary principle put forth by the International Polar Heritage Committee of ICOMOS is that previous human activity in the polar areas "has a potential significance for the documentation and the understanding of the history of these areas and should be expertly assessed with an eye to possible designation as a cultural heritage site before being altered or removed".[66] This type of provision would be necessary to preserve space heritage given that those regions would also be sparsely populated and not easily monitored. Also, if heritage sites are relatively isolated, then the development of customary international law is less likely to emerge given the paucity of activity and interaction among Member States.[67]

More recently, the UNESCO Convention on the Protection of the Underwater Cultural Heritage has promoted underwater archaeology, conservation and both natural and cultural heritage management.[68] The Convention

[e]ncourages States Parties to join forces in the protection, management and valorization of humanity's common underwater cultural heritage. In particular, it offers a unique mechanism to cooperate in the protection of archaeological sites located outside national jurisdiction and territorial waters.[69]

Moreover, the Convention expressly seeks to promote cooperation, information sharing, and understanding among countries that share a common cultural legacy.[70] For example, under the auspices of the Convention, recent efforts have included a UNESCO Workshop in waters surrounding Egypt with an underwater exploration of statuary in 2019, a joint virtual maritime exhibition among eight Latin American countries in 2020, and a joint maritime archaeological training with eight Arab countries in 2021.[71]

Although space-faring nations have tended to be wealthy and industrial, world heritage site designation by UNESCO offers national economic development through the promotion of tourism. Zurab Pololikashvili, the Secretary-General of the United Nations World Tourism Organization, stated in 2020

Around the world, in countries at all development levels, many millions of jobs and businesses are dependent on a strong and thriving tourism sector. Tourism has also been a driving force in protecting natural and cultural heritage, preserving them for future generations to enjoy.[72]

Ethiopia, for example, benefited as a developing nation in the 1960s and 1970s from the expansion of tourism and global interest when UNESCO identified several of Ethiopia's scenic sites for world heritage designation.[73] Some have argued that, in this context, developing nations are subject to and perhaps complicit in a predominately Western reimagining of national identity and power.[74] However, as more diverse nations join the Artemis Accords[75] and other space treaties, seeking to take part in the economic and political opportunities that space exploration offers, space tourism and the designation of protected heritage sites will impact nations large and small.

As the complex and competing interests in space heritage preservation are addressed below, it is important to remember the potential benefits of cooperation in preserving human heritage, particularly in fostering peace. As Secretary-General Pololikashvili stated: "The [tourism] sector has come a long way from being seen as just a frivolous leisure activity – it has now become an established part of national and global development and a key pillar of the sustainable agenda".[76] Space tourism has a role in heritage preservation and diplomacy, even if the concept of heritage and the desire to control outer space is fraught with uncertainty and competition.

### How UNESCO Addresses Competing Military and Commercial Interests

The role of heritage preservation in international relations requires some consideration of the substantial competing military and commercial interests which have funded much of early space exploration, although an in-depth analysis is beyond the scope of this discussion. Commercial and governmental drilling, logging and farming, for example, have presented an ongoing threat to world heritage sites on Earth.[77] Despite decades of growing UNESCO preservation efforts and legal development, commercial interests continue to object to heritage status,[78] and the World Heritage Convention remains surprisingly unclear on mining restrictions at protected sites.[79] In 2021, NASA reportedly awarded $500,000 to develop technology to engage in mining operations on the Moon.[80]

The Artemis Accords recognise a "mutual interest in the exploration and use of outer space for peaceful purposes"[81] and include protection of space heritage sites. However, its membership is still limited and it does not resolve the question of competing commercial interests. As of May 2023, there were 20 members of the Accords, far fewer in number than the near 200 nations that have ratified the World Heritage Convention.[82] Section 9 of the Accords is entitled "Preserving Outer Space Heritage" and broadly provides:

1 The Signatories intend to preserve outer space heritage, which they consider to comprise historically significant human or robotic landing sites, artifacts, spacecraft and other evidence of activity on celestial bodies in accordance with mutually developed standards and practices.

2. The Signatories intend to use their experience under the Accords to contribute to multilateral efforts to further develop international practices and rules applicable to preserving outer space heritage.[83]

The United States White House National Space Council stated in 2021 that the Accords "represent a shared vision for principles grounded in the Outer Space Treaty to create a safe and transparent environment which facilitates exploration, science, and commercial activities for all of humanity".[84] The Accords do not clearly define a heritage site, and discord exists on the interpretation of the agreed-upon use of commercial activities of space resources. Under Section 10 (Space Resources), the Accords state:

> The Signatories affirm that the extraction of space resources does not inherently constitute national appropriation under Article II of the Outer Space Treaty and that contracts and other legal instruments relating to space resources should be consistent with that Treaty.[85]

Article II of the Outer Space Treaty of 1967 simply states that "[o]uter space, including the Moon and other celestial bodies, is not subject to national appropriation by claim of sovereignty, by means of use or occupation, or by any other means".[86] The Moon Treaty of 1979 addresses these issues in Article 11(1),[87] but only 18 States have ratified the treaty as of 2021, a small consensus which includes neither the United States nor Russia.

Military and commercial interests often merge. For example, commercial satellites and other space technology may be used for both civilian and military communications, as well as intelligence efforts involving close observation of activities on Earth.[88] Public–private partnerships can both undermine and reinforce heritage site sustainability. For example, in a positive light, heritage preservation can establish goodwill internationally or prove economically viable as a tourist attraction. Of course, even when States have the authority to designate a precious natural or cultural site for world heritage designation, it does not mean that they will choose to do so and protect the site from lucrative economic development.[89]

Commercialisation of space is the new space race and a costly endeavour, inevitably enticing major public–private partnerships. In 2020, US President Trump issued an Executive Order which stated, "[s]uccessful long-term exploration and scientific discovery of the Moon, Mars, and other celestial bodies will require partnership with commercial entities to recover and use resources, including water and certain minerals, in outer space".[90] The United States does not currently appear to view outer space as a global commons. The United Nations, however, has expressed that:

> [g]lobal commons have been traditionally defined as those parts of the planet that fall outside national jurisdictions and to which all nations have access. International law identifies four global commons, namely the High Seas, the Atmosphere, the Antarctica and the Outer Space.[91]

Instead, the United States distinguishes between resource exploitation and an exercise of sovereignty. Under the United States Commercial Space Launch Competitiveness Act of 2015, one section seeks to facilitate resource use,[92] while the next states, "[i]t is the sense of Congress that the United States does not, by enactment of this Act, assert sovereignty or sovereign or exclusive rights or jurisdiction over, or ownership of, any celestial body".[93]

Unlike colonial exploration and frontier conquest on Earth, humanity currently is entering a vast region of space that is unpopulated, without the risk of subjugating or displacing other populations and communities. Some of the environmental concerns of mining on Earth, such as adding toxic metals to waterways,[94] may not be a concern on unpopulated celestial bodies. A voracious interest in commercialisation without limit is easily anticipated, if the last centuries of colonialism and exploration are any guide. However, an interest in conservation is a lesson humanity has already learned on Earth, not only to preserve and maintain resources but to preserve and appreciate the diverse natural and cultural heritage of humanity.

## Beyond UNESCO: National Efforts to Preserve Space Heritage

The nations that have begun to consider legal measures to preserve human heritage in space are understandably among those with the first space programmes: the Russian Federal Space Agency, the European Space Agency, the National Aeronautics and Space Administration in the United States, the Indian Space Research Organisation, the Japan Aerospace Exploration Agency and the China National Space Administration.[95] Space-faring nations have enacted national legislation to identify their property and jurisdictional interests in space where permitted under international law. In the context of preservation of space heritage, such as artefacts and spacecrafts, this national approach would be effective.

For example, under federal law, the United States provides for criminal jurisdictional authority over its vessels on, and aircraft flying over, the high seas, which are "out of the jurisdiction of any particular state".[96] With respect to its spacecraft properly registered under international space treaties, the United States exerts statutory authority

> from the moment when all external doors are closed on Earth following embarkation until the moment when one such door is opened on Earth for disembarkation or in the case of a forced landing, until the competent authorities take over the responsibility for the vehicle and for persons and property aboard.[97]

A space tourist who departed from Earth on an American spacecraft and was transported directly to an American space heritage site, such as a retired space station, may rely on national legal protections, supported by international law and a potential extension of UNESCO's World Heritage Convention.

In the United States, federal legislative bills to promote and regulate space tourism have been sponsored since 2003.[98] In addition, several unsuccessful federal

**144** Jennifer A. Brobst

legislative bills have been proposed since 2013 to create a national park on the Moon to protect the Apollo landing sites (1969–1972).[99] The legislation would have provided that the US Secretary of the Interior of the National Park Service would work with NASA and the Smithsonian Institute to monitor the landing sites, manage access, catalogue findings and work with other nations.[100] The proposed legislation also would have required a submission by the United States to UNESCO to nominate the lunar landing site as a world heritage site.[101] Nearly a decade later, the One Small Step to Protect Human Heritage in Space Act of 2020 was enacted by Congress.[102] While less encompassing than previously proposed bills and offering no regulatory licensing authority, the Act empowers NASA with loose oversight regarding commercial space activities and best practices in heritage preservation of the Apollo Lunar Landing sites.[103] The Act specifically states:

> (7) Such landing sites – (A) are the first archaeological sites with human activity that are not on Earth; (B) provide evidence of the first achievements of humankind in the realm of space travel and exploration; and (C) contain artifacts and other evidence of human exploration activities that remain a potential source of cultural, historical, archaeological, anthropological, scientific, and engineering knowledge.[104]

NASA had already adopted a space heritage preservation report in 2011, which the One Small Step Act references and promotes.[105] The report justified its recommendations, "[b]ecause there is no precedent for this situation throughout nearly 50 years of spaceflight, [and] there are no USG [government] guidelines or requirements for spacecraft visiting the areas of existing USG-owned lunar hardware".[106] Recognising the interim nature of the guidelines, NASA noted they would be in use "until more formal USG guidance is developed and perhaps a multilateral approach".[107] The goal was "to inform lunar spacecraft mission planners interested in helping preserve and protect lunar historic artifacts and potential science opportunities for future missions" and to create a dialogue with foreign space agencies.[108]

Therefore, in an environment without sovereign rule, reminiscent of the UNESCO experience with maritime and Antarctic heritage sites, nations should recognise that cooperation is possible and beneficial beyond the preservation of the heritage itself. In fact, bilateral cooperation between nations in park preservation has proven possible. For example, the United States and Canada have collaborated in their management and funding of more than one international park, one of which is a UNESCO World Heritage Site.[109] Botswana and the Republic of South Africa have co-managed the Kgalagadi Transfrontier Park since 1999, spanning the border of both nations.[110] Of course, local governance of heritage sites is another alternative to broad international oversight through UNESCO, a prospect beyond the scope of this analysis. However, bilateral or multilateral local control may permit greater mutual accountability,[111] as shown by the joint national ownership of the International Space Station,[112] itself a potential site for historic preservation in the future.

## Chapter Conclusion

Whether on Earth or in space, that humanity cares to preserve and protect its natural and cultural heritage is an aspect of tourism that is noble, but also concerning if it reflects competitive proprietary interests. The UNESCO World Heritage Convention offers a legal framework to prepare cooperatively for future space parks that may become increasingly accessible to the public as space travel expands. The "world" available as future world heritage sites does not have to be limited to Earth. Nations, such as the United States, have already considered legislation towards this end, identifying the Apollo landing site on the Moon for potential world heritage site protection. However, because of limits on national sovereignty and appropriation of territory in space under the Outer Space Treaty, natural heritage preservation in space will require a new international legal framework, perhaps inspired by existing agreements related to the high seas and Antarctica.[113] In 2023, ICOMOS announced that it had formed a new international scientific committee on Aerospace Heritage, in recognition that shared heritage from space launch sites on Earth to deep space probes and robotic spacecraft in orbital and outer space "connects all cultures across the planet".[114] Jointly managed international parks among nations are already a reality on Earth, which should lend credence to the hope that international cooperation in space will generate amazing scenic parks regardless of sovereign status. The history of national and international heritage preservation on Earth has shown that the dedication of the UNESCO World Heritage Convention to a shared humanity is a goal embraced by many. It serves as a reminder of a critical need to preserve humanity's shared heritage and its legacy in the cosmos.

## Notes

1 See Abraham Bell and Gideon Parchomovsky, 'Of Property and Antiproperty', *Michigan Law Review*, Vol. 12, 2003, pp. 1–70 at p. 8 (identifying parks as unique public goods "typically open to the public at large, and thus susceptible to the problem of overexploitation").

2 Budapest Declaration on World Heritage, 28 June 2002, WHC-02/CONF.202/25, §2.

3 UNESCO Convention Concerning the Protection of the World Cultural and Natural Heritage, 27 UST 37, 1037 UNTS 151(adopted 23 November 1972) [World Heritage Convention], Preamble.

4 See generally Catherine E. Parsons, Comment, 'Space Tourism: Regulating Passage to the Happiest Place on Earth', *Chapman Law Review*, Vol. 9, 2006, pp. 493–526 at p. 499 (outlining the early history of space tourism in Russia and the United States, including liability waivers for private citizens); A. Kerrest de Rozavel and F.G. von der Dunk, 'Liability and Insurance in the Context of National Authorisation', in Frans G. von der Dunk (ed.) *National Space Legislation in Europe: Issues of Authorisation of Private Space Activities in the Light of Developments in European Space Cooperation, Studies in Space Law*, Vol. 6 (Netherlands: Martinus Nijhoff Publishers, 2011) p. 125 (addressing the role of States in sharing liability with private enterprises pursuant to Article VII of the Outer Space Treaty (1967) and the Space Liability Convention (1972)); Patrick Zurita, 'The New Orient Express: Current Trends and Regulations in Space Tourism and the Need for Commercial Hypersonic Point to Point Travel', *Global Business Law Review*, Vol. 4, 2014, pp. 56–91 at p. 78 (discussing the history

**146** Jennifer A. Brobst

of commercial space regulation and the risk-sharing models that were intended to "spur the commercial spaceflight industry until the insurance market could stabilize and account for the potential catastrophic loss associated with a commercial space vehicle").

5 'Virgin Galactic', available at <https://www.virgingalactic.com/> Last visited, 31 August 2022 (promoting British entrepreneur Richard Branson's luxury suborbital flight service). See also Gitanjali Poonia, 'Virgin Galactic's Ticket Sales to Space Are Open. The Deposit Is $150,000', *DeseretNews*, 15 February 2022, available at <https://www.deseret.com/2022/2/15/22935898/virgin-galactics-ticket-sales-space-deposit-richard-barnson> Last visited, 3 May 2023 (listing the price of a single trip on Virgin Galactic at approximately US$450,000, with over 700 tickets sold and reserved in its first year).

6 Associated Press, '3 Visitors Heading to the Space Station Are Paying $55 Million Each, All Meals Included', *NPR*, 8 April 2022, <https://www.npr.org/2022/04/08/1091661900/spacex-space-station-launch-axiom> Last visited, 3 May 2023.

7 Glenn Harlan Reynolds, 'Not Your Father's Space Program', *Atlantic Monthly*, 5 June 2008, in Christopher Mari (ed.) *The Next Space Age* (New York: The H.W. Wilson Co., 2008) pp. 65–67 at p. 67.

8 Bernhard Gissibl et al. 'Introduction, Towards a Global History of National Parks', in Bernhard Gissibl et al. (eds.) *Civilizing Nature: National Parks in Global Historical Perspective* (New York: Berghahn, 2012) pp. 1–27 at p. 8.

9 Howard E. McCurdy, 'Has Spaceflight Had an Impact on Society? An Interpretative Framework', in Steven J. Dick and Roger D. Launius (eds.) *Societal Impact of Spaceflight* (NASA, 2007) pp. 3–16 at p. 9.

10 Linda Billings, 'Overview: Ideology, Advocacy, and Spaceflight – Evolution of a Cultural Narrative', in Steven J. Dick and Roger D. Launius (eds.) *Societal Impact of Spaceflight* (NASA, 2007) pp. 483–499 at p. 495.

11 'Museum of Cosmonautics', available at <https://kosmo-museum.ru/?locale=en> Last visited, 31 August 2022 (built on 4 October 1964).

12 *Supra* note 8, at 6.

13 *Id.*, at 1.

14 Eyder Peralta, 'Sally Ride, First American Woman in Space, Is Dead', *NPR*, ds23 July 2012, available at <https://www.npr.org/sections/thetwo-way/2012/07/23/157250870/sally-ride-first-american-woman-in-space-is-dead#:~:text=%22Studying%20whether%20there's%20life%20on,m%20certain%20that%20will%20continue.%2> Last visited, 3 May 2023.

15 James R. Hansen, 'Great Hero Yang', *Smithsonian Magazine* (Air and Space), March 2007, available at <https://www.smithsonianmag.com/air-space-magazine/great-hero-yang-15632584/> Last visited, 3 May 2023.

16 Budapest Declaration on World Heritage, 28 June 2022, WHC-02/CONF.202/25, § 1.

17 For example, the first Space Mountain ride at The Magic Kingdom in Disney World in the United States was opened in 1975 during the height of the international space race, weaving in numerous references to real space travel firsts. See Joshua Whitworth, 'The History of the First Walt Disney World Mountain: Space Mountain', *DIS* (Disney Information Station) (9 October 2019), available at<https://www.wdwinfo.com/history/the-history-of-the-first-walt-disney-world-mountain-space-mountain/> Last visited, 3 May 2023.

18 'International Dark Sky Parks', *International Dark-Sky Association*, available at <https://www.darksky.org/our-work/conservation/idsp/parks/> Last visited, 3 May 2023.

19 Declaration in Defence of the Night Sky and the Right to Starlight [La Palma Declaration], 19–20 April 2007 (Starlight Initiative, 2007) p. 3. See also UNESCO Convention for the Safeguarding of the Intangible Cultural Heritage, 4 May 2006, 2368 UNTS 3 (addressing the intangible and culturally diverse relationship of humans with nature and the universe).

20 *Supra* note 16.

21 See *Portal to the Heritage of Astronomy*, UNESCO (2010), available at <https://www3.astronomicalheritage.net/index.php/show-theme?idtheme=21> Last visited, 3 May 2023.

22 See generally 'Astronomy and World Heritage', *World Heritage*, Vol. 54 (UNESCO Publishing, October 2009), available at <https://whc.unesco.org/en/review/54/> Last visited, 3 May 2023.

23 *Museum of Cosmonautics* (Moscow, Russia), available at <https://kosmo-museum.ru/?locale=en> Last visited, 31 August 2022; 'Space Race', *National Air and Space Museum, Smithsonian Institute* (Wash. D.C., USA), available at <https://airandspace.si.edu/exhibitions/space-race> Last visited, 31 August 2022 (museum exhibit closed in 2023).

24 See Sarah A. Boyle, et al. 'High-Resolution Satellite Imagery Is an Important yet Underutilized Resource in Conservation Biology', *PLOS ONE* (23 January 2014), available at <https://journals.plos.org/plosone/article?id=10.1371/journal.pone.0086908> Last visited, 3 May 2023 (using remote high-resolution imagery to study the human-induced impact on forest conservation in Paraguay); 'Rare Clear View of Alaska', *NASA.gov* (19 June 2013), available at <https://www.nasa.gov/multimedia/imagegallery/image_feature_2534.html> Last visited, 3 May 2023 ("The absence of clouds exposed a striking tapestry of water, ice, land, forests, and even wildfires.").

25 Treaty on Principles Governing the Activities of States in the Exploration and Use of Outer Space, including the Moon and Other Celestial Bodies[The Outer Space Treaty], 27 January 1967, RES 2222 (XXI), 610 UNTS 205, Art. II.

26 *Id.*, Art. III.

27 See *supra* note 3.

28 'List of World Heritage in Danger', *UNESCO*, available at <https://whc.unesco.org/en/danger/> Last visited, 3 May 2023 (pursuant to Article 11(4) of the World Heritage Convention).

29 *Id.*

30 See Michael Viets, 'Piracy in an Ocean of Stars: Proposing a Term to Identify the Practice of Unauthorized Control of Nations' Space Objects', *Stanford Journal of International Law*, Vol. 54, 2018, pp. 159–212 at p. 192 (analogising maritime and drone piracy to the need for legal definitions of space piracy).

31 Oliver Wendell Holmes, Jr., *The Common Law* (New York: Barnes & Noble 2004 ed., originally published in 1881) p. 132.

32 'UNESCO World Heritage Convention' (States Parties), available at <https://whc.unesco.org/en/statesparties/> Last visited, 3 May 2023 (194 States to the Convention as of 23 October 2020).

33 UNESCO, Operational Guidelines for the World Heritage Committee, CC-77/CONF.001/8, 30 June 1977, § 1.

34 World Heritage List, UNESCO, available at <https://whc.unesco.org/en/list/> Last visited, 31 August 2022.

35 *Supra* note 8, at 9.

36 UNESCO World Heritage Convention, Review of Nominations to the World Heritage List, Second Session of the World Heritage Committee, Decision CONF 010 VIII.38 (inscribed 1978), available at <https://whc.unesco.org/en/decisions/2127> Last visited, 31 August 2022.

37 UNESCO World Heritage Convention, L'Anse Aux Meadows National Historic Site, available at <https://whc.unesco.org/en/list/4/> Last visited, 3 May 2023 ("The remnants correspond with the stories told in the Vinland Sagas, which document the voyages of Leif Erikson and other Norse explorers who ventured westward across the Atlantic Ocean from Iceland and Greenland to find and explore new territory, a significant achievement in the history of human migration and discovery.").

38 See World Heritage List, UNESCO, available at <https://whc.unesco.org/en/list/> Last visited, 31 August 2022.

39 See, for example, Air and Ténéré Natural Reserve in Niger, UNESCO World Heritage List, available at <https://whc.unesco.org/en/list/573> Last visited, 3 May 2023 (describing it as the largest protected area in Africa); New Zealand Sub-Antarctic Islands, UNESCO World Heritage List, available at<https://whc.unesco.org/en/list/877/> Last visited, 3 May 2023 (identifying outstanding universal value in a set of islands and their marine environments near Antarctica, with "unique and remarkable biodiversity").

40 See UNESCO World Heritage Centre, Operational Guidelines for the Implementation of the World Heritage Convention, 31 July 2021 [2021 Operational Guidelines], WHC.21/01, Art. II.A § 50 ("States Parties are invited to submit nominations") and Art. III.A (Preparation of Nominations).

41 *Id.*, Art. III.G (Decision of the World Heritage Committee).

42 *Id.*, Art. II.D (Criteria for the assessment of Outstanding Universal Value).

43 *Id.*, II.A, § 49.

44 *Id.*, II.D, § 77.

45 *Supra* note 3, Art. 4 & 5.

46 For example, Article 22 of the World Heritage Convention provides that World Heritage Fund assistance may include research studies, expertise, training, equipment, low-interest or interest-free loans, and nonrepayable subsidies.

47 *Supra* note 3, Art. 25.

48 *Id.*, Art. 29.

49 *Id.*, Art. 11(4). See also Peter Dykstra, Comment, 'Defining the Mother Lode: Yellowstone National Park v. The New World Mine', *Ecology Law Quarterly*, Vol. 24, 1997, pp. 299–331 at p. 328 ("[T]here is no enforcement mechanism to ensure that member countries comply with the Convention.").

50 UNESCO World Heritage Committee, State of Conservation of the Properties Inscribed on the List of World Heritage in Danger, 20 May 2019, WHC/19/43.COM/7A, 4 (emphasis added).

51 *Supra* note 25, Art. VI.

52 See Elizabeth Howell, '8 Cool Destinations That Future Mars Tourists Could Explore', *Space.com* (24 July 2018), available at <https://www.space.com/41254-touring-mars-red-planet-road-trip.html> Last visited, 3 May 2023.

53 UN Convention on the Law of the Sea, 10 December 1982[UNCLOS], 1833 UNTS 397, Art. 19.

54 *Id.*, Art. 87(1).

55 *Id.*, Art. 89.

56 See also *id.*, Art. 192 ("States have the obligation to protect and preserve the marine environment.").

57 *Supra* note 33, at II.D (Criteria for the assessment of Outstanding Universal Value).

58 Julian Jackson, 'What You Need to Know and Do to Protect the High Seas', *Pew Charitable Trusts*, 17 August 2021.

59 *Id.*

60 *Supra* note 53, Art. 217(8) ("Penalties provided for by the laws and regulations of States for vessels flying their flag shall be adequate in severity to discourage violations wherever they occur.").

61 See *id.*, Art. 235(1) ("States are responsible for the fulfilment of their international obligations concerning the protection and preservation of the marine environment. They shall be liable in accordance with international law.").

62 See Bryan Lintott, ICOA916 'Antarctica: Human Heritage on the Continent of Peace and Science', in ICOMOS 19th General Assembly and the Scientific Symposium "Heritage and Democracy," New Delhi, India (2018); see also Bryan Lintott, 'Arctic and Antarctic Heritage at Risk', Polar Heritage at Risk, ICOMOS 6ISC 2020, available at

<bjlintott.com> Last visited, 3 May 2023 (addressing anthropogenic risks and benefits to polar heritage, including the rise in sea level from climate change which has impacted heritage sites "on a global scale").

63 *Id.*

64 *Id.*

65 *Id.*

66 'Goals of the International Scientific Committees', *International Council on Monuments and Sites* (International Polar Heritage Committee) [ICOMOS] (15 November 2011), available at <https://www.icomos.org/en/about-icomos/committees/scientific-committees/goals-of-the-iscs> Last visited, 3 May 2023.

67 *Compare* Hjalte Osborn Frandsen, 'Customary International Law as a Vessel for Global Accord: The Case of Customary Rules of the Road for Governing the Orbital Highways of Earth', *Journal of Air Law and Commerce*, Vol. 87, 2022, pp. 705–757 at p. 746 (discussing the opportunity for customary international law due to frequently used space highways).

68 UNESCO Convention on the Protection of the Underwater Cultural Heritage, 2562 UNTS 45694, 2 November 2001 [Underwater Cultural Heritage Convention]. For an early critique of the development of the Convention, including a proposal to foster wider interest from tourists and amateur archaeologists, see David J. Bederman, 'The UNESCO Draft Convention on Underwater Cultural Heritage: A Critique and Counter-Proposal', *Journal of Maritime Law& Commerce*, Vol. 30, 1999, pp. 331–354.

69 UNESCO, '20 Years of Enhancing the Protection and Presentation of Underwater Cultural Heritage' (11 February 2021), available at <https://en.unesco.org/news/20-years-enhancing-protection-and-presentation-underwater-cultural-heritage> Last visited, 3 May 2023.

70 Underwater Cultural Heritage Convention, *supra* note 68, Art. 19(1) ("States Parties shall cooperate and assist each other in the protection and management of underwater cultural heritage under this Convention, including, where practicable, collaborating in the investigation, excavation, documentation, conservation, study and presentation of such heritage.").

71 *Id.* See also Nada Deyaa', 'UNESCO's Workshop Tackles Underwater Cultural Heritage for the First Time in Egypt', *Daily News Egypt*, 11 November 2019 <https://dailynewsegypt.com/2019/11/11/unescos-workshop-tackles-underwater-cultural-heritage-for-the-first-time-in-egypt/> Last visited, 3 May 2023.

72 Zurab Polokashvili, 'Responsible and Inclusive Growth at Heart of Tourism's Recovery', *Arab News* (8 December 2020), available at <https://www.arabnews.com/node/1774391> Last visited, 31 August 2022. See also UN World Tourism Organisation, available at <https://www.unwto.org> Last visited, 3 May 2023 (quoting Polokashvili's Arab News opinion article).

73 See Marie Huber, 'Developing Heritage – Developing Countries', in Joël Glassman et al. (eds.) *Africa in Global History Series*, Vol. 1 (Berlin/Boston: De Gruyter, 2021) pp. 21–24.

74 *Id.*, at 15 ("Heritage-making, from a state perspective, is not only an institutional and scientific but also a territorialising practice.").

75 See Tariq Malik, 'Romania Signs the Artemis Accords for Space Exploration Cooperation', *Space.com* (6 March 2022), available at <https://www.space.com/romania-signs-artemis-accords> Last visited, 31 August 2022.

76 *Supra* note 73.

77 *Id.*

78 See Matthew Machado, 'X. Mounting Opposition to Biosphere Reserves and World Heritage Sites in the United States Sparked by Claims of Interference with National Sovereignty', *Colorado Journal of International Environmental Law & Policy*, 1997, pp. 120–129 at p. 124.

79 Natasha Affolder, 'Mining and the World Heritage Convention: Democratic Legitimacy and Treaty Compliance', *Pace Environmental Law Review*, Vol. 24, 2007, pp. 35–66 at p. 44 (identifying the lack of express prohibition in the text of the World Heritage Convention against mining on protected sites, as well as a lack of agreement as to whether a sweeping prohibition against mining on world heritage sites could be implied).

80 Mike Wall, 'NASA Awards $500,000 to Develop Moon-Mining Tech', *Space.com*, 20 August 2021, available at <https://www.space.com/nasa-moon-ice-mining-challenge-awards> Last visited, 3 May 2023 (NASA's Break the Ice Lunar Challenge). See also William M. Callif, 'Be Wary of the Trojan Horse: A Commercial-Friendly Reading of the Outer Space Treaty as the Key to De-escalating the Emerging Space Race between the United States and China', *Suffolk Transnational Law Review*, Vol. 45, 2022, pp. 277–343 at pp. 311–312 (identifying China's plans to explore the Moon and establish a lunar scientific research station to gain economic and industrial advantage).

81 The Artemis Accords, Principles for Cooperation in the Civil Exploration and Use of the Moon, Mars, Comets, and Asteroids for Peaceful Purposes (adopted 13 October 2020) [The Artemis Accords], available at <https://www.nasa.gov/specials/artemis-accords/img/Artemis-Accords-signed-13Oct2020.pdf> Last visited, 31 August 2022.

82 U.S. Dept. of State, 'France Becomes Twentieth Nation to Sign the Artemis Accords', 7 June 2022, available at <state.gov> Last visited, 3 May 2023 (adding Bahrain, Colombia, France, and Singapore in 2022). See also Malik, *supra* note 75 (listing 16 State members as of March 2022, including Australia, Brazil, Canada, Israel, Italy, Japan, Luxembourg, Mexico, New Zealand, Poland, the Republic of Korea, Romania, Ukraine, the United Arab Emirates, the United Kingdom and the United States).

83 *Supra* note 81.

84 The White House National Space Council, 'Renewing America's Proud Legacy of Leadership in Space, Activities of the National Space Council and United States Space Enterprise' 16 (January 2021), available at <https://trumpwhitehouse.archives.gov/wp-content/uploads/2021/01/Final-Report-on-the-Activities-of-the-National-Space-Council-01.15.21.pdf> Last visited, 31 August 2022.

85 *Supra* note 81.

86 Outer Space Treaty, *supra* note 25, Art. II.

87 See *supra* note 30, at n. 69 ("[A]s the principles unique to the Moon Agreement cannot be fairly characterized as representing international customary law, its influence is limited to the few nations that have signed it and it is only of marginal relevance to space law generally.").

88 See Phillip C. Saunders, 'China's Space Ambitions: Implications for U.S. Security', *Ad Astra* (Spring 2005), in Christopher Mari (ed.) *The Next Space Age* (New York: The H.W. Wilson Co., 2008) pp. 42–46 at p. 43.

89 See Sarah C. Aird, 'China's Three Gorges: The Impact of Dam Construction on Emerging Human Rights', *Human Rights Brief*, Vol. 8, No. 2, 2001, pp. 24–37 at p. 36 (highlighting China's failure to designate regions with significant archaeological significance as world heritage sites, despite being a signatory to the World Heritage Convention, opting instead to permit destruction of the sites by building the world's largest hydroelectric dam on the Yangtze River).

90 US White House, Executive Order on Encouraging International Support for the Recovery and Use of Space Resources (6 April 2020) § 1, available at <https://trumpwhitehouse.archives.gov/presidential-actions/executive-order-encouraging-international-support-recovery-use-space-resources/> Last visited, 3 May 2023 (citing in support the Commercial Space Launch Competitiveness Act of 2015 (Public Law 114-90)).

91 UN System Task Team on the Post-2015 UN Development Agenda, Global governance and governance of the global commons in the global partnership for development

beyond 2015 (January 2013), available at <https://www.un.org/en/development/desa/policy/untaskteam_undf/thinkpieces/24_thinkpiece_global_governance.pdf> Last visited, 3 May 2023; see also *Black's Law Dictionary* (West Publishing Co., 6th ed. 1990) p. 278 (defining the term "commons" as "pleasure grounds and spaces or open places for public use or public recreation owned by towns or cities – in modern usage usually called 'parks'").

92 U.S. Commercial Space Launch Competitiveness Act of 2015 (Public Law 114-90)), § 402.

93 *Id.*, § 403. See also Jaime José Hurtado Cola, 'Tort Liability of Non-State Actors for Violations of the Outer Space Treaty', *Tort Trial & Insurance Practice Law Journal*, Vol. 57, 2022, pp. 541–604 at p. 556 (asserting that if Americans are recognising a right to explore and extract resources in space, then they will likely provide a legal tort remedy in the event that such a right is impaired).

94 See *supra* note 49, at 303.

95 Many other nations have governmental space agencies, even if they have yet to place astronauts in space. See 'Worldwide Space Agencies', *United Nations Office for Outer Space Affairs* (UNOOSA), available at <https://www.unoosa.org/oosa/en/ourwork/space-agencies.html> Last visited, 3 May 2003.

96 Special maritime and territorial jurisdiction of the United States defined, 18 U.S.C. §§ 7(1) and (5) (2018).

97 18 U.S.C. § 7(6) (2018).

98 For an early review of national space tourism legislation, see *supra* note 4, at 509–515.

99 Apollo Lunar Landing Legacy Act, 113th U.S. Congress, 2013–2014 (HR 2617) (attempting to establish the Apollo Lunar Landing Sites National Historical Park on the Moon as a unit of the National Park System).

100 *Id.*

101 *Id.*

102 One Small Step to Protect Human Heritage in Space Act, 116th U.S. Congress (2019–2020) (P.L. 116-275).

103 *Id.*

104 *Id.*, § 2(7).

105 'NASA's Recommendations to Space-Faring Nationals, How to Protect and Preserve the Historic and Scientific Value of U.S. Government Lunar Artifacts' (20 July 2011), available at, <https://www.nasa.gov/pdf/617743main_NASA-USG_LUNAR_HISTORIC_SITES_RevA-508.pdf> Last visited, 3 May 2023.

106 *Id.*

107 *Id.*

108 *Id.*

109 Jarrod H. Becker, Note, 'The Role of International Parks in Promoting Species Retention and Biodiversity', *Syracuse Journal of International Law & Commerce*, Vol. 29, pp. 371–398 at pp. 393–395 (Roosevelt Campobello International Park located on Campobello Island, New Brunswick, Canada; and Waterton-Glacier International Peace Park spanning the border between the countries and designated as a world heritage site).

110 *Id.*, at 396.

111 *Supra* note 79, at 44 ("While climate change, ozone depletion, and the law of the sea may be accepted as environmental concerns appropriate for international regulation, decision-making surrounding land use, heritage protection, and natural resource extraction are more fiercely guarded as issues of local governance.").

112 European Space Agency, 'International Space Station Legal Framework', available at <https://www.esa.int/Science_Exploration/Human_and_Robotic_Exploration/International_Space_Station/International_Space_Station_legal_framework#:~:text=This%20means%20that%20the%20owners,Partner%20on%20the%20Space%20Station> Last visited, 3 May 2023 ("[T]he owners of the Space Station – the United

States, Russia, the European Partner, Japan and Canada – are legally responsible for the respective elements they provide.").

113 See generally Yutaka Osada, 'Governance of Space Resources Activities: In the Wake of the Artemis Accords', *Georgetown Journal of International Law*, Vol. 53, 2022, pp. 399–511 at p. 421 (noting that outer space heritage would fall within the scope of the World Heritage Convention but for the fact that heritage sites must be situated on the territory of a State party).

114 'New ICOMOS ISC on Aerospace Heritage', ICOMOS, 13 Feb. 2023, available at <icomos.org> Last visited, 3 May 2023.

# 10

# CONTRACTUAL OBLIGATIONS IN THE CONTEXT OF SPACE TOURISM

*Rohan R. Pillai and Arshi Alam*

## Introduction

There was a time when an astronaut travelling to space was an oddity of astronomical proportions. However, much has changed since 1969, marking man's first step on the moon; since then, non-governmental personnel have increasingly made their presence felt in the space voyage business, beginning in 2001 with Russia sending private persons to the ISS.[1] Today companies like SpaceX, Blue Origin, and Virgin Galactic have successfully created a business model to offer private persons a taste of the anti-gravity experience. Several people have already taken these trips, and according to Virgin Galactic's estimates, these numbers are set to rise to a couple of thousands in the near future.[2] That said, space tourism is far from attaining the status of being a "regular exercise" with established rules and governing regime.[3] Owing to which examination of the obligations of the tourist and their operator becomes vital as questions of liability and insurance are bound to arise in case of the incidence of a misadventure.

## Regimes and Consent: A Liability

### Placing Space Tourism

The incompatibility of space tourism with the governing space law regime arises from the innate nature of the term itself. Defining space tourism connotes an element of pleasure or recreation.[4] Although personal scientific curiosity might be an auxiliary objective, it cannot be equated with an interest in benefiting humanity. This gains significance given that Article I of the Outer Space Treaty requires the use of outer space to be for the benefit and in the interest of all countries.[5]

DOI: 10.4324/9781032617961-10

The legal status of space tourists is, at best, muddy; it is difficult to argue that they fit the terms employed in the governing space law regime.

The term "astronaut" as described in Article V of the Outer Space Treaty describes them as being "envoys of mankind". The broader and humane Rescue Agreement of 1968[6] deals with assistance in events of emergency landings, accidents and distress. The Rescue Agreement employs in its text the term "personnel of a spacecraft".

According to Hobe, to fit space tourists in either of these terminologies is difficult, where "envoy of mankind" has a more humane connotation, and an "astronaut" has scientific or explorative meaning. Hobe further adds that "personnel" has a more functional meaning. On their short visit, space tourists do not perform any function relating to the spacecraft's operation. They also do not perform any beneficial function or scientific exploration. Therefore, they cannot be considered to fit any of these terms.[7]

Additionally, applying the aviation law regime to space travel has its own issues. A craft that carries tourists to space travels through the air and outer space. However, where air ends and space begins has not reached a consensus. (For this chapter's purposes, assumed to be beyond the Von Kármán Line, that is, 100 km above sea level.)[8]

This discussion gains significance in the context of determining liability for damage arising from space tourism, as these liabilities may be based on the governing legal regime, that is, space law or air law. Some have theorised the application of both regimes to a single journey. However, such an application could complicate the determination of liability for damage. Air law has long-established rules on the operator, passenger and third-party liability. In contrast, provisions of space law are all State-centred; additionally, they have yet to undergo judicial interpretation.

In light of the above discussion, the contractual establishment of rights and obligations between the space tourist and the operator becomes a key element. Away from the theoretical consideration of kilometres determining air space from outer space, these changes are highly pragmatic. Entry and re-entry in and out of outer space and into the atmosphere pose significant risks, as seen in the fatal Space Shuttle Columbia disaster. There is a substantial risk of the shuttle flaring up or myriads of other potentially fatal inadvertencies. This calls for monitored tourist/operator relations to ensure that the terms of their agreement are fair and the tourist is informed of the risks involved.

### Informed Consent Regime

The Americans have been quite at the forefront of regulating this. Currently, there are two federal laws governing space tourism organisations at the federal level. These are the Commercial Space Launch Amendments Act of 2004, its implementing regulation 14 CFR Section 460.9 and Section 460.45 and the Federal Aviation Administration (FAA) regulation of December 2006.

The US federal law refers to space travellers as space flight participants rather than passengers. Thus, their legal status and protections are not put on the same level as other passengers using conventional methods of travel like air passengers.

The regulation *inter alia* aims to guide the contract between the space tourist and their operators. The rules establish requirements for human space flight, emphasise an acceptable level of safety to the general public and inform the tourist of risks associated with launch and re-entry. At the core of it, these laws establish an informed consent regime similar to that associated with high-risk adventure sports like bungee jumping or air diving. In this chapter, we will attempt to analyse these laws to understand the outlines of principles on which space tourism contracts may be based.

### Re-entry and Launch Risk

What §460.45 does is impose a pre-requisite on the part of the operator as obligations towards the space flight participant, forbidding an agreement to conduct a space flight activity or receiving any compensation for it. Such pre-agreement requisite essentially translates into clauses in the tourist operator agreement declaring the fulfilment of these obligations, thus forming the skeletal structure of the tourist–operator agreement.[9]

The section does not indicate what language is to be employed by the operator in giving effect to its requirements, irrespective of which the flight participant is requested to attest to understand the risks involved.

Thus, the contract or communication prior to the contract must inform the "flight participant" of the risks, including a description of the known and potential unknown hazards. Other than the general obligation of disclosing risks of launch and re-entry and safety records, the operator is especially required to identify in writing "each" known hazard that could result in disability, serious injury, death or partial physical or mental disability. The emphasis on identifying "each" known hazard entails a detailed description and identification of known factors, thus containing an exhaustive list.

This also calls for a vehicle type-based hazard analysis.

### Technical Detail

The above-quoted section also emphasises presenting the information in a manner that is readily understandable with no special training. Provisions such as these serve a dual purpose. The first objective is clear, resulting from an adjustment to the peculiarity of space tourism. Anyone with enough money, irrespective of their technical qualification, can participate and requires the risk disclosure in a form that is easily accessible.

However, the second objective this standard achieves is protecting proprietary information. A detailed disclosure might violate export control regulations or sensitive data. Thus the particular hazards identified only need a disclosure on a general level. For example, suppose a hazard exists in the propulsion system. In that case, it may be informed by the general categorisation of hazard level. Classifications such as "catastrophic" or "inconsequential" may be used. These are easily understandable terminology that gives the participant awareness of the associated risk. At the same time, they protect proprietary information of the system design, disclosure of vehicle safety records and system vulnerabilities.

Non-certification Statement

The regulation also imposes an obligation on the operator to inform the participant that the government has not certified the vehicle as safe for carrying passengers.

This provision is peculiar to the United States as the FAA is not congressionally authorised to certify occupant safety. It acts as a stop-gap measure while also representing the state of disjunction between the air law and space law regimes worldwide. Space tourism is already a reality, despite which States are still not equipped to deal with it. Most States haven't established agencies to regulate space travel as they regulate air travel. Tourists, therefore, cannot expect the same level of safety as they are accustomed to the national domestic air travel safety standards.

Safety Record

§ 460.45(c)[10] of the FAA regulation requires information pertaining to the following:

- safety records
- the number of fatalities or severe injuries in sub-orbital or orbital flights
- catastrophic failures of launch and re-entry

to be provided to the tourist prior to and proximate to the launch, as material changes in safety records can present a higher risk than the participant consented.

Further provisions provide additional disclosure concerning the individual vehicle and its history. Thus a clause for disclosures of material events that alter the risk level and updates the passenger on the likelihood of risk involved is essential.

*Immunity from Liability*

Interestingly, the Act remains silent on the effect of compliance with these provisions; thus, the Act does not offer informed consent to immunise the operator from tortuous liability.[11] It can be said that there is a trend to establish personal responsibility for flight participation on the participant's part and establish their status as an informed consumer.[12] The informed consent provisions were not intended to act as contractual waivers,[13] which is perhaps demonstrated by the regulation requiring an express waiver of claim against the US Government.[14]

Thus there exists ambiguity in the distribution of risk. International liability for damage from space objects is fixed on the launching State; this raises questions about commercial space flights and their liability distribution. An argument can be made regarding relief from liability for negligence in light of informed consent.

States have enacted legislation to immunise operators from liability resulting from harm caused to space flight participants to encourage space tourism. Virginia passed such a law in 2007, which exempts tortuous liability from operators for injuries to the flight participants arising from "the risks of space flight".[15] It, however, has an exception for injuries caused by gross negligence or intentional injuries. This immunity is provided on the requirement to sign a "warning and acknowledgement form" by the flight participants.

Similar immunities are provided by Florida and New Mexico. Florida allows this immunity to be claimed by the flight operator and manufacturers and suppliers of components that the FAA has reviewed as part of its licensing procedure.[16] Further, US law also requires the operator to indemnify the US Government against the third-party claims up to $500 million.

### Principles Governing Liability

Given that there is no concrete law governing the distribution of liability between space tourists and operators, the general law of negligence governs such liability issues. In the event of a mishap, the liability is likely to be fastened based on the doctrine of assumption of risk and the doctrine of waiver, as seen in adventure sports. The current liability regime of *corpus iuris spatialis in iuri gentium* is narrowly defined and ill-equipped to tackle the fast-developing commercial evolution of space travel.[17] The delineation between air space, near space and outer space will clarify rights and obligations and enhance the margin of safety for aircraft or space vehicles.[18]

### Assumption of Risk

The repeated comparison of space tourism to adventure sport perhaps indicates the applicability of the doctrine of assumption of risks. The doctrine stipulates a complete bar on liability if an agreement is reached to relieve the other party of their duty to care for protection and assumption of risks by the participant.

This results in a change in the nature of the duty imposed. It transforms from a duty to protect to a duty to make conditions as safe as they appear to be.[19] If this lower bar is met, the duty is fulfilled, and the operator is free from liability; this must be read in line with the disclosure requirements discussed above. Thus, it would depend on the nature and scope of consent received and the tourists' understanding.

## Express Waiver

Like other recreational activities, the tourist operator contract will likely have an express waiver clause. But to what extent can such a waiver be relied upon is questionable. Law of waiver changes jurisdictionally; some States allow for enforcement of waiver of rights clause while others don't. Due to its exculpatory nature, such a clause would generally have the imposition of high standards; such a waiver would have to be crystal clear in its scope and effect. Even so, the general inapplicability would apply when found to be against public policy, suffering from gross negligence.[20] Common law jurisdictional limitation to waiver would apply too, which will vary from State to State. At the least, an express waiver clause is likely to be present irrespective of its enforceability in tourist operator agreements until a uniform law governing their arrangement appears.

### *Passenger Liability*

Application of the Montreal Convention is possible in cases where harm is suffered while aboard the airship and its two-stepped scheme could also be applied for determination of passenger liability. The Montreal Convention provides provisions for carriers' unlimited responsibility in circumstances of passenger damage or death. However, if the carrier can establish that "all reasonable steps" were undertaken to avoid the loss, limited liability may apply to damage in the case of a delay. Other damages are restricted to 100,000 Special Drawing Rights (SDRs) if the service provider can demonstrate that it wasn't its or its agents' omission or negligence that caused the damage or that there were other third parties which were wholly responsible for the damage through their omission or negligence. The Montreal Convention, on the other hand, only pertains to "international air transport of humans". Such transport is international if "the points of departure and destination... are located... inside the boundaries of two States Parties... in accordance with the parties' agreement...". Because the journey on board an aircraft ends there, the point where the sub-orbital vehicle separates from the airplane may be considered the "place of destination". If the moment of separation occurs within the airspace of the State from which the aircraft took off, international carriage may be called into question. Even if the Montreal Convention criteria did not apply to the transfer of the (combined) aircraft, the aircraft's flight would be governed by the relevant rules of national aviation law. Because the Montreal Convention aims to bring into consonance the liability requirements of national air laws, whether the Montreal Convention provisions or the various national accountability rules apply makes little difference in practice. However, the Montreal Convention does not apply to transportation on board the space vehicle upon separation from the airship. Space law may apply to the solitary vehicle that uses rocket propulsion for thrust. The Liability Convention imposes absolute liability on a launching State for injury caused by a "space object on the Earth's surface or to aircraft in flight". The launching State's fault-based responsibility extends to injury caused by a space

Contractual Obligations in the Context of Space Tourism **159**

object when not on Earth's surface, to another launching State's space object, or to persons or property on board such space object. It is unclear if the Liability Convention applies to passengers aboard spacecraft. Article VII of the Liability Convention expressly stipulates that the Liability Convention does not apply to injury caused by a launching State's space object to nationals of that same State or to third-party nationals or "foreign nationals at such time as they are engaged in the operation of that space object". This suggests that the Liability Convention does not apply to passengers, whether they are nationals of the launching State of the space object or passengers who are not citizens of that launching State but are participating in the functioning of the space object. It might be claimed, however, that the Liability Convention applies to passengers because they are not normally "involved in the operation" of the space object. Space passengers, on the other hand, knowingly put themselves in danger by taking part in a space mission. In light of this, the launching State's entire accountability for harm caused to passengers of its space object looks unacceptable. Furthermore, Article III of the Liability Convention clearly refers to instances involving third parties, meaning that passengers are not subject to fault-based liability. As a result, passengers will likely not be able to seek compensation under the Liability Convention. This has been called into question because passenger safety is crucial to the industry's profits. However, as commercial space flight becomes more prevalent, State responsibility and accountability become less acceptable.[21]

If the Liability Convention is not applicable, liability can be decided by using national law. It is enough to summarise the fundamental characteristics of the various national systems here. Passenger liability can be formed by contract or by illegal or tortuous behaviour, assuming the relevant national legislation allows it. A choice-of-law clause can be included in a contract. Acts conducted on board a space object are subject to the criminal and tortuous legislation of the State of registry. The United States recently established national space legislation that specifically mentions passengers, or "space flight participants". The plan may serve as a catalyst for more legislation at the international and national levels. The law in the United States has some repercussions for reciprocal releases of claims, which exempt the parties from liability. Some exclusions are required by law, while others are permissible but not required. Important requirements of applicable law in the United States, for example, include:

1   The licensee is required to make a reciprocal waiver of claims with "its contractors, subcontractors and customers…". Since a space flight participant is not a "customer" the provision does not apply to passengers. However, the operator is not prevented from making a waiver of liability a condition of an agreement with the space flight participant.
2   Moreover, the licensee has to make a reciprocal waiver of claims with the US Government under which each party agrees to be responsible for property damage or loss it sustains, or for personal injury to, death of, property damage or

loss sustained by, *inter alia*, space flight participants, if the damage results from an activity under the licence. Such waiver of claims only applies to any amount exceeding the insurance or demonstration of financial responsibility required under subsection (a)(1)(B) of section 70112, that is, to an amount exceeding US $100 million.

3 The space flight participant must hold harmless and indemnify the US Government and its agencies, servants, agents, subsidiaries, employees and assignees from and against liability, loss or damage arising out of claims brought by anyone for property damage or bodily injury, including death, sustained by, *inter alia*, a space flight participant, resulting from licensed or permitted activities.[22]

The method used by the United States demonstrates that liability waivers are permissible in certain circumstances. The FAA made it plain in the final regulations that exemptions include claims stemming from an individual's own death. After all, the Liability Convention does not yet apply to passengers, as previously stated. As a national law, US legislation has limited global application, while it may serve as a catalyst for future legislation on both the national and international levels. So far, international space law lacks comprehensive regulation on accountability for damage incurred by space flight participants. Because the Montreal Convention may not be relevant to the second leg of the voyage and the Registration Convention has flaws, future changes to current instruments, or possibly the creation of a new instrument entirely, may be required.

### Third-Party Liability

The Rome Convention governs third-party responsibility for aircraft transportation. The Rome Convention only allows the operator, presumably the owner of the aircraft, and not the tour operator, to be held liable if it can be proven that the damage on the surface was caused by an aircraft in flight or by any person or item falling from it. As a result, liability is restricted. However, if the person who suffers harm establishes that it was caused by "a willful act or omission of the operator... done with the intent to cause damage", the operator's culpability is limitless. Because so few governments have accepted the Rome Convention, its applicability is restricted.[23]

The International Civil Aviation Organization (ICAO) is now debating whether to renew the third-party Liability Convention, which might be based on a two-tier structure similar to the Montreal Convention on passenger liability. The vehicle should not be deemed an aircraft after separation, rendering the Rome Convention inapplicable. However, third parties may be entitled to seek reimbursement under the Liability Convention. The Liability Convention applies to situations in which third parties are concerned about losses that are not due to the launching State of the space object that caused the harm.

Contractual Obligations in the Context of Space Tourism **161**

According to Article VII(a) of the Liability Convention, the Liability Convention does not apply to damage caused to nationals of the "launching State". As a result, the launching State's own citizens must rely on national rules, which often only provide for fault-based accountability. National space law can address this imbalance. The Liability Convention, as an international convention, applies solely between nations. Thus, only a launching State, as defined in Article I(c) of the Liability Convention, shall be accountable for harm under the Liability Convention's provisions, not nationals of the launching State who caused the damage. If national space legislation allows it, the launching State may have recourse against its nationals. Liability under the Liability Convention may be a requirement for the launching State's right of remedy under its national space legislation. Notably, an injured national may be on the opposing side of these claims. It is up to the State in question whether or not to file a claim on behalf of such a plaintiff. Indeed, several national space laws provide for such a right of redress.[24]

Recent legislation in the United States may serve as an example of current and possibly future legislation. Risk sharing is established by Section 701 of Title 49 of the US Code. The licensee must obtain liability insurance or demonstrate financial responsibility for the maximum likely loss arising from third-party claims and claims by the US Government for damage or loss to government property, in order to compensate the United States if it is held liable for damages under the Liability Convention or the Federal Tort Claims Act. The maximum insurance coverage necessary for third-party liability is $500 million in the United States. Section 70113(a)(1) provides for the conditional payment of claims by the US Government for third-party liability in excess of the statutory financial obligation up to $1.5 billion. Following such restrictions, the licensee is liable for any claims. As a result, the licensee is liable for losses up to US $500 million, which must be covered by insurance or shown financial responsibility. The US Government rewards genuine claims for amounts over $500 million up to $1.5 billion. The licensee is responsible for payments in excess of US $1.5 billion. The law in the United States is clearly only of national scale, but it may signal a trend for future national and international legislation. When a space capsule is launched by a rocket, the legal responsibility regime is solely determined by international and national space law. Air law regulations would not apply since both items may be classified as space objects.[25]

In summary, the Montreal Convention governs passenger liability in aviation law, whereas the Rome Convention governs third-party liability for aircraft damage if they are participating in space activities. The Liability Convention does not apply to passenger liability for damage caused by space object(s). According to national legislation, liability for passenger damage may instead be proved through contract or by criminal or tortuous activity. Although the Liability Convention covers third-party losses, it only applies directly between nations. However, if national law allows it, governments may have recourse against their citizens who cause the damage.[26]

## Insurance in Space Tourism

As a result of space tourism, insurance companies will have new options. Space tourists spend a lot of money on tickets and are also aware of the perils of space flight, resulting in a distinct risk profile. Space insurance is a highly technical subject that necessitates a thorough grasp of launch vehicles, satellites and other associated issues. The existing space insurance policy, on the other hand, exclusively covers astronauts and ship crew members and makes no provisions for space tourists' passenger duty. Space Adventures sought to address the problem of insurance by obtaining personal accident insurance for its clients' safety and well-being. It imposes the need as a result of the significant development in the prospects of space travel. The uncertainties surrounding the legal status of a space tourist, the liability regime and the rules and legislations provide an additional threat to the insurance sector.

Several countries now require private firms with launch and operating certifications or permits to get appropriate insurance to protect their space objects and launch facilities, as well as third-party and product liability. As a result, private space tourism businesses will very definitely be obliged to get the necessary insurance to reimburse them in the case of claims by States attempting to recover damages suffered by space travellers and other parties. Because of the high risks involved, it is doubtful that the current space insurance market will be able or even willing to cover space tourism operations at this time.

Given that individuals are now purchasing tickets on commercial spaceflights, the urgent need for a new space tourism insurance model to analyse the specific risks involved and ensure the payment of compensation is self-evident.

While some may claim that space travel insurance cannot be provided because it is too risky, one must examine insurance history. In response to increased trade demand, several insurers began in the late 1600s by insuring ships. It might even be argued that embarking on a multi-week ocean voyage was riskier than taking an 11-minute ride into space due to weather, illness and navigational mistakes.

There are several factors to consider when determining whether a risk is insurable. They frequently include features such as[27]:

- A high number of homogenous exposure units are required. The loss must have been unintended and unintentional. The loss must be determinable, quantifiable and certain. The loss should not be systemic in the sense that multiple risks are exposed to the same occurrence, possibly culminating in catastrophic loss.
- The possibility of loss must be calculable.
- The premium must be financially viable.

Insurance firms cover pure risk, which is defined as any situation in which there is a danger of financial loss but no chance of financial gain. As a result, an insurable risk should include the possibility of accidental loss, which means that the loss must be the product of an unintended activity and occur at an unanticipated time and scale.

The notion of insuring exposures in space is not new to the insurance industry. Carriers like as Allianz, AXA XL, and Munich Re have been insuring space equipment such as rockets and satellites for a long time and understand how to underwrite such risks. This comprises revenue loss and material damage, as well as insurance for prelaunch, launch and in-orbit. Furthermore, liability insurance is significantly more usually required in the case of causing harm to other people's property in space or on Earth.

However, when it comes to passenger insurance, a different situation emerges. Even the world's wealthiest billionaires, Richard Branson and Jeff Bezos, did not have insurance readily available to support their space flight endeavours. Although XINSURANCE provided coverage to Jeff Bezos and Blue Origin passengers immediately before the launch, it is unheard of whether Bezos accepted the offer.

According to a *New York Times* DealBook newsletter story, Virgin Galactic and Blue Origin are not required by law to offer passengers with insurance. According to the report, there is no evidence that Virgin Galactic or Richard Branson obtained insurance for the perilous voyage of the firm CEO. The spaceship, VSS Unity, was definitely insured. Virgin Galactic has even suggested that at some time in the future, its passengers would be asked to sign a contract making them accountable for their own safety.[28]

Furthermore, the coverage for space flight through a life insurance policy is questionable. Historically, life insurance plans did not cover or charged a higher premium for dangerous hobbies such as personal flying, skydiving and hanggliding. Life insurance companies are unlikely to contemplate space flight since it has not been made available to everybody and is not accessible to the general population. While commercial aviation has not been banned from life insurance, it is possible that commercial space flight will be insured.

To accommodate space travel, the contract's language will need to be changed significantly. As we are seeing now, a strongly commercialised environment would very certainly require liability covering for passengers similar to current airline laws. The history of space travel insurance may be similar to that of aviation insurance. The first air travel policy was created in 1911, but it didn't take long for pioneers like Charles Lindbergh to complete a transatlantic flight insured for $18,000.[29]

Perhaps insurers will initially insert stipulations saying that they will bear no liability if someone dies. Still, as more information about the threats becomes available, safety is proven and flying frequency increases, the limitations will be gradually lowered. Over time, the aviation insurance industry has evolved to be a multibillion-dollar industry. Once the space travel industry becomes large enough, it may be integrated into ordinary commercial aviation, given the dangers and any future regulation are expected to be comparable.

Insurers may be increasingly ready to write policies when the focus of space flight shifts from high-net-worth individuals to the general population. Even discounting all reported space trash, there is an inherent risk in travelling into space. Still, technology will move forward with time, safety will constantly precede when

## 164  Rohan R. Pillai and Arshi Alam

the public is concerned and space flight becomes commercialised. Space travel insurance may be required by law and so acquired by businesses, or it may be required by travellers of different net worth and purchased directly by passengers.

The insurance sector will collect data needed to complete appropriate underwriting and pricing as space trips become more common. Space flight will develop and may eventually meet the criteria for an insurable risk. Any modifications in mainstream transportation would be covered by the insurance sector, especially if there is a need for profit.

Furthermore, Lloyds of London believes that the space insurance industry has averaged $550 million in yearly premium payments over the last decade. However, the majority of these have been satellites and non-human cargo transported to the International Space Station. Neil Stevens, senior Vice-President of space products at insurance broker Marsh, told the *New York Times*, "The insurance sector must decide if this is more like aviation insurance or present space plans. There has never been a time when insurance markets have not stepped up". He believes that this is only one tiny step towards turning space travel into a full-fledged tourist industry.[30]

The risks' prototype nature, combined with a high degree of new technology and an inadequacy or absence of relevant historical information, needs a case-by-case evaluation by expert underwriters. As a result, with its methodical technical analysis and tailored coverage, the space insurance market would be more positioned to manage this risk than the aviation insurance market. Because it is more accustomed to dealing with huge fleets, common design patterns and mass transportation, the aviation insurance market is ill-equipped to cope with such unique/new risk. When vehicles acquire appropriate levels of dependability, design and equipment commonality, flying frequency and commercial viability, insurance market forces and underwriters will propose less one-of-a-kind insurance solutions.

Passenger liability insurance is not required under current federal regulations in the United States. Under this legal framework, potential space tourists will be travelling at their own risk, having signed a waiver of redress based on informed consent. In the United States, trial attorneys are disputing the legal significance of these waivers. If the waiver law is not approved at the State level, it will very certainly be challenged in State courts in the United States. Because of the unclear nature, extent and availability of the information to be provided to the potential passenger, as well as its inherent impenetrability to non-professionals, defining the critical informed consent need may likewise represent an impossible aim. Space tourism firms will respond in the case of such an incidence, guided by a solid risk management plan.

## Chapter Conclusion

Looking back upon the above analysis, it becomes clear that the current laws governing space tourism are, at best, patchworks and stop-gap measures. Locating space tourism in the international regime itself is an arduous task. Often essential questions are left unaddressed, opening the field wide for a contractual recusal from all kinds of liability. The lack of governing law in most States, the ambiguity regarding air travel and space travel demarcation, and the lack of consensus on the status of space tourists further complicate the matter. The distribution of risk and uncertainty regarding insurance leaves plenty of room for future litigation. Given the rising commercial space tourism, these problems will increase manifold.

The US FAA regulation for all its flaws provides, at the least, a guideline based on whose principles such contracts can be formulated. Requirement of compliance and incorporation of legally mandated clauses can bridge the gap that is currently evident and provide for a just distribution of risks. The informed consent regime appears to be titled towards the flight operator; however, such an assertion remains conjectural in the absence of significant litigation. The insurance industry appears to be developing an appetite for space tourism; however, much remains dependent on the fate of space tourist flights in the coming days.

This wide-ranging uncertainty and confusion regarding space tourism will not only hamper the development of the commercial space travel industry but will likely lead to contentious litigation. The researchers believe that the calls for establishing a new space tourism law regime on an international level are well-founded in their foresight and are increasingly becoming necessary.

## Notes

1 Gabriella C. Sgrosso, *International Space Law* (Vicchio di Mugello: Logisma Editore, 2011) pp. 266 & 267.
2 Mark J. Sundahl, 'The Duty to Rescue Space Tourists and Return Private Spacecraft', *Law Faculty Articles and Essays, Journal of Space Law*, Vol. 35, 2009, pp. 163–200 at p. 165.
3 Tanja Masson-Zwaan L., 'Regulation of Sub-Orbital Space Tourism in Europe: A Role for EU/EASA?', *Air and Space Law*, Vol. 35, No. 3, 2010, pp. 263–272 at p. 264.
4 Tanja Masson-Zwaan and Steven Freeland, 'Between Heaven and Earth: The Legal Challenges of Human Space Travel', *Acta Astronautica*, Vol. 66, No. 11 & 12, 2010, pp. 1597–1607 at p. 1599.
5 Treaty on Principles Governing the Activities of States in the Exploration and Use of Outer Space, Including the Moon and Other Celestial Bodies, 27 January 1967, 610 UNTS 205, 18 UST 2410, TIAS No 6347, 6 ILM 386 (entered into force on 10 October 1967) [Outer Space Treaty], Art. I.
6 Agreement on the Rescue of Astronauts, the Return of Astronauts and the Return of Objects Launched into Outer Space, 1967, RES 2345 (XXII), Preamble.
7 Stephan Hobe, 'Legal Aspects of Space Tourism', *Nebraska Law Review*, Vol. 86, No. 2, 2007, pp. 439–458 at p. 446.
8 Thomas Neger and Edith Walter, 'Space Law - An Independent Branch of the Legal System', in C. Brünner and A. Soucek (eds.) *Outer Space in Society, Politics and Law* (Vienna: Springer, 2011) pp. 219–489 at p. 240.
9 Electronic Code of Federal Regulations, 14 CFR, Chapter III (C) §460.45 (2015)
10 *Id.*
11 70 Fed. Reg. 77269.
12 Rebekah Davis Reed, 'Ad Astra Per Aspera: How Shaping A Liability Regime for the Future of Space Tourism', *Houston Law Review*, Vol. 46, No. 2, 2009, pp. 585–613 at pp. 599.

13 71 Fed. Reg. 75627 ("Neither Congress nor the FAA mandated waivers of claims against an operator"); 70 Fed. Reg. 77269.
14 14 C.F.R. § 460.49.
15 Virginia Space Flight Liability and Immunity Act, Va. Code. Ann. §§ 8.01-227.8 to 8.01-227.10 (West 2010).
16 *Id.*
17 Dimitrios Buhalis and Carolos Costa, *Tourism Business Frontiers: Consumer, Products and Industry* (Amsterdam: Butterworth Heinemann, 2006) p. 157.
18 *Supra* note 7, at 439–458.
19 *Turcotte* v. *Fell* (1986) 502 N.E.2d N.Y.
20 Walter T. Champion, *Fundamentals of Sports Law* (New York: Clark Boardman, 1990) p. 3.
21 Ram Jakhu and Raja Bhattacharya, 'Legal Aspects of Space Tourism', *Proceedings of the Forty-Fifth Colloquium on the Law of Outer Space*, 2002, pp. 112–129 at p. 120.
22 14 C.F.R. § 440.17(e)-(f) (2007).
23 Convention on Damage Caused by Foreign Aircraft to Third Parties on the Surface ("Rome Convention") Oct. 7, 1952, 310 U.N.T.S. 181
24 Valigrie Kayser, *Launching Space Objects: Issues of Liability and Future Prospects* (R. Jakhu et al. Eds., 2001) p. 52.
25 E. Jason Steptoe, 'United States Government Licensing of Commercial Space Activities by Private Enterprise', *Proceedings of the Twenty-Seventh Colloquium on the Law of Outer Space*, 1985, pp 191–196 at p. 240.
26 See Stephan Hobe, 'Legal Aspects of Space Tourism', *Nebraska Law Review*, Vol. 86, No. 2, 2007, at p. 86
27 Richard C. Frese, 'Will Space Travel Insurance Become as Common as Auto Insurance?' available at https://www.milliman.com/en/insight/will-space-travel-insurance-become-as-common-as-auto-insurance Last visited, 22 January 2022.
28 Sara Lewis Kallop, "Cover Me to the Moon: Will Insurers Provide Coverage for Space Tourism Travel?" available at <https://www.jd*Supra*.com/legalnews/cover-me-to-the-moon-will-insurers-8693355/> Last visited on 22 January 2022.
29 Willis Towers Watsonm, 'Insurance Marketplace Realities 2021 Spring Update – Aerospace', available at <https://www.willistowerswatson.com/en-US/Insights/2021/04/insurance-marketplace-realities-2021-spring-update-aerospace> Last visited on 22 January 2022.
30 *Supra* note 23.

# 11

# SPACE TOURISM

## Possible Crimes and Their Adjudication

*G.S. Sachdeva*

### Introduction

With commercial travel to space having started with flights by Virgin Galactic, Blue Origin and SpaceX, space tourism appears just around the corner. To begin with, it may start with sub-orbital flights for gravity thrills, then orbiting space stations as entertainment dens leading to celestial hotels and space habitats for vacationing and longer residence, respectively. Roscosmos is also buoyed by the mission of 8 December 2021 that carried Japanese billionaire Yusaku Maezawa and his assistant to the International Space Station (ISS). It thus seems ready to fight for this niche business of space tourism for its market share and supremacy.[1] The Russian view is that space tourism is the future and it is not for money but "It's national prestige…".[2]

The safety of space flights has been repeatedly demonstrated and sustained. Tariff rates are also bound to become affordable with multiplicity of space carriers and ensuing competition. The space carriers are promising exhilarating views of the planet Earth in cosmic perspective and *lumiere* splendour that could be surreal and mesmerising. The touristic offers will progressively become more interesting and attractive, for example, a package of wedding ceremony in a space station, honeymooning on the Moon[3] or golfing and other sports on celestial bodies. The space hospitality industry may, later, proffer thematic tours on the celestial bodies or longer stays for research.

It is to be expected that space groupings would be cosmopolitan with the multiplicity of nationalities, ethnicities, cultural backgrounds, a mindset of values and behavioural attitudes. Moreover, humans would naturally carry their instincts of pugnacity, ego and revenge even to the outer space domain. Each factor would pack the gathering with differences making it endemic to disagreements, conflict

DOI: 10.4324/9781032617961-11

**168** G.S. Sachdeva

and resultant crimes. Moreover, the conditions of cramped claustrophobic living in space as also the travails of blast-off, the effects of velocity, spin and g-factor would make even a trained person uncomfortable and irritated, bodily and mentally, and this overwhelming feeling of continued uneasiness may erupt into a crime, minor or major.

The existing corpus of space law has no specific rules for handling such situations. In fact, Outer Space Treaty (OST) did not visualise such contingencies and the need for remedies because astronauts then were highly trained professionals with ingrained discipline. But tourists may be rich persons derived from different cultural and family backgrounds and may turn out to be spoilt brats and demanding grown-ups. And their stay in cramped hotel accommodation and the claustrophobic environment with scant comfort and little privacy may cause annoyance. Added to these can be the adverse effects of blast-off, reduced gravity and the hazardous environment of space. The cumulative effect of all these factors could cause provocation and, in the ultimate, crimes.

Acts of crime in space hotels may pose problems in adjudication due to conflicts of jurisdiction and hassles of extradition. Of course, help can be legitimately sought from the tenets of international law, but this may not be enough to settle all issues. This dilemma leads to a need for a *specialis* treaty to regulate the handling of space crimes with requisite procedures. Again, OST does not permit the operation of national sovereignty on the celestial bodies. Hence outer space remains an ungoverned domain with no policing of compliances or enforcement of treaty provisions. Confusion and defiance can be visualised easily, which may lead to disorder and conflict and clamour for enforcement of the rule of law.

It can be logically argued that there is need for a governance body for the composite outer space, which has been suggested as Space Superintendence Authority (SSA)[4] or World Space Organisation (WSO),[5] as an organ of the UN with a suitable charter, professional staffing and adequate funding to administer this ungoverned domain. A proposal is now mooted that the defunct Trusteeship Council may be revived and repurposed for the task of this governance. This organ of the UN, earlier also, discharged a similar function and would be eminently suited for the administration of "the province of all mankind" and management of Common Heritage of Mankind by executing leases of celestial realty for commercial mining of natural resources and managing spaceports and space traffic with safety in order to promote space activities in the best interests of humankind.

As regards crimes, the executive organisation of outer space can, at best, report these as committed in outer space but cannot act in the judicial dispensation. Of course, the first reference would be to the concerned States to assume jurisdiction under principles of territoriality or nationality or universality or supra-territoriality, either legislated or claimed by possession. But these parameters may not be sufficient for the purpose and may conflict with claims of extradition or that enough evidence for trial may not be available to the country assuming jurisdiction. Such hassles through diplomatic processes tend to be long drawn. So, a solution

Space Tourism: Possible Crimes and Their Adjudication **169**

has been proffered to establish an International Court of Space Crimes (ICSC) as a specialised bench of the International Court of Justice (ICJ) or International Criminal Court (ICC) for adjudication in long-drawn, disputed, complex and multi-nationality cases.

It is conceded that the proffered solutions are not simple decisions but would need prolonged negotiations and diplomatic consultations to build consensus on all the three suggestions, *viz.*, concluding a new treaty, deciding on resuscitation of Trusteeship Council and establishing a specialist bench as ICSC for trial of complicated and disputed space crimes. Also, my submission may have to be suitably modified and honed to the objectives intended. And space law fraternity is urged to cogitate and comment on the wisdom and viability of the recommendations. For the very reason of dilatory processes involved, proactive initiatives are requested to be taken by the United Nations and the COPUOS so that an appropriate and predictive enforcement system is in place and in time to tackle the problems contingent on the popularity of space tourism and rush of tourists.

It will be prudent to define the scope of this chapter at the beginning itself. On the positive side, it will visualise crimes by humans, as conventionally understood, in the space domain. It will also discuss business crimes which may or may not attract corporeal punishment but would certainly incur liability and compensation. The discussion also intends to allude to crimes against humanity that may be caused by any component of space tourism, irrespective of the mode and method of retribution. Thus, violations by the States in breach or defiance of treaties, like weaponisation of outer space[6] and militarisation of celestial bodies or commercial colonisation of celestial natural resources or claims of pseudo-sovereignty,[7] in establishment of heritage parks would be excluded from the purview of this chapter.

## Viability of Space Tourism: Assumptions

Commercial space travel has commenced with the efforts and investments from the private sector of the economy, particularly the United States, though other countries like Russia, China and India may soon follow. Dennis Tito, the first fare-paying passenger, is believed to have paid $2 billion to Roscosmos for his week-long trip to the ISS. That was indeed a fortune, but the current tariff for a Virgin Galactic sub-orbital flight is pegged at $2.5 million per passenger. It is also public news that its anticipated flights for the next five years are already booked or optioned out. SpaceX, Blue Origin, Bigelow and others are also in the race as commercial space carriers. No doubt, with mounting competition, the tariff rates for space travel will progressively reduce and become more affordable.

It is, therefore, natural that space travellers would expect space hospitality with some sort of novel experience, a promise of new entertainment and conducting of unique sports to keep them engaged, in their spare time, while in space. Most of these touristic requirements are being actively discussed and meticulously planned. Expectedly, the touristic offerings would include a spectacle of earth-lights at night,

**170** G.S. Sachdeva

an exhilarating view of the universe, a marriage ceremony in space, honeymooning in a low-gravity environment, fun trips in leisure time and unique sports to keep the tourists engaged. Space visitors would also have theme tours in mind and select itineraries of geological interest or archaeological/historic sites or heritage parks or even customised tour to satisfy personal interest and purposeful objectives.

It is expected that the US quarters of the International Space Station (ISS) are due to be commercialised through lease or sale as the budgetary provision for its maintenance will end by 2025. So, its commercial utility is being mulled for different purposes like a filming studio, for advertising by billboard transmissions[8] or even as a multi-purpose floating motel in space, among others. Japan is planning to hoist a space station for movies and videos while China is already building one. Axiom Space is also intending to build a movie production studio on the refurbished ISS by 2024.[9] More ideas and options will follow. Similarly, visits to celestial habitations could be for researchers in astronomy, geology, space agronomy, mineral exploration, space psychology, effects on biology or a tour of celestial heritage sites and so on. Hence, research authentication visit, circuit tour of heritage parks or purposed visit for unique space-sports or sheer fun tourism is expected to be on the menu for leisure, pleasure and entertainment.

Apart from short space trips, the public worldwide has shown interest in one-way tickets to celestial residencies on the Moon, the Mars and even deep in space, if feasible and liveable. In this regard, the concepts of Woerner's Moon village[10] or Mars colony or exo-Mars deep-space camps and habitats appear promising and worth promoting. These prospects are neither oneiric visions nor a crazy idea but an anticipatable reality of the near future and an integral part of the programmes and projects of the twenty-first-century tourism industry. Thus, space tourism is just on the cusp of progress with State impetus, substantial promotion and public enthusiasm.

The boost also comes from the reactivation of NASA plans for lunar real estate development as a base camp for deep-space probes. Other reasons for this revived interest in space habitats are: to create new lands to accommodate population expansion; to create a refuge for the survival of humanity in the event of a total disaster on Earth; and to create wealth by exploiting natural resources on celestial bodies.[11] Another reiteration from NASA comes in a recent statement announcing its plan "of sending humans to the Mars appears optimistic and realistic".[12] No wonder the bandwagon of space tourism has been cranked well and is gaining traction.

## Components of Space Tourism

Before we embark on our discussion on crimes, it will be prudent to enlist the components or stakeholders in space tourism. This aspect becomes pertinent because each component, by its nature, character, level of interaction and extent of involvement, would account for space crimes. Our understanding of crimes is mostly of those prohibited or mandated acts as defined in legal codes and either committed or omitted by human beings. But actions by other entities, public and private, can also be tantamount to grave situations, like crimes, more so in space which is an unsparing environment. It is, therefore, important to clarify that the term "space crimes" used here is very generic in scope and has a broad, even loose, connotation to cover near-crimes, dereliction in duty, lapses in responsibility, incurring of liability, and cognate acts, situations and interpretations. Nevertheless, the crimes discussed will be related to the space domain, whether committed in space, directed towards space or emanated from space.

## The Space Tourist

Among the major components of space tourism or, in other words, stakeholders, the first and most important one is the space tourist, who is a passenger for the space carriers and a guest for the hospitality industry and becomes the core and the reason for space tourism. In the past, astronauts who went into space were highly disciplined professionals from the defence forces, and even fare-paying passengers were either State-sponsored or were rich businessmen. Moreover, astronauts were pampered with the haloed status of "envoys of mankind", which attracted certain responsibility also. Hence chances of actual space crimes were minimal, and the few occurrences that happened were either condonable or punished with leniency.

Space tourists of the next decade and later would be drawn from the civilian populations of all ages and from different countries; hence, despite pre-trip training, their discipline threshold may not be high. Moreover, most of them would be the ones spending their lifetime savings for such an experience, so their expectations may be high to demand value for money despite constraints of the spatial environment and the operational hazards of space flight. Thus, the fare-paying passenger may be, at times, highly assertive, unreasonably demanding, wary of the discomforts and un-adjusting to fellow passengers. Further, the bio-psycho-effects of velocity, g-factor and gravity in blast-off, and micro-gravity later may also make the passenger indisposed, nervous and unwell. Perhaps, the seeds of conflict and crime may be sown at this stage that may grow into ugly events later.

## The Space Carrier

The next stakeholder is the space carrier. Safety of passengers is of paramount importance as contractual duty and under the tort law. Ergo, there should be no compromises relating to technical upkeep and space-worthiness of the vehicle as also the availability of full information about space situational awareness for space traffic manoeuvres and emergencies. Thus, the carrier's culpable commissions and omissions may not constitute conventional crimes, yet these deficiencies and defaults are punishable in other ways of liability and compensation. At the same time, it is pertinent to note that any negligence in space operations can be grave

**172** G.S. Sachdeva

because the space environment is unsparingly hazardous and rarely gives another chance for survival. Hence, due diligence and abundant caution in space operations would be legally expected and would call for the highest care and attention.

### Business of Space Hospitality

In the activity of space tourism, the hospitality business assumes a central position, and its core responsibility is to provide residential infrastructure and guest services with reasonable comfort and privacy. In the 1970s itself, space planners had visualised and created blueprints of infrastructure for huge colonies that were feasible on the Moon and the Mars. Space tourism was in view and realisable through these planetary villages, which had other purposes and objectives also. These habitats or space galleries were additionally intended to create new lands to accommodate human population explosion, to ensure the survival of humanity in an eventuality of global disaster annihilating mankind and to create wealth by exploiting the natural resources of outer space.[13] This ideation has progressed but not as fast as envisaged initially.

However, an important mandate for any orderly and enjoyable living in orbital tourist stations or planetary hotels or celestial resorts would be to ensure safety and security of the guests, tourists and residents during their stay. At the same time, these residencies should also include approved plans and SOPs (Standard Operating Procedures), which would need to be activated and executed for their exit and evacuation in case of emergencies. Adequate food options on the menu and their sufficiency in availability would be another veritable demand of the guests.

Visitors on such a trip would also need entertainment, fun engagement and games for their pleasure and leisure time. Towards this end, an alliance of experts in space-sports and the entertainment industry are designing and developing games exclusively for low or micro-gravity playing fields. A group known as the Space Games Federation has already identified a number of the prospective game concepts like guiding a magnetic ball through hoops in space-to-space dodge ball. The central theme and focal point of these activities are just fun and pass-time. However, these would require new playing fields, new rules of the game and a new competitive spirit. The proposals under consideration are being evaluated by sports visionaries and games experts on the parameters of fun concept, play-feasibility, game strategy and community involvement. The accepted ideas will be defined, characterised and formalised as space-sports, which will be open to volunteering competitors without any discrimination.[14]

Allan Shepard of the Apollo 14 mission is known to have hit a golf ball on the surface of the Moon, and it travelled 22 m.[15] People were fascinated with the stroke, and golfing on the Moon may become an elitist fad. In due course, competitive sports and athletic endeavours in space, though initially for sheer fun, light exercise and occupation of spare time, will eventually become more challenging than anything on Earth. Thus, space-sports will create and throw up new public idols called "astroletes",[16] who will be individuals with the core skills of an astronaut and harbouring the competitive spirit of an athlete. Further, sportsmen have often been leaders of global friendship and informal ambassadors of peace-building and global amity. At the same time, crimes in the sports fraternity are not unknown and would *ipso facto* travel to the space domain.

### The Authorising State

The next component of space tourism would be the State that would "authorise and permit" the space activity. This aspect assumes importance because "States parties to the Treaty shall bear international responsibility for national activities in space"[17] irrespective of the character of the entity carrying out the same. This provision further mandates that such activities "shall require authorisation and continuing supervision by the appropriate state party to the Treaty".[18] In other words, this Article requires that national space activities should be in conformity with the Treaty principles and that the State shall be duty-bound to ensure compliance with the same.

Another responsibility that rests on the launching State, though coupled with jurisdiction over control on and ownership of the space object,[19] relates to international liability for any damage caused to another State party.[20] As the risk threshold is high in outer space, the liability aspect assumes greater importance. But experts often lament that the safety element in space flights is a neglected area because neither the States have evolved safety regulations to govern space-worthiness nor space carriers have bound themselves to any safety standards. In fact, space carriers have, in practice, not even maintained any historical record to prove that their technology and operations are safe.[21] Hence accountability for any disaster is completely lacking, and this lawlessness is reinforced by the US Congress Moratorium on Safety Regulations established in 2004.[22]

There is, however, an allied duty of the State under the Outer Space Treaty[23] and also laid down in an amplificatory convention which command that space objects launched into outer space shall be registered in the national registry.[24] It further requires that details of the same launchings be "furnish[ed] to the Secretary-General of the United Nations, as soon as practicable...".[25] In the past, derelictions in compliance with this requirement have been observed, perhaps, for classified secret missions, particularly by China.

## Crimes in Space

### General Discussion

Crimes and humanity have travelled together in history, from Adam in heaven to Cain on Earth and also with their descendants in mankind. Humans have tended to offend others on some cause or pretext to incur reciprocal wrath or disapproval of the elders. Possibly, breach of clan norms and other such defiance were unacceptable, to the community leaders and the society at large, forcing retribution or punishment. However, with the passage of time, the then normative irritants and inimical disputes have now grown into moulds of legal classifications and coded crimes. Normative or codified, some such condemnable acts may reflect an element of malice or volitional ill-will (*mens rea*), which is a peculiar characteristic of human beings alone. Interestingly, animals harbour no *mens rea* against each other and fight only for hunger and survival.

Psychologists inform, certain instincts like self-survival, pugnacity, revenge and greed, among others are biologically and psychologically wired in our DNA. These innate propensities tend to recur as reflex actions with a surprising frequency of repetition and uniformity in individual behaviour. Although these traits improve with conscious effort, training and experience yet, original predilections, personal kinks or repressed anger do wake up under provocation or similarity of encounter. Therefore, humans being human tend to carry their inherited and acquired baggage of genetic personality, inborn temperament, individual experiences, basic disposition, nurtured habits and personal eccentricities wherever they venture out, even to the space domain. And some of these traits may not be agreeable to or compatible with others in heterogeneous social groups and hence, the possibility of objections, disputes, clashes and crimes on some pretext or cause.

Crimes, "generally so understood",[26] remain crimes irrespective of the domain where committed, whether on the Earth, on the sea, under sea, in the air, in the outer space or on the celestial bodies. But crimes must contain two components of specificity: first is the *acteus*, either an act that is specifically prohibited or an act mandated yet not performed. The second component is *mens rea* or intention behind the act. Despite these near-universal conditionalities, human perception on crimes, even of the same crime, varies in different countries and communities due to historical factors, cultural legacies, religious injuncts, economic development, educational standards, constitutional guarantees, geographical compulsions, social influences, familial values or personal fixations, to mention only a few. Beset with varied grooming, predilections and experiences, different mindset and at different times, may look at the same or similar event or action to evoke different responses and varying levels of gravity of reaction.

Such situations do confront us on the Earth also, even within the same country, province or community where our opinions may vary, responses may be disparate and views may be incongruous or conflicting. These dissimilarities or dissent, however, would become more pronounced and manifest in internationally and ethnically and generationally mixed groups of tourists in space stations in orbit, space resorts on celestial bodies or residents in planetary habitats. These differences could be aggravated by the quality and quantity of direct or tangential relationships between them or the nature and extent of unavoidable contact in common areas of utilities and facilities. And experiences from these contacts can also influence individual opinions and perceptions which may tend to differ towards the same behaviour or action and so would reactions, creating a predicament for dissension and conflict leading to crimes. These inherences surely follow humans to the outer space in some form or the other.

Our dilemma would further increase due to pressures of specific influences of the space environment, working hazards in an unfamiliar milieu and associated mental anxiety for personal safety. It is to be expected that space passengers, hotel guests and planetary residents would constitute multi-nationality, multi-ethnicity and multi-generational groups with different habits, attitudinal mindsets, living styles and cultural values. And space stations and space habitations would, perforce, provide cramped spaces, unergonomic work stations, not-too-comfortable living and scant privacy. Added to these could be the deprivation of the affections of families and familiars. Therefore, under such conditions of cumulated mental tension, disputes, conflicts and crimes may erupt easily. In fact, humans are mentally wired with anger and pugnacity, and resultant expressions under deprivation or frustration, stress or provocation could be predictive triggers of actual or near-crimes.

Therefore, under such tense conditions, actions deemed innocuous, non-aggressive or non-provocative on Earth may elicit surprising or unpredictable responses urging to boldly express disapproval or precipitate dissent that may escalate to a conventional crime. On the other hand, an act of unmistakable crime on Earth may reveal disparate contributory factors or proximate causation in space. Possibly, the same or similar action in a space environment may draw a seemingly unexpected retort or an unnecessary provocation leading to gross reactions that may prompt or result in the commission of acts which could constitute patent crimes. Thus, Earth and space constitute dissimilar locus and background for the causation of crimes that may appear seemingly the same or similar in action and intent.

### Crimes by Tourists

Tourists, being human, would commit crimes in space as on the Earth but a shade grosser, a little oftener, which may be environmentally induced and under circumstantial tension. Thus, a tourist may commit a physical crime alone and by oneself on another or more, ranging from battery to injury to murder, and may even commit jointly with help or complicity on sudden provocation. These can also be conspiratorial with joint planning or to take revenge for past misdeeds. There can be collective crimes, like riots, or disturbance of law and order or creating nuisance in a public place.

Individual crimes may be of theft, misappropriation, embezzlement and other possessory crimes of illegal gains, stealing etc., crimes of mental harassment, hurting sentiments or spreading hate between countries, communities and denominations. Crimes against the State could be sedition, causing disaffection against legitimate authority, mutiny and uprising or waging war against the established State. This category could also cover terrorist acts, organised crimes and complicit acts by the mafia in parallel to and in defiance of the State authority.

**176** G.S. Sachdeva

### Near-Crimes by Space Carriers

Space carriers as operators of a public transportation system would attract several mandatory duties under tort law and other germane legislation. The primary imperative devolves in relation to the safety of the passengers during carriage to destination. Therefore, this mandate requires that there are no lapses in the standards of all-round safety, abidance of the space traffic management (STM) rules and that there are no compromises in space-worthiness of the capsule or satellite and its launch vehicle. This would also mean that there should be no dereliction in operational duty, advertent or inadvertent, by the employees and agents of the carrier. It commands due diligence in performance and actions in *abundanti cautela*. Deficiencies, derelictions and lapses may rarely lead to corporeal punishment or incarceration, yet liability for loss or damage caused to the contracting party, as also to the third party, would be binding and compensable.

It is also pertinent to mention that even under contract for carriage into space, a passenger would be entitled to liability and compensation in *restitutio in integrum* for death or injury in the event of an accident. It is possible that the carriers may contract out their liability under the doctrine of *volenti non fit injuria*, meaning voluntary action suffers no injury. There are other contractual clauses also to cut or mitigate the burden of liability, e.g. force majeure, *ad impossibilia* etc., for known or labelled hazardous activities. Ethically, a passenger must be properly informed of the risks entailed in the activity and truncations of liability, if any, before the contract is concluded. UN COPUOS can help create a standard contract format for space travel and stipulate liability regimen for space carriers duly protecting the legitimate interests of the passenger; as also shift the evidentiary burden for defence on the carrier under the doctrine of *res ipsa loquitur*, meaning facts speak for themselves. This evidentiary clause was introduced in the contracts for carriage by air under the Warsaw Convention, 1929.[27]

### Near-Crimes by Hospitality Business

Space hospitality is the critical element of space tourism and a vital link in the safety and security of the guests. The prime responsibility with criminal overtones relates to providing safe and secure residence to the guests, fail-proof infrastructure, fully working support utilities and necessary facilities for comfort and enjoyment. Any promised theme tours or historical trips should be conducted on time and in the best manner. Expectedly, space tourists would be a pampered lot and would overpoweringly demand value for their fortune spent on a once-in-a-lifetime trip. In a way, this is their valid right, and any deficiencies or lapses in performance would be a criminal denial as also a contractual breach. Alongside, guests deserve the best space-specific foods on their menu with utmost hygiene and sufficiency in availability.

Despite elaborate medical check-ups before launch, pink of health, at all times, cannot be guaranteed during the trip. Hence, hospitality agents should cater for

Space Tourism: Possible Crimes and Their Adjudication **177**

in-house arrangements of the medical staff of all categories, appropriate facilities and necessary medicines for dispositional health emergencies. Again, accidents and disasters cannot be predicted for the time of their occurrence or gravity of damage. And celestial bodies being exposed to radiation hazards from the Sun and other sources would need protective shelters for the safety of guests as the first priority. This facility of distress-shelters should be freely open to every guest in need, without discrimination. In dire necessity, the space treaties permit international cooperation, seeking safe shelter in facilities run and operated by other States.[28]

There may arise circumstances when the situation may so aggravate in a disaster or accident that the only judicious option for the safety of the guests may be evacuation to Earth. For this purpose, hospitality entities should also have contingency plans and backup systems to ensure shelter till safe return. Further, the process of evacuation must be transparent, without any preferences or bias, arbitrariness or discrimination, of any kind whatsoever, in facilitating rescue and departure to Earth so as not to cause any anguish or harm to any guest.[29] Else, it may attract action under Human Rights Convention or International Humanitarian Laws for torture and other imputations, as relevant.[30] This view may seem odd today, but its relevance will become apparent with time, necessity and repetition. Space law needs new jurisprudence of equality, equity and justice.

## Crimes against Humanity

Commercial space travel that commenced with Dennis Tito in 2001 has now got a boost in 2022 with the efforts of space tycoons like Branson and Bezos. Other competitors are following suit and will soon join the league of commercial space carriers. Hence, commercial space travel may become operational to the public in the right earnest. Market analysis reveals that a large number of prospective passengers worldwide are queuing up for ticket reservations or for booking of options.[31] If the commercial transportation system rolls safely, then space tourism is not far behind, and the number of launches will escalate exponentially over the years. Thus, growing space travel and tourism may lead to adverse effects on the Earth's atmosphere, space tourist sites and humanity. Further, the so introduced tourism facilities would augment the numbers of tourists that may pose problems of security screening to obviate anti-social elements from sneaking into space habitats.

### Adverse Effects on Earth's Atmosphere

There are yet many unknown adverse effects of space activities on the sustenance of the environment of the Earth. One such effect recently realised and appreciated is the impact of increased space launches on the ozone layer around the Earth, which is so vital to the health and well-being of humans. The concern becomes graver in view of the progressively increasing frequency of commercial space flights. Operators of spacelines are confident of the long queues for sub-orbital flights, and reliable projections estimate that the number and frequency of commercial space flights may increase from 10-a-year to about 360 annually in a decade[32] subject to opportunity windows. Hopes are that with increasing number of competing carriers and ensuing tourist rush, the estimates may be surpassed much sooner. The consequent adverse impact on the ozone layer can be well appreciated.

However, scientists caution about the impending possibility of pollution of the stratosphere by rocket exhausts from the burning of solid fuels. Their despondence increases because hybrid fuels, as propellants, have also revealed no major drop in the pollution level. The emitted carbon particles from exhaust, howsoever small in size and light in weight, tend to stay put almost *in situ*, for extraordinarily long periods. In the 1990s, a research team led by Dr. Rosenlof and others drawn from NOAA, NASA and the US Air Force studied pollution by Shuttle launches. It revealed the presence of chlorine emissions from launch rockets and their chemical reaction showed an adverse influence on ozone reserves.[33] Regrettably, there has not been much research and development towards safe fuels and rockets generating ozone-damaging substances are still used as work-horses.

It is conceded that the studies conducted so far have been preliminary in scope, limited in time and localised in space (over Florida), indicating a need for the latest and empirical data collection and analysis for better understanding and corrective action. Nevertheless, results from existing studies indicate that the atmosphere and stratosphere are undergoing specific changes in their character and content yielding strong hints of adverse impact on global climate and weather patterns with existential threats. As a result, the ecosystem of the total atmosphere seems vulnerable and at great risk.

In fact, the World Meteorological Organisation has already observed the widening of the ozone holes and hinted at the possibility of creating new such holes over spaceports, which are mushrooming worldwide (with four of them coming up in Japan alone), and has accordingly declared rockets as a potential future concern and a possible detriment to the well-being of mankind.[34] This calls for dedicated research on fuel substitutes that are less polluting and more friendly. But engineering history shows that these objectives may gain only incremental development through in-service evolution rather than quantum leaps in technology.[35]

An allied problem of concern would be the increased frequency of launches and noise pollution around the spaceports. This may ultimately affect the mental health and hearing faculties of those residing in nearby areas. Thus, there is a reason for "eco-anxiety" with a shaky validation for the *cause celebre* of space tourism. Possibly, the cost-benefits of sustained space travel, space hospitality and planetary habitations may turn out to be unconscionably high and equally unpredictable in consequences for humanity. Anyway, space travel may have to be held accountable for the pollution caused in the process and at the same time, we need to find ways to co-exist. Perhaps, one option could be to restrict the launches for commercial space travel in the current decade and concurrently accelerate research for greener fuels and evolve measures for eco-controls. It will be wise to act in time, in the larger interest of mankind, before it is too late and beyond redemption.

## Risks of Terrorist Activities in Space

Terrorism has plagued the world for many decades, and it has assumed many manifestations, from simple threats to hijacking to blowing up of aircraft. Cultural values have deteriorated and perceptions blurred by biases; as a result, terrorists take to anti-social and violent acts for perceived grievances and illusory wrongs. These outfits and believers usually select soft targets to avenge themselves and blitz their cause. It is logical to surmise that vulnerable space tourists and unsecured space assets appear just the right and opportune victims for such criminal elements.

Terrorism is not a physical entity or a weapon but a mindset and conviction that travels like a virus in the psyche of susceptible people. The infection spreads fast, and it becomes difficult to detect and isolate the infected ones. Therefore, valid apprehensions exist that tight security and fool-proof screening of space passengers and tourists may be a tall order, and there may be gaps in compliance. Such slip-ups can be highly dangerous all around. Further, space carriers and hospitality entities in their enthusiasm for competition and to harvest early profits of the nascent business may permit, by inadvertence or complicity, certain non-State actors or terrorist-minds to travel and stay as guests in a celestial hotel or planetary habitat. Good governance and efficient policing need to be localised in space because it cannot be efficiently operated or controlled from the Earth.

The presence of such a person in space environment can create a high-voltage situation of imponderable vulnerabilities. This aspect assumes prominence because a modern terrorist need not smuggle a bomb or hide a weapon, the carrying of which is prohibited and whose presence may be detected in security checks. With the easy availability of modern and advanced digital technology, it seems highly probable that a terrorist can cause more damage with a laptop keyboard or cyber applications than a kinetic bomb or weapon. The ominous threats could be existential to humanity. Perhaps, vigilant security of the highest order may, at best, mitigate such a threat.

## The Hazards of Space Debris

It is a well-known fact that the existing launch vehicles, despite technological advances, leave certain "sheddings" like discarded vehicle stages, used-up fuel containers and even blasted nuts and bolts. Added to this is the trend to launch huge constellations of small satellites with not-so-long operational life. And given a small population of zombie satellites, all these add to a major problem of space debris which causes safety scares to astronauts in the space stations as also other operational satellites, which are not only high-value assets but also so vital for our daily communications and entertainment needs on the Earth.

As a result of debris pollution, the low Earth orbit is so dense that it is becoming difficult to find an appropriately timed window of opportunity to launch satellites. Such safe slots are becoming fewer and narrower in time. Given the promising

**180** G.S. Sachdeva

possibility of commercial space travel and tourism, the number of launches will increase tremendously and add more clutter. Thus, the resultant accumulation of space debris will almost choke any opportunity for launch and degrade the sustainability of the environment for such exploratory or commercial activities for our posterity. This is no wisdom and can be deemed a crime against humanity.

It, therefore, becomes imperative that we clean up the caused clutter in space. This requires systematic, concerted and planned efforts at remediation. For future mitigation, best practices, as recommended, must be adopted by all space-faring countries[36] to reduce future induction of space debris. Partly, improved technology of lesser stages of rockets is also helpful in this regard. The other aspect of the problem relates to the remediation of the past accumulations of space debris and the consequences of their natural implosions and explosions. Not to forget that thousands of pieces have been added by the ASAT experiments in the destruction of defunct satellites.

The situation is hurtling towards utter "irremediation" and calls for stern measures and salvage operations to be mandated by a new treaty and, in tandem, supported by national laws and technical practices. Scavenging outer space is becoming possible with techniques developed by Switzerland and Japan. The cleansing process, however, needs resources and these may be mustered from the respective polluting countries on the principles of "polluter pays" and "proportional responsibility", which have already been internationally mooted, accepted and almost practised under agreements germane to climate change. Not cleaning up outer space for posterity would be as bad as a crime.

## Some Challenges Posed by Space Tourism

Space tourism may be a once-in-a-lifetime aspiration of space enthusiasts, a laudable ambition of the business tycoons for company prestige as also a vision of a profitable industry which may create a multiplier effect in national economies. Granting the benefits, this activity, nevertheless, faces some challenges, of which important ones are flagged here for attention and action at different levels, national and international. But a breach or defiance of existing law would be a near-crime. Apropos, a couple of suggestions are put forward in succeeding paragraphs.

### *Space Traffic Management*

Space launches need precise space situational awareness as also meteorological information at the exact time of the blast-off. The launch windows are generally narrow in time and need punctual launch effort. In sporadic launch cases, such information may be obtained from data agencies, but when such space flights regularly move up and down from different spaceports from the Earth and from celestial bodies, space traffic management (STM) would become an imperative necessity. This can be operated and controlled on the lines of air traffic control system management. But to ensure accident-free space transportation, STM would require uniformity in operations, intense international cooperation, inter-agency coordination and an authoritative control organisation to enforce discipline and ensure compliance.

### Spaceports Infrastructure

At present, space flights are few, by select operators and at rather infrequent intervals, more or less like inaugural or chartered air flights. However, with the advent of space tourism and ushering in commercial space flights, certain regularity and certainty in schedules would be lawfully necessary as a public transportation system. Moreover, in today's context, flights may be few and planned that can operate from State agency launch-pads as maintained by NASA. But commercial transportation to feed space tourism would need to avail of independent paid services of private spaceports coming up in other countries for launches.

Japan is known to be developing four private spaceports on scattered islands for commercial space launches. These facilities will be open for use on a hire basis. Similar private launch facilities are also being developed by China to be offered on a pay-and-launch system. The costs and modalities of charging for casual launches are yet to be decided. On the other hand, space-port facilities need colossal investments, which will have to be capitalised and amortised. And these will also demand regular maintenance and incidental expenses. Thus, launch costs would be heavy.

### Celestial Realty for Tourist Resorts

Space tourism would need, apart from orbiting resorts, hotels on the celestial bodies, to begin with on the Moon and the Mars. For constructing such residential accommodation and ancillary infrastructure, the industry would need real estate either as an outright purchase or long-term lease. This is not permissible under existing space law[37] which does not permit national appropriation or claim of sovereignty by States in outer space. The Moon Agreement, 1979 also treats the Moon and other celestial bodies as the province of all mankind (Article 4) and "Common Heritage of Mankind" (Article 11). But there is no governing body or established authority to regulate and execute leases of celestial realty of the common province, recover rentals thereon and ensure their demise on expiry of the term.

The dilemma is serious and insurmountable under the incumbent legal order of space, and unless resolved soon, may provoke defiance of the established Outer Space Treaty provisions. Such a defiant State practice may be obviated by solutions. Therefore, it can only be resolved by authorising a UN organisation to manage developmental aspects, private appropriation and commercial utilisation of outer space and celestial bodies. It has earlier been proposed that a World Space Authority[38] may be established under the UN umbrella. But a better and speedier option for implementation would be to revive and repurpose the defunct

**182** G.S. Sachdeva

Trusteeship Council for the total governance, developmental superintendence and holistic management of the outer space, including celestial bodies. Else, breaches of treaty law would occur.

### Health Concerns in Outer Space and on Celestial Bodies

Empirical studies on the health of astronauts have revealed changes in body structure and on body organs. Therefore, physical health and mental fitness are important for space tourists and would be so stipulated by the carriers because space travel is no bullock-cart ride and requires the highest standards of sustainable physique, mental agility and psychological preparedness for this unique trip of tourism. Space travel and hotels will involve inconveniences of physical spaces with a claustrophobic environment which, for some, may be difficult to withstand and endure. Further, space travel entails accelerations at high speed and spiral motion on launch and effects of high g-factor, which may cause bodily discomfort in lower limbs and excessive blood rushing to the brain. This condition may cause vomiting, black-out and other sicknesses despite training and acclimatisation. Again, a zero-gravity environment would require practice of a "new-walking" habit and other unaccustomed effects of living in space. Not sounding despondent, the predicament may be really hard to contend with. Therefore, only hard-core enthusiasts may venture.

The Red Planet is the next interesting touristic base and a future home for humans, but it may offer worse conditions and be riskier also. Despite the technological viability, space radiation imposes limitations in terms of comfort and longevity of stay. The scientists have been studying two main types of hazardous radiation – solar energetic particles (SEP) and galactic cosmic rays (GCR). By analysing photographs and with inputs sent by Ingenuity probes, it appears possible to stay safely on the planet for up to four years only.[39] Howsoever mentally strong be the tourists, yet risk-prone stays, hazardous environs and absence of contact with terra firma would keep them tense for "anchored" safety of life, and they could blow up on minor annoyance or provocation. Thus crimes, minor or major, are enmeshed in space tourism, in different ways.

### Adjudication of Space Crimes

Having established that humans everywhere will commit crimes, and more so in the space environment, it becomes pertinent to consider their trial or adjudication by a competent court. The primary purpose of a trial is to evaluate the evidence to determine the crime of the accused or find a reason for exoneration or acquittal. In case the accusation is proved beyond a reasonable doubt, then follows punishment and quantum of sentence or award. The sentence may be mitigated, quantitatively or qualitatively, for several considerations like accidental act, under provocation, age of the accused, the possibility of reformation and so on. While for some reasons, such as for deterrence in the future or to curb recidivism by a habitual offender, maximum awardable punishment may be decided.

First, it is pertinent to note that at the time of negotiations on OST, crimes were not considered for the inclusion of a suitable provision. It could not even be imagined if astronauts, with their military training and regimented behaviour, could indulge in such acts, and space tourists were not at all in the reckoning. So, the Treaty has no Article for such contingencies except the mention of "jurisdiction and control" over astronauts.[40] This claim to jurisdiction was derived from the principles of territoriality and nationality under international law and facilitated the settlement of jurisdiction and competence of the court to seize the case for trial.

Secondly, outer space and celestial bodies remain an ungoverned and un-policed domain, so bringing a culprit to an appropriate court would not be easy. It will be more so because treaties generally do not define procedures for breach, defiance or criminality. State practice prescribes that option and remedial measures. Thirdly, there could be conflicting claims for the extradition of the accused. Such assertions are generally based on bilateral treaties, but where no such treaty exists, the wrangles may involve diplomatic channels. And permission to extradite is not only based on the legalese but nuanced by political and other considerations. Thus, negotiations could be dilatory and prolonged.

Lastly, there is a dictum that justice delayed is justice denied. Therefore, in cases of inordinate delay in dispensation of justice, the matter could be elevated to the International Court of Justice, or its specialised bench on space crimes, or International Court of Space Crimes (ICSC) could take cognisance of the matter and adjudicate on the specifics of the crime with the help of amicus curiae, as necessary, from the respective countries of the defendant and the complainant.

This aspect of "particularised" advice to the court assumes importance in social justice because the legal codes of the nationals in dispute may differ, and the respective awardable sentences could vary. Further, even individual perceptions of the crime and the verdict may evoke conflicting responses due to variations in social norms, cultural fixations or individual mindsets due to economic or educational or social background. Hence, the emphasis could be on social justice rather than sheer legalistic dispensation based on judicial option. It seems rather imperative that the judgment should be viewed as neutral, just and impartial by both parties involved.

## Chapter Conclusion

The history of crimes and humans is inalienable. Perhaps, such acts are born out of inherited instincts which have mutated with social change and economic prosperity. There is no reason to believe that humans shall not carry this inherited baggage and acquired predilections to outer space and celestial bodies. May be, circumstances of outer space would be more stressful due to mixed populations and their differentials in perception. Hence, greater proneness to commit crimes.

**184** G.S. Sachdeva

In such cosmopolis situations, crimes may involve persons from different nationalities, the locus may not clearly define the jurisdiction and claims to extradition for non-judicial reasons may undermine the competence of the court. Procedure for prosecution is another deficiency in international law which makes it lame for trial. Further, evidence for the court may be scattered or not accumulable within the competence of the trial court. These imponderables may render the trial of space crimes difficult and inefficient, leaving both parties grumbling and dissatisfied. Thus, the existing corpus of space law reveals its inadequacies to the challenge.

These hassles suggest the need for a *specialis* treaty that can regulate activities with the least friction or conflicts, and can comprehend and tackle the flagged issues to provide solutions in the best interest of all parties. Moreover, as discussed earlier, outer space and celestial bodies are an ungoverned domain where national sovereignty is not exercised. Hence, for the administration and governance of the composite domain, the UN may repurpose and task Trusteeship Council. This organisation, thus, could manage the real estate of celestial bodies, provide an impetus for its commercial development to benefit humanity and ensure its sustainability for posterity to enjoy space tourism and other commercial benefits. The initiative for this would lie with the UNCOPUOS.

For consideration of jurisdiction, judicial handling of crimes and punishment of offenders, the principles of international law, e.g. nationality, territoriality and universality, may be legitimately invoked. But in case the matter is not brought to any appropriate domestic court in reasonable time due to dilatory tactics and diplomacy, then the victim or the heirs should be permitted legal access to the special bench of ICJ or to the ICSC, if then existing. In the end, a caveat that the justice dispensed may not be purist or legalistic but suitably tempered to accommodate differences in social norms, ingrained customs and variations in national legal codes. Thus, justice granted may be suitably balanced by such prevailing divergences as also the circumstantial pressures of outer space and celestial bodies. This will humanise justice for space crimes and instil a more honourable perception.

In conclusion, it must be accepted that space activities are progressively expanding with commercial overtones and profit motivations. It is also true that space law, today, is not expressly permissive of such appropriation or ventures by private enterprise. But let us not scuttle this nascent development on flimsy legalities, lack of modalities, procedural lacunae or a rigid mindset. These challenges can be overcome, and the need is to evolve new idioms of law, new space jurisprudence, rational interpretations and adaptive approaches rather than stall or resist opening up new vistas, like space tourism, for the betterment of humankind.

Thus, the second-generation space law will, perforce, have to be cognitive of multi-disciplinary approaches, intrinsically interactive, perceptibly liberal, resilient in character, responsive to contingencies and conducive to new opportunities that usher in collective gain and common benefit to humanity. Therefore, space tourism demands a predictive and progressive regime of space law, domain governance and adjudication that ensures unhindered growth, affords desired economic fillip, permits permeation of gains to the common tourist, assures equitable treatment and is proactive in its approach. In such a benign regimen and conducive atmosphere, space tourism is sure to flourish and benefit all stakeholders meaning the State will benefit from taxes, the economy with a multiplier effect, private enterprise from profitable business and the tourist from a competitive tariff. Hence, all contributors to the success of space tourism must consciously and conscientiously endeavour to keep it safe and secure from space crimes by innovative policing methods and by maintaining public law and order.

## Notes

1 AFP report, 'Russia Ready to Fight for Space Tourism Supremacy', *Times of India* (Chandigarh edn), 20 December 2021, p. 10.
2 *Id.*
3 However, space is no place to get pregnant and gestate. Experiments on rats in Soviet Cosmos-1129 in 1979 showed that despite fertilisation, the pregnancies were "resorbed". Longer stays in space have led to reduced sperm count and shrunken testes in males and ovaries shut-down in females.
4 G.S. Sachdeva, 'Space Tourism—Some Legal Implications', in Sandeepa Bhat (ed.) *Space Law: The Emerging Trends* (Kolkata: Eastern Law House, 2018) pp. 95–122 at p. 114.
5 G.S. Sachdeva, 'Space Tourism: Need for Legal Radicalism', *Indian Journal of International Law*, Vol. 45, No. 4, 2005, pp. 487–509 at p. 500.
6 For example, FOBS, Fractional Orbital Bombardment System of Russia. This project has since been abandoned.
7 For example, Russia claims that Venus is their planet because they were the first to successfully land there and have found methane on the ground and gas phosphene in the atmosphere which is a sign of life. See 'Venus Is a Russian Planet, Says Kremlin Space Chief after Sign of Life Found', *Times of India*, (Chandigarh edn) 9 September 2020, p. 14.
8 Mike Brown, 'SpaceX to Launch Billboard into Space: Is It Legal? Experts Weigh In', *Shutterstock*, 17 August 2021, available at <http://www.shutterstock.com> Last visited 17 May 2023.
9 'Axiom Space to Build a Movie Production Studio on ISS by 2024', *Space.com*, 25 January 2022, available at <https://www.space.com/axiom-space-station-movie-studio-module> Last visited, 18 May 2023.
10 Dr. Woerner, a scientist, created a concept-design of the Moon Village. See Jan Woerner, 'Moon Village: A vision for Global Cooperation and Space.4', available at <https://blogs.esa.int/janwoerner/2016/11/23/moon-village/> Last visited, 16 May 2023.
11 Karl Tate, 'A Village in Orbit: Inside NASA's Space Colony Concepts (Infographic)', *Space.com*, 5 August 2013, available at <https://www.space.com/22228-space-station-colony-concepts-explained-infographic.html> Last visited, 18 May 2023.
12 *Supra* note 4, at 97.
13 *Supra* note 11.
14 Leonard David, 'Let the Space Games Begin! Ideas for off-Earth Sports Move to Center Court', *Space Insider*, *Space.com*, 5 January 2022, available at <https://www.space.com/space-sports-ideas-microgravity-games> Last visited, 18 May 2023.

15 Elizabeth Howell, '50 Years Ago, an Apollo 14 Astronaut Played Golf on the Moon, Here's the Inside Story', *space.com*, 4 March 2019, available at <https://www.space.com/apollo-14-moon-landing-golf-shot-analysis> Last visited, 18 May 2023.

16 This term has been coined by Linda Rheinstein, Founder of Space Games Federation, see Leonard David, 'Let the Space Games Begin! Ideas for Off-Earth Sports Move to Center Court', available at <https://www.space.com/space-sports-ideas-microgravity-games> Last visited, 17 May 2023.

17 Outer Space Treaty, Art. VI.

18 *Id.*

19 *Id.*, Art. VIII.

20 *Id.*, Art.VII.

21 Tereza Pultarova, 'Do Space Tourists Really Understand the Risk They're Taking' on *Twitter@Spacedotcom*, 17 September 2021.

22 *Id.*

23 Outer Space Treaty, Art. VIII.

24 Convention on Registration of Objects Launched into Outer Space 1975, Art. II (1).

25 *Id.*, Art. IV (1). Words in parenthesis added for verb correction.

26 The qualification, "generally so understood", has been added because human perception on crimes varies in different countries and communities for different reasons.

27 Convention for the Unification of Certain Rules relating to International Carriage by Air 1929 and its subsequent amendments. For a detailed analysis, refer G.S. Sachdeva, *International Transportation: Law of Carriage by Air* (New Delhi: Deep & Deep Publications, 1987).

28 Outer Space Treaty, Art. IV. Although it pertains to astronauts, it can be extended to tourists on the principle of reciprocity and international cooperation under Article XI of OST. The Moon Agreement 1975, Art. 10(2) also endorses this.

29 There is a raging controversy in UK where the Prime Minister prioritized rescue of pets (cats and dogs) over people during the evacuation process from Afghanistan. Report from NYT, London, 'UK PM Faces Fire over Claims He Prioritized Pets Over People during Afghan Evacuation', *Times of India*, (Chandigarh edn), 28 January 2022, back of front cover page.

30 The Geneva Conventions 1949 and Protocol on Torture.

31 David M. Ashford, 'Space Tourism-How Soon Will It Happen?'. A paper presented at the IEEE, *AeroSpace Conference at Snowmass, Colorado*, USA, 1–8 February 1997, available at <http://ieeexplore.iiie.org>document> Last visited 17 May 2023.

32 Tereza Pultarova, 'The Rise of Space Tourism Could Affect Earth's Climate in Unforeseen Ways, Scientists Worry', *Twitter@Spacedotcom*, July 2021.

33 *Id.*

34 World Meteorological Organisation, *Report on Scientific Assessment of Ozone Depletion*, 2018, available at <https://csl.noaa.gov/assessments/ozone/2018/> Last visited, 16 May 2023. Such reports are prepared every four years.

35 *Supra* note 31. Also refer G.S. Sachdeva, *Space Tourism: Industry of the 21st Century*, Monograph published by Foundation for Aviation and Sustainable Tourism, New Delhi, 1999.

36 UN Space Debris Mitigation Guidelines 2007.

37 Outer Space Treaty, Art. II.

38 G.S. Sachdeva, *Space Commercialisation: Prospects, Challenges and Way Forward* (New Delhi: Pentagon Press LLP, 2019) pp. 136 & 137.

39 Amit Chaturvedi, 'How Long a Mars Mission Should Last? Scientists Say 4 Years, Explain Why', *Hindustan Times*, New Delhi, 7 September 2021.

40 Outer Space Treaty, Art. VIII.

# 12

# ISSUES OF OWNERSHIP AND TOURISM IN OUTER SPACE

*Attila Sipos and Simran Upadhyaya*

## Humankind and Outer Space

On 2 December 1942, the scientists Enrico Fermi (1901–1954) and Leo Szilárd (1898–1964) induced the first nuclear chain reaction, a regulated "atomic bonfire".[1] Thereby, humankind had fetched the Sun from the sky to the Earth. Due to this step, a new era of human civilisation commenced: the "Atomic Age". Humankind did not confute itself, and by the preparation of nuclear weapons, it got trapped in an awful chain of causation, which in its entirety unfolded itself in the Cold War (1947–1991). However, beyond the horrors of war, the development of strategic weapons, especially the increase of the effective range of missiles (further experiments in the interest of reaching the destination by weapons of mass destruction) facilitated the rapid development of technology, which has directly promoted that humankind entered outer space as soon as possible. Development is irresistible and to date space tourism increasingly resembles air transport, which has transformed from the luxurious journey of the privileged into public transport. To that extent, space travel, which was previously restricted to astronauts as "envoys of mankind", now extends to space tourism mainly for recreational purposes.[2] Space tourism has been defined as "any commercial activity offering customers direct or indirect experience of space travel".[3] While the term of space tourist refers to "someone who tours or travels into, to, or through space or to a celestial body for pleasure and/or recreation",[4] the activities of space tourism include but are not limited to "long-term stays in orbital facilities, short-term orbital or sub-orbital flights, and parabolic flights".[5]

The space is much busier than it used to be as an increasing number of space objects (mainly satellites) are being launched into orbit with each passing year.[6] No doubt, space tourism has also considerably grown over the past few years.[7] A

DOI: 10.4324/9781032617961-12

**188** Attila Sipos and Simran Upadhyaya

commentator suggests that space traffic will rise to five million space passengers per year by 2030.[8] This estimate clearly reflects the growing demand among potential tourists. Accordingly, due to increasing space traffic and space tourism just about to set off, certain pressing legal issues – whether activities related to space tourism comply with the Outer Space Treaty[9] – emerge.

### Walking a Tightrope

The chances of survival for human civilisation have significantly diminished mainly by reason of the existence of an extraordinary multitude and diversity of ammunition of weapons of mass destruction.[10] This risk in itself is inconceivably vast. Humankind has become vulnerable (according to Stephen Hawking, climate change, asteroid strikes, epidemics and overpopulation will incur our downfall)[11] and in their conceit, humans considered the Earth their world-empire and ventured into outer space as well. One of the most intriguing eras, the "Space Age", commenced on 4 October 1957 with the launch of Sputnik-1 (*спутник: fellow-traveller*). *The Sputnik was the first satellite of human civilisation, the first space device revolving in outer space. On that day, humankind flung open the door into outer space.* Undoubtedly, we have reached spiritual altitudes and humans proclaimed in a resounding manner: "we have conquered outer space". Indeed, science as a collective enterprise encompassing human generations has helped humans reach outer space. As a result, our astronauts can do research in outer space for peaceful purposes. Currently, with the emergence of space tourism, humans apart from astronauts can travel into outer space as well.[12] Previously, space adventure had implied travelling into outer space and returning, but the reusable space vehicles of the 1980s were introduced to promote commercial space use.[13] However, with the growing popularity of space tourism, humans have started paying visits to outer space.

Overcrowding raises important questions about the possible coincidence on the one hand of the right to exploration and scientific research for the benefit of mankind, on the other hand, of the right to ownership. Accordingly, we need to follow the timeless message of our first astronauts setting foot on the Moon: "We came in peace on behalf of all mankind!"[14] which may convey more profound meaning. This is a splendid heritage! The intellectual adventure introduced us to outer space. Although we made it into outer space, despite the great steps, we have to realise that our rocket technology is obsolete since our spaceships still do not facilitate to reach, for instance, Proxima Centauri, the star which is at a distance of 4.24 lightyears and is the closest one to our Sun (star) always shining at us (that is, while travelling with the speed of light, covering 300,000 km per second, the journey would take 4.24 years). By relying on contemporary technology, this interstellar journey would take about 18,000 years.[15] There are no miracles in the skies. What is more, we do not possess a privileged place in the universe.[16] While technical development preceded our moral development by far, we keep living mainly off the benefits of proprietorship based on our instincts rooted in the material world.

It is hard to declare, but the disappearance of humankind would remain unnoticed in distant galaxies. Albeit man has exited from the gravitation of the Earth and has indeed reached several planets, our telescopes span billions of light-years, and this distance is still rising, yet, in possession of the multitude of knowledge and experience, we may declare: man has not conquered outer space![17]

Even so, it has become almost inevitable for humankind to expand into outer space. We need to expand since the global community has jeopardised and thoroughly exploited our sole liveable environment: the Earth. In addition, humankind has not confuted itself this time either: we have trashed even the place where we are heading. The space trash of more than 30,000 objects weighing over 9,855 tonnes (which exceeds the weight of the Eiffel Tower), circling in outer space, poses a danger to human activities carried out in outer space.[18] Moreover, with the potential increase in space tourism, a rise in space traffic will automatically lead to the multiplication of space trash, air pollution,[19] high levels of waste, not to mention radiation problems, etc. The numbers are alarmingly increasing; therefore, the halt of "trashing" requires an international, legally enforceable and controllable solution. Environmental protection poses unprecedented challenges to humankind. We are lagging behind by several decades as to the protection of the environment in outer space, therefore, not only new basic principles are necessary, but the consistent enforcement of the existing ones is vital.[20]

## Is It Possible to Exploit the Possession of All of Us?

### Ours and Mine

Outer space belongs to all of us. It is freely utilisable and cannot be appropriated in any form. Its appropriation is inadmissible either owing to the fact of first presence or by the disposal of the symbols of State power (e.g., State emblems, armour, national flag). These basic principles are laid down under the Outer Space Treaty signed in 1967 in the midst of the Cold War. The Outer Space Treaty is the basic agreement on international space activity; it contains basic principles recognised by the international community. Essentially, the treaty determines the pursuit of human activities related to outer space and its framework. The principal objectives[21] were the protection of outer space in its foundations from the races of armament and acquisition of property, thereby, the minimisation of the possibility of the contingent formation of a prospective armed conflict.

The rule is unambiguous and we have to adhere to the letter of the law. At the same time, it is confusing that objects freely utilisable by all are appropriated by some entities. How is it feasible to sell and purchase at auctions cosmic materials deriving from outer space, to market and purchase real estate (with extraction rights) on the Moon and other celestial bodies, to conceal mineral substances collected on the Moon in the framework of the Apollo Programme, then sell them and make a fortune therefrom?

Throughout history, besides the United States, Chinese, Soviet and Japanese experts managed to bring down rock specimens from the Moon. In 1993, the Soviets sold a minor part of the "collection" brought down to the Earth by the LUNA-16 Moon-Probe (1970). Three rock samples with a weight of 0.2 g could be sold with the assistance of Sotheby's Auction House for US $442,500. Then, these tiny and light rock specimens were again put up for auction after years by the nameless owners, who could sell them to the new, again anonymous customers at much higher prices.[22]

When the States stipulated the rules of property law, they did not think of the prospective possibility of the emergence of private capital besides the States in space research. Therefore, the express prohibition of ownership pertained solely to nations. However, some profiteers took advantage of the unregulated situation speculatively when they started selling "parcelled" estates on the Moon or other celestial bodies. Many people purchased the peculiar and simultaneously cheap Moon estates or the areas of other celestial bodies[23] disregarding the basic principle of Roman law and civil law effective until today: *nemo plus iuris transferre potest, quam ipse habet*, that is, nobody can transfer more rights than their own, which means that ownership can be obtained solely from an owner. In addition, it proceeds from the logic of the law that a private agreement may not annul public law (that is, *privatorum conventio juri publico non derogat*). Namely, the individual cannot have more rights than the nation itself because the individual may not rise above the community. Not talking of the fact that such a sale targets an impossible object, which means the nullity of the contract since the possession of the estate, the harvest of its fruit or its visit is unfeasible for the individual.[24]

The Unites States transferred 270 pieces of Moon rock specimens as gifts to foreign countries, primarily for scientific reasons; however, a part of them disappeared. For instance, about 184 pieces of the 370 samples shipped by the Apollo 11 and 17 missions are missing, 160 rock specimens were transferred abroad, while in the United States 24 pieces were obtained by unauthorised persons.[25]

Albeit the instances above did not entail sanctions, essentially, they are illegal. At the same time, we can also get access lawfully to cosmic materials. With a stroke of luck, we can stumble upon such rocks in the nature, while very rarely the most fortunate ones come across them in their own garden. Meteorites, cosmic debris from the Moon or other celestial bodies, reach the surface of the Earth naturally (this implies that they do not burn upon entrance into the atmosphere of the Earth), but as it has happened several times, they have been brought down by humans.

The substantive scope of the Outer Space Treaty does not encompass materials striking the Earth (mainly meteorites), thus, it is not inadvertent that several countries in their national legal system (if it applies in their source of law regulating the national activity of space research) provide for the legal fate of such cosmic materials. In the majority of States (for example, in the United States or France), the individual by discovery or first seizure of the object having become unmastered on the Earth (*res nullius*) turns into an owner according to the principle of *res nullius credit primo occupanti.* At the same time, in the case of cosmic materials explored in the depth of the Earth, the individual will not become an owner since the materials are subject to the national law concerning the rules of mining (mineral rights).[26]

Some States in their national legal system consider these cosmic materials to be strictly State property. The discoverer is obligated to transfer the object to the State. Such objects are usually studied and deposited in museums (e.g. India[27] or the United Arab Emirates).[28] For example, in India, all fallen aerolites together with the documentation relating to them should, in the first instance, be transferred to the National Geological Museum in Kolkata.[29] All local governments and the national government require compliance with the resolution. The Museum is under the control of the Director of Geological Survey in India. No compensation is paid to finders, and a new finding needs to be transferred to a representative of the Geological Survey of India or the local police. In the United Arab Emirates, federal law on the space sector declares that "any meteorite falling within the State Territory is the property of the Emirates".[30] Furthermore, any person owning a meteorite in a legitimate manner can be requested by the Emirates Space Agency to lend it for scientific or research purposes.[31]

The situation is not so simple when humans land rock specimens on the Earth. Mainly because this requires outer space industrial activity taking lengthy time as well as particularly human missions involve high risks and they are terribly expensive (merely the spacesuit of a NASA astronaut costs US $12 million).[32] In addition, humankind, with superhuman efforts, has brought down minuscule quantities to the Earth so far. In 2006, for the first time in the "Space Age", NASA gathered and brought to the Earth 1 mg stardust deriving from the Wild-2 Comet with the help of the STARDUST Probe. This mission in itself cost about US $200 million. Formerly, in 2003, the researchers of the Japan Aerospace Exploration Agency (JAXA) had launched the Hayabusa (*Peregrine falcon*) probe to reach the '25143 Itokowa' asteroid, from where in 2010 they brought back less than 1 mg sample material. The mission cost about US $100 million. The JAXA Hayabusa-2 returned on 5 December 2020 and managed to bring a sample of 0.1 g to the Earth. The mission cost US $150 million. In 2016, the OSIRIS-Rex asteroid researcher Space Probe was launched by NASA with the objective to gather samples from the '101955 Bennu' asteroid near the Earth. The mission has met with success and on 24 September 2023, the Space Probe returned to the Earth with samples weighing about 250 g in its capsule. The largest shipment was realised in the framework of the Apollo Programme (1961–1972): a quantity of 382 kg (842 pounds) rock specimen was landed on the Earth.[33]

International law facilitates to land rocks and mineral substances as samples from the Moon and other celestial bodies on the Earth.[34] The cosmic materials delivered to the Earth have functioned as samples for scientific purposes, so they are landed as being in possession of the launching State or other States. To a certain limit, the owner of the samples becomes entitled to examine the rock specimens and also to dispose of them, but this rule cannot be construed broadly, that is, upon

## 192 Attila Sipos and Simran Upadhyaya

extraction in large quantities, the materials landed on the Earth cannot be handled under this legal title as they are subject to the primary responsibility of the sovereign State.

### Exploitation in the Province of All Mankind and the Common Heritage of Mankind

The first UN General Assembly Resolution concerning outer space law[35] and the Outer Space Treaty settle property relations in their foundations, but they do not provide for the exploitation and utilisation of resources in storage in outer space. As a general basic principle, the exploration and utilisation of outer space, including the Moon and other celestial bodies (naturally with the exception of the Earth), including the trajectories surrounding them and leading to them, shall be carried out for the benefit and in the interest of all countries irrespective of their degree of economic or scientific development. *Scilicet*, all States on a basis of equality and in accordance with international law, without discrimination of any kind, may do research freely and utilise resources in a manner that the work carried out in outer space must be regarded as "the province of all mankind".[36] Namely, all aspects of the activity need to serve humanity, even if this declaration in principle cannot really be enforced in a legal dispute. During research, the interests of other States may not be injured, the work carried out – regarding the interests of present and future generations – may not be impeded and experiments causing the disruption of the balance of nature may not be done. The Contracting Parties guarantee the right for the States which, due to technical and economic under-development, cannot participate in the research of outer space, but which later may have such capacity, to get involved based on equality.

In the Moon Agreement,[37] the drafters instituted a new legal formula favouring the less developed countries as well: "the common heritage of mankind". This scope encompasses the planets of the Solar System, with the exception of the Earth, with all their treasures and the trajectories leading to and surrounding them. The objective of the drafters was to protect future generations, to allocate the benefits acquired in outer space to all and not to let the natural resources be freely exploited.

To date, 18 States have ratified the Moon Agreement and further four States have signed it (Guatemala, France, Romania and India). The Moon Agreement facilitates the acquisition of samples by the States and disposition over them for scientific and educational purposes.[38] The term of property, just like in the Outer Space Treaty, does not appear here either, thus, the mineral substance specimens and other samples brought down to the Earth cannot be appropriated. Exclusively activities for peaceful purposes can be carried out, which promote the interests of the international community, observe the rules of international law and are in conformity therewith.

The legal institution of 'the common heritage of mankind' is propitious,[39] nevertheless, it hinders mining activities to be carried out in the future on the

Moon and other celestial bodies, since it generates limitations by the stipulation of the obligation to share the materials, the "fruits" extracted on the Moon under the management of an international organisation, with other countries irrespective of the fact to what extent they have contributed to the success of the enterprise. This severely deters venturesomeness since the extractor is interested primarily in generating profit, whereas, due to the observance of rigorous technical and safety prescriptions, they may have to incur serious expenditures that deters profit-making. Exploitation has a sole method: the recovery of mineral substances pursuant to an international system of rules. This solution is not unprecedented, since the international seabed has been utilised under the supervision of the International Seabed Authority (ISA).[40] One of the principal tasks of this institution established by an international regime is the supervision of the equitable allotment of the profit proceeding from the resources among the parties, with special respect to the interests and needs of developing countries and to the efforts of the States directly or indirectly engaged in exploitation. Despite the fair distribution, the legal institution of the 'common heritage of mankind' has not found a sufficient number of adherents. The 'common heritage of mankind' initiative hinders commercial development. Consequently, it is necessary to review these principles to gain support from various countries and create opportunity for space exploration activities.

### Space Tourism and Outer Space Treaty Violations

The Space Treaties have been drafted broadly only to encompass exploratory space activities undertaken by governmental agencies.[41] As a result, these treaties are ill-equipped to deal with modern-day space adventures, which may potentially violate the provisions of both the Outer Space Treaty and the Moon Agreement. Accordingly, the evolution of space tourism with constant human presence in outer space may have certain legal implications.

As established previously, the drafters of the Outer Space Treaty emphasise that the exploration and use of outer space shall serve the benefit of mankind. However, the activity of private space tourism for recreational purposes, which is reserved for the wealthy, does not comply with the requirement of "the benefit of all mankind". This raises questions as to whether an activity for leisure and entertainment (including collecting souvenirs) can be equated with an activity of exploration for the benefit of mankind. As mentioned above, the Outer Space Treaty clearly states that in outer space, States can freely engage in space activities (exploration and use) on a basis of equality and in accordance with international law without making claims for sovereignty (Articles I, II). The same principle is reiterated in Articles 2 and 6(1), further Article 11 (4) of the Moon Agreement.

In essence, outer space is free for use by all, including the freedom of injecting and launching objects into outer space without the prior permission of other States.[42] All nations can freely gain access to outer space. Clearly, the evolution of space tourism will increase human presence in outer space. In addition to satellites, the launch of other objects will also proliferate and with more objects in space, the presence of debris increases the chances of collision and aggravates the risk of damage to vital satellites.[43]

Currently, developed countries are the forerunners of contemporary activities of space tourism,[44] so they solely account for the rise in space traffic. This may prevent the free movement of other space objects launched for the purpose of research by developing countries. Every nation has an equal right to conduct space activities, but in the future the dumping of space objects and excessive space tourism will prejudice other countries' rights to freely conduct space activities for reasons apart from leisure. This will interfere with the obligation of developed countries to provide scope for developing countries to access space or carry out scientific research.

Pursuant to Article II of the Outer Space Treaty, outer space is not subject to national appropriation on the grounds of sovereignty. Similarly, Article 11(2) of the Moon Agreement also prohibits national appropriation. The fundamental principle of "non-appropriation" is that outer space is beyond the territorial jurisdiction of any State.[45] States are free to engage in space activities while respecting the sovereign claim of other States.[46] These treaties emphasise purposefully that nations cannot claim a segment of space as their own and they declare that exploration needs to be carried out for the benefit/common interest of mankind. However, the collection of rock specimens as souvenirs serves merely personal rather than common interest. Thus, as both treaties prohibit the appropriation of space resources, they may be violated by prospective commercial space tourism.

It is also argued by commentators that with the development of the activity of space tourism, the demand for hotels on the Moon and other celestial bodies will emerge.[47] Accordingly, the construction of such facilities will entail the concept of the "ownership" of estates. Naturally, such legal protection will infringe the sovereignty claim denied under Article II. Further legislation needs to ensure the establishment of such a legal title under international space law.[48] Additionally, granting the right of ownership might create scope for dispute over interference with another nation's space object.

The protection of the environment in outer space is an obligation under Article IX of the Outer Space Treaty. However, the growth of space tourism will also increase the chances for littering the space environment, which is ultimately bound to lead to the pollution of pristine areas.[49] Ever since space exploration began, NASA has traced about 9,000 man-made objects in space. Furthermore, of the objects identified in year 2000, some pose threat to space vehicles and will bring about catastrophic damages.[50] It is also likely that activities of space tourism will be the world's primary source of carbon dioxide emissions and will also aggravate the situation of space debris.[51] Thus, it is imperative that activities of space tourism are minimised before the situation exacerbates further. It is also imperative to find an equilibrium between the development of space tourism and environmental protection forming a part of outer space law.

Considering the potential difficulties that may arise with the full-fledged operation of space tourism in the future, it is necessary to deliberate on certain legal issues: What levels of activities of space tourism are appropriate? Are there any restrictions that must be imposed to contain the excessive use of outer space by tourists? In what directions does the Outer Space Treaty need to be amended to encompass modern-day space activities? Will it be possible to reformulate international rules to balance out the interests of the States and private entities?

### The Unilateral Concept Determines the Law

For the purpose of rendering the investment of money and energy in space industrial enterprises agreeable for private companies and aiding the growth of space tourism, the legislators need to guarantee the system of the conditions of ownership. The formation of a new regime is in progress and entails dismantling the legal impediments via unilateral steps.

On 6 April 2020, the President of the United States rejected the Moon Agreement under an executive order and requested American diplomacy to find allies via bilateral agreements for the enforcement of the peculiar interests of the United States. Essentially, the prohibition pertains to the expansion of State sovereignty, namely, territorial appropriation, while it does not extend to the resources thereon which will serve the missions: "Americans should have the right to engage in commercial exploration, recovery and the use of resources in outer space, consistent with applicable law. Outer space is a legally and physically unique domain of human activity, and the United States does not view it as a 'global commons'".[52] Thus, the resources may be extracted and freely disposed of by any entity capable thereof.

Celestial bodies, planets themselves are the treasuries of mineral substances. They hold important materials in excellent quality and enormous quantities. Modern technology is capable of extracting cosmic materials, then of their delivery to the Earth. However, the activity of extraction has not been done on a larger scale, an industrial scale yet, and it will not take place in the near future, either. Mining is a long-term vision. At the outset, preceding mining, material tests and the analysis of mineral substances will be necessary. As a matter of course, mining on the surface of the Moon or other celestial bodies has justification and immediate economic benefit. In the beginning, therefore, space borne energy resources need to be utilised in the cosmos for the purpose of the safe pursuit and support of human activities.

The countries opting for the unilateral path are motivated not only by the protection of their own investors, but also by the fact that effective international treaties are difficult to amend. The reason is that international law is a conservative discipline, it requires mutual compromise concerning solutions, which through diplomatic and governmental channels take a lot of time and effort. Nevertheless, it is even more difficult to frame a new treaty among the States favouring the establishment of the status quo or reliance on the United Nations Committee on the Peaceful Uses of Outer Space (UNCOPUOS) based on consensus. Concerns are remounting since the law concerning the issues of outer space activity does not give adequate answers, or, if it does, the answers do not become community-level models of unification. In addition, time has also shortened: competition has sharpened and we are witnessing irreversible processes.

With the increasing regulation of national space law, currently, 36 States recognise its benefits (the latest one is Thailand).[53] For example, of the 22 Member States of the European Space Agency (ESA), 17 States dispose of special national legal documents pertaining to outer space activities subject to their jurisdiction. Of course, this does not mean that the given State defies international legal regimes, but the national regulation determines rights and obligations with respect to safety and security (primarily to environmental protection), to authority and surveillance, to jurisdictional (registrational) and litigious (controversial) issues, and to the underlying assumption of responsibility by the State.[54] The enforcement of particular interests sets an example many times prospectively and motivates other States and industrial performers or compels them to take action. There is no need to set the world on fire this time either, for example, the International Law Association (ILA) created a standard, the Model Law on National Space Legislation, thereby assisting the work of national legislators.[55]

Rightly, the enterprises cannot wait for international law to follow up with technical development or industrial demands. However, it is already evident that there is no thronging in the mining department, namely, not every entity is capable of the organisation or implementation of such activity. Besides the United States, the national rules of the United Arab Emirates, Luxembourg and Japan also deal with the appropriation of resources deriving from the activity of mining. These are encouraging models, their objective is the unilateral dissolution of the existing multilateral system so that more adherents accede thereto, and thereby, it can give rise to a new multilateral alliance in the future.

- The United States determines the resources located in outer space under a statute. The scope of this law extends to citizens and legal entities (under certain conditions to foreign companies as well). The legislators believe that the appropriation does not result in ownership of the territory, but the resources may be extracted and exploited, that is, they may be owned and delivered, and eventually, also sold.[56]
- The Luxembourgian law protects investors, explorers and candidates for mining rights. The law defines the framework for authorisation to utilisation and grants ownership to private companies over the exploited resources.[57] The system framed by the statute consisting of altogether 18 Articles is attractive for foreign States as well, since Luxembourg as a member of the European Union functions as a financial, investment-attracting hub and an intermediary towards other industrially developed European Union Member States.

Issues of Ownership and Tourism in Outer Space **197**

- The national law of the United Arab Emirates facilitates private companies to appropriate a "prize" entirely.[58] The legal grounds of this conception is simply the fact that on the high seas (international waters), the legal status of which coincides with that of outer space, after fishing in the territory, where the common things are freely utilisable by all, the capture may be sold on the market. "If the fish does not belong to you, why do you go fishing on the seas?"
- Japan's Parliament adopted legislation which grants Japanese companies permission to search for, extract and utilise various space resources. Japan's legislation is similar to the provisions stipulated by US regulations. The law grants companies rights to the resources that they extract, but does not allow property rights to celestial bodies.[59]

Besides national legislations, all of the above four States are signatories to the Artemis Accords, which endorses authorisation to recover and use space resources.

The unilateral approach is also encouraged by the fact that bringing down rock specimens from the Moon or other celestial bodies or their utilisation has never been frowned on by other States, thus, due to a dispute by reason of the breach of the Outer Space Treaty no proceedings have been instituted at court.[60] The advantage of the unilateral world is the opportunity of the establishment of coalition units, namely, if more and more States take the same or proximate stand in their national rules, they can intervene in these issues by supporting each other. What is more, in an ideal case, the largest possible number of States can lay the foundations of a new international treaty. Furthermore, if other States, for instance, India, commence mining activities in outer space, they may expect with good reason that the above-mentioned countries and their partners will not criticise the space mining activity of India, and they will not contest the appropriation of cosmic resources by India.

At the same time, Russia rejects the unilateral approach providing solutions on a national level and urges the establishment of a multilateral unity,[61] while Brazil promotes broader consultation. The demand is growing that the UNCOPUOS stipulates international rules in which the States prioritise the protection of celestial bodies. Currently, the organisation of the UNCOPUOS has 102 members, thereby it is one of the largest committees in the system of the UN.[62] Therefore, this is not a simple task since the decision-making mechanism based on consensus excludes the possibility of a uniform decision on such issues of great importance. At the same time, the fact that merely a few countries are concerned directly by the exploitation of outer space, their unilateral seeking ways and means may amalgamate into coalitions, which may gain ground in new dimensions, for instance in the Artemis Accords.

### The Artemis Accords

Subsequently to the Apollo Programme, currently, it is the Artemis Mission that motivates the international community. The objectives of the mission to be implemented by NASA include the landing of people on the surface of the Moon in 2025, the commencement of the establishment of a space base on the celestial body and the extension of the international cooperation via the involvement of other partners.

The framework of cooperation is extended by the Artemis Accords (namely, Principles for Cooperation in the Civil Exploration and Use of the Moon, Mars, Comets, and Asteroids for Peaceful Purposes), to which 24 States have acceded so far.[63] The Accords is not an international treaty, therefore, it cannot be enforced legally. Of the 24 signatory States, Australia (in 1986) and Mexico (in 1991) are the only countries which ratified the Moon Agreement and later signed the Artemis Accords. (*Note*: Saudi Arabia also signed the Artemis Accords, but withdrew from the Moon Agreement on 5 January 2023, effective 5 January 2024.) The Accords contain principles for "a Safe, Peaceful and Prosperous Future". The Accords' substantive scope extends to the Moon, Mars, comets, and asteroids, their surfaces and below surfaces. Among the ten progressive principles contained in the package of measures, there are two which have a potentially important message with respect to proprietorship.

- The Accords facilitate the extraction and utilisation of resources but solely in compliance with the rules of the Outer Space Treaty (Space Resources – Section 10.2).

- In the interest of the prevention of conflicts deriving from space activity with the objective of the enforcement of obligations under the Outer Space Treaty, the establishment of security zones around the facilities is admissible (Section 11). This solution resembles the concept of artificial islands applied in maritime law, around which under adequate conditions a zone of 500 m may be founded.[64] The boundary of the zone is not demarcated, obviously, if the territory expands, the boundary of this zone may shift as well.

Related to the two basic principles above, the question arises as to what extent the foundation of a security zone means appropriation, even if implicitly. Also, to what extent these rules contradict the basic rules laid down in the Outer Space Treaty (Articles II, IX, XII), i.e. access to the space object open on the basis of reciprocity, free movement, peaceful utilisation and the possibility of control?[65] The Accords is open for signature by the States embracing the objectives, thereby, it creates a new forum and institution for unified intervention.

## Chapter Conclusion

All of us are aware that estates cannot be acquired in outer space as no appropriation of the territory is admissible, furthermore, extraction in outer space is not entirely free, either. In order to render the activities of extraction and exploitation more attractive for investors and entrepreneurs, the achievement of these goals, carrying out activities of recovery should be promoted and protected on the level of international law. However, an according uniform international regime has not been framed yet. Currently, we are witnessing the proliferation of national regulations, unilateral solutions, which with the establishment of coalitions pave the way for securing the acceptance of the conception that the acquisition of property with the intention of gaining sovereignty above the territory is prohibited, but the acquisition of property in case of the recovery of mineral resources is permitted.

Beyond this, we need to consider issues deriving from space tourism such as the pollution of the environment, the consequences of appropriation (investment, establishment of destinations, hotels and shops), all of which entail new legal challenges. The legislators need to provide comprehensive responses, thus, uniform regulations are indispensable, since the legal disputes generated by citizens with different nationalities would lead to legal insecurity.

The unilateral path does not intend to defy international law and guarantees both the prohibition of appropriation of the territory with the claim of sovereignty and the admissibility of the appropriation of extracted mineral resources. Notwithstanding, more guarantees would be necessary. Mining qualifies as dangerous operation, which, beyond the real hazards, can with good reason generate international disputes. Framing a genuinely new international system of rules in conformity with the rules of international law could guarantee that the enterprises, while not injuring the interests of other States during extraction, can sell the extracted materials for the purpose of the generation of profits. We can carry out mining for profit in the interest of humankind, while terrestrial life has never been so hazardous before; therefore, our responsibility and engagement have become increasingly overpowering. It is a distressing fact that the most precious and most important subsoil wealth of space mining is not platinum or gold but water itself. Man is capable of shaping nature, but cannot conquer either nature or outer space, even if at the outset they were convinced about the opposite.

## Notes

1　New York Herald Tribune, 'Man Behind the A-Bomb – Dr. Leo Szilard Dies', available at <https://library.ucsd.edu/dc/object/bb0479342v/_1.pdf> Last visited, 1 October 2022.
2　Steven Freeland, 'Up, Up and… Back: The Emergence of Space Tourism and Its Impact on the International Law of Outer Space', *Chicago Journal of International Law*, Vol. 6, No. 1, 2005, pp. 1–22; Ankit Kumar Padhy, 'Legal Conundrums of Space Tourism', *Acta Astronautica*, Vol. 184, 2021, pp. 269–273.
3　Stephan Hobe and Jiirgen Cloppenburg, 'Towards a New Aerospace Convention? Selected Legal Issues of 'Space Tourism', *47th Colloquium of the International Institute of Space Law*, 2004, 377–385 at p. 377; *Id.*, at 6.
4　Zeldine Niamh O'Brien, 'Liability for Injury, Loss or Damage to the Space Tourist', *47th Colloquium of the International Institute of Space Law*, 2004, pp. 386–396 at p. 387.
5　Stephan Hobe, *supra* note 3; Stephan Hobe, 'Legal Aspects of Space Tourism', *Nebraska Law Review*, Vol. 86, No. 6, 2007, pp. 439–458 at p. 439.

6 In 2020 alone, Elon Musk's Starlink programme launched more than 800 satellites into space. Ramin Skibba, 'As Space Traffic and Tourism Rise, the World Needs an International Space Treaty', available at <https://science.thewire.in/law/space-tourism-orbital-debris-international-space-treaty-biden-administration> Last visited, 15 May 2023.

7 John Adolph, 'The Recent Boom in Private Space Development and the Necessity of an International Framework Embracing Private Property Rights to Encourage Investment', *The International Lawyer*, Vol. 40, No. 4, 2006, pp. 961–965; Steven Freeland and L. Tanja Masson-Zwaan, 'Between Heaven and Earth: The Legal Challenges of Human Space Travel', *Acta Astronautica*, Vol. 66. No. 11–12, 2010, pp. 1597–1607 at p. 1600.

8 Steven Freeland, *supra* note 2, at 3.

9 Treaty on Principles Governing the Activities of States in the Exploration and Use of Outer Space, Including the Moon and Other Celestial Bodies, 27 January 1967, 610 UNTS 205 [Outer Space Treaty].

10 Merely in our days altogether over 13,000 nuclear weapons are registered officially in nine countries of the world. Over 90% are in the United States and Russia, with the remainder in China, France, India, Israel, North Korea, Pakistan and the United Kingdom. Ploughshares Fund, 'World Nuclear Weapon Stockpile Report', available at <https://ploughshares.org> Last visited, 15 May 2023.

11 Stephen Hawking, 'Humanity only Has 100 Years Left on Earth before Doomsday', available at <https://futurism.com/stephen-hawking-humanity-only-has-100-years-left-on-earth-before-doomsday> Last visited, 15 May 2023.

12 Roger R. Bate, Donald D. Mueller, and Jerry E. White, *Fundamentals of Astrodynamics* (New York: Dover Publications, 1971) pp. 151–176; Thomas R. Rankin, 'Space Tourism: Fanny Packs, Ugly T-Shirts, and the Law in Outer Space', *Suffolk University Law Review*, Vol. 36, No. 3, 2003, pp. 695–716 at p. 697.

13 Thomas R. Rankin, *id.*

14 Norman Mailer, *Moonfire. The Epic Journey of Apollo 11* (Viersen: Taschen GmbH, 2010) pp. 266 & 267.

15 May Clery, 'U.S. Lawmaker Orders NASA to Plan for Trip to Alpha Centauri by 100th Anniversary of Moon Landing (in 2069) Science', available at <https://sciencemag.org/news> Last visited, 15 May 2023.

16 The same natural laws determine the movement of objects on celestial bodies and on the Earth.

17 Attila Sipos, *International Civil Aviation Law: Regulations in Three Dimensions* (London: Springer Nature, 2024).

18 The European Space Agency, 'ESA's Annual Space Environment Report', available at <https://www.sdo.esoc.esa.int/environment_report/Space_Environment_Report_latest.pdf> Last visited, 15 May 2023.

19 Ankit Kumar Padhy, *supra* note 2, at 273.

20 B. Sandeepa Bhat, 'Application of Environmental Law Principles for the Protection of the Outer Space Environment: A Feasibility Study', *Annals of Air and Space Law*, Vol. XXXIX, 2014, pp. 323–354.

21 United Nations, Office for Outer Space Affairs, 'Travaux Préparatoires of Outer Space Treaty', available at <www.unoosa.org/oosa/en/ourwork/spacelaw/treaties/travaux-preparatoires/outerspacetreaty.html> Last visited, 15 May 2023.

22 Kiona N. Smith, 'Soviet Lunar Samples Sell for $855,000 at Sotheby's, But More May Be on the Illicit Market', available at <https://forbes.com/sites/kionasmith> Last visited, 15 May 2023.

23 Lunar Land, 'The Earth's Oldest, Most Recognized Celestial Real Estate Agency', available at <https://lunarland.com/moon-land>; <https://indianexpress.com/article/technology/science/planning-to-buy-a-piece-of-the-moon-sorry-but-thats-not-possible-for-now-5238827> Last visited, 15 May 2023.

24 *Supra* note 17.

25 Mark Bosworth, 'What Has Happened to NASA's Missing Moon Rocks?' *BBC World Service*, available at <https://www.bbc.com/news/magazine-16909592> Last visited, 15 May 2023; Denise Chow, 'NASA Has Lost Hundreds of Its Moon Rocks, New Report Says', available at <https://www.scientificamerican.com/article/nasa-has-lost-hundreds> Last visited, 15 May 2023.

26 For example, in Australia the people generally own only the upper surface of the land. Everything below that (minerals) belongs to the Crown. Minerals are widely construed as it is declared "modern landowners may not even own the soil on their land". Brendan Edgeworth, *Butt's Land Law*, 7th ed. (Australia: Thomson Reuters, 2017) p. 218; Coal Acquisition Act 1981 No. 109, 5 (1), Vesting of Coal in the Crown.

27 The Resolution of the Government of India, Revenue and Agriculture Department, No. 45G–22–13, 28 April 1885 at Simla. Circular Letters No. 14870–14883–119 dated 19 December 1914 and No. M–1184 of 9 June 1925.

28 UAE Federal Law No. (12) of 2019, On the Regulation of the Space Sector. Issued on 19/12/2019 Corresponding to 22 Rabi' Al-Akhar 1441H. [UAE Federal Law No. (12) of 2019].

29 Douglas G. Schmitt, 'The Law of Ownership and Control of Meteorites', *Meteoritics & Planetary Science*, Vol. 37 (Supplement), 2002, pp. B5–BII, available at <https://uark.edu/meteor> Last visited, 15 May 2023.

30 UAE Federal Law No. (12) of 2019, Art. 30 (2–3).

31 UAE Federal Law No. (12) of 2019, Art. 30 (8).

32 Alexander Donovan, '13 Out of This World Facts About Spacesuits That You Should Know', available at <https://interestingengineering.com> Last visited, 15 May 2023.

33 Lunar Rocks and Soils from Apollo Mission. NASA Sample Collection, available at <https://.curator.jsc.nasa.gov/lunar> Last visited, 15 May 2023.

34 Moon Agreement, Art. 6.

35 UNCOPOUS Res. 1721 (XVI), International Co-operation in the Peaceful Uses of Outer Space, 20 December 1961.

36 Outer Space Treaty, Art. I; Moon Agreement, Art. 4.

37 UNOOSA RES 34/68, Agreement Governing the Activities of States on the Moon and Other Celestial Bodies, 1979.

38 Moon Agreement, Art. 6.

39 *Id.*, Art. 11.

40 Ricky J. Lee, *Law and Regulation of Commercial Mining of Minerals in Outer Space* (Dordrecht: Springer, 2012) pp. 229–256.

41 Outer Space Treaty, Art. VI & IX; Moon Agreement, Art. 11.

42 North Sea Continental Shelf Cases (*F.R. Germany* v. *Denmark; F.R. Germany* v. *Netherlands*), (1969) I.C.J. 3, 230 (dissenting opinion of Judge Lachs); Steven Freeland, *supra* note 2, at 8.

43 Chelsea Munoz-Patchen, 'Regulating the Space Commons: Treaty Space Debris as Abandoned Property in Violation of the Outer Space Treaty', *Chicago Journal of International Law*, Vol. 19, No. 1, 2018, pp. 233–259 at p. 240.

44 Ramin Skibba, 'As Space Traffic and Tourism Rise, the World Needs an International Space Treaty', available at <https://science.thewire.in/spaceflight/space-tourism-orbital-debris-international-space-treaty-bidenadministration> Last visited, 15 May 2023; Rankin R. Thomas, 'Space Tourism: Fanny Packs, Ugly T-Shirts, and the Law in Outer Space', *Suffolk University Law Review*, Vol. 36, No. 3, 2003, pp. 695–716 at p. 697.

45 Steven Freeland, *supra* note 2, at 4.

46 *Id.*

47 *Id.*, at 5.

48 *Id.*, at 14.

49 *Id.*, at 21.

50 John Adolph, 'The Recent Boom in Private Space Development and the Necessity of an International Framework Embracing Private Property Rights to Encourage Investment', *The International Lawyer*, Vol. 40, No. 4, 2006, pp. 961–965 at p. 983.

51 M.P. Ferreira Snyman, 'Legal Challenges Relating to the Commercial Use of Outer Space, with Specific Reference to Space Tourism', *Potchefstroom Electronic Law Journal*, Vol. 17, No. 1, 2014, pp. 1–50 at p. 8.

52 Executive Order 13914, 'Encouraging International Support for the Recovery and Use of Space Resources', 6 April 2020, Billing code 3295-FO-P, Section 1, available at <https://federalregister.gov/documents> Last visited, 15 May 2023.

53 Si-soo Park, 'Thailand Moving to Enact Space Activities Act', *Space News*, available at <https://spacenews.com/thailand-moving-to-enact-space-activities-act> Last visited, 15 May 2023.

54 Kumar Abhijeet, *National Space Legislation for India* (Singapore: Springer, 2020) pp. 1–16.

55 Sandeepa B. Bhat and Arthad Kurlekar, 'A Discourse on the Remodelling of ILA Model Law on National Space Legislation', *Journal of Space Law*, Vol. 41, No. 1, 2017, pp. 1–28; Res. No. 6/2012, 75th Conference of International Law Association (ILA), 26–30 August 2012.

56 Commercial Space Launch Competitiveness Act, Space Resource Exploration and Utilization (Sec. 402), H.R.2262, U.S. (2015).

57 Law on the Exploration and Use of Space Resources, No. 674, 28 July 2017.

58 The law, which consists of 9 Chapters and 54 Articles and regulates space activities in the Unites Arab Emirates, took effect in December 2019.

59 Law Concerning the Promotion of Business Activities Related to the Exploration and Development of Space Resources, Space Resources Act No. 83 of 2021, 23 June 2021.

60 Commercial Space Launch Competitiveness Act, Title IV, Space Resource Exploration and Utilization, H.R. 2262, U.S. (2015), Sec. 402.

61 Director General of Roscosmos, Dmitry Rogozin called for a "system of regulations" to address those issues at an international level instead of the adoption of national laws like the new Japanese space resources law. "Russia believes that the States must not adopt any laws and regulations on a unilateral basis because the space is our common heritage and belongs to everyone." Global Space Exploration Conference, St. Petersburg, 15 June 2021.

62 UNCOPUOS Membership Evolution, 'GA Resolution 77/121', available at <www.unoosa.org/oosa/en/ourwork/copuos/members/evolution.html> Last visited, 15 May 2023.

63 Australia, Bahrain, Brazil, Canada, Colombia, the Czech Republic, France, Israel, Italy, Japan, Luxembourg, Mexico, New Zealand, Nigeria, Poland, the Republic of Korea, Romania, Rwanda, Saudi Arabia, Singapore, Ukraine, the United Arab Emirates, the United Kingdom and the United States of America, available at <https://www.nasa.gov/artemis-accords> Last visited, 15 May 2023.

64 United Nations Convention on the Law of the Sea, 10 December 1982, 1833 U.N.T.S. 397 (entered into force 16 November 1994), Art. 60.

65 Frans von der G. Dunk, 'The Artemis Accords and the Law: Is the Moon 'Back in Business?' Science & Technology', available at <https://thebigq.org> Last visited, 15 May 2023.

# 13

## SPACE TOURISM

### Learning from the Antarctic Experience

*Aaditya Vikram Sharma*

### Introduction

On 11 July 2021, a small rocket plane soared more than 80 km into the Earth's atmosphere.[1] It carried four passengers who reached the edge of space and landed back on Earth.[2] One of the passengers was Sir Richard Branson, the founder of Virgin Galactic, which had operated the spaceflight.[3] Similar feats were to follow. On 20 July 2021, the 'New Shepard' Crew Capsule developed by Blue Origin, LLC achieved a ten-minute-long sub-orbital flight with four passengers on board, along with its founder Jeff Bezos.[4] This was followed by the Inspiration4 mission of Space Exploration Technologies Corp. (SpaceX) on 16 September 2021.[5] The mission successfully ended on 18 September 2021 when their spacecraft 'Dragon Resilience' was recovered from the Atlantic Ocean.[6] All these missions herald a new beginning in the realm of international space tourism.

Space tourism is not a new development. Almost 20 years ago, on 30 April 2001, Dennis Tito (an American entrepreneur) paid a hefty sum to the Russian Space Agency Roscosmos and spent a week on the International Space Station (ISS).[7] Six more space tourists followed him, with the last one leaving the station in 2009.[8] Subsequently, no such event took place until 2021. Since then, private companies have continuously experimented with and honed their space-faring skills. Some of them, such as Virgin Galactic,[9] focus on sub-orbital space tourism. They have now figured out the mechanism and are commercially selling space tourism packages to potential buyers.[10]

However, international law has not been able to keep up with these strides in technology, and many legal issues have arisen.[11] For instance, if the space object launched by a private operator causes some damage, then who will be liable? Further, what are the responsibilities of the private actor for protecting the space

DOI: 10.4324/9781032617961-13

**204** Aaditya Vikram Sharma

environment? Additionally, humanity has only been in space for a very short time, and its presence needs to be preserved, so how will the heritage in space be protected? International space law has been unable to answer these questions adequately.[12]

In this chapter, it is analysed whether the experience of the ATS can be applied to the regulation of space tourism. Just like space, Antarctica is a remote environment, presents a unique set of challenges to access it and has been regulated through several treaties.[13] Further, it has faced issues such as sovereignty and jurisdiction similar to space.[14] Like space law, the Antarctic Treaty[15] was designed to foster scientific research, protect the environment and maintain international peace.[16] However, unlike international space law, the ATS is highly developed in guiding tourists as well as tour operators.[17] So, the ATS can be the basis for devising space tourism norms. Being a comparatively mature treaty, it can shed light on what States must focus on when it comes to space tourism.

The chapter is divided into six parts. Part 1 is the Introduction which gives the idea of the study and outlines its methodology. Part 2 deals with the international legal frameworks wherein the history, development and contemporary status of international space law and the ATS are discussed. Then, Parts 3 and 4 outline the initiatives in tourism in space and Antarctica, respectively. In doing so, the legal setup applying to each region with specific reference to tourism is covered. Subsequently, in Part 5, a thorough study is done on how or whether the ATS can be used to formulate remedies for legal issues in space tourism. Part 6 is the concluding section, where the findings of the chapter are summarised with suggestions.

## The International Legal Frameworks

### International Space Law

Space law is a body of international treaties, agreements, conventions, United Nations General Assembly (UNGA) Resolutions, rules and regulations given by other international organisations and lastly, national rules that address the issue of utilisation of outer space by human beings. According to the United Nations Office of Outer Space Affairs (UNOOSA), space law can be described as the "body of law governing space-related activities".[18]

The genesis of international space law was the launch of a Soviet satellite named Sputnik on 4 October 1957.[19] This was followed by the launch of the Explorer-1 satellite by the United States. A 'space race' was to follow,[20] and it became clear that there was no regulation in the area as this was beyond the scope of air law.[21] On 18 December 1958, the need for international cooperation and conventions for the peaceful use of outer space was recognised by the United Nations General Assembly (UNGA).[22] The UNGA was "Wishing to avoid the extension of present national rivalries into this new field". The UNGA also established an *Ad Hoc* committee to deal with problems of law involved in space activities.[23] Subsequently, a permanent

Space Tourism: Learning from the Antarctic Experience **205**

body called the Committee on the Peaceful Uses of Outer Space (UNCOPUOS) was established on 12 December 1959.[24] UNGA resolutions were adopted, which emphasised the peaceful use of outer space. Ultimately, the Treaty on Principles Governing the Activities of States in the Exploration and Use of Outer Space, including the Moon and Other Celestial Bodies, 1967 (Outer Space Treaty or OST) came up.[25] It formed the cornerstone of international space law and the treaties which followed.[26] Of these, the Agreement on the Rescue of Astronauts, the Return of the Astronauts and the Return of Objects Launched in Outer Space, 1968[27] (Rescue Agreement) and the Convention on International Liability for Damage Caused by Space Objects, 1971[28] (Liability Convention) are of relevance to space tourism. Further, various other GA resolutions and international conventions have also come up.[29]

A variety of matters are covered by international space law. These include the preservation of the space environment, settlement of disputes arising from acts in space or of space objects, the rescue of astronauts and international cooperation. Further, it also covers any liability owed by one nation to another for damage caused by space objects and sharing of information about any potential threats in space.[30]

However, UN Space treaties do not directly address space tourism as it was not an issue when they were being drawn up.[31] The law of outer space purports to create a legal environment that would enable the achievement of the common goals of mankind. These common goals and interests also include the peaceful utilisation of outer space. Pertinently, space represents the applicability of the concept of "common heritage of mankind".[32] The concept predominantly clarifies that certain territories are available to all mankind – no one State can lay claim to them. While the term is not used in the Convention, under the 1967 Outer Space Treaty, Articles I, II and III explicitly adopt the principle of common heritage.[33] From these articles, the following can be inferred:

a   Outer space, Moon and celestial bodies are accessible and available to all mankind (and to all countries) for any space activity.[34]
b   All human beings have access to outer space based on equality and international law.[35]
c   International cooperation in the scientific investigation of outer space, Moon and celestial bodies is promoted.[36]
d   No nation can appropriate outer space, the Moon and celestial bodies.[37]
e   International law applies to all activities in outer space, on the Moon and the other celestial bodies. The aim is to maintain international peace, security, cooperation and understanding.[38]

These principles reflect the idea that outer space is a common heritage of mankind. The Moon Treaty expands this concept. However, it has not received accessions from most space-faring States and thus, does not carry as much 'hard power'.

**206** Aaditya Vikram Sharma

Nevertheless, even with OST, certain limitations apply to the usage of this term. For instance, Triggs notes that:

> Consensus as to the common heritage principle does not, however, apply to the more precise question whether Outer Space Treaty and the Moon Treaty prohibit the unilateral exploration of non-renewable resources of outer space.[39]

Based on the above, it can be construed that the treaty permits space tourism as all human beings are allowed to access outer space. Their nationality is immaterial, and for our purposes, the use of outer space for tourism is neither prohibited nor directly regulated by international law.

### The Antarctic Treaty System

Antarctica was discovered in the year 1820. By the time of the Cold War, seven countries had claimed different parts of it. These were Argentina, Australia, Chile, France, New Zealand, Norway and the United Kingdom. According to Shaw, these claims were dubious at best.[40] Later on, the Antarctic Treaty was signed by 12 countries in Washington D.C., United States, in 1959. Along with the above-mentioned countries, representatives from Belgium, Japan, South Africa, the United States and the Union of Soviet Socialist Republics (USSR) acceded to it.[41] The Antarctic Treaty established a demilitarised zone that would be utilised for scientific research.[42] Notably, the treaty froze States' territorial claims without explicitly denying or supporting them.[43] Any activity on this frozen continent does not constitute any claim/denial of sovereignty.[44] As it is a product of the Cold War, the treaty forbids all parties from testing nuclear weapons and disposing of radioactive waste on the continent, *inter alia.* The members were bound indefinitely with a review scheduled to take place after 30 years. In 1991, a protocol was added and signed by the Member States. The protocol strives to protect the Antarctic environment and bans exploration of resources for 50 years.

The Antarctic Treaty is the basis for establishing the ATS.[45] Under Article IX, parties to the treaty undertake to meet at regular intervals to discuss matters pertaining to

a  use of Antarctica for peaceful purposes only;
b  facilitation of scientific research in Antarctica;
c  facilitation of international scientific cooperation in Antarctica;
d  facilitation of the exercise of the rights of inspection provided for in Article VII of the Treaty;
e  questions relating to the exercise of jurisdiction in Antarctica;
f  preservation and conservation of living resources in Antarctica.[46]

All the treaties that have been concluded in furtherance of the consultative meetings have addressed the Antarctic environment.[47] Major treaties and protocols include the Convention for the Conservation of Antarctic Seals 1972,[48] the Convention on the Conservation of Antarctic Marine Living Resources 1980 (CCAMLR),[49] the Convention on the Regulation of Antarctic Mineral Resource Activities 1988[50] and the 1991 Protocol on Environmental Protection to the Antarctic Treaty (Madrid Protocol).[51]

## Space Law and Tourism

Space tourism is now a reality. Private space corporations actively provide tourism services to those who can afford them. Successful ventures such as Axiom Space, Blue Origin, SpaceX, Virgin Galactic, etc., have launched tourists into space.[52] However, at this juncture, it is necessary to understand the issues in space tourism and the nuances of the different kinds of space tourism.

### The Definition of Space

To date, there is no clarity on where outer space begins.[53] Experts say that space starts when orbital dynamic forces gain prominence vis-à-vis aerodynamic forces.[54] In 1957, Theodore von Kármán, a Hungarian-American engineer and physicist, determined that the boundary between the atmosphere and outer space lies at around 80 km above sea level.[55] The Fédération Aéronautique Internationale[56] (FAI) has determined that the 'Kármán Line' is 100 km above sea level.[57] However, this is not the final word on the boundary between space and atmosphere as there is no consensus on this limit.[58] For instance, Australia has demarcated the boundary at 100 km above sea level[59] while the United States gauges that space begins after 80 km above sea level.[60] States have their interpretations regarding this, so the delimitation of the boundary is not final.[61] Fitzgerald has argued that perhaps the International Civil Aviation Organisation (ICAO) can take up the task.[62] But, until May 2022, the matter remained unresolved.

### Different Kinds of Tourism

The two main kinds of space tourism are orbital and sub-orbital. Further, there is a proposed mechanism known as Intercontinental Rocket Transport.

When a spacecraft reaches the boundary between the Earth's atmosphere and space and then falls back to the planet, it is known as sub-orbital tourism.[63] The object falls back to the Earth as it lacks escape velocity.[64] Even then, passengers on any such craft can experience weightlessness by being almost into space.[65] This type of space tourism is being heralded by Virgin Galactic.[66]

On the other hand, orbital space tourism is how tourism to space is conventionally imagined. A spacecraft carries tourists beyond the gravitational pull of the Earth and gets into orbit.[67] The spacecraft remains in orbit, and afterwards, it plunges back to Earth in the form of a controlled re-entry.[68] SpaceX has provided tour services via this method.[69]

## 208 Aaditya Vikram Sharma

Intercontinental rocket transport has been proposed as another method of transporting people on the planet. It involves the use of rocket technology developed for spaceflight. According to Elon Musk, the aim is to fly people around the planet within 30–60 minutes.[70] However, this method is still theoretical and has not taken flight yet – literally.[71]

### Regulation of Space Tourism

International space law does not directly address space tourism. However, there are ancillary agreements in the domain of space law which deal with related aspects. The first international treaty which dealt with space was the Outer Space Treaty of 1967. It established liability for actions done in outer space. For the purposes of tourism, Article VII of the treaty is relevant. This article makes launching States liable for any mishap which occurs in outer space if their personnel/objects are responsible for the damage.[72] The Liability Convention, 1971 complements this article. The Liability Convention concerns itself with two kinds of damages – one which takes place on Earth and another which takes place in outer space. In the case of the former, the strict liability doctrine applies,[73] whereas for the latter, the negligence liability applies.[74] However, the Convention makes States, rather than the private party, liable for any misfortune. This fact is relevant because, currently, private actors are providing space tourism services.[75] It is also pertinent to note that these conventions create third-party liability only, that is, damage done to parties not involved in the operation.[76]

Further, the astronauts are treated as government employees and labelled as "envoys of mankind" to whom the Rescue Convention would apply.[77] However, these regimes are inadequate. For instance, neither is the protection of the environment covered nor is the issue of licensing and liability of private parties. There are other legal problems as well. For instance, unlike orbital flights, sub-orbital flights do not reach orbit.[78] As discussed above, there is no clarity on where outer space begins. So, are sub-orbital flights in the Earth's atmosphere or in outer space? This is relevant because different legal regimes would apply in each case.

Further, when it comes to air law, it is very well defined, and the whole idea of jurisdiction, regulation, etc., is settled. But international space law is ill-defined and does not clarify the type of rules applicable to the craft. This makes it pertinent to define the boundary where space begins because different legal instruments will apply accordingly (that is, air law below space and space law afterwards). Due to these inadequacies, domestic legislation has been filling up the gaps prevalent in international law. For instance, international space law, in addition to the US rules given by the Federal Aviation Authority regulates both orbital and sub-orbital tourism as all the private space tour companies are operating from that country.[79]

## Antarctica and Tourism

Tourism to Antarctica is booming.[80] The number of tourists has risen exponentially, and the tickets are getting cheaper.[81] This has led to the creation of a hefty tourism industry that spans simple sightseeing[82] to luxury cruises.[83] Access to the continent is permitted to all persons under the Antarctica Treaty System, which has allowed the industry to develop.[84] The tourism industry regulates itself through a voluntary code of conduct prescribed by the International Association of Antarctica Tour Operators (IAATO).[85]

### *The Beginning*

Tourism to Antarctica started in 1957–1959 when it was visited by Argentinean and Chilean ships with tourists on board.[86] The icy continent received widespread public attention through the works of Richard E. Bryd,[87] Vivian Fuchs[88] and Edmund Hillary.[89] This led to a gradual increase in the number of tourists visiting Antarctica. Tour operators soon started providing services with small cruise ships regularly bringing in 50–120 passengers.[90] The number of passengers kept rising with the large cruise ship, 'Ocean Princess', with the capacity of 400 persons being pressed into service between 1990 and 1993.[91] In February 2020, the *New York Times* reported that another cruise ship, 'the Coral Princess', traversing the region with tourists, has 2,000 berths.[92] To quote the IAATO, "Since the beginning of the modern Antarctic travel industry in the 1960s, the number of visitors to Antarctica has grown from a few hundred to 50,000 each year."[93]

### *Beyond Tourism: Discovery of Minerals*

When the Antarctic Treaty was signed in the year 1959, the region was believed to be rich in biological resources but not in mineral resources. This was because only 1% of the continent was exposed to rock, and so the presence of ores of any element was next to none.[94] Since the 1970s, however, offshore resources of petroleum have been found, and many nations have taken up oceanographic research of the region.[95] In 1988, the Convention on the Regulation of Antarctic Mineral Resource Activities was adopted by the ATS and signed by 19 States.[96] Pertinently, it was never ratified. It should be mentioned here that the Convention aimed to allow mining activities to take place in Antarctica with stringent regulations. But, soon all the efforts to exploit the vast Antarctic resources came to a grinding halt.

### *Environmental Problems*

The rise in the number of tourists poses a challenge to the Antarctic environment. The ecosystem is fragile, and it can take decades for any ecological imbalances to be corrected.[97] Visitors may unknowingly carry seeds and spores, which may be

**210** Aaditya Vikram Sharma

invasive to native life.[98] Further, an increase in the number of ships also raises the probability of catastrophic events such as oil spills.[99]

The fears were realised when on 28 January 1989, a tourist ship named 'Bahia Paraiso' operated by the Argentine Navy ran aground in Antarctica. All the passengers and crew on board were rescued. Unfortunately, the damage to the ship caused diesel to leak, killing the local flora and fauna.[100] This incident demonstrated the fragility of the Antarctic environment. Similar instances were reported in February and November 2007, respectively.[101] On the other side of the planet, on 24 March 1989, the Exxon Valdez oil spill occurred in the Gulf of Alaska, United States. Exxon Valdez was an oil super tanker that hit a reef and spilled almost 37,000 tonnes of crude oil in the surrounding waters. According to National Geographic,

> The final death toll included 250,000 seabirds, almost 3,000 sea otters, 300 harbour seals, 250 bald eagles, 22 killer whales, and billions of salmon eggs. Populations of Pacific herring, a cornerstone of the local fishing industry, collapsed. Fishermen went bankrupt.[102]

While this ship was located in the Arctic, the event highlighted that accidents can occur even if all the preventive measures are taken.[103]

The events in 1989 laid bare the truth that a mechanism was required to regulate the Antarctic environment. In furtherance of the same, the Protocol on Environmental Protection to the Antarctic Treaty was concluded in Madrid, Spain, on 4 October 1991 and came into effect in 1998. The Protocol was a game-changer that created new principles to be applied for protecting the environment in Antarctica. It directly led to the creation of the IAATO, which has regulated tourism in Antarctica ever since.[104]

The Protocol on Environmental Protection to the Antarctic Treaty, 1991 contains 27 articles, one schedule and six annexures. It is a comprehensive treaty that aims to save its protectorate from harm. It does so by

- Designating Antarctica as a "natural reserve devoted to peace and science"[105]
- Establishing that certain environmental principles have to be compulsorily consulted in the planning and conduct of all activities[106]
- Prohibiting any activity related to mineral resources (in effect prohibiting mining)[107]
- Making any activity contingent on a successful environmental impact assessment[108]
- Creating the Committee for Environmental Protection,[109] which shall "provide advice and formulate recommendations to the Parties in connection with the implementation of this Protocol"[110]
- Formulating an Emergency Response Action mechanism to tackle any environmental emergency in Antarctica

The schedule creates a dispute resolution mechanism for the parties.[111] This is followed by the six annexures which form an integral part of the Protocol.[112] Annexure I *deals* with environmental impact assessment. Annexure II pertains to the conservation of wildlife in the region. Annexure III gives guidance regarding waste disposal and management. Annexure IV gives guidelines to prevent marine pollution in Antarctica. Annexure V further gives guidelines for the protection and management of the Antarctic Region. Finally, Annexure VI concerns itself with liabilities which arise from environmental emergencies.

In 2021, the ATCM adopted the General Guidelines for Visitors to the Antarctic.[113] As per the guidelines, "All visits to Antarctica should be conducted in accordance with the Antarctic Treaty, its Protocol on Environmental Protection, and relevant Measures and Resolutions adopted at Antarctic Treaty Consultative Meetings (ATCM)."[114] It then lists the general advice for visiting Antarctica while simultaneously making sure that the environment is not affected.[115]

Further, in 2018, the Antarctic Treaty Consultative Meeting adopted the "Guidelines for the assessment and management of Heritage in Antarctica" (Heritage guidelines).[116] Under the terms of the guidelines, parties must protect the historic sites, structures and objects present in Antarctica.[117] It is also noted that this protection is necessary because the presence of human beings in Antarctica has been chronologically very short.[118] Consequently, this limited historical evidence is extremely important.[119]

### The IAATO and Its Regulation

When the 1991 protocol was formulated, seven major tour operators in Antarctica founded the International Association of Antarctica Tourist Operators.[120] IAATO is an international non-profit organisation that aims to protect the Antarctic environment.[121] Indeed, it is understandable that a tourism organisation will aim to maintain the pristine environment of the region from where its members reap their livelihood. IAATO has members from across the globe. According to its official website,

> Today, IAATO's membership is truly international. Member companies hail from Argentina, Australia, Belgium, Canada, Chile, France, Germany, Italy, Japan, Netherlands, New Zealand, Norway, People's Republic of China, Russia, South Africa, Sweden, Switzerland, United Kingdom, United States and the U.K. Overseas Territory-Falkland Islands (Islas Malvinas).[122]

In its goals, IAATO mentions that it wishes to conserve and manage the pristine environment in Antarctica. Indeed, IAATO has done a stellar job with self-regulation, having achieved its objectives.[123]

Analysing the functioning of the IAATO is an interesting exercise. The Association gives guidelines for both tourists and tour operators. Its website lists three guidelines for visitors – the Antarctic Treaty General Guidelines, the IAATO 'Don't Pack A Pest' guidelines and General Information for Wildlife Watching.[124]

The Antarctic Treaty General Guidelines for Visitors to the Antarctic give the visitors a bird's-eye view of the Antarctic Treaty, the Protocol and all the measures adopted by the ATCM.[125] It's a succinct read which makes the reader aware of their responsibilities. It aims to ensure that the Antarctic environment is not affected by tourist visits.[126] The IAATO Don't Pack a Pest! Flyer informs readers about the non-native species in Antarctica and how they can be harmful.[127] It gives tips and methods on how tourists should prepare their belongings before and during the voyage.[128] Finally, the IAATO General Information for Wildlife Watching aims to minimise the potential environmental impacts on the wildlife in Antarctica.[129] It ostensibly aims to achieve the purposes given under Article II of the Protocol.[130] The guidelines are quite comprehensive and deal with multiple scenarios that may affect the fauna.[131] IAATO has gone a step further by incorporating visitor briefings[132] and information for tourists arriving on yachts.[133]

Tour organisers also abide by a hefty set of guidelines given by the IAATO.[134] All the tour companies operating in Antarctica have to give an Environment Impact Assessment report to their respective governments.[135] They also need to abide by guidelines given for land-based activities, sea-borne tourism, helicopter operations, Zodiac (a type of inflatable boat) operations, remotely operated vehicles, etc.[136] The guidelines and SOPS (Standard Operating Procedures) are quite comprehensive.

The bottom line is that the Antarctic region was designated as a global common. A treaty was designed in 1959, which has successfully lasted to date. Further, the ATS committee has continued evolving new treaties and instruments. The IAATO has been working on the basis of the treaty to maintain the Antarctic environment as it is in its own interests to do so. This shows the maturity of the ATS and especially when it comes to the protection of the environment and tourism.

### Learning from the Antarctic Experience

Space tourism and Antarctic tourism are niche areas of the travel industry. They are very recent and lack binding treaties for their regulation. However, in the case of Antarctica, a voluntary set of guidelines under the auspices of the ATS (especially the Madrid Protocol) has worked well. These can be taken up to understand and regulate space tourism which is at a relatively nascent stage.

In this study, various gaps have been discovered in the regulation of space tourism. To summarise, the following lacunas are broadly identified in space law:

1 There is no clarity on where space starts and ends.
2 There is no specific regulation of 'Space Tourism' and the current treaties do not adequately address the privatisation of the space industry.
3 The legal status of space tourists as astronauts and their rescue is unclear.
4 The liabilities and duties of space tourists and operators are not specified.
5 The threats to the space environment and heritage are not adequately addressed.

Space Tourism: Learning from the Antarctic Experience  **213**

The list is not exhaustive.[137] However, it contains the most critical legal issues which haunt space tourism. Can these questions be addressed by referring to the Antarctic Treaty System?

### Boundary of Space

The first issue is regarding the boundary between air and space. The Kármán Line is not endorsed as the final boundary between air and space by all international bodies and countries. So, this matter is as of yet unresolved. Unfortunately, it cannot be adequately resolved by looking at the Antarctic Treaty System. This is because Antarctica is a solid land mass with well-defined boundaries.[138] On the other hand, the delimitation of outer space is not an easy task involving both scientific and political hurdles. Therefore, to resolve this issue, States will have to look elsewhere.

### Regulation of Space Tourism

However, for the second issue, reference can be made to the Antarctic Treaty. When the Antarctic Treaty was drafted, there was no provision for regulating tourism. But, once the Madrid Protocol was adopted in 1991, the tour operators and the stakeholders decided to create a voluntary mechanism regulating tourism.[139] This mechanism was created by multiple operators coming together under the guidance of the ATS as well as the new environment legislations.[140] As discussed above, the voluntary guidelines have worked well, and the problems concerning tourism in Antarctica have been mitigated.[141]

A system could be devised on similar lines under space law wherein multiple operators such as SpaceX, Virgin Galactic, etc. come together to create voluntary guidelines which they would abide by when operating in space. This organisation of International Space Tourism Operators could take it upon itself to regulate tourism. The guidelines would, of course, be based on the current international space law. A new treaty could be devised in the future which regulates the space environment. But a better path would be to develop a treaty not only to protect the space environment but also to regulate space tourism. This would remove the dependency on voluntary guidelines and make space tourism legally regulated. However, it is not certain whether the industry would take stringent norms in a positive light as they reason that it hampers research and development.[142]

### The Definition of 'Astronaut'

The fourth issue could also be resolved via Antarctic law. While the ATS would not be of much assistance in defining who exactly is an astronaut, it could help in finding out what are the liabilities and responsibilities of astronauts while they are in space. Of course, this idea would not only extend to astronauts but also to tourists (as and when the definition is devised) and tour operators. The ATS already lays down what are the responsibilities of people coming to Antarctica. These include the maintenance of the environment and making sure that there is a minimum effect on the Antarctic region. Further, the legislations aim to prevent issues such as oil spills, damage to natural life, heritage, etc. These can be used in drafting binding guidelines on the stakeholders reaching outer space. It is conceded that the ATS cannot be of much assistance in drafting protocols unique to space (such as extra-terrestrial life). Nevertheless, it is still helpful for other issues which occur when mankind accesses any 'pristine' area. Both the regions are remote and have their own intricacies that do not attach to any other land mass or biosphere or region that we know of and have lived on. Accordingly, it is essential that these mechanisms be devised for space, and they can be based on what has already been done with the ATS, which carries an institutional experience of over 60 years.

*Protection of Environment and Heritage*

We are already confronted with the reality that space junk has become a big problem.[143] The remains of old defunct satellites, rocket parts and debris as a result of anti-satellite rocket tests have made space a very delicate environment to navigate.[144] If the activity in space increases due to commercial activities such as tourism, it would be necessary to make sure that the environment is protected. There are already near-misses (and occasional collisions) with debris occurring daily in space.[145] The International Space Station routinely has to be moved away from a collision course with space debris.[146] While this is a general issue, the increase in space tourism will only add to the debris already in space.[147] Therefore, very stringent guidelines will have to be devised to protect the environment of space by keeping it clean and debris free. In this regard, the Antarctic Treaty can be followed, which does not allow any such harm to come to the environment.[148] As highlighted above, the Madrid Protocol has assisted operators in creating voluntary guidelines, which are very helpful in mitigating any damages caused due to tourism. In this manner, sustainable tourism could be achieved in space too.

The issue of space heritage can also be addressed via Antarctic Treaty System. According to Losier, the protection of landing sites and objects in space is consistent with the heritage legal theory.[149] Further, the 2018 Heritage guidelines given by the Antarctic consultative meeting are very much relevant. They aim to preserve the heritage present in Antarctica, especially because the time spent by humans over there has been very short. The same logic can also be applied to space, and similar guidelines could be adopted for the protection of heritage in space. Examples of heritage sites could include tangible assets such as Neil Armstrong's footprint on the Moon,[150] the defunct rovers on Mars,[151] the Moon impact probe of the Indian lunar space probe Chandrayaan-1 on the Moon[152] and so on. The creation of a group similar to IAATO would, of course, lie on the collaborative tendencies of the current actors in space law, especially as it would be a voluntary act.

## A Pinch of Salt

Of course, even with all their similarities, Antarctica and outer space have a number of differences. The first major one, of course, is they are both different environments with very different realities facing them. While Antarctica has become relatively accessible and is now also being affected by global warming,[153] these points do not apply to outer space as of yet which would have its own unique set of challenges. Antarctica also has the Antarctic Treaty System, which allows governments to devise guidelines, protocols or treaties regularly. This allows contemporary issues to be addressed. However, in the case of space law, the developments are very slow. While there are regular meetings[154] of the Committee on the Peaceful Uses of Outer Space (COPOUS) under the aegis of the UNOOSA, there have not been any landmark breakthroughs in a long time. This is why it is also suggested that an overhaul of international space law in the manner of the ATS can be done.

## Chapter Conclusion

The final frontier of space has already been breached. The scenario had changed from 1967, when the idea was to prevent a second Cold War from taking place in space. Now, space has become a domain of private parties which are easily able to access it and utilise its potential. Subsequently, the regulation of space tourism and an overhaul of international space law are issues which need to be urgently addressed. While some scholars have argued that workarounds can be arranged through the treaties that are available right now, it is always better to have a more specific law in place. Private tourism operations will also need to be addressed accordingly. This is because while legislation can easily regulate them, some countries might not be as stringent as others. For instance, when it comes to the law of the sea, registration of ships is compulsory. However, the regulations of certain countries are much more stringent than in others. Thus, having an international treaty that puts the same set of regulations on all the actors across the world would be much more pertinent than relying on domestic legislation alone. For this, reference can be made to the Antarctic Treaty System. It is a mature system which has existed since 1959. It has a mechanism for revising its mandate and taking into account contemporary issues. It has also got a lot of experience and faced issues similar to what we are facing in outer space. Due to these reasons, the ATS presents a viable resource through which international space law can be overhauled and space tourism regulated.

An adaptation of the ATS would allow States to regularly give guidelines and new regulations. This would result also in mitigation of new issues with their solutions being drawn up with new ideas and implementing them together in regular meetings that might happen annually or biannually. While the biggest contribution of the ATS could be to mitigate the issues that already exist in space law, an even bigger contribution could be the completion and the creation of a new space treaty/ system drawn on similar lines to it. This has worked well for Antarctica, and while there would be reservations, it would not be a bad idea, especially in light of the current space law.

The necessity of regulating space tourism right now should not be lost on anyone. The number of trips by private operators is only going to increase. Even State actors such as Roscosmos have entered the fray because of the highly lucrative space tourism industry. In fact, there are certain other developments which need to be looked into at the same time. The experiences of the ATS would be highly beneficial in understanding the development of international space law. We do not need to repeat the same mistakes that we made while the international treaty for Antarctica was being drafted or when it started working. The experience of the ATS itself can be taken to develop the regulations in international space law. Of course, these regulations shall be different from those in the Antarctic Treaty System. This is because of the uniqueness of space and its industry. Space has different applications and therefore it needs its own set of guidelines for regulating it developed specifically for it. While this is not the only way of resolving the issues plaguing this industry, it is one mechanism which can be utilised to solve the contemporary problem of regulating space tourism.

## Notes

1 Kenneth Chang, 'Highlights from Richard Branson's Virgin Galactic Flight', available at <https://www.nytimes.com/live/2021/07/11/science/virgin-galactic-launch-richard-branson> Last visited, 23 April 2022.
2 *Id.*
3 *Id.* See also Michael Greshko, 'What Virgin Galactic's Milestone Flight Means for the Future of Tourists in Space', available at <https://www.nationalgeographic.com/science/article/what-virgin-galactic-milestone-flight-means-for-the-future-of-tourists-in-space> Last visited, 23 April 2022.
4 Gradatim Ferociter, 'Blue Origin Safely Launches Four Commercial Astronauts to Space and Back', available at <https://www.blueorigin.com/news/first-human-flight-updates/> Last visited, 23 April 2022.
5 Amy Thompson, 'SpaceX Launches Four Civilians into Orbit on Historic Inspiration4 Flight', available at <https://www.space.com/spacex-launches-inspiration4-civilian-orbital-mission> Last visited, 27 April 2022.
6 *Id.*
7 *BBC World News*, 'World's First Space Tourist 10 Years On: Dennis Tito', available at <https://www.bbc.com/news/science-environment-13208329> Last visited, 23 April 2022.
8 Małgorzata Polkowska, 'Space Tourism Challenges', *Review of European and Comparative Law*, Vol. XLV, No. 2, 2021, pp. 153–182 at p. 156. See also BBC World News, 'Japanese billionaire blasts off to International Space Station', available at <https://www.bbc.com/news/world-asia-59544223> Last visited, 27 April 2022.
9 Jonathan Amos, 'Virgin Galactic's Spaceship Makes Solo Flight', available at <https://www.bbc.com/news/science-environment-11511604> Last visited, 27 April 2022.
10 Kate Duffy, 'What Will Space Tourists Get When They Fly with SpaceX, Blue Origin, and Virgin Galactic? Spacesuits, sleeping bags…and Jeff Bezos', available at <https://

www.businessinsider.in/tech/news/what-will-space-tourists-get-when-they-fly-with-spacex-blue-origin-and-virgin-galactic-spacesuits-sleeping-bags-and-jeff-bezos/articleshow/84294254.cms> Last visited, 27 April 2022.

11 Loh Ing Hoe, 'Lacuna of Outer Space Law in Governing Space Tourism and Malaysia Stands', *American-Eurasian Journal of Agricultural & Environmental Sciences*, Vol. 15, Special Issue on Tourism & Environment, Social and Management Sciences, 2015, pp. 73–81.

12 *Id.*

13 Armel Kerrest, 'Outer Space as International Space: Lessons from Antarctica', in P.A. Berkman, M.A. Land, D. Walton, and O.R. Yound (eds.) *Science Diplomacy: Antarctica, Science and the Governance of International Spaces* (Washington D.C.: Smithsonian Institution Scholarly Press, 2011) pp. 133–142 at p. 133.

14 *Id.*

15 The Antarctic Treaty, 1 December 1959, 402 UNTS 71 (entered into force on 23 June 1961).

16 *Id.*

17 Secretariat of the Antarctic Treaty, 'Tourism and Non-Governmental Activities', available at <https://www.ats.aq/e/tourism.html> Last visited, 28 April 2022.

18 UNOOSA, 'Space Law', available at <https://www.unoosa.org/oosa/en/ourwork/spacelaw/index.html> Last visited, 28 April 2022.

19 E.B. Editors, 'Sputnik', available at <academic.eb.com/levels/collegiate/article/Sputnik/69273> Last visited, 30 April 2022.

20 Carlo Focarelli, 'International Law in the 20th Century', in Alexander Orakhelashvili (ed.) *Research Handbook on the Theory and History of International Law* (Northampton: Edward Elgar Publishing Inc., 2011) pp. 478–526 at p. 501.

21 *Id.*

22 UNGA Res. 1348 (XIII), (18 December 1958).

23 *Id.*

24 UNGA Res. 1472 (XIV), (12 December 1959). The Committee uses consensus decision-making and has been deemed as a success. See: Shirley V. Scott, *International Law in World Politics: An Introduction* (Colorado: Lynne Rienner Publishers, 2012) p. 173.

25 Treaty on Principles Governing the Activities of States in the Exploration and Use of Outer Space, Including the Moon and Other Celestial Bodies, 27 January 1967, 610 UNTS 205, 18 UST 2410, TIAS No 6347, 6 ILM 386 (entered into force on 10 October 1967) [Outer Space Treaty].

26 I.H. Ph. Diedricks-Verschoor and V. Kopal, *An Introduction to Space Law* (The Netherlands: Kluwer Law International BV, 2008) p. 3.

27 Agreement on the Rescue of Astronauts, the Return of Astronauts and the Return of Objects launched into Outer Space, 22 April 1968, 672 UNTS 119 (entered into force on 3 December 1968) [Rescue Agreement].

28 Convention on the International Liability for damage caused by Space Objects, 29 March 1972, 961 UNTS 187 (entered into force on 1 September 1972) [Liability Convention].

29 A compilation has been prepared by the United Nations Office for Outer Space Affairs. See: UNOOSA, 'United Nations Treaties and Principles on Outer Space and related General Assembly Resolutions', available at <http://www.unoosa.org/res/oosadoc/data/documents/2008/stspace/stspace11rev_2_0_html/st_space_11rev2E.pdf> Last visited, 3 May 2022.

30 *Id.*

31 Steven Freeland, 'Fly Me to the Moon: How Will International Law Cope with Commercial Space Tourism?', available at <http://classic.austlii.edu.au/au/journals/MelbJIL/2010/4.html> Last visited, 27 April 2022.

32 G.D. Triggs, *International Law: Contemporary Principles and Practices* (New Delhi: LexisNexis, 2006) p. 326.
33 *Id.*
34 Outer Space Treaty, Art. I.
35 *Id.*
36 *Id.*
37 Outer Space Treaty, Art. II.
38 *Id.*, Art. III.
39 *Supra* note 33, at 327 & 328.
40 Malcolm N. Shaw, *International Law* (Delhi: Cambridge University Press, 2017) p. 399.
41 EB Editors, 'Antarctic Treaty', available at <academic.eb.com/levels/collegiate/article/Antarctic-Treaty/7752> Last visited, 22 April 2022.
42 *Id.*
43 The Antarctic Treaty, 1 December 1959, 402 UNTS 71 (entered into force on 23 June 1961), Art. IV.
44 *Id.*, Art. IV (2).
45 Karen Scott, 'Institutional Developments within the Antarctic Treaty System', *International and Comparative Law Quarterly*, Vol. 52, No. 2, 2003, pp. 473–488 at p. 474.
46 The Antarctic Treaty, Art. IX (1).
47 *Supra* note 46.
48 Convention for the Conservation of Antarctic Seals, 1 June 1972, 1080 UNTS 175 (entered into force on 11 March 1978).
49 Convention on the Conservation of Antarctic Marine Living Resources, 20 May 1980, 1329 UNTS 47 (entered into force on 7 April 1982).
50 Convention on the Regulation of Antarctic Mineral Resource Activities, 3 October 1981, 30 ILM 1461 (not in force).
51 Protocol on Environmental Protection to the Antarctic Treaty, 4 October 1991, 2941 UNTS 9 (entered into force on 14 January 1998).
52 Ram Mohan, 'Space Exploration: Companies Breach New Frontiers', available at <https://economictimes.indiatimes.com/news/science/space-exploration-companies-breach-new-frontiers/bigelow-aerospace/slideshow/76243311.cms> Last visited, 29 April 2022.
53 Nadia Drake, 'Where, Exactly, Is the Edge of Space? It Depends on Who You Ask', available at <https://www.nationalgeographic.com/science/article/where-is-the-edge-of-space-and-what-is-the-karman-line> Last visited, 27 April 2022.
54 *Id.*
55 *Id.*
56 The Fédération Aéronautique Internationale is the international governing body for air sports. Notably, it also devices definitions for human space flight.
57 S. Sanz Fernández de Córdoba, '100km Altitude Boundary for Astronautics', available at <https://www.fai.org/page/icare-boundary> Last visited, 28 April 2022. In 2018, the FAI was deliberating whether the Karman Line should be reduced to 80kms. See- FAI, 'Statement about the Karman Line', available at <https://www.fai.org/news/statement-about-karman-line> Last visited, 28 April 2022.
58 For instance, see the responses received from countries and permanent observers of the Committee on the Peaceful Uses of Outer Space (COPUOS) in-UN Doc. A/AC.105/1112/Add.9, available at <https://www.unoosa.org/oosa/oosadoc/data/documents/2021/aac.105/aac.1051112add.9_0.html> Last visited, 25 April 2022.
59 Space (Launches and Returns) Act 2018, No. 123 of 1998. The definition of 'space object' is as follows: "(a) an object the whole or a part of which is to go into or come back from an area beyond the distance of 100 km above mean sea level; or (b) any part of such an object, even if the part is to go only some of the way towards or back from an area beyond the distance of 100 km above mean sea level."

60 National Environmental Satellite Data and Information Service, 'Where Is Space?', available at <https://www.nesdis.noaa.gov/news/where-space> Last visited, 26 April 2022.

61 For further reading, see the presentation given by Pedrazzi in the IISL/ECSL Symposium, 2011 – Marco Pedrazzi, 'Are There Indications for Upper and Lower Limits for Air Space and Outer Space in Air Law, Space Law and National Legislation?', available at <https://www.unoosa.org/pdf/pres/lsc2011/symp03.pdf> Last visited, 27 April 2022.

62 P. Paul Fitzgerald, 'Inner Space: ICAO's New Frontier', *Journal of Air Law and Commerce*, Vol. 78, No. 4, 2014, pp. 3–34.

63 Erik Seedhouse, 'Space Tourism', available at <https://www.britannica.com/topic/space-tourism> Last visited, 26 April 2022.

64 Om Marathe, 'Suborbital Flight: Fast Enough to Reach Space, Not Stay There', available at <https://indianexpress.com/article/explained/explained-fast-enough-to-reach-space-not-stay-there-7400009/> Last visited, 29 April 2022.

65 *Id.*

66 Virgin Galactic, 'Virgin Galactic Spaceflight', available at <https://www.virgingalactic.com/#horizontal-scroll> Last visited, 30 April 2022.

67 *Supra* note 64.

68 *Id.*

69 ANI, '4 SpaceX Tourists Return to Earth after 3-Day Extra-terrestrial Excursion', available at <https://www.business-standard.com/article/current-affairs/4-spacex-tourists-return-to-earth-after-3-day-extra-terrestrial-excursion-121091900071_1.html> Last visited, 30 April 2022.

70 Sean O'Kane, 'Elon Musk Proposes City-To-City Travel by Rocket, Right Here on Earth', available at <https://www.theverge.com/2017/9/29/16383048/elon-musk-spacex-rocket-transport-earth-travel> Last visited, 28 April 2022.

71 Dom Galeon, 'Is Elon Musk's Fast Earth Travel via Rocket Possible?', available at <https://futurism.com/is-elon-musks-fast-earth-travel-via-rocket-possible> Last visited, 29 April 2022.

72 Rescue Agreement, Art. VII.

73 Liability Convention, Art. II.

74 *Id.*, Art. III.

75 The Russian Space Agency Roscosmos has provided services as well but they are also in collaboration with the private tour agency 'Space Adventures'.

76 Frans G. von der Dunk, 'The Regulation of Space Tourism', in Erik Cohen and Sam Spector (eds.) *Space Tourism: The Elusive Dream* (Bingley: Emerald Publishing, 2019) pp. 177–199 at p. 184.

77 *Supra* note 28.

78 *Supra* note 64.

79 For instance, see the 'Guidance on Informing Crew and Space Flight Participants of Risk Given by the Federal Aviation Authority of the US', available at <https://www.faa.gov/about/office_org/headquarters_offices/ast/regulations/media/Guidance_on_Informing_Crew_and_Space_Flight_Participants_of_Risk.pdf> Last visited, 30 April 2022. Also, readers should note that the Federal Aviation Administration (FAA) of the US places the boundary at 80 km, while NASA has demarcated it to be at an altitude of 76 km.

80 Paige McClanahan, 'Tourism in Antarctica: Edging Toward the (Risky) Mainstream', available at <https://www.nytimes.com/2020/02/26/travel/antarctica-tourism-environment-safety.html> Last visited, 3 May 2022.

81 *Id.*

82 Readers may visit the website of 'Antarctica Flights', an Australian Tour Operator at <https://www.antarcticaflights.com.au/> Last visited, 1 May 2022.

83 'Silversea Cruises Ltd. Is Another Tour Operator in Antarctica', Available at <https://www.silversea.com/destinations/antarctica-cruise.html> Last visited, 3 May 2022.

84 Mehr Gill, 'Explained: How to Have a holiday in Antarctica, and What It Will Cost', available at <https://indianexpress.com/article/explained/explained-how-to-have-a-holiday-in-antarctica-and-what-it-will-cost-6144379/> Last visited, 27 April 2022.

85 IAATO, 'About IAATO', available at <https://iaato.org/about-iaato/> Last visited, 28 April 2022.

86 United Nations Environment Programme, *Tourism in the Polar Regions: The Sustainability Challenge*, (Electronic edition: UNEP, 2007) p. 12.

87 Bryd was part of the documentary film "The Secret Land" which featured real-life scenes of *Operation High jump*. Admiral Bryd was tasked to explore Antarctica to gauge its potential for conducting military operations. The film won the American Academy Award for Best Documentary Feature Film in 1948.

88 Sir Vivian Ernest Fuchs led the British expedition which completed the first overland crossing of Antarctica.

89 Globally renowned as the first person to climb Mount Everest, Sir Edmund Hillary also co-authored the book 'The crossing of Antarctica' with Vivian Fuchs.

90 *Supra* note 87, at 12.

91 *Id.*

92 *Supra* note 81.

93 *Supra* note 86.

94 British Antarctic Survey, 'New Map Reveals How Little of Antarctica's Rock Is Ice-Free', available at <https://phys.org/news/2016-08-reveals-antarctica-ice-free.html> Last visited, 29 April 2022. The research done by the British Antarctic Survey has revised the ice-free rock area from 'less than 1%' to 0.18%.

95 For instance, see Robert Perkins and Rosemary Griffin, 'Russia Stokes Political Tensions with Hunt for Antarctic Oil', available at <https://www.spglobal.com/commodityinsights/en/market-insights/latest-news/oil/022120-russia-stokes-political-tensions-with-hunt-for-antarctic-oil> Last visited, 30 April 2022.

96 New Zealand Foreign Affairs & Trade, 'Current Status of the Convention', available at <https://www.mfat.govt.nz/en/about-us/who-we-are/treaties/convention-on-the-regulation-of-antarctic-mineral-resource-activities/> Last visited, 29 April 2022.

97 BBC Bitesize, 'Impacts of Tourism', available at <https://www.bbc.co.uk/bitesize/guides/z782pv4/revision/3> Last visited, 30 April 2022.

98 *Id.*

99 *Id.*

100 United States Congress: Office of Technology Assessment, *Polar Prospects: A Minerals Treaty for Antarctica* (Washington D.C.: Congress of the US, 1989) p. 138.

101 Reuters Staff, 'Antarctic Fuel Spill after Ship Runs Aground: Scientist', available at <https://www.reuters.com/article/us-antarctica-spill-idUSL0193180820070201> Last visited, 1 May 2022. See also The Associated Press, 'Sunken Antarctic Cruise Ship Left Oil Spill', available at <https://www.nbcnews.com/id/wbna22039975> Last visited, 1 May 2022.

102 Stephen Leahy, 'Exxon Valdez Changed the Oil Industry Forever – But New Threats Emerge', available at <https://www.nationalgeographic.com/environment/article/oil-spills-30-years-after-exxon-valdez> Last visited, 1 May 2022.

103 *Supra* note 101, at 140.

104 IAATO, 'The History of IAATO', available at <https://iaato.org/about-iaato/our-mission/history-of-iaato/> Last visited, 1 May 2022.

105 Protocol on Environmental Protection to the Antarctic Treaty, Art. 2.

106 *Id.*, Art. 3.

107 *Id.*, Art. 7.

108 *Id.*, Art. 8.

109 *Id.*, Art. 11.
110 *Id.*, Art. 12.
111 The schedule designates Arbitration as the preferred method of dispute resolution with the forum being the Permanent Court of Arbitration.
112 Protocol on Environmental Protection to the Antarctic Treaty, Art. 9.
113 Resolution 4 (2021). These guidelines are updated annually or biannually.
114 *Id.*
115 *Id.*
116 Resolution 2 (2018) Annex.
117 *Id.* at 4.
118 *Id.*
119 *Id.*
120 *Supra* note 105.
121 *Id.*
122 *Id.*
123 Daniela Haase, Machiel Lamers and Bas Amelung, 'Heading into Uncharted Territory? Exploring the Institutional Robustness of Self-Regulation in the Antarctic Tourism Sector', *Journal of Sustainable Tourism*, Vol. 17, No. 4, 2009, pp. 411–430 at p. 413.
124 IAATO, 'Preparing for Your Expedition', available at <https://iaato.org/visiting-antarctica/preparing-for-your-expedition/> Last visited, 3 May 2022.
125 IAATO, 'The Antarctic Treaty General Guidelines', available at <https://iaato.org/wp-content/uploads/2020/04/Antarctic-Treaty-General-Guidelines.pdf> Last visited, 3 May 2022.
126 *Id.*
127 IAATO, 'Don't Pack a Pest', available at <https://iaato.org/wp-content/uploads/2020/04/IAATO_Don_t_Pack_a_Pest.EN_190070.pdf> Last visited, 3 May 2022.
128 *Id.*
129 IAATO, 'General Information for Wildlife Watching', available at <https://iaato.org/wp-content/uploads/2020/04/IAATO-General-Information-for-Wildlife-Watching_072030.pdf> Last visited, 3 May 2022.
130 *Id.*
131 *Id.*
132 IAATO, 'Mandatory Briefing Slideshow for Visitors', available at <https://iaato.org/visiting-antarctica/visitor-briefings/> Last visited, 3 May 2022.
133 IAATO, 'Information for Yachts', available at <https://iaato.org/visiting-antarctica/information-for-yachts/> Last visited, 3 May 2022.
134 (Agenda Item 11) ATCM XXV IP 72 Guidelines for Tourist Operations in Antarctica by the International Association of Antarctica Tour Operators (IAATO).
135 *Id.*
136 *Id.*
137 For instance, the depletion of the ozone layer, the high price and 'eliteness' of accessing space, safety concerns, licensing requirements etc. For further reading, see Future Learn, 'Is Space Tourism Good for the Planet?', available at <https://www.futurelearn.com/info/blog/is-space-tourism-good-for-the-planet> Last visited, 3 May 2022. See also Rebecca Heilweil, 'How Bad Is Space Tourism for the Environment? And Other Space Travel Questions, Answered', available at <https://www.vox.com/recode/22589197/space-travel-tourism-bezos-branson-rockets-blue-origin-virgin-galactic-spacex> Last visited, 3 May 2022.
138 However, by the time the Antarctic Treaty was signed, multiple States had already laid claim to it. In the case of space law, the Outer Space treaty prevented this from happening by disallowing the application of sovereignty to outer space and celestial bodies. In this sense, the OST answers the question better than the AT which freezes such sovereign claims in time.

139 *Supra* note 105.
140 *Id.* See also B. Stonehouse, 'IAATO: An Association of Antarctic Tour Operators', *Polar Record*, Vol. 28, No. 167, 1992, pp. 322–324.
141 Michael Wenger, '30 years of IAATO', available at <https://polarjournal.ch/en/2021/05/18/30-years-of-iaato-our-mission-endures/> Last visited, 3 May 2022.
142 Christian Davenport, 'Richard Branson and Jeff Bezos Will Fly to Space at Their Own Risk. Does That Make It Right for Everyone?', available at <https://www.washingtonpost.com/technology/2021/06/23/space-tourism-faa-regulation/> Last visited, 28 April 2022.
143 Mark Garcia (ed.), 'Space Debris and Human Spacecraft', available at <https://www.nasa.gov/mission_pages/station/news/orbital_debris.html> Last visited, 29 April 2022.
144 *Id.*
145 PTI, '27,000 Man-Orbit, and Counting: Space Junk Is Here to Stay', available at <https://www.firstpost.com/world/27000-man-made-objects-in-earth-orbit-and-counting-space-junk-is-here-to-stay-10342421.html> Last visited, 30 April 2022.
146 Gabrielle Tétrault-Farber, 'International Space Station Swerves to Dodge Space Junk', available at <https://www.reuters.com/lifestyle/science/international-space-station-swerves-dodge-space-junk-2021-12-03/> Last visited, 30 April 2022.
147 This does not mean that tourists would be throwing materials on to the Earth's orbit; however, it is not something which cannot be expected with tourists always wanting to leave their immemorable traces in time. These problems already confront ancient buildings and heritage structures on Earth.
148 Kevin A. Hughes, Peter Convey and John Turner, 'Developing Resilience to Climate Change Impacts in Antarctica: An Evaluation of ATS Protected Area Policy', *Environmental Science & Policy*, Vol. 124, 2021, pp. 12–22. With respect to climate change, the treaty is critiqued by the authors as 'lacking'.
149 Marlène Michèle Losier, 'Cultural Heritage in Outer Space: Identifying International Legal Principles that Define and Promote Its Safeguarding within a Space Law Framework', available at <https://www.unoosa.org/documents/pdf/copuos/lsc/2021/tech-10E.pdf> Last visited, 30 April 2022.
150 Nadia Drake, 'Should Neil Armstrong's Boot Prints Be on the Moon Forever?', available at <https://www.nytimes.com/2019/07/11/science/moon-apollo-11-archaeology-preservation.html> Last visited, 2 May 2022.
151 To date, there have been six active rovers on Mars. Five of them are American in origin, while one is Chinese. See NASA, 'Mars Exploration Rovers', available at <https://mars.nasa.gov/mer/> Last visited, 2 May 2022. See also Rahel Philipose, 'Explained: What Is China's Zhurong Rover, Set to Explore Mars?', available at <https://indianexpress.com/article/explained/explained-all-you-need-to-know-about-chinas-zhurong-rover-set-to-explore-mars-7316365/> Last visited, 3 May 2022.
152 ISRO, 'Water on the Moon', available at <https://www.isro.gov.in/water-moon> Last visited, 3 May 2022.
153 United Nations, 'Antarctica "Should Not Be Taken for Granted" Scientists Declare, Amid Extreme Weather Uptick', available at <https://news.un.org/en/story/2022/04/1115342> Last visited, 3 May 2022.
154 UNOOSA, 'COPUOS History', available at <https://www.unoosa.org/oosa/en/ourwork/copuos/history.html> Last visited, 3 May 2022.

# INDEX

accident 7, 20, 30, 31, 45, 46, 47, 52, 57, 80, 102, 104, 106, 118, 120, 154, 162, 176, 177, 181, 210
aerodynamic: alleviation 3; forces 207; lift 3, 18
aerospace: heritage 145; industry 43; jurisdiction 24; planes 43; technologies 22; vehicle 3, 4
aircraft 2, 3, 4, 9, 18, 19, 20, 22, 23, 29, 83, 106, 143, 157, 158, 160, 161, 179
airspace 2, 3, 4, 17, 21, 22, 23, 25, 81, 106, 158
Allianz 163
alumina 119, 121, 122
Anousheh Ansari 28, 30, 114
Antarctic: environment 206, 209, 210, 211, 212; heritage 144; resources 209; tourism 212; travel 209; treaty 140, 204, 206, 207, 209, 210, 211, 212, 213, 214, 215, 216
anti-satellite test (ASAT) 60, 61, 62, 63, 64, 180
applicable law 2, 3, 4, 10, 50, 159, 195
Appropriate State 6, 78, 80, 81, 82, 84, 85, 87, 88, 89, 90, 173
appropriation 136, 138, 142, 145, 175, 181, 184, 189, 194, 195, 196, 197, 198, 199
Artemis 1 123; Accords 34, 141, 197, 198; Mission 197
asteroid 191, 198; strikes 188
astronaut 2, 7, 8, 10, 16, 17, 18, 19, 24, 25, 28, 29, 30, 31, 32, 33, 34, 35, 36, 37, 38, 43, 44, 45, 46, 47, 48, 49, 50, 51, 53, 55, 56, 57, 60, 69, 89, 100, 101, 102, 103, 104, 105, 107, 108, 115, 116, 134, 153, 154, 162, 168, 171, 173, 179, 182, 183, 187, 188, 191, 205, 208, 212, 213; Wings 24, 35
atmosphere 3, 9, 18, 19, 21, 56, 59, 107, 110, 116, 117, 119, 121, 122, 123, 125, 126, 135, 142, 154, 177, 178, 185, 190, 203, 207, 208
authorisation 6, 61, 78, 80, 81, 89, 90, 106, 173, 196, 197
aviation 3, 9, 19, 20, 24, 89, 106, 107, 110, 121, 163; insurance 104, 163, 164; law 2, 4, 5, 9, 10, 102, 106, 107, 154, 158, 161; personnel 9
AXA XL 163
axiom 37, 116, 170, 207

black carbon (BC) 119, 121, 122
Blue Origin 1, 2, 16, 28, 38, 42, 43, 101, 115, 120, 121, 123, 153, 163, 167, 169, 203, 207
Budapest Declaration on World Heritage 133, 135

cabin crew 34
Canso 118
carbon 119, 121, 178; dioxide 9, 123, 194; emission 122, 123; footprint 123, 124
celestial bodies 7, 8, 10, 32, 44, 70, 78, 86, 124, 135, 136, 137, 138, 141, 142,

**224** Index

143, 167, 168, 169, 170, 174, 177, 180, 181, 182, 183, 184, 187, 189, 190, 191, 192, 193, 194, 195, 197, 198, 205
Challenger 30
chemical 9, 121, 178
Chicago Convention 4, 9, 106
China National Space Administration 143
Chorzów Factory 70, 76
collision 5, 58, 59, 60, 61, 83, 86, 117, 118, 194, 214; avoidance 57, 59; risk 56, 58, 59, 61, 64
commander 30, 32, 85
Commercial Space Launch Act 33, 34
Commercial Space Launch Competitiveness Act 143
commercial space tourism 1, 2, 6, 11, 25, 42, 43, 44, 46, 47, 48, 49, 50, 53, 88, 89, 90, 134, 165, 194
common heritage 139, 168, 181, 192, 193, 205, 206
consultation 23, 57, 63, 169, 197; rights 62
contractual obligations 153
Convention on International Liability for Damage Caused by Space Objects (Liability Convention) 9, 10, 23, 43, 52, 81, 83, 85, 86, 90, 104, 105, 107, 124, 158, 159, 160, 161, 205, 208
Convention on the Law of the Sea (UNCLOS) 20, 139
COPUOS 24, 35, 57, 58, 59, 169, 176, 184, 196, 197, 205
Corfu Channel 70, 75, 81, 88
cosmonaut 33, 37, 60, 102, 103
cosmos 100, 108, 145, 195
crimes 84, 102, 106, 167, 168, 169, 170, 171, 173, 174, 175, 176, 182, 183, 184, 185; against humanity 169, 177
cultural heritage 133, 134, 135, 136, 137, 138, 140, 143, 145
customary international law 44, 49, 51, 70, 78, 140

damages 22, 82, 102, 106, 158, 161, 162, 194, 208, 214
debris 9, 38, 58, 59, 60, 62, 63, 107, 117, 118, 121, 124, 125, 179, 180, 190, 194, 214
Declaration in Defence of the Night Sky and the Right to Starlight 135
delimitation 2, 17, 21, 24, 83, 207, 213
demarcation 2, 3, 4, 24, 25, 165

Dennis Tito 1, 28, 42, 100, 101, 114, 169, 177, 203
distress 7, 30, 31, 32, 34, 36, 44, 45, 46, 47, 50, 51, 52, 53, 57, 154, 177, 199
due regard 60, 64

Elon Musk 28, 115, 116, 208
emergency 7, 8, 9, 30, 31, 34, 44, 45, 46, 47, 48, 50, 52, 57, 102, 105, 154, 210
environment 9, 28, 36, 37, 42, 51, 55, 63, 64, 108, 109, 114, 116, 118, 119, 123, 124, 125, 134, 135, 137, 139, 142, 144, 163, 168, 170, 171, 172, 175, 177, 179, 180, 182, 189, 194, 199, 204, 205, 206, 208, 209, 210, 211, 212, 213, 214, 215
environmental impact 119, 139, 210, 211, 212
envoys of mankind 7, 8, 30, 31, 35, 45, 46, 49, 56, 105, 154, 171, 187, 208
equitable 185, 193
European Space Agency (ESA) 56, 109, 117, 143, 196
exploration 16, 17, 31, 36, 48, 49, 61, 62, 63, 70, 101, 107, 108, 123, 124, 126, 135, 136, 137, 138, 139, 140, 141, 142, 143, 144, 154, 170, 188, 191, 192, 193, 194, 198, 203, 205, 206
Express Waiver 157, 158
extraction 142, 189, 192, 195, 198, 199
extradition 168, 183, 184
extra-terrestrial 102, 108, 124

Federal Aviation Administration (FAA) 3, 19, 24, 34, 35, 89, 154, 156, 157, 160, 165
flight crew 32, 34, 89
functional approach 3
functionalist 3, 17, 18; approach 17, 19, 20

global commons 142, 195
government astronaut 33, 37, 43

hard law 24, 44, 45, 50
harmful: contamination 9, 61, 124; interference 5, 62, 63
health hazard 52
human: occupant 34; space flight 42, 155
humankind 108, 135, 144, 168, 184, 187, 188, 189, 191, 199
hybrid law 4
hydrazine 118, 120
hypersonic weapon 118

Index **225**

Indian Space Research Organisation
(ISRO) 109, 143
informed consent 154, 155, 156, 157, 164,
165
Inspiration4 2, 28, 42, 101, 116, 203
Inter-Agency Space Debris Coordination
Committee (IADC) 58, 59, 60
Inter-Governmental Agreement on ISS 10
International Association of Antarctica Tour
Operators (IAATO) 209, 210, 211,
212, 214
international cooperation 64, 135, 145, 177,
181, 198, 204, 205
International Council on Monuments and
Sites (ICOMOS) 140, 145
International Court of Space Crimes 169,
183, 184
International Dark-Sky Association 135
international responsibility 6, 61, 77, 78,
79, 81, 82, 84, 90, 106, 138, 173
international space law 2, 4, 10, 31, 37, 38,
44, 101, 105, 108, 109, 110, 124,
160, 194, 204, 205, 208, 213, 215,
216
International Space Station 1, 25, 28, 30,
33, 42, 43, 56, 58, 59, 60, 99, 100,
101, 102, 107, 109, 114, 133, 136,
144, 164, 167, 170, 203, 214
International Telecommunication Union
(ITU) 5
Iran-US Claims Tribunal 72, 74
ISS Crew Criteria 102, 103

Japan Aerospace Exploration Agency 143,
191
Jeff Bezos 2, 16, 28, 42, 101, 115,
163, 203
Julian Huxley 136
jurisdiction 6, 7, 10, 22, 24, 31, 45, 57, 82,
83, 84, 85, 86, 87, 88, 102, 106,
140, 142, 143, 158, 168, 173, 183,
184, 194, 196, 204, 206, 208

Karman Line 3, 16, 17, 18, 19, 20, 25, 115,
121, 154, 207, 213
kerosene 117, 119, 120, 122
Kessler Syndrome 117
Kodiak Island 118

launching state 2, 4, 6, 11, 45, 46, 47, 52,
83, 85, 86, 87, 88, 157, 158, 159,
160, 161, 173, 191, 208
liability 2, 9, 10, 17, 22, 23, 34, 43, 46, 52,
81, 82, 83, 85, 86, 90, 100, 102,

104, 105, 106, 107, 124, 133, 153,
154, 156, 157, 158, 159, 160, 161,
162, 163, 164, 165, 169, 171, 173,
176, 205, 208
Low Earth Orbit (LEO) 36, 37, 55, 56, 58,
59, 60, 61, 62, 64, 69, 109, 117,
118, 179

Maritime Launch Service (MLS) 118
Mir 101, 114, 133
mission specialist 30, 32
mitigation of space debris 58
Montreal Protocol 121
Moon Agreement 7, 8, 32, 43, 45, 50, 181,
192, 193, 194, 195, 198
Museum of Cosmonautics 134, 135
mutual cooperation 17, 23

National Aeronautics and Space
Administration (NASA) 3, 19, 28,
30, 32, 35, 36, 37, 58, 100, 109,
115, 116, 117, 120, 122, 133, 141,
170, 178, 181, 191, 194, 198; Air
and Space Museum 135; Space
Council 142
natural and cultural heritage 133, 134, 136,
140, 143, 145
New Shepard 16, 17, 115, 120, 203
Nicaragua 70, 72, 73, 74, 75, 77, 79, 80,
81, 88
Non-Certification Statement 156

One Small Step to Protect Human Heritage
in Space Act 144
Operational Guidelines (for the
Implementation of the World
Heritage Convention) 136, 137
operator 2, 5, 6, 10, 11, 32, 56, 57, 59, 60,
61, 63, 64, 86, 88, 89, 90, 117, 153,
154, 155, 156, 157, 158, 159, 160,
165, 176, 177, 181, 203, 204, 209,
211, 212, 213, 214, 216
orbital: allocation 5; slot 5, 6; tourism 1
Outer Space Treaty (OST) 6, 7, 8, 9, 10, 16,
30, 32, 43, 44, 48, 49, 56, 60, 61,
62, 63, 69, 70, 78, 79, 80, 81, 82,
83, 84, 85, 86, 87, 88, 89, 90, 105,
124, 126, 135, 138, 142, 145, 153,
154, 168, 173, 181, 188, 189, 190,
192, 193, 194, 195, 197, 198, 205,
206, 208
ownership 71, 136, 143, 144, 173, 187,
188, 190, 194, 195, 196
ozone: hole 17; layer 102, 121, 177, 178

**226** Index

parks movement 134, 135
passenger liability 158, 159, 160, 161, 164
payload specialist 30, 32
peaceful: purpose 141, 188, 192, 198, 206;
 use 17, 21, 22, 36, 57, 108, 109,
 196, 204, 205, 215
personnel 7, 8, 9, 10, 25, 31, 32, 34, 38, 44,
 45, 47, 48, 49, 50, 51, 53, 57, 86,
 153, 154, 208
pilot 19, 29, 30, 32, 34, 115, 123
pollution 117, 118, 120, 121, 122, 135, 139,
 178, 179, 189, 194, 199, 211
Prevention of an Arms Race in Outer Space
 (PAROS) 125
privatisation 87, 109, 212
propellant 116, 119, 120, 121, 178
Protocol on Environmental Protection to
 the Antarctic Treaty 207, 210, 211
province of all mankind 6, 168, 181, 192

registration 4, 5, 6, 9, 10, 17, 22, 43, 85, 86,
 87, 88, 105, 215; Convention 4, 5,
 43, 86, 87, 105, 107, 160
rescue 7, 8, 31, 32, 42, 44, 45, 46, 47, 48,
 49, 50, 51, 52, 53, 57, 177, 205,
 210, 212; Agreement 7, 8, 9, 43, 44,
 45, 46, 47, 48, 49, 50, 51, 53, 57,
 105, 154, 205
Reusable Launch Vehicle 43, 89
Richard Branson 2, 16, 28, 42, 101, 115,
 163, 203
Richard Garriott 115
Rio Declaration 125
Russian Federal Space Agency
 (Roscosmos) 120, 122, 143, 167,
 169, 203, 216

safety 2, 6, 34, 56, 57, 60, 64, 89, 101, 108,
 110, 125, 133, 155, 156, 157, 159,
 162, 163, 167, 168, 171, 172, 173,
 175, 176, 177, 179, 182, 193, 196
sally ride 134
salvage 51, 52, 180
satellite 3, 19, 55, 56, 57, 58, 59, 60, 61, 62,
 63, 64, 86, 87, 88, 117, 118, 135,
 142, 162, 163, 164, 176, 179, 180,
 187, 188, 193, 194, 204, 214
social justice 183
souvenirs 193, 194
sovereign 20, 24, 81, 99, 100, 106, 138,
 139, 144, 145
sovereignty 2, 17, 18, 19, 20, 21, 22, 23,
 73, 83, 87, 106, 109, 136, 138, 139,

142, 143, 145, 168, 169, 181, 184,
 192, 193, 194, 195, 199, 204, 206
space: activities 1, 2, 3, 4, 5, 6, 7, 8, 11,
 17, 22, 23, 24, 33, 34, 35, 53, 55,
 56, 60, 61, 62, 63, 69, 78, 79, 80,
 81, 82, 83, 84, 85, 86, 89, 90, 99,
 100, 102, 104, 105, 106, 108, 109,
 110, 116, 123, 144, 161, 168, 173,
 177, 184, 193, 194, 195, 196, 204;
 adventures 1, 100, 101, 114, 162,
 193
space border 16, 17, 18, 19, 21, 22, 23;
 boundary 17, 18, 19, 21, 22, 23, 24;
 commercialisation 4; crimes 168,
 169, 170, 171, 182, 183, 184, 185;
 Industry Act 34; insurance 102,
 104, 108, 162, 164; mining 197,
 199; mission 9, 61, 99, 100, 101,
 102, 104, 105, 107, 108, 109, 159;
 object 3, 4, 5, 6, 7, 10, 17, 22, 23,
 24, 29, 31, 33, 42, 45, 46, 47, 55,
 56, 57, 58, 59, 60, 62, 63, 64, 80,
 81, 83, 86, 87, 88, 90, 104, 106,
 119, 137, 157, 158, 159, 160, 161,
 162, 173, 187, 194, 198, 203, 205;
 operation 16, 23, 45, 49, 171, 172;
 parks 134, 145; shuttle 30, 32,
 120, 154; situational awareness 57,
 171, 180; technology 42, 43, 142;
 tourism market 2, 6, 43; tourist 1, 5,
 6, 7, 8, 9, 10, 11, 23, 25, 29, 30, 32,
 34, 35, 36, 37, 44, 48, 49, 50, 51,
 52, 53, 69, 89, 99, 100, 101, 102,
 103, 104, 105, 106, 107, 108, 109,
 110, 114, 124, 133, 143, 154, 155,
 157, 162, 164, 165, 171, 176, 177,
 179, 182, 183, 187, 203, 212; traffic
 management 5, 6, 57, 176, 180;
 travel 25, 35, 42, 43, 44, 45, 47,
 49, 50, 52, 100, 121, 124, 125, 135,
 139, 144, 145, 154, 155, 156, 157,
 162, 163, 164, 165, 169, 176, 177,
 178, 180, 182, 187; treaties 7, 43,
 44, 45, 46, 47, 49, 50, 51, 52, 53,
 56, 60, 141, 143, 177, 193, 205
spacecraft 7, 19, 20, 22, 25, 29, 31, 32, 34,
 38, 42, 43, 44, 45, 48, 49, 50, 51,
 52, 55, 56, 57, 58, 59, 64, 100, 101,
 104, 114, 115, 116, 120, 122, 123,
 126, 141, 143, 144, 145, 154, 159,
 203, 207
spaceflight participant 33, 34, 36, 101, 102,
 103

SpaceX 1, 2, 9, 28, 37, 42, 43, 56, 58, 101, 109, 115, 116, 117, 120, 122, 133, 153, 167, 169, 203, 207, 213
spatial approach 3
spatialist approach 17, 18 ,19, 23
*specialis* treaty 168, 184
standard of care 62
Starlink 56, 58, 117, 200
state of registry 5, 6, 7, 31, 45, 86, 87, 88, 89, 90, 159
state responsibility 69, 70, 74, 76, 77, 78, 79, 80, 81, 83, 85, 86, 88, 90, 159
sub-orbital tourism 37, 43, 207, 208
supervision 6, 61, 78, 80, 81, 89, 90, 100, 106, 173, 193

tort law 171, 176
tour operator 5, 6, 10, 160, 204, 209, 211, 213
Transitionary Outer Space Zone (TOSZ) 17, 20, 21, 25
Trusteeship Council 168, 169, 182, 184

UDMH 120
United Nations Educational, Scientific and Cultural Organization (UNESCO)

119, 133, 134, 135, 136, 137, 138, 139, 140, 141, 143, 144, 145
United Nations 5, 17, 18, 20, 31, 45, 47, 49, 50, 53, 57, 86, 87, 107, 124, 125, 133, 135, 136, 140, 142, 169, 173, 196, 204; Environment Programme (UNEP) 124
United States 3, 10, 19, 22, 29, 32, 33, 34, 43, 44, 50, 61, 62, 70, 72, 73, 74, 75, 84, 85, 87, 89, 90, 121, 134, 142, 143, 144, 145, 156, 159, 160, 161, 164, 169, 190, 195, 196, 204, 206, 207, 210, 211
universal value 137, 138, 139

vertical launch 2
Virgin Galactic 1, 2, 16, 17, 28, 38, 42, 43, 101, 115, 120, 121, 122, 133, 153, 163, 167, 169, 203, 207, 213

water vapour 119, 121, 122, 123
World Heritage: Committee 136, 137, 138; Convention 133, 134, 135, 136, 137, 138, 139, 141, 143, 145

XINSURANCE 163

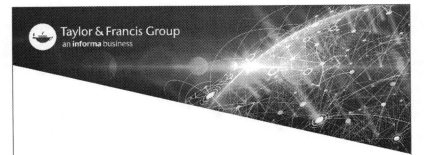

Printed in the United States
by Baker & Taylor Publisher Services